ML

This book is to be returned on
the last date

The John Fraser-Robinson Direct Marketing Series

ADVERTISING THAT PULLS RESPONSE

Advertising That Pulls Response

Graeme McCorkell

McGRAW-HILL BOOK COMPANY

London · New York · St Louis · San Francisco · Auckland
Bogotá · Caracas · Hamburg · Lisbon · Madrid · Mexico
Milan · Montreal · New Delhi · Panama · Paris
San Juan · São Paulo · Singapore · Sydney · Tokyo · Toronto

Published by
McGRAW-HILL Book Company (UK) Limited
Shoppenhangers Road, Maidenhead, Berkshire, SL6 2QL, England
Telephone 0628 23432
Fax 0628 35895

British Library Cataloguing in Publication Data

McCorkell, Graeme
  Advertising that pulls response.
  1. Advertising
  I. Title II. Series
  659.1

  ISBN 0–07–707320–7

Library of Congress Cataloging-in-Publication Data

McCorkell, Graeme
  Advertising that pulls response / Graeme McCorkell.
     p.   cm. –
  (The John Fraser-Robinson direct marketing series)
  Includes index.
  ISBN 0–07–707320–7
  1. Advertising media planning. 2. Advertising. I. Title
  II. Series: Fraser-Robinson, John.
  John Fraser-Robinson direct marketing series.
  HF5826.5.M35   1990
  659.1—dc20   90–37507

12345 BP 93210

Typeset by Computape (Pickering) Ltd, North Yorkshire and
printed and bound in Great Britain by The Bath Press, Avon

Contents

Introduction to the series

If you're the kind of person that likes value for money then *Advertising that pulls response* is a book for you. Equally, the subject of this whole series is probably for you too.

Direct marketing. In sales, marketing and advertising it is almost a synonym for value for money.

Direct marketing offers such value because it provides a powerful combination of selling power and advertising power inextricably linked together. To fail to understand, master and exploit both these forces is to deny yourself the maximum that direct marketing can give you.

Nowhere, in my opinion, does the true potential of these siamese twins focus more than with off-the-page, direct response advertising. A fact brought sharply to light when my own book—*The Secrets of Effective Direct Mail*, published by McGraw-Hill—was featured by Britain's specialist mail order booksellers, Wyvern.

Wyvern is run by someone who bucked the trend. His name is Michael Herbert. He, a good idea, and some good people have been very successful at finding a niche for themselves in the business of selling books through direct marketing.

If ever you meet Michael you can ask him about 'the pull-through effect'. It's a phenomenom he discovered quite early on in the development of Wyvern and which you would think would move him, in the eyes of the retail bookstores at least, from some kind of Maverick competitor to a white knight and friend.

Michael has discovered that for almost every book he sells off the page, two, sometimes three or more, sell through retail stores. The pull-through effect.

Michael is not the first to discover it. Do you remember those off-the-page ads that started in the seventies for briefcases, luggage sets, digital watches and the like? At one time they threatened—and almost succeeded—in turning the Sunday colour supplements into mail order catalogues with added editorial. As well as successfully selling their merchandise and building profitable customer bases for the advertisers, these ads also sent people across the nation scurrying into briefcase shops, luggage shops and digital watch shops.

Sir Clive Sinclair, in quite a short space of time, saw the power of the advertising effect work for him and against him. First with his computers where they achieved sales, but also built up massive levels of consumer awareness and huge corporate (and for that matter personal) imagery all of which, when he finally went retail through conventional outlets, must have proved an enormous negotiating power. The asset value of the brand built up and delivered free on top of the sales.

Then with the C5, Sir Clive was to see that same advertising effect working so powerfully against him, the company and the product. Acting as it did to spread the word like some deadly, unstoppable bush fire.

The secret, of course, is to harness the twinned powers for your own benefit. One delighted store owner told me recently how he had learned this lesson. 'Marvellous!' he said, 'I sell enough off-the-page to more than pay for the ads. And we're selling more—over twice as much through our distributors. And then, on top of that, the ads are doing a marvellous job building the brand. Pushing the corporate image too. What do you say to that?'

'You're right', I agreed, 'it's marvellous.'

In Europe now, I believe there is one man who knows more about this whole subject than the others. And so when I approached him and found him willing to join the series, I was delighted. Apart from all else, as competitors and as friends we go back a long way. Indeed Graeme McCorkell was, I think, the very first advertising person I met to appreciate, value and understand direct marketing.

Now, I have the advantage over you. I've read, learned, laughed, sighed and cheered my way through this book. In many ways, you may find Graeme uncompromising in his views. I think that will work to your benefit. The advertising you do for your business in the future will perform better, sell more, make greater profits through his experiences, knowledge and wisdom.

You will reach for this book in times of need. Treat it like a friend. It will surely return its own value to you many thousandfold. As indeed will each of the books that make up this direct marketing series.

John Fraser-Robinson

Preface

'You are so beautiful I can hardly keep my eyes on the meter,' says Woody Allen to Diane Keaton as they taxi expensively downtown in 'Manhattan'.

If successful direct response ads are not always so beautiful, it is, perhaps, because their creators are keeping a beady eye on the meter. They certainly don't get much time or production money to lavish on their work.

But the standards by which most advertising is judged are irrelevant, certainly to direct response advertising. People allow themselves to be confused by the fact that ads have to be written and designed. This does not qualify them to be viewed as works of art. You don't buy from a salesman because he speaks in blank verse or his gestures seem artistic. You buy because you believe what he is telling you.

Having the (professional) misfortune to live in a country where anything which smacks of moving merchandise is viewed from well beneath a raised eyebrow, I understand why many advertising people wish to associate themselves more closely with Shaftesbury Avenue than Petticoat Lane. However, they are wrong to do so and their clients should not allow them to get away with it.

Evidence of the aesthetic values of the citizenry can be found by comparing the content and circulations of the newspapers which are available to them.

If your motive for being in marketing, advertising, sales promotion or direct marketing is to elevate public taste, this book is not for you. On the other hand, if you see nothing wrong in trying to help yourself or others to an honest buck, it will help you keep your eyes on the meter.

The book is intended for reference, more than for bedtime reading. I don't expect you to begin at Chapter 1 and plough a lonely furrow all the way to Chapter 12.

At the beginning of each chapter is 'The proposition'. Read it to see if the chapter will cover what you want to know. If you think it does, read 'The pay-off' at the end to confirm your impression. Only then, dip into the chapter. You will find the margins are wide so that you can make pencil notes.

Graeme McCorkell

Acknowledgements

I want to thank all those who allowed me to use their work to illustrate points in the text. In particular to my distinguished panel of contributors to the Great Ad Gallery: Chris Albert, Chris Barraclough, Drayton Bird, Bruce Collins, Terry Hunt, Chris Jones, Roger Millington, Graeme Robertson, Chris Rudd and George Smith.

A most important thank you is due to the good folks at CIA Direct in general and Ian Prager in particular, without whom I doubt that there would have been a chapter on media planning and buying.

Finally, a tribute to the salesmanship of John Fraser-Robinson and Mike Adams, who talked me into writing this book when I thought there were more enjoyable ways to pass the time.

1 Advertising that pulls response

The proposition

Direct response advertising in newspapers is almost as old as advertising itself. In the nineteenth century, *The Times* carried front page advertisements (ads) for *Encyclopaedia Britannica* as part of a business agreement between the two publishers on a shared-profit basis. This was the forerunner of the PI (charge per-inquiry) and Affinity Group deals favoured by the direct marketers of today.

Some of the most famous of all ads, and some of the longest running, have been direct response ads. Nothing made John Caples' name more revered in the advertising business than an ad he wrote for a correspondence course as a young man: 'They laughed when I sat down at the piano, but then I began to play . . .' This ad ran for seven years.

Direct response advertising in newspapers and magazines has never been regarded as a speciality in quite the same way as in direct mail, perhaps because the media employed are familiar to anyone in advertising. Yet the majority of advertising carrying a response mechanism, and almost all of that planned and executed in a thoroughly professional manner, has been the preserve of the direct marketers in mail order, publishing and direct selling.

It is a more recent phenomenon to see the widespread attachment of response mechanisms to ads for retail distributed products; often ads whose primary objective is the communication of a specific product benefit rather than the capture of direct enquiries.

Such advertising has been dubbed variously as 'across-the-line advertising' or 'double-duty advertising'. These terms apply irrespective of the vehicle employed—be it TV, or print media advertising, or direct mail. The distinguishing feature of such advertising is that it carries a dual objective and its achievement is measured by its advertising value as well as by the quantity and quality of response that it produces.

The growth of across-the-line advertising has revitalised

interest in the techniques of direct response. It accounts for the astonishing fact that close to two-thirds of all advertising expenditure in the USA goes on advertising that carries some form of response mechanism.

Later we shall examine the reasons for this growth, but at the moment it will suffice to say that the economics of maintaining a private one-to-one marketing database of enquirers, trialists and regular users have, in the late-eighties, become suddenly more attractive. To construct such a database requires a source of names and addresses and one such source is across-the-line advertising.

Marketers are, rightly, becoming more demanding of the money they outlay on media advertising and are, as a result, taking an increasing interest in the measurement of its effectiveness. Direct response provides a quantification, an objective measurement which may not be sufficient to portray the whole effect of advertising but has, at least, the merit of total impartiality.

Is direct response different?

Few advertisers would be content if their advertising merely complied with its dictionary definition: making known their goods or services. Advertising is required to do more: it is required to persuade, and to persuade it must elicit a positive response. This response may be measured by direct sales or enquiries or it may have to be evaluated, through research, against less direct measures.

However, this is a difference of means. It is not a difference of principle. The ultimate object of any advertising is to persuade its audience to do what the advertiser wants them to do, or think what the advertiser wants them to think.

It was my frustration in being unable to measure the results of my advertising labours in clear, unequivocal terms, combined with my excitement at discovering the delights of direct response, that led me to leave mainstream advertising and become a practitioner of direct marketing. It is a decision I have not regretted for one moment. Yet I still feel some resentment at the way in which advertising and direct marketing have been neatly labelled and boxed separately. I have yet to meet the major advertiser who does not also require to employ direct marketing, sales promotion and PR skills. The more these, usually, separate communications appear to speak with one voice, the more they are likely to add up to a whole greater than the sum of the parts.

The poster at the airport, the TV commercial, the personalised invitation mailing, the loose insert in the magazine, the sign on the shop window and the 'take one' application in the restaurant are all part of the persuasion process to have and to use a Visa Card. To describe some of these as 'above-the-line' and others as 'below-the-line' may be convenient, but does nothing to aid our understanding of the communication process.

At some level in any client organisation, it is essential that someone understands all of these activities, not only to allocate scarce resources with optimum efficiency, but to ensure that they are used in harmony. So this book is for you, as a marketing person. If this understanding can be acquired by those responsible for the creation of the messages and the media plans, then the client's job becomes considerably easier, or at least, possible. So this book is also for you as an agency person. My purpose in writing the book is to make one part of this whole mix of communications more familiar and easier to understand. If it kindles your enthusiasm for directly measurable advertising, then I can promise you enormous satisfaction and interest, not to mention first night nerves, in joining the growing band of people who stick their necks on the block week-in, week-out while the computer tells them what they have achieved.

Many years ago, while working for a conventional mainstream advertising agency, I started to do direct response advertising because one of my clients was in mail order. Later, I started to use direct mail. To me it was just another advertising medium, albeit one I used exclusively for direct response. Of course, I had never heard of direct marketing because the term had not been invented. Now that I have made my living from direct marketing for over 20 years, direct mail is still just another advertising medium to me. And direct response is still just another way of using advertising.

'If that is all there is to it, why write a book about it?' you may ask. And now you have forced me to admit that there are important differences, philosophically as well as practically, between what I do now and what I did then. There are differences in the technique and the planning of any advertising which produces a directly measurable response. These differences have to be understood if we are to avoid making potentially catastrophic errors.

More than this, there is a difference in the way a direct

marketing person approaches and solves a business problem. We have to realise this to understand why we should trouble to engage in advertising that produces a specific response.

A different way of thinking

I can best explain this difference by oversimplifying, though only slightly. Let us suppose you are a media planner. Your brief gives you a definition of the target market. Let us say, BC1 (middle market) homemakers aged 25–44. Your plan will seek to cover this market with optimum frequency as broadly as your budget will permit.

When your plan is finished you reckon you have done a pretty good job. You have run a number of alternative solutions and the computer has told you which is best.

What you have not done is made any distinction between one BC1 25–44-year-old homemaker and another. But some of them are regular buyers, some are occasional buyers and some will never buy. Of course, you may have made some allowance for this through TGI data, or whatever, but since you do not know which individuals buy and which do not, that is as far as you can go.

And what about the campaign brief? There is probably a market share objective. But does the brief make it absolutely clear how this is to be achieved? Is the objective to maintain loyalty, to get regular users to buy more, to get trialists to buy regularly, or to get non-trialists to become trialists? 'All of these', is the answer I usually got, but perhaps things have become better since then.

Direct marketers set about their plan in quite a different way. They construct their market share objective from unit sales, but also work out how many of these can be made for nothing, how many at low cost, how many at average cost, and so on until it is unprofitable to continue. The cheapest sales to make are those that are made to regular buyers, the next cheapest are to occasional buyers, the next to people who have identified themselves as interested, and the most expensive sales are to people who are theoretically in the market for the product but are not *known* to be potential buyers. Other marketing people may follow a similar methodology but they may construct their target purely on the basis of how many units they can push through each group of retail outlets—with a certain weight of advertising, with tailor-made promotions and so on.

What direct marketers require in order to be able to do what they do, is a marketing database which lists individuals—a one-to-one marketing database. They will use this to describe their potential market as, perhaps:

- Advocates (regular buyers who introduce trialists)
- Regular buyers
- Trialists
- Prospects (people who have identified themselves as potential buyers)
- Suspects (people who are theoretically in the market)

The direct marketers consider this list as a hierarchy, or ladder, which their marketing plan helps consumers to ascend. The more people that can be enticed on to the higher rungs, the lower will be the cost-per-unit sale.

Clearly, if we have a retail distributed product, it makes sense to build a model which takes account of both the channels of distribution and consumer behaviour. Using direct marketing technology we can do this, as well as taking into account predicted competitive behaviour.

Direct marketers seek to build a consumer franchise on a more exclusive basis, so that it is less vulnerable to the behaviour of both retail outlets and competition.

Their one-to-one marketing database depends utterly on being able to identify prospects, trialists and regular buyers as individuals. If a direct marketer is running a mail order or direct sales business, this is comparatively simple. Not surprisingly, therefore, marketing database technology was developed first by such businesses and most quickly emulated by banks, building societies and insurance companies, because they already held lists of account holders' addresses.

User databases for retail distributed products are a much more recent development and are often fairly simple and less complete (i.e. do not represent the universe of users). The fact that this is so does not negate their value: it is good business to capture as many of your product users as you can, and the information you hold about these people enables you to target potential consumers with far greater accuracy.

In my experience, more than half—perhaps as much as three-quarters—of advertising expenditure goes on maintaining user loyalty. If we can communicate with users on a one-to-one basis, this is more precise, efficient, powerful and flattering. It also means we can devote more of our advertising and sales promotion effort to securing trial. The more you can increase the lifetime value of one customer, the more you can afford to spend on recruiting another customer.

The rapid growth of this activity has been fostered by

three factors: the first is escalating media costs; the second is increasing market segmentation; the third is diminishing data capture and retrieval costs. The combination of the first two factors has had a deadly effect on the profitability of promoting many products through mass media advertising. It simply does not make sense to talk to, say, only 200,000 regular users of a brand across a TV screen. The cost of audience wastage is colossal.

The third factor has made practicable what has long been possible, but simply uneconomic for most advertisers. The huge advances in semi-conductor technology brought a PC up to the power of a roomful of mainframe computers in a span of not more than 20 years.

The aim of being able to converse with product users on a one-to-one basis, generally by mail, does not imply that the relationship must start on this basis. Indeed, it is difficult to be so precise in defining the potential users of many products that direct mail would be a good medium for prospecting. It is an expensive medium in cost-per-thousand audience terms, and is not a medium to use unless we have good reason to suppose that we can be extremely accurate in our targeting.

Inducing trial will therefore always be heavily dependent on 'above-the-line' media, on in-store promotion and house-to-house distribution of coupons or leaflets. Neither is it a necessity that all advertising designed to induce trial should contain a direct response mechanism. It is merely very advantageous, providing that the addition of such a mechanism does not damage the communication delivered by the ad.

Allowing prospects to identify themselves

Now, it may surpise you that anyone engaged in direct response could admit to the possibility that a response mechanism might impair the quality of any piece of communication. But we must accept that the mood of certain advertising might indeed be adversely affected by a heavy-handed attempt to convert interest into immediate action. But the attempt need not be heavy-handed and not all that many of the advertising messages that compete for our attention each day would be damaged by offering the consumer a means of identifying himself or herself as a potential buyer.

The offer of more information than it is possible to give in an ad, the offer of a sample, the offer of a money-off voucher, the offer to send the product—gift wrapped, to a friend—are all devices that can enhance the value of an advertising message to the recipient. Whenever Noting and Reading scores are produced for all the ads in any given magazine, it is a virtual certainty that a disproportionate quantity of the highest performing ads will be direct response ads. The highest performers of all will usually be ads that seek to complete a sale off-the-page.

Why should this be? The fact is that people do not read or avoid reading ads because they are clever or not-so-clever. They read what interests them. Ads which contain hard information about a product out of necessity—because the advertiser wishes to sell it off-the-page—are of more interest. Ads which the reader can act upon immediately are of more interest. These are indisputable facts which cannot be denied—however much they might like to do so—by creative people who resent the intrusion of reply mechanisms into their lovingly created ads.

So, let us lay the ghost of the notion that there is a conflict between an ad designed to create awareness and one designed to create a response. Far from conflicting, these two aims are entirely compatible. The presence of a response mechanism *increases* the attention value of an ad. Furthermore, it is my experience that readers will accept, indeed desire, far more information from ads than most advertisers are willing to give. The conventional wisdom is that people are bored by ads, so if we posterise the ads we can make the message as brief and as entertaining as possible.

The application of this misguided philosophy has resulted in automotive advertising which so frustrates the consumer through its lack of information (even the offer of information) that the consumer is driven to buying specialist magazines to garner the data the advertiser has withheld. So the advertiser drives the potential buyer into the arms of a specialist publisher whose predeliction this month may be for a competitive model.

In the same market, a specialist American agency devised a floppy disk ad for Buick which could be played on an Apple Mackintosh computer. The disk was promoted in the Apple Mackintosh User Magazine. Sixteen per cent of the circulation sent for it; 96 per cent recalled at least a substantial part of the information on the disk; and 80 per cent passed it on to a friend. The number seriously considering Buick increased from 10 per cent to 20 per cent. The average time spent playing the disk was about 30 minutes. The conventional media ads, which contained virtually no hard information, had done nothing to shift the low-tech image of the brand and had no discernible effect on sales.

The point of this story is that advertising and marketing people who lack direct response experience constantly underrate the consumer's desire for information. In my view, they also underrate the consumer's intelligence. The reason for this is that they lack a definitive measure of the effectiveness of their ads and most rely on fundamentally unsound, unscientific research tools on which to base their advertising judgements.

Specious research

Alvin Achenbaum—latterly a partner in the marketing consultancy of Canter, Achenbaum Associates and formerly a director of both J. Walter Thompson and Grey Advertising in the USA—views copy testing with distaste. At a breakfast conference of the American Marketing Association in New York on 7 February 1985 his masterly address included a sharp rebuke to those who deliver the results of such activity as 'research findings':

> To take the most prevalent technique used today—so-called recall tests—irrespective of the number of studies done which show that recall measurements are irrelevant, that they are not in fact related to consumer purchase proclivities or purchasing behavior, marketeers continue to use and rely on that measuring stick.... But copy tests lack for more than a relevant measurement device. The fact is that they fail on almost every aspect of good research design—from the small samples they use to the unrealistic stimuli involved, to name only two.
> Frankly, the money spent on all this foolish research is a waste....

Achenbaum is far from alone in holding this view. Much wasted effort has been devoted to pre-testing of ads. One famous campaign which failed in pre-tests (twice) was that for Heineken ... 'refreshes the parts which other beers cannot reach'.

At the time of writing, the campaign has been running for 16 years. The reason it ran at all is that the client and his agency had the guts to back their judgement rather than the alleged 'findings' of specious research. How many other potentially famous campaigns have foundered upon the hollow rocks of so-called copy testing?

Many years ago I recall that most perceptive researcher, Bill Schlackman of William Schlackman Ltd, telling me that he had never been able to prove to his own satisfaction any effect of advertising beyond its capacity to make the advertised commodity better known. He was not saying there was no other effect; merely that advertising research could not *prove* any other effect.

I, for one, would hate to have the fate of my copy decided by specious research. Much better to argue it through with an intelligent client who has a clear understanding of the objective and is not afraid to make a decision. For copy testing is a lottery. 'We'll put it out to research' is code for 'We can't decide so we'll waste some money with the research company.' The alleged research will most usually be conducted in a highly unscientific manner with a sample too small to produce a statistically signficant finding, even if it had been soundly constructed. Yet every week, in some agency or other, you will see long faces or faces wreathed in smiles because the campaign 'researched badly' or 'researched well', according to the quack who conducted it.

This practice has even been extended to the selection of agencies. Campaigns submitted by agencies in competitive pitches have been 'put out to research'. Doubtless, the advertisers responsible for this ridiculous waste of money congratulate themselves on their objectivity. It would be equally objective, and less expensive, to draw the winning agency's name out of a hat. Unfortunately, the chosen course of action has much to commend it to marketing people who lack the self-confidence to make management decisions and are concerned to build evidence that will protect their backs.

Because such a dismissal begs the question 'Is there a better way?' let me digress for a moment to describe it. John Meszaros of Audi Volkswagen told me how he and a former colleague chose Bartle Bogle Hegarty as the Audi agency. They spent a month collecting videos and tear-sheets of ads they admired. They then met together and short-listed the ads they agreed upon and found out which agencies were responsible. They toured the agencies and picked the people who looked like a team with which they could form a good working relationship. John's point was that they did not expect a new agency to produce a campaign which would run and run until it had had the chance to get right inside the company and its products. He was right. It took a while before the commercials tagged, '*Vorsprung durch Technik*' were created and lifted the image of the marque. If you decide to select an agency on the strength of its creative capabilities, it would be hard to find a more sensible way of doing it than this.

The list of eminent marketing, research and advertising people who are, at best, dubious and at worst, contemptuous, of copy testing is almost endless. Why, then, do the peddlars of this nonsense continue to survive and to prosper? Surely, the answer must lie in our desire to find some objective and rational measurement of what we cannot help reacting to subjectively and emotionally.

For 50 years research people have tried, but failed, to find the answer. It is a reasonable assumption that they will not find it before the end of this century. Yet direct response people know the answer and have known it since the end of the last century. The answer lies, perhaps *can* only lie, in measuring behaviour.

A better way to gauge effectiveness

To measure behaviour we must include some form of response mechanism in our ads. There is no other way to demonstrate whether one ad, or one campaign, will be more effective than another. It is quite impossible to compare live-test response results of many alternative ads without learning more about what makes ads work. I know far more about advertising now than I did when I was engaged in it full time. Paradoxically, I am presumed to know far less, because I am now a direct marketing person.

There is, of course, an objection to using response behaviour as a measure of effectiveness. It is that the aim of a campaign may be something else entirely. Let us suppose we are trying to persuade our target market to choose our, hitherto unknown, brand of champagne when they go to the supermarket or off-licence. To do this we must establish a high awareness level in the market and convey the notion that our brand is somehow preferable to the competition. We shall probably try to give it a cachet, a snob value, which suggests that the sort of people who know champagne, and drink it regularly, prefer our brand.

You could, with some justification, maintain that attaching a response mechanism to an ad which sought to convey this would be an irrelevant artifice; that response would not be a reliable measure of whether the campaign would achieve its objective. How could the most dedicated direct response enthusiast argue with that?

Yet, I now submit for your consideration this proposition: suppose the offer were to send a gift-wrapped bottle to a friend or business associate? All you, the recipient of this message, have to do is to call a toll-free or freefone telephone line and quote your credit-card number. Then a gift-wrapped bottle will be sent to your friend with a greetings card in your name.

Your purpose in responding may simply be to demonstrate your affection, or it may be to impress someone with your good taste and thoughtfulness. Either way, you would probably like the esteem in which your friend holds you to increase, rather than be diminished, by your kind gesture. Therefore, you will want to send a brand that is a testament to your good taste and thoughtfulness.

Now let us suppose that what we are really doing is testing one ad against another. I submit to you now that if ad A pulls 50 per cent more gift orders that ad B, it is *more likely* that ad A will make the basis of a campaign that will achieve your objective more quickly and for less outlay than ad B. If you doubt this, consider the alternatives. You could use research, which has been proved over and over again to be entirely specious. Or you could, more reasonably and at less cost, back your hunch.

So how good is your hunch? Pretty good? Let us say you have been in marketing or advertising a good few years now. You have not got to where you are by making too many mistakes. Or have you? How can you *know* this? On what scientific evidence do you base such an assertion?

The dubious value of expert judgement

In October 1983, I was speaking at the Direct Marketing Association International Convention in Miami. One of the other speakers was Stan Rapp, co-author of *Maximarketing* and one of the founders of the Rapp & Collins direct marketing agency. Picture the scene. There were 270 hard-bitten direct marketing professionals packed into the darkened theatre when Stan Rapp rose to his feet. He held three $100 bills up high. He would give them, he said, to the first three people in the theatre who could predict the results of the ten split-run ad and mailing tests he was about to show. Split runs, in which alternative offers, headlines, copy treatments, designs, mailing formats and even direct marketing agencies are tested, are the life blood of direct marketing. Results of such head-to-head encounters are measured by the response they produce, the business that results and the eventual profitability of each ad or mailing.

The tests were drawn from the USA, the UK, France, Switzerland and Australia. To make it harder, some of the splits were not just A, B splits in which alternate copies are seen by alternate readers (a perfect random sample, you will note) but three- or four-way splits and, in one case, even a six-way split.

Pretty tough to judge. Still, with 270 *bona fide* experts in the room there were bound to be some winners, were there not? I got six out of ten right and I already knew one of the results. I could not find anyone who claimed better than seven. Not noted as a gambler, Stan knew his money was safe. Experience had told him that when it comes to predicting results, the experts were not much better than random guessers.

It is a sobering thought. When I told you I knew more about advertising now than when I was engaged in it full time, I did not tell you that the most important thing I have learned since is how fallible I am. Every direct marketing person of any experience has this self-awareness. That is why we seek to substitute empirical evidence for so-called rational judgement at every opportunity. That is why we understand the desire to test copy but we are not deluded by the artificial and fundamentally unsound research methods that are all too commonly used today.

So much for conventional copy research. And so much for our infallibility. Is the measure of direct response to our champagne offer beginning to look more attractive to you? It should. Accepting its limitations, which are purely to discover whether ad A or ad B is *more likely* to be efficient in achieving our objective, it has two overwhelming advantages.

Firstly, the sampling technique is sound. We have sampled the true audience to our campaign by running the test in the media we shall be using. And we have conducted the test on an A, B split-run basis, so our two sub-samples are perfectly matched. (Incidentally, with the exception of cable, we cannot do this on TV. We have to test regionally.) Secondly, our measurement is of actual purchaser behaviour. True, it is not a retail purchase. But the purchaser is still making a statement about himself when he commissions us to send a bottle to his friend: 'I am a thoughtful person who appreciates this champagne and I think you will, too.'

Note that I have not claimed that such a test will demonstrate whether either of the two ads would be successful, but only that one ad is more likely to be successful than the other. No one has yet discovered whether a test market will be successful without conducting it. That is why marketers have to go to that expense.

We have, however, substituted an objective measurement of behaviour for subjective judgement or inaccurate measurement of an irrelevancy. Incidentally, if we keep the offer going when we roll out the winning ad, we also now have a captive list of donors and recipients. This not only has a marketing value, as touched on earlier in this chapter, but also is productive of a wealth of information. For example, we know which credit cards our buyers prefer to use. From their post or Zip codes, and those of their gift recipients, we can access a great deal of geo-demographic and lifestyle data which will assist us in our media planning and tell us the store locations which represent high potential for the product. We have executed a copy test and produced a valuable set of media and marketing data as a bonus.

Single-minded advertising

It is impossible for me to forget my advertising training and lose my awareness of the importance of single-minded advertising. Thus, when we talk of taking advertising across-the-line, we must not forget the objective. Advertising with a single objective very often achieves it; advertising with a number of objectives rarely achieves any of them. It is for this reason that I admit the danger implicit in measuring the likely effect of advertising for a retail-distributed product by means of direct response.

What I fear is that, insensitively handled, the addition of a response mechanism can be crass. Later in this book you will learn of all sorts of techniques and tricks that you can use to increase direct response. One can all too readily envisage a scenario in which an insecure and ignorant client may forget the true objectives of a campaign and demand more, and yet more, direct response. It is not hard to deliver this response but it may be at the cost of an image that has been carefully nurtured and developed over many years.

The limitations of response as a measurement of the success of a campaign created to induce retail sales must not be forgotten. As with any business enterprise, the goal for the campaign must remain visible so that the shortest route to it is followed.

Fortunately, this potential conflict between the development or preservation of a brand or corporate image and efficiency in achieving direct response does not always emerge. Indeed, as we have seen earlier, the consumer prefers advertising that contains hard information and an immediate opportunity to act upon it. We have learned this through long experience of the testing and measurement of alternative ads—not simply from reading and noting scores. Ads which satisfy the reader's demand for information (this varies according to the nature of his commitment) outpull ads with short, clever copy. Ads with a prominent reply mechanism outpull those with a discreet coupon. We have learned that the consumer prefers ads which engage his or her interest on the merits of what is being sold rather than through artifice.

The value of clear communication

Reproduced on pages 15 and 16 are two ads cut from the same magazine. They are both direct response ads, though each ad is also concerned with branding. One ad, that for The Carphone Group (Fig. 1.1), is rather obviously produced by hard-bitten direct response professionals— actually from my old agency, MSW Rapp & Collins. Clearly, the priorities are response first, corporate identity second. The second ad (Fig. 1.2) is for Laura Ashley. It advertises a new spring clothing catalogue and the framed design features the telephone number that you can call (at no charge) to receive a free copy of the catalogue. Those responsible for this ad were, presumably, more concerned with the stewardship of the image than the volume of requests they would generate.

Reproduced in small size and black and white, it is probably not too difficult to discern the displayed telephone number in the Laura Ashley ad. In its original full colour, full *Sunday Times Magazine* size, it was easily possible to see each delicate drawing of a garment which made up each digit of the telephone number. It was, however, next to impossible to see what the patterns represented. I discovered the telephone number by reading the body copy. Thinking that this might be a peculiarity of my own perception (or lack of it) I showed the ad to four other people. None of them twigged that the drawings of clothes added up to the telephone number.

It is not possible to see the ad in its full glory here. But, take my word for it, it was carefully crafted and painstakingly put together. Yet I believe it was destroyed by a misguided attempt to be clever. For, after all, what is the point of advertising the availability of a free catalogue unless you want readers to take advantage of your offer?

I said at the time that I believed the creators of the

A powerful mobile phone that doesn't tie you to your car from just £6.95* a week.

This is a transportable. A powerful cellular phone that can be used in or out of your car.

You can call from almost anywhere

A transportable can make or take calls anywhere within the UK's cellular coverage area. So whether you're in a car, in a restaurant, on a remote building site or on the train home, you will always be in touch.

It clips into and out of your car

In fact, you get all the benefits of a carphone but with the extra flexibility of a fully portable phone. A transportable clips in and out of your car with ease. And now The Carphone Group can supply you with a hands free version –
so you don't even have to lift the handset to dial or speak.

19,000 Carphone Group customers

There's more to choosing a cellular phone than checking a list of features. It's just as important to ensure your phone is installed and serviced properly. That's why over 19,000 people have chosen to buy their mobile phones from The Carphone Group.

More experienced than other companies

The Carphone Group have been in the business of supplying mobile phones for 9 years. Our engineers are highly qualified and carefully trained.

And our offices are nationwide. So you are guaranteed professional and individual attention on a local basis.

Send for the free fact pack now

The Carphone Group have produced a FREE FACT PACK all about mobile phones. How to choose the best one, where to have it installed and serviced and information on other associated services. Claim your fact pack *free* by calling our HOTLINE or returning the coupon. Or call your local office – they're listed at the bottom of the page.

The FREE FACT PACK gives you details

Features available on our range of transportables.

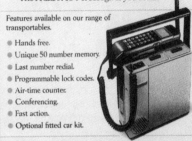

- Hands free.
- Unique 50 number memory.
- Last number redial.
- Programmable lock codes.
- Air-time counter.
- Conferencing.
- Fast action.
- Optional fitted car kit.

on the other phones in The Carphone Group range (including in-car phones and handportables). On Cellnet and Vodafone systems. Send for yours today.

For a faster response call our HOTLINE TODAY on 01-749 9572.

*Offer includes free demonstration, and is based on a five year lease rental agreement, 3 months down payment with installation, network subscription and calls extra. Subject to availability.

LONDON 01-749 9572. BIRMINGHAM 021 455 7999. BRISTOL 0272 276 719. EDINBURGH 031 312 8000. LEEDS 0532 420777. MANCHESTER 061 872 3312. MILTON KEYNES 0908 560148. SOUTHAMPTON 0703 339773.

Figure 1.1 The Carphone.
The straightforward approach. The telephone is actually a tipped-on card.

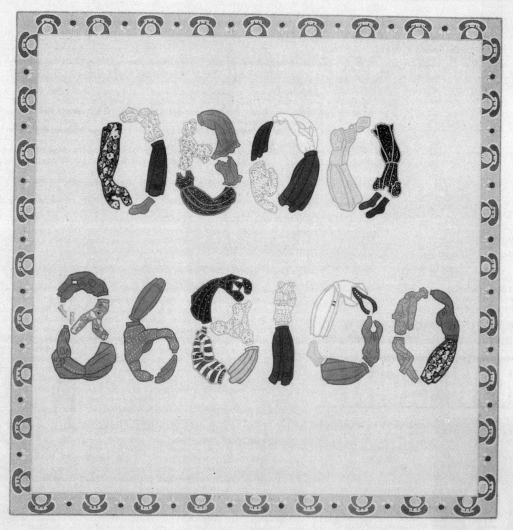

THE LAURA ASHLEY CLOTHES LINE.

Ring free phone 0800-868100 and you will receive a catalogue of our new Spring Collection.

Our new Mail Order service gives prompt delivery and the convenience of settling by credit card.

You can add a breath of fresh air to your wardrobe without venturing outside.

Figure 1.2 Laura Ashley.
You are invited to phone for Laura Ashley's catalogue. Misplaced ingenuity?

Carphone ad could have sold more copies of the Laura Ashley catalogue at £2 each, than those responsible for the Laura Ashley ad could give away.

Just look at the difference. The Carphone ad leads with a benefit headline above a clear cut-out illustration of what they are offering. The copy is peppered with sub-heads, acting as alternative start points to the reader. It is made very clear how to respond and the copy makes plain exactly what information is available to responders. The ad is, however, less carefully crafted in its appearance. The typographer was not worried by leaving the odd 'widow' here and there. Personally, I do not think this detracts from a busy, interesting-looking ad that is packed with information of interest to anyone on the brink of deciding to have a mobile telephone.

Readers not yet ready to respond will have been rewarded by the informative nature of the Carphone ad. It will have done the image of The Carphone Group no harm at all in their eyes.

Seeing with the consumer's eyes

The harsh reality of being confronted with statistical evidence of one's errors forces the direct response professional to adopt the viewpoint of the consumer. Time is not wasted on irrelevancies, points that will be noted only by people engaged full time in advertising. The reader is given what the reader wants. Is this really so bad for the image of the commodity being advertised? The ads achieve high noting and reading scores. Readers spend more time on ads of that type.

On one of my all-too-many commuter rail rides I observed a man poring over a direct response ad featuring a number of different items. He spent ten full minutes with the ad. I know this because I timed him. Yet, I do not have a single friend in the advertising business who would have done other than dismiss the advertisement as being appallingly badly designed. I would not have dared to enter it even for a direct response creative award. If I had, it would have been tossed aside in the preliminary judging.

But can you seriously believe that the ad harmed the image of the advertiser with this man? Or that he would forget who the advertiser was? Anyone who knows the market well enough to engage people's attention for a matter of minutes with an ad deserves applause, not brickbats. Still, the advertiser is doubtless cheered by the cash receipts.

Nor is this an isolated instance. The week before I sat down to write this chapter, a free-standing (loose) insert fell out of one of the Sunday magazines at home. It was an A5 size 36-page speciality catalogue. My wife, whom I thought would have been starting work on lunch, instead spent 20 minutes—yes, I timed her, too—absolutely engrossed by this catalogue. That is almost as much time as she would have spent with the rest of the newspaper, which contained, say, around 200 ads.

A better way to measure media effectiveness

Just as the measures of copy effectiveness which are conventionally applied to advertising are totally misleading, so are the techniques of head counting media research increasingly irrelevant when one ad has the capacity to engage attention for minutes on end and another fails to rate a second glance. Of course, we are not all the same and what interests one reader may turn off another. Yet, those ads that engage attention for more than a few seconds are nearly always ads with a response mechanism and with a satisfactory information content.

The experience of analysing direct response from media advertising gives an insight into the qualitative differences between one medium and another. Such differences are assumed and taken into account by any good media planner. But how can the planner test assumptions or give a number value to the belief that one medium seems, editorially, to be more compatible with the product or advertising message than another? It is impossible. Any plan is, therefore, a mix of mathematics and hunch.

If we are able to analyse response data from test insertions, we know better. Even if our main objective is not to secure direct response, it is surely a measure of the relative interest in our message in alternative media. I was first struck by the scale of qualitative differences between media more than 20 years ago when working for a catalogue mail order client. We used two large-circulation women's weeklies, *Woman* and *Woman's Own*. Their circulations were, in fact, very similar. The readership profile data showed no significant differences. As a mere male, I could not see any obvious distinction between the type and tone of the editorial in *Woman* and the editorial in *Woman's Own*. Even the make-up, typography and picture content were much the same. Yet one magazine pulled 40 per cent more response than the other. Subsequent test insertions produced a consistent result.

Since then, I have encountered far more dramatic differences, though seldom from such similar media. Even now I cannot see how the most perceptive of media planners could anticipate qualitative differences on this scale.

Direct response also gives us a basis for making inter-media comparisons between whole media groups: newspapers versus magazines, even print advertising versus broadcast media. In making such comparisons we need to keep in mind the effect of the reply mechanisms available to us. Obviously, the options open to us with broadcast media are restricted and, if direct response is not the main objective of the campaign, our inter-media comparison may be impaired if we take only direct response into account.

A better use of space

Often of greater practical interest are less ambitious comparisons: between alternative space sizes or colour versus black and white, for example. It was in the late 1950s that Brian Copland drew attention to the relatively high efficiency of small spaces by producing a formula derived from *noting scores*. Taking two media—a mass-circulation Sunday newspaper and a women's weekly magazine—he examined the noting scores of different sizes of ad. He concluded that noting increases in line with the square root of the increase in size. Thus an ad twice as big produced only just over 40 per cent more notings. I have no idea how conclusive his findings were and, of course, his thesis is long out of print. (Later Starch research in the USA indicated an even smaller gain.)

Nevertheless, it is almost uncanny how often doubling the size of a direct response ad increases the response by little more than Copland might have estimated. We might even attribute the slight extra benefit of a larger size to either extra informative copy, an easier-to-complete coupon, or to the extra importance accorded to the advertiser by a larger ad.

More recent studies have confirmed that noting rarely increases in arithmetic proportion to size. However, I have found that certain product categories do not follow this rule when it comes to response. One such category at the present time is life insurance. Full-page newspaper ads work for sell-off-the-page insurance, even though it is possible to condense the same quantity of information to fit a smaller space. It was therefore with great interest that I read that noting scores are also out-of-step with the norm when it comes to financial advertising. (I am indebted to the Reader's Digest Association's library for this information, derived from an analysis of Starch INRA Hooper Noting and Reading Scores in the United States, undertaken by Edwin Bird Advertising.)

Table 1.1 shows the effect of increasing size from full pages to double-page spreads in four business magazines. Financial ads are compared against a base of all other ads.

Edwin Bird Wilson concluded, '... a low interest product category has more to gain from larger advertising units than a high interest product category.' This is surely true for, if a page ad achieves a noting score of 67 per cent then it is impossible to improve this score by more than 50 per cent. However, there is likely also to be a dominance factor at work. If the whole of a page or spread is taken up with a low interest ad it is harder to escape from it than if the ad has to compete for attention with other, more interesting items within the same area.

It is not my objective here to suggest that there is a direct relationship between noting and response. Indeed, I know that there is not. Clearly, far more people note an ad than read the whole of it, and far more people read the whole ad than respond to it. Nor would I suggest that the rather artificial measures of noting and reading, as measured in research studies, are any substitute for the recording of the 'real life' behaviour that is available from counting coupons or telephone calls. An ad has to do more than get noticed, although getting noticed is a good start.

What I do find interesting is that two pieces of objectively

Table 1.1 Advantage of spreads v. pages

	Business Week	Dun's	Forbes	Fortune
Noting—all ads	+ 30%	+ 45%	+ 33%	+ 31%
Noting— banking/finance	+ 81%	+ 92%	+ 81%	+ 90%
Reading most— all ads	+ 38%	+ 50%	+ 29%	+ 43%
Reading most— banking/finance	+ 150%	+ 150%	+ 150%	+ 217%

derived information tend to point in the same general direction. It is not a direction that finds much favour with many of my former colleagues in general advertising. In 1986, I received a distress call from a senior account handler in the London office of a well-known international agency, which better remain nameless. The agency had run full-page newspaper ads for a product and, for the first time, had included a response device. The response had been abysmal. Could I tell him where they had gone wrong? There were many things wrong, of which the size of the ads was probably the least important. Nevertheless, I asked why the ads, which contained scarcely any information, were designed as full pages. He assured me that his job would be in danger if he briefed the creative department to produce anything smaller.

Appalled by this revelation, I telephoned a friend who was a director of the same agency. He assured me that the poor fellow was under a misapprehension. Yet the atmosphere of ignorance and fear of creative colleagues which could engender such a mistake simply could not exist in an environment where all concerned are supplied with a regular flow of factual information about their performance. The notion of creative infallibility is quickly seen to be ludicrous and everyone becomes a little wiser, or at least more knowledgeable, as a result.

Direct response also gives us a measure of the value of colour. Again, colour gives an advantage to noting and reading scores—broadly similar to that gained by doubling the size. However, some products are highly 'colour sensitive', while others are not. It would be tempting to suggest that this is a matter that can be resolved by the application of a little common sense—although sometimes it can, but this is not always the case. Very often advertisers run straight adaptations of colour ads in black and white. And very often they do not work. But if we create the ad as a black and white ad to start with, we can often make it at least as cost-efficient as the colour ad. This is something we can only discover from direct response test experience.

Understanding the effect of frequency

The media insights that we gain from our direct response experience do not stop at media selection, space size and use of colour. Possibly the most interesting of all is that which challenges the generally held notions on frequency. The direct response specialist knows that he is already experiencing sharply diminishing returns when he is distributing advertising impacts with far less frequency than many media planners would consider an acceptable minimum.

I can illustrate this point most clearly by calling upon my television experience. Many years ago, when I was a media planner, it was drummed into me that unless I could achieve 400 rating points in as many weeks, preferably with an even frequency distribution, I was simply wasting the client's money. Anything less than 400 rating points (equivalent to each viewer seeing the commercial four times) was virtually useless. Not many advertisers could afford such a high frequency today. Yet, when I first used TV as a direct response medium, I never even considered this frequency. My first campaign for a learn-with-play course was directed towards young mothers using day-time TV. Because I was aiming at a specific audience segment I thought I could get away with a low-frequency campaign using a relatively large number of 60-second spots, each achieving a low audience rating. The whole campaign notched up just over 100 rating points over four weeks and we were experiencing diminishing returns by the last week. Over the years, as TV became more expensive, we cut back and back. By the fourth year we were down to 63 rating points using 30-second commercials. It was not a brilliant success but, discounting airtime cost inflation, the fourth-year campaign was marginally more efficient than the first year of the campaign.

It would take a timebuyer of unusual imagination to believe that such a low-frequency campaign could have any impact at all. Yet, time after time, direct response experience in all media keeps suggesting that conventional notions of necessary minimum frequency may not be well founded. In print media few mail order products can stand a frequency of much more than one appearance in four weeks in any one publication. I can think of one product that suffers diminishing returns with more than three pages in weekly colour magazines over a 12-month period.

Of course, we must recognise that there is a difference between the effect of advertising on coupon or telephone response and its effect on retail sales which, by definition, are made at a later time and in a different place, doubtless with many intervening distractions. In a retail environment the cumulative benefit of advertising is likely to count for more, and the weight of competitive pressure may need to be counteracted. Yet, if the effect of advertising is necessarily cumulative, why is there never a detectable cumulative benefit in a direct response campaign? Much is made of the fact that response is instantaneous. The first time we see a message we decide to respond to it or discard it. Subsequent exposures make little difference. Yet, if this is the case for direct response ads, why is it not the case for non-response ads? And, if it is the case for direct response ads, why do responses come in—sometimes in quite large numbers—for weeks, or even months, after the ad has appeared? What has triggered a late response? Clearly, the decision to respond must have been made earlier—and the coupon, the ad, or the complete publication put on one side. But what has finally prompted the decision to respond? It could well be the sight of a later ad in the same campaign, a competitive ad, or some external influence. Then, of course, there is the effect of pass-on readership. Generally, direct response advertisers expect to receive only about half the response they will get from the *Reader's Digest* in the first month after their ad appears. The remainder may come in over a period of 18 months or longer, although 95 per cent will generally be received within three months.

All these complicating factors make it difficult to compare the ideal frequency of a direct response campaign with that of any other campaign. Perhaps it is enough to say that direct response experience suggests that the effects of advertising are more subtle and more complex than many advertising people recognise; that, in some measure, advertising is effective at much lower weights than most realise, and that direct response experience affords us the best chance of pinning down the true effects of advertising investments in the years to come.

The advertisers who add a response mechanism to their ads cannot help but learn more about the effect of their advertising as a result. The more alternative ideas they test, the more they will learn.

The pay-off

Direct marketers know they cannot survive on new business alone. That is why they have always maintained lists of customers to whom they can mail catalogues or one-shot product offers. They have been doing this almost since postal services began although, until the invention of the computer, list maintenance was a laborious and cumbersome process.

Nevertheless, repeat sales were invariably cheaper to make than new business sales.

Direct marketers have not been alone in recognising the vital importance of repeat business. Few businesses could survive without taking action to secure the loyalty of their customers. At one time, it might have been sufficient to ensure that the quality of the product matched competition; but increasingly aggressive use of 'offensive marketing' tactics made it essential to take more positive steps, through advertising and loyalty promotions, to keep customers faithful to a brand or a retail store.

In this respect nothing has changed. What has changed is that the combination of more narrowly targeted products (niche marketing) and the escalation of broadscale advertising and promotion costs have raised the penalty for inaccuracy. It is no longer viable in most markets to talk to customers while also talking to everyone else. These changes have taken place in an environment in which the consumer desires more information and increasingly wishes his or her individuality to be respected. The consumer increasingly wishes the vendor of merchandise to talk *with*, and not *at* him or her. The consumer wants an informed dialogue, not a repetitious monologue.

The astonishingly rapid reduction in the cost of building and maintaining one-to-one marketing databases makes it possible for many more companies to treat consumers as intelligent individuals. It is no longer necessary to be running a mail order business, a bank, or an insurance company to build and maintain a customer database.

What is necessary, however, is the persuasive skill to make prospects and customers want to enter a dialogue with the manufacturer or supplier of goods and services. Media advertising is only one of a number of vehicles that can be harnessed for this purpose. However, it is in many markets by far the most important.

Such media advertising may have as its sole objective the collection of enquiries or first-time buyers. Or it may serve a dual purpose, with the collection of names, addresses and, possibly, telephone numbers seen by the advertiser as a bonus. It is the contention of this book that, in reality, all advertising has the dual purpose of creating a clear-cut, favourable identity for a brand or business and making immediate sales. The notion that one course can be pursued to the exclusion of another is artificial. For what is the purpose of creating a favourable image unless it is to complete a sale? And how can we argue that we can undertake direct response advertising without some effect, adverse or favourable, on the image of the advertiser? If so, is it not better that the effect should be favourable?

The questions which direct response activity raises in our minds—whether we are patrons or practitioners, entrepreneurs or creative people—are entirely healthy. They are healthy because the activity is measurable and can be related, directly or indirectly, to bottom-line profit. The direct response specialist lives in the real world and has to listen to what the consumer is saying. These questions are also healthy because they are based on factual evidence, derived from actual consumer behaviour and not primarily from research of variable quality. Sample research measuring past behaviour is generally more or less as reliable as the sample composition. Research seeking to measure future behaviour is less so. The direct response specialist substitutes live tests for predictive research. He is therefore substituting the measurement of past behaviour for the forecasting of future behaviour.

It is impossible not to increase one's learning-rate when bombarded with evidence in this way. The instructive process leads us to question what few other advertisers have very seriously questioned, and we keep coming up with the answers that would disturb many. These answers may not be absolutes and may not hold good for all time. Yet our capacity to test and to continue testing enables us, more often than not, to stay one step ahead.

Earlier we have asserted that most advertisers underrate the consumer's desire for information—indeed, underrate the consumer's intelligence. We have arrived at this conclusion from observation of response to advertising. Yet supporting evidence from other sources abounds. In recent years, we have seen a proliferation of successful consumers' guide magazines, advising on the purchase of everything from an insurance policy to a car. We have seen the introduction of more informative food packaging, the growth of financial and holiday features in newspapers, on TV and the radio. Yet much of the non-direct response advertising we see today denies the consumers the information they crave.

Far from being less attractive to the reader, ads which supply information and promise an opportunity to respond—either by placing an order or requesting additional information—are more attractive. More people look at such ads, and more people read all or, at least, the biggest part of them. People spend more time with them. The supposition that readers find ads boring, and the ads should therefore be as short as possible is totally fallacious. Equally misguided is the notion that readers have to be 'conned' into looking at ads by artifical attempts to be 'clever' or 'entertaining'.

The rigid differentiation between ads and editorial is in the mind of the advertising person, not the reader. Readers read what interests them. They make a decision to focus on, or reject, both pieces of advertising and editorial content more or less instantaneously.

Readers simply do not bother to look at ads which do not promise a reward for so doing. That is why ads that contain a benefit in the headline and supporting illustration most frequently outperform ads that do not.

The good news is that interesting, informative, benefit-led advertising works even in comparatively small spaces, with comparatively sparse frequency. If we are to believe our results, most non-direct response advertising is too concentrated in short bursts, probably in too narrow a range of media, and with over-indulgent space sizes. This inefficient type of schedule could turn profit into a loss of almost catastropic proportions for a mail order advertiser. Even bearing in mind the differences between brand advertising and mail order, it is possible that the advertiser who can measure the efficiency of his advertising with precision knows something the other advertisers do not.

Direct response experience suggests that many advertisers waste a substantial part of their budgets by over-concentration of investment. That is to say, they use excessively large spaces, too frequently, over too short a campaign period, in too narrow a range of media. As a result their advertising investment delivers diminishing returns.

These, however, are matters on which you, the reader, will wish to make your own judgements. This book merely gives you a guide as to how to plan and execute direct response campaigns. It will guide you whether your interest is in across-the-line advertising, sales lead generation or selling off-the-page. In following it, you cannot help but learn things about advertising that will be entirely new to you.

2 How advertising works

The proposition

Much of what we have discussed in our opening chapter is contentious. It apparently does not fit with research-based theories of how advertising is used by consumers to help in the selection process of any commodity which may involve a long or complex decision process. I am conscious that the breadth of the territory covered in the first chapter prevented me from doing justice to the counter argument. Since this argument is powerful, to leave it unexpressed and unanswered would be an omission of unforgivable proportions. It would leave the advocate of across-the-line advertising exposed to the charge of partiality or, worse still, ignorance.

So, before venturing into a deeper study of our subject, I shall endeavour to do justice for classical advertising thinking and to explain why the view expressed in Chapter 1 is soundly based.

Fortunately the evidence to support classical advertising theory is not in dispute. It is based, not upon specious advertising effectiveness research, but upon research into the thought processes of the potential consumer. Too much of this research has charted the buying decision process in a similar fashion for even the most dogmatic direct response protagonist to dismiss the conclusion as mere hypothesis. The underlying facts, then, are common to both arguments. The only difference is in their interpretation.

It is tempting for the direct marketing specialist to sweep aside non-response advertising as unaccountable and, therefore, of doubtful value. Indeed much of it is. However, this would do a grave injustice to good advertising which not only does work, but can and has been proved to work on the evidence of correctly executed research and, indeed, sales. I use the term non-response as shorthand. I mean, of course, non-direct response. All good advertising provokes a response. All good advertising people are interested in evaluating this response and quantifying it.

Any major purchase involves a selection process which is

quite complex and may take a considerable time. This process may begin almost unconsciously long before the potential consumer is faced with making a firm decision. In this chapter we shall examine the process and see the contribution advertising makes to steering the consumer in the desired direction. We shall examine the arguments for separating the messages delivered at different stages in the process (the arguments for non-response advertising) and the arguments for truncated communications (the arguments for across-the-line advertising).

The selection process

There is a little dispute in the advertising business about the steps which form a potential buyer's selection process, although they are not always described in exactly the same way. A graphic illustration of the process that particularly appeals to me is one I saw at the London agency, KHBB, and I hope I may be forgiven for borrowing it.

The analogy used is one of a bucket (Fig. 2.1) which, of course, has a large open top and is tapered. To make our examination more concrete, let us assume that Mr Prospect, our consumer, has taken the decision to buy a car.

To enter the bucket the consumer has first to be aware of the alternatives. Some of the alternatives may be relevant, others not. The purpose of advertising at this stage is to ensure that the potential buyer is aware of our car before seriously considering the acquisition of another car. Indeed, the process of building awareness may have started long before Mr Prospect was in a position to buy a car at all, perhaps as a child. If we fail to achieve a high level of awareness among the target market we have defined, fewer people will enter the bucket. Our car will not be considered because it is not within our prospective buyer's consciousness—hence, the preoccupation of advertising people with 'intrusive' advertising. Clearly, advertising which establishes awareness even before the potential buyer has entered the market will be more effective than advertising that has to start from behind. To be effective before the consumer is seriously interested, the ad has to be effective at engaging attention through its sheer impact. This should not be confused with stridency. It may achieve impact through its entertainment value or its aesthetic appeal. How advertising accomplishes its task may depend on who our potential buyers are. Its capacity to raise the

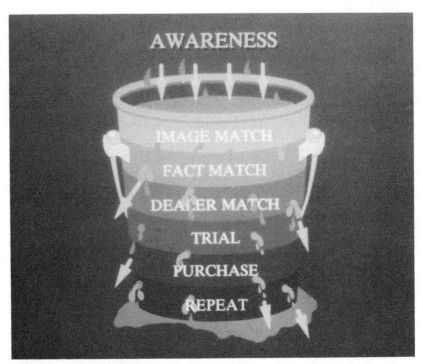

Figure 2.1 Bucket.
The consumer steps in selection. The KHBB Bucket.

level of awareness among our target market is a legitimate measure of advertising effectiveness. It is not a complete measure, but it is a vitally important one. Our prospect will not enter the bucket unless he is aware of what we offer. While it is always possible for our product to enter the list of candidate purchases at a later stage in the selection process, it is at a disadvantage unless it was among the original candidates. Sticking with our car example, it would be too late at the test drive stage. Most dealers sell only one or two marques. Even at an earlier stage in the process it may be an intruder, dismissed by the potential buyer as an unwelcome disturbance to a selection process already well under way.

Image matching

At the top of our bucket, the *image match* is the first stage of the selection process. In this stage, our consumer, Mr Prospect, matches the advertised car with his own image requirement. If he wishes to project an image of success he is most likely to be attracted by advertising which conveys status and luxury. If he sees himself as a dynamic go-getter with lots of aggression, he is more likely to be attracted by advertising which conveys high performance and handling characteristics. These attitudes to marques can become so entrenched that it is difficult for the manufacturer to launch a model that has characteristics not matching the consumer's perception of the marque. These perceptions can only be changed gradually and with an intensive effort. Few of us would disagree that the process of image matching, particularly in the car market, follows immediately on that of awareness, before serious practical considerations apply. Nevertheless, it would be absurd to suppose that such considerations are totally excluded from the potential buyer's mind. No one with a family of six, who can afford one car only, is seriously in the market for a Porsche. However, such facts as may intrude on the buyer's thinking process at this stage are fairly basic. The process is more a dreaming process, or wishing process, than a conscious, rational thought process.

The business of assisting the consumer in the image-matching process is nearly always simultaneous with the business of establishing awareness. Although the two stages can be expressed sequentially, this is not how advertising is generally used. Advertising people would regard advertising as wasteful if it did no more than establish awareness. Advertising has also to establish relevance. Since the consumer, more often than not, uses image matching to establish relevance, advertising must also project an unambiguous image for the product. Thus our potential buyer is not only aware of the car, but is also aware of its relevance to his need to project an image of himself. The converse is also true. He may become aware that the image projected by the car does not match the image he wishes to project of himself. Thus our potential buyer is aware of more cars than those which match his image requirement. The bucket leaks. It has holes in the sides.

Leaving aside any question of targeting, television is the most powerful mass-audience medium for promoting awareness and for surrounding a product with the desired imagery. It is not a good medium for conveying much factual information. This does not matter since our consumer will shortlist on the basis of image matching with scant knowledge of the practical considerations applying to each candidate. Only those candidates that offer an image match will merit further consideration. Thus the advertising plan will use the media which best support its objectives, while reaching the target market as efficiently as possible. The

advertising plan will also reflect a need to build up
awareness over a period of time.

Fact matching

If it has achieved its twin objectives of establishing a high
degree of awareness and offering an image match to a large
number of potential buyers, many people will enter the next
level down the bucket. This level is the *fact match*. At this
level our consumer is closer to the day of decision. He is now
ready to start collecting the information he will need to
make his final decision. This process may be much more
thorough for some people than it is for others. Many will
have found a perfect image match with one car. They do not
want to be confused by the facts. They only need enough
information to post-rationalise a decision which, to all
intents and purposes, they have already made. The facts
may even be collected solely to rehearse a rationale for their
decision that can be presented to their spouse or to friends.
For these prospects the car's designers and the advertising
people have done their job, and only the prospects' friends or
the dealer have any chance of talking them out of buying
their dream car. They may not even take a proper test
drive. They are nearly as good as money in the bank.
Suckers!

For others the fact match is a more serious undertaking.
Possibly more than one model offers a near-perfect image
match. Possibly there is a potential conflict between
aspiration and practical considerations. Our potential buyer,
Mr Prospect, now displays heightened awareness of
advertising and editorial road test reports. He may buy
specialist magazines and discuss his potential choice with
friends. At this stage, advertising still has a role to perform.
Advertising will appear in the car magazines the
fact-matcher is collecting. Print advertising may also appear
in newspapers offering low-cost finance or some other deal to
bias the facts in our favour. The expenditure on this
advertising will be much less since it is directed only at
those people who have entered the second level down the
bucket. They are also only at that level for a short period of
time. So our audience is smaller. And because of the
audience's heightened interest we do not have to swamp it
with advertising. One exposure to our fact-match message
may be enough.

Our bucket tapers and there are holes in the side all the
way down. At fact-match stage our car will be eliminated by

many who found it satisfying at image-match stage. Perhaps our potential buyer read a road test report in which our car was damned with faint praise or even panned. Maybe there were a dozen other favourable road test reports he could have read but he had to pick on one of the few bad ones. Perhaps the car does not stand up well on trade-in value, economy, rear leg-room or some other feature which is important to our potential buyer.

Possibly, the presentation of the facts disturbed the image. The way in which facts are presented can inadvertently be at variance with imagery surrounding the car at image-match stage.

Dealer matching

Those remaining in the bucket now descend to a level at which they are ready to start kicking a few tyres or picking up some brochures. They need to find out about dealers. This is the *dealer-match* level and, at this level, local newspaper and yellow page directory advertising is likely to be used for reference. The car manufacturer's or distributor's influence over the image presented by dealers may be crucial, for again there is a good chance this may be inconsistent with the imagery that got the car short-listed earlier. If totally antipathetic, the image projected by the dealership can destroy Mr Prospect's dream. This disturbance may occur before he gets to the dealership or while he is there.

On his first visit he may not get beyond looking at the stock and taking away a brochure. But the dealer will want him to enter the *test-drive* stage when he should be gently persuaded to buy, accepting an agreed trade-in price for his old car.

Once he has made his purchase, Mr Prospect will make his judgement about whether he was right or not fairly quickly. His judgement will depend on whether the car lived up to his image of it, whether it performs reliably, and the quality of the after-sales service he gets. He is already starting the process all over again, congratulating himself, or contemplating a switch next time round.

Through research it is possible to establish how many people enter the bucket, how many leak out at each level, and the reasons why they leak out or descend to the purchase level. The effectiveness of advertising, together with other influences, can be measured at awareness and image-match stage. Much leakage between image-match stage and fact-match stage may suggest that the image projection is unrealistic or wrongly targeted. Alternatively, we could blame the product.

This sequence of processes can be, and often is, used to justify the elimination of irrelevant fact and response mechanics from advertising which has been sensitively and intelligently designed to establish awareness and assist image matching. The objectives are clear and logical. Since the consumer must be made aware of our product and will initially short-list it on how well the image matches his or her self-image, there is no point in disturbing this process by trying to throw in the kitchen sink. Bombarding a prospect with facts too early will upset the process of assimilating the imagery with which we want to surround the product. The facts are better left until the consumer is ready to descend to the fact-match level. It is difficult enough to buy awareness and carve out a desirable and clear-cut image without attempting to truncate the whole buying decision process. We must first appear seductive before we present our more mundane virtues. Trying to present both qualities at once ensures that we shall communicate neither.

A more direct approach

I used to believe all that. Many people more intelligent than I, still do. It is a logically supportable argument. More than that, at one level it is entirely true. It is perfectly correct to say that a mood commercial for a sporting car could be utterly destroyed by rattling off a stream of performance data, price information, or an invitation to take a test drive. But this is not what I would advocate. Such advertising would not be across-the-line advertising, merely bad advertising.

So what, then, are the arguments in favour of a more direct approach? Firstly, there seems to be general agreement that advertising should seek to accomplish more than establish awareness of the existence of a product. Since image matching is assumed, in most cases, to be the first of a series of sifting processes, we can afford to double up the tasks of establishing awareness and projecting an image. Indeed, the accomplishment of the second task reinforces the first since we are describing who should buy our product. Already, then, our advertising is performing two tasks in the space of one advertisement. We are declaring both the availability and the relevance of the product in one message. Is this not enough?

The difficulty with this argument is that, even if the buying decision stages were invariably in the sequence we have described, our advertising audience are not all at the same stage. Those who will look at our advertising with the greatest of interest are those closest to a buying decision. They may be about to make it or may have just made it. The closer they are to the buying decision, the less satisfying our image advertising is. They know we are desirable, they want to know we are attainable. Our advertising is not greasing the sides of the bucket so that they can slip down it effortlessly. Unless we help them to slide down the bucket we may remain what we said we were—a beautiful image. What we have done is to leave it to chance how they will tackle the fact-match stage. Unless they go through this process with our car the odds are they will buy a different car. If we do not make the process easy for them they may well tackle it, but in their own way. Instead of our presentation of the facts, they will use someone else's presentation of the facts. This presentation may or may not satisfactorily answer their questions. It may or may not be favourable. It is likely to be in the form of what they can easily find from road test reports or capsule descriptions in car magazines. If the verdict is not in our favour, our carefully nurtured image will be of no avail.

The factual information they may obtain about our car from magazines may be compared with the manufacturer's own information about a competitor's car. Consumers cannot be expected to act fairly or particularly thoroughly. If a competitor makes it easier to undertake the fact match, the competitor will probably get the business. In my view, the competitor will deserve to get the business.

A second difficulty with the classical advertising argument is that not all consumers go about contemplating a purchase in the same way. The consumer's image of who should drive a particular car may depend more on who he knows is already driving one than the impression the advertising gives. If a successful neighbour or colleague is driving that type of car, that may be more desirable than if it is not the case. The potential buyer may wish to emulate a real person rather than a fictional character in a commercial. He or she has moved into the fact-match stage without the aid of advertising or with advertising playing a subordinate role. What he or she needs to know now is where more information can be found.

Others—in the case of cars, they are often women—are less concerned with using a car to project their own self-image. They want it to project them and their passengers from one physical location to another. The image match assumes much less significance than the fact match. Now it is possible to generalise and say that such people as I describe would short-list cars with an image of economy, reliability or safety. That they are, in fact, undertaking image matching first. Yet I believe the dividing line between choosing a car as a projection of oneself and choosing it for another virtue, such as economy, cannot be explained away entirely as a characteristic of the car. Clearly, the cheaper a car is, the more likely it is to be chosen for practical virtues. But no car is so cheap that the buyer could not instead purchase something cheaper secondhand. The difference between buying a new East European car and an old sports car is not one of price. The former buyer is primarily concerned with facts and the latter primarily with self-image. The balance of fact and imagery is infinitely variable and will be different in different people's decision process to buy even the same type of car.

The assumption that the consumer selects first on image match, without any real consideration of fact, is largely true but is not entirely true. Some consideration of fact is necessary to involvement in the message. There is no point in desiring a Rolls-Royce if we can only afford the hub caps. Then again, how do we separate image from fact. Is not the price of the Rolls-Royce, which is fact, not a most important aspect of its image? Does not the claim, '0–60 mph in 7 seconds', help the image along a little bit? What is to one person an aspirational purchase is, to another, highly practical. Whatever the balance between imagery and fact, between emotion and rationality, we must give the consumer every assistance to slide down our bucket easily or a prospective buyer may escape through the holes.

Greasing the sides of the bucket

I do not suggest that it is always necessary or even desirable to present much by way of factual information in advertising whose purpose is to establish awareness and create a personality for a product. However, if it does not communicate factual information, that is no reason why it cannot offer a source of information. Indeed, since there is no point whatever in letting potential buyers enter the top of our bucket unless we wish them to reach the bottom, there is every reason why we should do all we can to help them on their way down. Unless they go to the fact-match level they will not, except in a few eccentric cases, buy. Advertising is purely a means to an end and it will work better when the linkage between awareness and purchase stages is strong. Each stage should contain a link with the next. The awareness ad should tell us where we can find out more, perhaps by phoning for an information pack. This information should tell us where we can inspect the product, discuss it, test it and buy it. The whole sequence should be a painless process. I am sorry if the suggestion of adding a phone number to the end of the commercial is offensive to some advertising people. I understand, but I do not sympathise. Advertising has no intrinsic value, it is purely a means to an end. It is wasteful to let people slip through the sides of the bucket and, while we cannot keep them all in, we can at least make the effort to keep in as many as we can.

Sometimes, of course, a direct response mechanism may be an image killer. More often it is not. I look forward to the day when a case has to be made for leaving out a response mechanism. At present a case has to be made for putting one in. Since the sole purpose of advertising is to bring people closer to purchasing, this strikes me as rather strange.

Sooner or later, the potential consumer must make the sometimes enormous leap from the dream of the product generated by advertising and the reality of the dealership, or the dealer's local newspaper ads. This is where good linkage pays off. If our awareness ad offers us more information by phoning a toll-free or freefone number, we can now assimilate facts presented in a way that is consistent with the image. Instead of having to read these facts in car magazines, they are presented on glossy pages surrounded by seductive pictures of the car. We are controlling the fact-match process and ensuring that the facts are presented in a way that is not dissonant with our image. Our presentation of the facts is personally addressed to our enquirer. With these facts will come a personal test drive invitation from the local dealer or a promise of a phone call from the dealer. No need to look up dealerships in a local directory or find our dealer's ad, peppered with secondhand car bargains, in the local newspaper. Instead, everything is presented and handled in a way that is consistent with the image we have presented.

The addition of a response mechanism to an ad is a small price to pay for a seamless communications process in which the values of the product are maintained from first awareness to the moment of purchase and beyond. To ignore the fact that there is a big gap between the glossy imagery of an expensive commercial and the crude reality of what will greet the potential buyer in his local newspaper or on the dealer's forecourt is comfortable but unprofitable. Sooner or later the consumer will find, in the process, a gap which is hard to bridge, and the more control we exercise over communications throughout, the easier it will be to close the gap.

The example of the car buyer can be continued beyond the purchase decision and on as far as the replacement decision. Clearly, the more consistent the image promoted by the dealer's attention to after-sales service and mailed communications is with the image promoted by advertising, the more likely it is that our buyer will not be disappointed and will stay loyal to the marque.

Controlling the dialogue

In this context we see advertising as no more than the beginning of a dialogue which we wish to enter with our potential buyer. It is not good practice to hand over the responsibility for maintaining this dialogue to others and hope for the best. It is essential to control it through mailings, possibly through telemarketing, and through selection and education of dealers, so that we are seen to speak with one voice. We cannot control this process without inviting prospects to identify themselves to us.

The more control we exercise, provided we are doing the right things, the more successful we shall be. The more successful we are, the more selective we can be of our dealers and the more we can demand of them. The more successful we are, the higher will be the demand for secondhand models and the smaller will then be the depreciation of the new cars we sell. It is a success spiral. Manufacturers such as Ford and BMW are very demanding of their dealers, ensuring that the dealer delivers, in presentation as well as service, a package that is consistent with the image. It is no coincidence that Ford are the most advanced users of direct marketing technique in the automotive industry.

Many advertisers do not have such difficulty in controlling each stage of the decision process. In many cases the process is less agonising to the consumer because the purchase decision is less crucial, less irrevocable. In others, the advertiser is also the supplier, as in the case of an airline. Yet the principles remain the same, and the case for the sort of advertising that leaves the consumer high and dry with no signposts pointing to where he can find out more will get harder and harder to justify as advertisers seek to exercise greater control over the dialogue with potential buyers.

It is impossible to conduct a dialogue with consumers from the moment they enter our potential market until the moment they leave it without learning more about their decision-making processes with consequential benefits to all our communications. No one can afford to remain aloof from parts of the process that are not their direct responsibility. We have achieved nothing worthwhile until a sale has been made and nothing very much until a customer has been won. We have not won a customer until he or she is satisfied with the purchase and is prepared to buy again from the same source.

In the automotive market the word 'conquest' is used to describe a sale made to a new customer. My friend Uwe Drescher, president of Drescher, Heine, Rapp & Collins in Hamburg, made a presentation to Volkswagen in which he pointed out that the term was misused. The first sale was not a conquest. It was merely the first battle won. A conquest involved turning a prospect into a loyal subject, one who remained with the marque and, even, acted as an advocate for it. To make conquests we must be in direct touch with our prospects as early as possible and remain in touch with them for as long as possible. Advertising that does not help us to begin that process is short-changing us.

A classic example of a truncated image–fact–dealer test drive match was given to me by Stan Rapp, co-founder of Rapp & Collins Worldwide. He told me that in 1981 Giorgio fragrances were the first ever users of scent-strip inserts in magazines. It was a case of necessity being the mother of invention because this new company were unable to gain acceptance of their range in retail stores. Being a perfume manufacturer it would never have occurred to them to run anything but very stylish advertising with mood photography and minimal copy. Image-match advertising. The only difference was that the advertising was in the form of inserts which also incorporated a scent strip to 'test drive' the product and an order form so that you could buy it. The perfume sold in quantity. It sold in such quantity that stores were besieged with potential buyers and Giorgio were now in the nice position of magnanimously agreeing to supply. Giorgio continued to sell direct as well as supplying the stores. They recovered 30 per cent of their advertising investment out of the profit on direct sales so they were able to outspend the competition. By 1984 Giorgio was the number one brand. Now most of the major competitors were following suit and running scent-strip ads. Nevertheless, Giorgio were able to sell their company for $187 million in 1987 just six years after starting it.

Not every advertiser has the opportunity to truncate the process quite as dramatically as this. But that is no excuse for making it difficult for the prospective buyer to move down the bucket. Giorgio is living proof of the reward that can come from making the process as easy as possible.

The pay-off

The way in which consumers decide what to buy and what not to buy has been the subject of extensive well-executed research, not simply advertising effectiveness studies of the type we have already dismissed. This research leads us to believe that there are a number of decision stages in the process which direct marketing people will ignore at their peril. These stages are: IMAGE MATCH, FACT MATCH, DEALER MATCH and TEST DRIVE or TRIAL. Many products are excluded by consumers simply because they are unaware of them. The first and primary function of advertising is to make known to the potential buyer what we have to offer. Other products are known to the consumer but are eliminated with scarcely a conscious thought because their image does not match the consumer's self-image. This matching process will generally take place before any serious fact-collection has begun, often before the consumer is in the market for the product category. Fact matching takes place as the purchase decision looms near and this process may be serious or less serious depending on the value of the purchase and the strength of the desire to possess the product. Low-value commodities do not receive as much consideration as important purchases, such as cars or holidays. Similarly, where the image match is perfect, the motivation for fact collection may simply be to post-rationalise a choice that has already been made.

The dealer-match stage may be crucial when the product can be purchased from only one source in the consumer's locality or where the advice of the dealer is needed as reassurance. In some cases, mail order and car rental being two examples, the dealer and the advertiser are one and the same. In other cases the consumer may have many alternatives in the selection of the store from which to make the purchase. Depending on the satisfaction of the dealer match, the consumer will then take a 'test drive'. In the case of a perfume the test drive may involve the application of a small sample to the wrist. For wine, it will be a wine tasting. For furnishing fabrics it may be taking home a sample swatch of material. In mail order it may be 10-days' free trial. For many commodities, including almost all packaged goods, it is a trial purchase.

Many marketing and advertising people believe that any attempt to truncate these decision stages will confuse the consumer and lead to a loss of clarity in communicating the special quality of a brand. They are prepared to accept as inevitable the leakage that occurs between each stage in the decision process. It is this belief that is challenged by the across-the-line advertiser. The across-the-line advertiser argues that advertising communicates simultaneously to audience segments who are in different stages of the decision process. Some of the audience, perhaps the majority, are in the image-match stage. Others are in the fact-match stage. Because the latter are closer to a buying decision they will be more attentive to our advertising. If it neither supplies information nor directs the audience to where information is available, this advertising frustrates the fact-matcher and causes leakage.

The best way to minimise leakage at the fact-match stage is to control the fact-matching process. To do this we must allow fact-matchers to identify themselves to us. Since they are a minority of any media audience, and close to making a purchase decision, knowing their identity is very valuable information. It enables us to satisfy their thirst for facts in a way that is synergistic with our image and without confusing our mass media advertising. We can enter a private dialogue with our prospects, one in which they tell us a little about themselves and we tell them which of our products will suit them best.

By undertaking this dialogue with the consumers we are now less vulnerable to a potential mis-match at dealer stage. The consumers are more certain of the decisions they have made and are less susceptible to dealer advice. Their dependency on the dealer is reduced.

While the purchase of a car is very different from the purchase of a can of beans, the same logic applies. If the consumers know that our beans are nutritionally superior to, or have a lower calorie-count than, the retailer's own-label beans, the consumers are less likely to be switched by the retailer to the own-label product. This principle may even be extended to added value services such as hair colourant advice lines, diet plans, baby care information, or other services which can be introduced to our identified prospects at fact-match stage. Such services forge a strong link with consumers.

Unless we are an across-the-line advertiser we cannot enter into a private dialogue with a prospective purchaser, and cannot exercise any direct control over the decision process. Advertising is too expensive to waste in this way.

3 Eight kinds of direct response

The proposition

Direct marketing people, when talking of response, usually classify response as one-step or two-step: one-step is an order; two-step is an enquiry. While these broad divisions are useful shorthand descriptors, there are a good many kinds of two-step responses and several one-step responses.

A direct response may come in by mail or telephone; it may be accompanied by a credit card number or cheque; it may be in the form of a simple request; or it may be a completed questionnaire. The action that we invite our readers to take is only limited by the extent of our imagination and what is reasonable and practicable to do.

Unless we are attempting to complete a sale from our advertisement, our purpose in soliciting a response is to get our suspects to identify themselves as prospects. We are in complete control of how well qualified we want our prospects to be. The harder we make it for them to respond, the fewer will do so. But those who do respond will be hot prospects.

What determines our choice is its effect on total business or profitability. If it is relatively expensive to handle an enquiry, or if the subject matter is interesting enough to generate many casual enquiries, or if it is costly to follow up an enquiry (with a salesperson's visit, for example), then we shall be careful to ensure that our enquiries are well qualified. What we are doing is balancing the advertising cost of obtaining an enquiry against the cost of handling it. Depending on the ratio of advertising cost to handling cost we shall be more or less selective.

This same principle often applies to one-step advertising. We can increase the number of orders by invoicing with the goods. But we shall also increase returns, incur bad debt and increase our administrative expense. So it may be more economical to settle for fewer orders by insisting on a cheque or credit card number with the order. It depends on the advertising ratio, the size of the bad debt risk and the gross profit margin on the goods.

Two-step advertising response

The kinds of two-step advertising responses which are described below are not mutually exclusive. It is impossible for respondents to request information from us without telling us something about themselves. For even if they only give us their name and address and post code, this is sufficient to apply geo-demographic descriptors to their address. Or, if they work for a company, we shall probably ask for a job title and we may apply a Standard Industrial Classification to that company.

Information seeking

The first kind of two-step response we shall consider is INFORMATION SEEKING. Information seeking response includes brochure requests, booklet requests, audio or video cassette requests, requests for lists of stockists, etc., when the purchase will be consummated at a retail outlet or through an appointed distributor.

Information seeking response advertising is the most widely used of all forms of direct response advertising and, in its purest form, easily the least useful to the advertiser. Until comparatively recently, advertisers offering brochures and other information rarely kept the names and addresses they collected, scarcely ever passed them over to retail outlets, almost never bothered to classify them geo-demographically, and quite often failed to use them to analyse the relative cost:effectiveness of alternative media.

Yet, each name and address represents a sales opportunity. Until we have decided how we intend to use the opportunity we should not trouble to produce a brochure or take any Information Seeking response advertising.

It is not difficult to think of actions we could take to make the most of information seekers:

1. We can put them in touch with a specified dealer.
2. We can give them a discount voucher or other limited-time offer to prompt them to visit a dealer quickly.
3. We can send a follow-up mailing to find out if they have made a purchase and induce them to do so, if not.
4. If we incentivise our warranty or guarantee card system (with purchase), we can track enquirers through to purchase. We now know the relative conversion rate from

alternative media and can profile enquirers against purchasers.

5. From our collected enquiries, provided we keep the list clean (i.e. up-to-date, removing people who have changed address), we now have an enquirer database to market new products, to test market, to cross-sell and to undertake new product research.

6. We can profile enquirers using ACORN, MOSAIC, or the geo-demographic classification system of our choice. We can compare this profile with whatever profile data we have on the total market, media readership and known users.

7. From our response analysis we can obtain a guide to the relative cost:effectiveness of media, space sizes, colour, copy and offers.

Information providing

Although we can easily find ways to make information seeking response more useful, it still may not be useful enough. We may need to know more personal details to qualify our enquirer as a true prospect. This leads us to a discussion of our second type of response, which is INFORMATION PROVIDING.

Our information providing respondent's motive is not to provide us with information but to receive a benefit, in exchange for which the prospect is prepared to give us information. This method is used by companies who specialise in producing *Lifestyle* marketing databases for general direct mail use. Such companies collect questionnaire responses through guarantee cards, or loose inserts, or house-to-house distributed questionnaires, often with the incentive of money-off coupons. However, information providing response is increasingly being gathered by individual manufacturers, distributors and service companies. Among the first users were airlines (to identify frequent flyers), but FMCG manufacturers are increasing their use of this technique.

Early examples included Bristol Myers, to identify users of competitive hair-colourant brands, both in the USA and the UK. In the UK, colour page ads in magazines offered a free pack of Clairol in exchange for a competitive pack top. A further pack was offered in exchange for a completed questionnaire. By keeping in touch with the respondents and tracking their purchase behaviour, Bristol Myers would be able to gain much valuable information on product acceptance of Clairol among the users of each of the competitive brands.

A classic case was provided by Colgate Palmolive in Denmark. It was decided to launch a dishwasher detergent, Galaxy, using direct marketing techniques, because of the high wastage implicit in a large-scale mass media campaign. In any event, Galaxy could easily be outspent by the brand leader, Neophos, which enjoyed a 70 per cent market share. At the time of the launch, 23 per cent of Danish households owned a dishwasher. Had it been possible to identify those households individually, Colgate would simply have mailed them with an offer.

Instead, a double-page spread ad was taken in a free magazine offering roughly 100 per cent coverage of Danish households (2 135 000 circulation). A questionnaire was tipped-on to the ad. The incentive to complete the questionnaire was a 10 Kr money-off coupon against a purchase of Galaxy. Respondents had to identify which dishwasher they owned, which detergent they used and give various other items of personal information. Colgate got 46 600 responses, equivalent to 10.4 per cent of the 448 000 dishwasher owners. Of the 46 600, 14 000 completed a product usage questionnaire in exchange for a further 10 Kr. At this stage 26 000 coupons had been redeemed. A further promotion to the responder's file produced another 8000 new names from a recommend-a-friend offer. Colgate announced a final expectation of data capturing 25 per cent of all dishwasher owners and securing a 15 per cent market share by the end of the launch period.

An interesting adjunct was the use of telephone research among non-redeemers to gauge the effect of the promotion on them. The use of research to test the advertising value of promotions among non-respondents is becoming more commonplace. The uses of Information Providing response are almost endless. Indeed, as we have seen, any response is productive of at least some information. How much information we seek depends upon the uses we can make of it. The more information we seek, the less response we are likely to get. Alternatively, the more information we seek, the greater the incentive we must offer to secure a response. Each case is a trade-off between quantity of information and cost of response.

We should bear in mind that some information will be required from all respondents, while other information may only be required on a sample basis. The information required from all respondents is that which will drive our private marketing database communications. Remaining information, required for research purposes, is best left to a second stage after we have already captured the highest possible number of identified prospects or users.

The types of incentive we offer the information provider need not be a money-saving coupon or a free sample. It may be valuable information (e.g. a video cassette) or it may be free membership of a travel club, or an advisory service to young and expectant mothers, or any of a wide variety of other benefits.

Enquiry generating

ENQUIRY GENERATING response differs only from information seeking response in that we are now intending to complete the sale by mail or telephone. This whole process may be very rapid as, for example, if we secure a telephone enquiry for motor insurance and provide a quote and secure provisional acceptance in the same conversation. Or it may be very long drawn out. A coupon returned by a prospective home study course student may be followed up by six or seven mailings and, perhaps, a telephone call before the course provider gives up and places the would-be student on a bulk file of failed enquiries.

The considerations of advertising cost per enquiry, fulfilment (enquiry handling) cost and conversion rate are similar to information seeking response. The main difference is that the enquiry generating adviser is in a much more advantageous position to study the mathematics of alternative tactics. Since the advertiser knows precisely the number of sales and their value, the benefit of any change that is made can be calculated, whether that change is to advertising copy, media selection, offer, or follow-up procedures or materials.

The advertiser is balancing quantity of enquirers against their quality. It is a fascinating business and the correct tactics for any one advertiser are quite unlikely to be right for another. The correct tactics for the same advertiser may even vary between different media.

Here are 20 ways in which response quantity/quality can be adjusted:

1. Ask the respondent to pay postage.
2. Offer FREEPOST.
3. Use a loose or bound-in insert with pre-paid card.
4. Add an 0800 (toll-free) phone number.

5. Ask for the respondent's telephone number.
6. Ask for the respondent's business card.
7. Make the reply coupon bigger.
8. Illustrate a free brochure.
9. Offer a cassette.
10. Offer sample swatches of material, or other free sample.
11. Require the respondent to give personal data.
12. Offer a gift to reply.
13. Offer a gift against purchase.
14. Qualify the reader with long copy.
15. Emphasise the purchase stage in the copy.
16. Use a prize draw or competition.
17. Use full colour.
18. Alter media selection.
19. Offer a choice of free gifts.
20. Make the enquirer state which of several alternative products interest him.

This list is by no means comprehensive. It can be as long as human ingenuity and our capacity to analyse test results can make it. As the reader can readily deduce, some of these ideas are designed to increase response, others to inhibit casual response.

Years ago, the well-known horticulturalist, Ron Blom, was persuaded to test loose inserts to promote his bulb catalogue. The insert was in the form of a small postcard carrying a full colour shot of the catalogue. The respondent was invited to fill in his name and address and return the card. Naturally, it was a postage-paid card and response flooded in until it reached more than 5 per cent of the run. The cost-per-response was minimal but the catalogue wastage on unconverted responses was verging on the unacceptable. The solution was to make the respondent use a postage stamp to reply. In a split-run test of this modification against the original insert, cost-per-response scarcely altered. The reduction in response rate was counterbalanced by the saving in pre-paid postage. But the conversion rate increased sharply and so fewer catalogues were used up for each order obtained.

The problem with horticultural catalogues and travel brochures is that they are treated like free magazines. Many people send for them as a source of reference or entertainment with no serious intention of ordering. It is necessary to qualify the respondents by making them pay postage, asking them for personal data, or even charging for the catalogue if its appeal is sufficiently strong to withstand such a drastic step. It is not uncommon for catalogue charges to be imposed but refunded against the first order.

More often, however, the advertising cost-per-response looms large when compared with the enquiry fulfilment cost. Some injection is needed to stimulate additional response. Once, when I was visiting Pickfords Travel, I was asked if I had a business card on me. I handed it over and they turned it into a luggage label with the card sealed in a clear plastic cover with a slot punched in it to accommodate the leather strap.

This gave me the idea of an incentive to get business travellers to identify themselves as prospects to Pickfords Business Travel. I had my reply incentive and we were able to data capture accurate job title and address detail from the business card.

The components of the equation are: advertising cost-per-response, fulfilment cost and conversion rate. Often, fulfilment cost disappears under another budget caption and is ignored. Yet it may be a very significant item. Suppose we are mailing a brochure or catalogue which costs £2 postage paid. Magazine A pulls responses at £2.50 each and gives a conversion rate of 10 per cent. Magazine B pulls responses at £5 each but produces a conversion rate of 20 per cent. If we merely count the advertising cost, both media will give us the same cost-per-sale: £25. But, when we count in fulfilment cost, the true cost-per-sale from Magazine A is £25 plus £20 (for ten catalogues) = £45. Magazine B costs less. £25 plus £10 (for five catalogues) = £35. The tactics we adopt: to increase response, curb response to boost conversion rate, will depend on the relative values of each part of the equation.

Lead generating

Lead generating response will be followed up by a salesperson. Instantly, we can see that the ratio of advertising cost to follow-up cost is likely to be very different than it is in the case of enquiry generating response. The cost of a salesperson's time in making a presentation in the prospect's office or home may be anything from £100 to £250, or even more. If the salesperson is self-employed and depends on commission earnings, this cost does not disappear. If we give the salesperson 'loose', time-wasting leads, he or she will not be able to make a good living and will switch allegiance to another company.

The logic which this new cost equation may suggest to you

is that copy for lead generating ads or mailing should be much tighter, to produce 'qualified' leads. Yet practical experience does not support this logic. The reasons are, firstly, that any attempt to qualify enquiries always cuts out some people who would have bought and, secondly, it is generally possible to qualify leads at low cost after they have come in.

Leads may come in by mail or telephone. With live telephone answering, they may be converted to appointments on the spot. Mailed responses can be telephoned or, alternatively, may be sent an information package and invited to cancel the salesperson's intended call, if they wish, by contacting the advertiser.

The plain fact is that many more potentially willing buyers will respond for a free brochure, or even the vague 'further information', than will send back an enquiry form requesting a sales call. If this, admittedly, unexciting chapter is boring you I hope you will bear with me. On the other hand, you could do worse than pick up a copy of Alan Coren's *BUMF*. In it you will find quoted an ad from *Exchange & Mart*. It reads: 'Muratex Shelving Systems salesmen have an exciting tale to tell! Ring us NOW for an immediate call. You won't be disappointed.' Alan Coren fans will readily imagine the kind of exciting tale which his salesman told.

While appealing to Coren's highly developed sense of the ridiculous, the ad might also have appealed to people desperate to get their hands on some genuine Muratex shelving. But the point is that it over-qualifies the respondent and in the wrong way. Those most likely to be willing to face an over-enthusiastic salesman are those with the self-confidence to control the interview. Some years ago, when the Federal Trade Commission required the company selling *Encyclopaedia Britannica* to print a warning message (that a salesperson might call) on their ads in New York State, the response went down as you might expect. What you might not expect was that the conversion rate also deteriorated. Those not put off by a salesperson's intended call were those with most confidence in their ability to say 'No'.

The only extent to which a lead generating ad should attempt to qualify respondents is in terms of their interest in the product and their acceptability as a potential purchaser (e.g. creditworthiness, job status, etc.). A study of lead generating copy from experienced companies will show that, far from being longer and more explicit than enquiry generating copy, it is shorter—attempting to whet the appetite, not give the whole game away.

When one considers that most products and services justifying the cost of a salesperson's time are, by definition, relatively expensive and difficult to sell, it must be right to avoid overlapping the salesperson's function in the ad or the mailing. The purpose of the ad is to generate a potentially convertible lead. It is no more than that unless it is also to make the market aware of the product.

Nothing that an ad or a mailing can say will equal the power of a well-conducted face-to-face presentation. If it could, salespeople would cease to be employed.

The mathematics are simple enough. We have an advertising cost, a response-handling cost and a sales-call cost. To optimise our effectiveness we must juggle with these elements to get the right formula. The response-handling cost may include an incentive or there may be an incentive against purchase. The response-handling cost may also include a catalogue or brochure and a telephone call to book an appointment. The formula may look something like that shown as Table 3.1.

Table 3.1 Component costs

Cost of each component	£	
Advertising cost-per-lead	10.00	
Brochure despatch	1.50	
Telephone calls	2.50	
Sales calls	100.00	
Total cost of components		
Advertising leads (@ 1:10 per sale)		100.00
Brochures (@ 10 per sale)		15.00
Telephone calls (@ 10 per sale)		25.00
Sales calls (@ 3 per sale)		300.00
Total		£440.00

So far, so simple. The complicated part is that salespeople need places to go. If they are wholly dependent on advertising leads, the business of keeping them fully—but not too fully—occupied can be nightmarish.

What is required is a completely even flow of leads across sales weeks and across sales territories. This is an impossibility, although some levelling out can be achieved through the use of reply incentives in low-pull months and late deal newspaper advertising to plug gaps in the schedule.

Salespeople with too many leads in their pocket will start to select the ones they think are the best or most convenient to call upon. Salespeople with too few will start to lose confidence and, probably, income. No company which depends upon sales leads should leave itself without methods through which regional sales managers and representatives can generate their own. National advertising should never be the sole source of leads, but it can perform a valuable role as double-duty advertising, creating an environment within which it is easier to sell. It does this by making the product and the company better known and trusted.

Another complicating factor is the attitude of salespeople towards leads generated from particular offers, copy or media. Sometimes these are based on one experience and are completely fallacious, yet a negative attitude to an offer or a medium can spread like a bush fire through a salesforce. There is nothing one can do except rest the offer, the medium or the ad until the fire has died out. The belief that an ad generates loose leads becomes a self-fulfilling prophecy.

Some companies attempt to deal with this by disguising the source of leads so that they will be handled impartially. However, this may be denying salespeople information that is useful in the initial handling of the prospect. Sharing information will usually lead to a better result, with a two-way exchange of experience and ideas more than compensating for the occasional scrapping of a good idea that has a bad name with the salesforce.

Here are 15 ideas that can help you to execute effective lead generating response advertising:

1. Before you do anything talk to sales managers and representatives and go out on sales calls. Always check what you have found out with a senior manager because the experience may be atypical.
2. Gain a thorough understanding of the mathematics.
3. Allocate to media selection the first priority: media decisions are generally the most critical in determining quantity and quality of response.
4. As a general rule mailings (unless to a well-qualified list) will produce the loosest leads, followed by inserts, and space ads will produce the tightest leads. The cost-per-lead will probably be in reverse order.
5. In media that produce tight leads at high cost, consider the use of a reply incentive.
6. A free brochure will pull more response than a vague

offer of more information. If it is illustrated in the ad or mailing, the response will increase.

7. A prominent reply mechanism will increase response. Telephone replies may represent an immediate opportunity to convert to appointments.

8. Relatively few people are willing to request a sales call, although they are less reluctant to do so in business-to-business advertising. Those discouraged by the promise of a sales call are not necessarily less likely to buy.

9. The loss of response that may result from requesting the enquirer's telephone number will be more than compensated for by ease of contact if the advertiser intends to book appointments over the telephone.

10. It may be advantageous to allow enquirers a choice of follow-up. A check or tick box allowing urgent enquiries to short-circuit the free brochure and to request immediate contact often works. Up to 10 per cent of enquirers may respond in this way. They are hot leads.

11. Nothing gains a bad name with a salesforce faster than a sweepstakes response mechanism. Use only as a last resort.

12. Take every opportunity to maintain dialogue with salespeople. Pre-sell campaigns, share success stories. Their confidence in the advertising is crucial to its success. And they can give you good ideas.

13. Check on how your ads or mailings are being followed up regularly. Respond to them and get friends or colleagues to respond. You will sometimes be amazed by how easily things can go wrong.

14. Remember, your advertising can do more than generate an immediate response, without sacrificing its efficiency. Ensure it does a good branding job.

15. Even if there are no direct competitors, there are always other ads and mailings which are relevant. Collect them, study them and try to work out the strategy. Maybe there is something you can learn.

Your efficiency in lead generation will be heavily dependent on the efficiency of lead tracking in the sales organisation. It is absolutely vital that if it is less than perfect, you put it right or make such a nuisance of yourself that the person responsible puts it right. You cannot do good work or get good work done unless the facts are at your fingertips.

Credit applications

CREDIT APPLICATIONS are a specialised form of response which are, nevertheless, of great importance. Legal constraints will determine the size, shape and presentation of terms of the application form for a credit card or a fixed-term loan. Advances in the design and adoption of credit scorecards have led to a reduction in the number of enquirers who are accepted. The best answer to this is to generate enquiries from a pre-scored mailing list, but relatively few companies have developed the technology to make this possible. Thus a large number, perhaps the majority, of applicants are rejected.

A credit scorecard takes the factors that are known about a person living at a particular address and weights these, together with application form details and information about the area of residence, in proportion to their significance. It is an actuarial process, like working out a motor insurance premium. The problem is that the answer comes out as 'Yes' or 'No'. A 'No' does not imply that the applicant is a bad debtor, but merely that the risk that he *might* become a bad debtor is unacceptable to the company on the basis of what is known.

Thus a high reject rate may well lead to a number of creditworthy rejects who are unlikely to look upon the company in a favourable light. Clearly, this is a problem to be avoided in so far as possible. By far the most significant variable in this context is media selection. Nothing else will qualify applicants nearly as well as putting the inserts or ads in the right media or mailing the right lists.

It is not possible to qualify respondents by making a weak offer. Those who are most in need of credit and are, therefore, most likely to be rejected will apply anyway. Rather the reverse is the case. A powerful incentive, such as a high-quality gift will increase the average quality of response by attracting people with less need for an additional credit line. The problem with these latter people is that they may make limited use of credit once they are on board.

Contrastingly, an offer of a low interest rate for a credit card has two effects. It produces a high quality of response because it attracts serious people, and it produces extended credit users because people who use their credit card as a charge card are unconcerned with interest rate. These people are unprofitable to the credit card company.

There is no way round the legal constraints which cause most credit applications to look so forbidding. However, much can be done with the skilful use of a second colour to make the form look as easy as possible to fill in. More can be done to ensure the application is easy to seal and post. Loose inserts, tip-ons and mailings allow the maximum of convenience to be given to responders. This is important for credit cards, less so for fixed-term loans. A credit card may be applied for on an impulse, a fixed-term loan will not.

A one-step mail order ad for a dress may also be a credit application. However, since credit is the subordinate feature, the subject is best handled in a more appropriate section.

Order generation

ORDER GENERATION ads seek to complete a sale off-the-page. However, the sale will be conditional because the respondent has the right to return the goods with a request for a refund. It is an area of direct response which is intriguing to many advertising people and it is satisfying to complete sales from a mere page in a magazine (or, perhaps, a small space) when the ad is successful.

Nothing did more to change the attitudes to mail order of a generation of marketing people in the UK than the Scotcade ads of the 1970s. Unfortunately for Bob Scott, his immaculate ads produced many imitators, doubtless thinking there was easy money to be made in selling off-the-page. Almost all these imitators bit the dust because they had not thought the business through properly before they plunged in.

As much admired as the Scotcade ads in the UK were Joe Sugarman's famous JS & A ads in the *Wall Street Journal*, selling merchandise with narrative copy rather in the guise of a newsletter subscription ad, but written with more wit and great style. Such ads, devoting a full page to selling a single item, changed the face of mail order from multi-item modular ads or small bargain spaces, often featuring low-quality speciality products, to something altogether more widely acceptable.

Space ads are by no means the only example of order generating advertising. Single-item loose inserts or mini-catalogue inserts are widely used. Less commonly in the UK than in the USA, orders are generated by cold mailings (usually of catalogues) or off-the-TV-screen for single items. Order generating ads or catalogues are aimed at the credit card user and almost invariably offer a choice of ordering by telephone or post.

The subject of one-step advertising is large enough to merit a chapter on its own and it will suffice for the present to sketch in only enough of the picture to differentiate order generating advertising from other forms of direct response. Order generating advertising is used to sell a wide variety of commodities including clothes, hi-tech gadgets, hardware, collectables, newsletter subscriptions, even holidays—as well as many smaller business purchases.

The distinguishing feature is that the cash margin is sufficient to recover the cost of advertising (unless the purpose of the ad is really database building) and yet the percentage margin is not so high that it would make better sense to sell on a free trial (send no money) basis.

However, it is an axiom of direct marketing that the first sale you make will be the least profitable. It costs more to get a new customer by selling off-the-page than it does to keep that customer with good catalogues, good mailings and good customer relations. So, even the sell-off-the-page advertiser's pay-off comes from repeat business. Nevertheless, there is a limit to how much you can afford to pay for a new customer and a cash mail order company (as opposed to a credit or book club trading company) is generally unsound unless it is at least breaking even on the first transaction.

The reason is that a cash business does not have the built-in continuity of a credit or negative option club business. The mere acceptance of proprietary credit cards does not induce loyalty to the company. The more closely the item offered at the front end is a representative sample of what is to follow, the more likely it is that repeat sales will result. This, perhaps, explains why loose inserts in mini-catalogues have gained in popularity.

The use of the sell-off-the-page technique has spread to offers to merchandise direct from manufacturers who would normally sell through retail outlets. Impetus was given to this movement through the introduction of scratch-and-sniff cards, which Giorgio and Calvin Klein used highly successfully in the USA to launch fragrances direct to the public via magazine inserts. Sell-off-the-page has also been used to launch hi-tech products, the ads being used to educate the market on the capabilities of the product to pave the way for later volume sales through retail outlets. The failure of Sinclair Research in the small personal computer field, due to finance and production problems, should not blind us to what would otherwise have been a highly successful marketing strategy—one in which profit-making direct sell ads were used to influence many more potential consumers than those who ordered direct. The extraordinarily inventive Clive Sinclair was a pioneer of across-the-line advertising just as he was of ultra-low price computers and miniature TV receivers.

Before leaving our capsule description of Order Generating advertising, mention should be made of its somewhat chequered history. It is a business that can be entered into by almost anyone with minimal capitalisation. As such it represented a temptation to would-be get-rich-quick entrepreneurs who had no real understanding of the harsh mathematics we shall tackle in a later chapter. As a result, such advertising is now carefully regulated in most countries, e.g. in the UK through voluntary codes adopted by the media owners. Today's sell-off-the-page advertisers must satisfy the appropriate media associations of their ability to finance and supply the merchandise they advertise and may be required to set up an independently managed bank account for this purpose.

Trial generating

TRIAL GENERATING advertising works in precisely the same way as order generating advertising, except that the risk is transferred from the buyer to the seller. Whereas, in order generating ads, it is left to the dissatisfied buyer to return unwanted goods and claim a refund, in trial generating ads it is left to the vendor to collect payment for the goods.

The trial generating advertiser is, in effect, betting that the increased volume of business obtained through a free approval offer will more than compensate for the increased free approval returns, the bad debt, the adverse cash-flow and the extra collection expense. Put this way it may sound bad business, but this is far from the case.

Trial generating ads are most likely to be used in two circumstances. The first is when the cost of advertising (i.e., the cost of obtaining a new customer) is high and the margin available on the product is also high. We could consider books as a good example. The cost price of a book is generally about one-quarter of the selling price. The cost of advertising in this case is likely to be greater than the cost of the product. Since we can expect to double our response with a 'send no money' offer it makes sense to do this even though our net sales will not double, but may increase by about

75 per cent. The cost of bad debt will be relatively low because our product did not cost much to produce. Our advertising cost-per-sale will have decreased by over 40 per cent. This is more than enough to recover the additional expenses we shall have to meet.

The second circumstance in which send-no-money ads are likely to be used is when the advertiser wishes the respondent to open a credit account. The ad will then act as a 'sampler' of what is to come, which is goods delivered to the door on free approval with the opportunity to pay for them on continuous credit or, in the case of a business, on account. The biggest users of this type of advertising are catalogue mail order companies and the ads are most likely to feature women's clothing. Here, the margins are less attractive than in the case of books, the cost of merchandise being generally slightly more than half the selling price. Furthermore, free approval returns are a serious factor because of the fit, material and colour problems. In this case the advertiser does not expect to show a profit on the first transaction, but is willing to take the risk that he can win a loyal customer.

If the purpose of the advertising is not seen as making a profit on the first sale, but is seen as winning the maximum number of new customers for a given outlay, it makes sense to consider trial generating advertising. Furthermore, it gives the advertiser freedom from the restrictions of the voluntary codes mentioned above, and freedom to employ sweepstakes as a method of increasing response. Provided that freedom to enter is given to those who do not wish to order the merchandise, there is no problem in linking a promotion of this sort to a free approval offer. Partly because sweepstakes work most effectively in personalised mailings, a great deal of trial generating advertising is, in fact, by direct mail.

A more detailed discussion of the comparative mathematics of order generation versus trial generation is to be found in Chapter 6, 'How to plan—sell-off-the-page'.

Enrolment generating

ENROLMENT GENERATING advertising employs a loss-leading offer to induce the reader to enter a commitment to make future purchases. Most people think of book and record clubs as examples and, indeed, these are generally the biggest advertisers. However, wines and cosmetics are also sold in this way. Collectables may be sold on a subscription basis, as may continuity sets of books or craft cards.

Magazine subscriptions may be considered an example, but most magazine subscriptions are sold by trial generating advertising and some by order generating advertising. The distinction is that the subscription is usually for a fixed term and is paid in a lump sum early in the subscription period. An exception is the Consumers' Association. Their subscribers pay by direct debit and there is no fixed subscription term. Thus, the Consumers' Association is enrolling new members (or subscribers) with a loss leading offer in exchange for willingness to enter a commitment.

The Automobile Association and RAC also secure new members on a variable direct debit or continuous authority credit card basis. Open-ended commitments of this nature produce a higher loyalty rate than fixed subscription terms.

The great advantage of enrolment generation is that, after the first transaction, continuity is driven by negative option. The customer must cancel, or stop paying, to sever the relationship. Since most of us are lazy, this is likely to work much better than a positive option system which requires us to overcome our inertia to renew our subscription.

When the book club principle was new it was a licence to print money. The commitment might be to take only four books in the first year of membership. But the book club monthly newsletter, featuring the books available, contained the announcement of the book club's selection of the month. The subscriber automatically received this book unless he cancelled. Book clubs still operate on this principle, but today's sophisticated consumer—more often than not—ignores the book club's recommendation and either cancels that month's despatch or chooses an alternative book.

Enrolment generation is potentially the most profitable of all direct marketing activities because of the strength of negative option selling. It is only limited by the number of people willing to join, but this is a serious limitation. To join, people must foresee a benefit in the continued supply of a commodity or a service. There is a limit to the types of either which are perceived in this way. We may be prepared to buy books or wine through a club, or to subscribe to a private medical insurance scheme or a breakdown service, but the number of appropriate products and services is limited as is the number of potential joiners.

Book and record clubs offer what is called a 'subsidy' to make the front-end offer sufficiently attractive. This may cost at least twice as much as the advertising. The Consumers' Association employ sweepstakes. Continuity series book publishers may offer the first book free, together with the second on free approval. Gifts abound. It is a matter of adjusting the odds so that the consumer's greed overcomes his or her caution. After that, we must rely on the quality of our product and, possibly, the consumer's apathy.

The pay-off

Direct marketing people usually refer to direct response advertising as one-step or two-step. In reality, there are sub-divisions of these types so that there are, in all, eight distinctly different types of response advertising. All response advertising should be designed to win a customer rather than just a sale. However, the relative emphasis placed on doing the former rather than the latter determines the choice between the eight types of response advertising.

Two-step advertising
1. *Information seeking*. Advertising that offers the enquirer further information about the advertised product or product range. This is by far the most common type of direct response advertising.
2. *Information providing*. Advertising that seeks to collect information about respondents in exchange for providing them with a benefit, such as a money-off voucher.
3. *Enquiry generating*. Information seeking response is here converted to sales without the intervention of a dealer or a salesperson. The advertiser attempts to complete the sale by mail or telephone.
4. *Lead generating*. Information seeking response is controlled by the advertiser's own salespeople, usually after printed information has been despatched to the enquirer and an appointment has been made over the telephone.

One-step advertising
5. *Credit applications*. The respondent applies for a credit account or a personal loan subject to the credit provider's approval and his agreement to conform to the terms and conditions which must be stated in full at the time of application.
6. *Order generating*. Response comes in the form of an order with accompanying payment or credit card number and signature, unless the order is by telephone. A money-back

guarantee is obligatory. The most common form of one-step advertising.

7. *Trial generating*. The respondent does not send money but agrees to pay by the end of a stated approval period or requests later billing at the time of order.

8. *Enrolment generating*. The respondent does not send money but agrees to join or subscribe on the basis of stated terms and conditions. Where goods are offered (as in the case of a book club) these will be on free approval. In the case of a subscription, a free trial period may be offered using a post-dated direct debit or credit card continuous authority.

These, then, are the eight basic types of response although there may be variations and, in some cases, two-step response may in reality be multi-step, affording the respondent several opportunities to discontinue an enquiry. It is important for the advertiser to consider the potential lifetime value of a customer and to plan accordingly. It is only by looking at the customer's total value, or value over a considerable period, that the correct judgement is likely to be made about the initial offer. Unfortunately, while it is easily possible to test the effect on front-end response of each type of response advertising, it takes time to measure the resulting loyalty of the customers it produces. There is no substitute for knowledge of fall-out rates from alternative customer winning strategies and we shall give some consideration to these later.

All direct response advertisers, whichever of the eight basic types of response they are producing, must be acquainted with the regulations that govern the use of personal data. In most cases these are unlikely to affect business-to business advertising, but will certainly impact any consumer advertising that is productive of information about customers or prospects. The Data Protection Act 1984 is the relevant legislation in the UK at the time of writing.

Users of Order Generating advertising will, in the UK, be required to give undertakings to the Associations representing the media owners. See 'Media Organisations' in Chapter 13.

4 What makes people respond?

The proposition

What marks out the successful direct response advertising person from the also ran is what has always marked out good advertising people from the not-so-good. Some people call it 'insight'. But whatever word we may attach to this special quality, it is an ability to enter the mind of the reader, to adopt the reader's point of view.

The processes advertising people go through to do this are as varied as the individuals themselves. It is rather like an actor getting into a part until it becomes a second skin. A little while ago I was intrigued to hear Beryl Reid, the distinguished comic and dramatic actress, say that she started by getting the feet right. It struck me that this apparently eccentric approach had a marvellous quality of logic to it. She was literally putting herself into someone else's shoes. Good advertising people, like good actors, put themselves in someone else's shoes.

It is tempting to suggest that this behaviour is instinctive with some advertising people and others will never learn it. But no one is a 'born' advertising person and everything is available to be learned. Habit simply makes it easier.

The essentials are an interest in, and observation of, other people's behaviour. It is impossible to behave like a chameleon unless we know what colour we need to change to next. Like the good actor, the advertising person combines day-to-day observation in his personal life with painstaking research into the specific 'part'. The similarity between direct response advertising and a theatrical production is the shared ability to 'fine tune' according to audience reaction.

Although every product, every market and every media audience is different, we can nevertheless make useful generalisations about what it is that makes direct response advertising work. Human nature is not greatly changed by time or distance. An offer that works in Australia will generally work in France, or the UK, or anywhere else.

Let us then start with a simple proposition. It is this:

People respond to advertisements only when the immediate gain in responding exceeds the risk or cost of responding by an acceptable margin, and it appears easy to respond. Their response may be complete or incomplete. An incomplete response may be to clip a coupon and put it on one side or simply to put the whole magazine on one side. The longer it is left on one side, the less likely it is that the response will be consumated. This is why many offers are close dated.

Putting the offer up front

When we consider our simple proposition, it is easy to understand why book club ads and mail order catalogue ads are the way they are. 'Take any 4 books for only £1' may not strike the average advertising person as anything but tedious and hackneyed. But the reason it is tedious and hackneyed is because it has worked so well for so long. And the reason it has worked so well for so long you now understand, even if you did not before you started reading this book. It is because the offer has been used to elevate the immediate gain in responding by an acceptable distance above the penalty (cost) of joining the book club.

What enables the same 'boring' headline, or slight variations of it, to keep running is that refreshment is achieved by constantly replenishing the stock of 'lead' books that readers may choose from. The readers' greed or acquisitiveness is part of nature, and that is a constant. The books they want to read or, at least, own are a movable feast. To the advertising person who lacks the insight to enter the readers' minds, the ad never changes. But the would-be book club members see each ad as different because their attention is engaged by what is on offer. The ad is a shop window with a new display every month. The offer is there to engage their attention and to elevate the immediate gain above the perceived penalty.

If there is also an easy-to-complete coupon, no money required up front and no postage stamp to find, there is every chance our acquisitive book buyers will respond.

Such advertising is, perhaps, not a good showcase for direct response or across-the-line advertising. But it is a perfect example of the old adage, 'if its working, don't mend it'. This advertising is not disparaged by anyone who has enjoyed, or not enjoyed, the experience of looking at print-outs of the response to their own advertising. It is the way it is because it works.

A former colleague consulted me about a client who was a wine shipper. His client, Bordeaux Direct, had been successfully selling wine off-the-page, mainly from lesser known French wine regions. The cost of recruiting new customers in this way had always been high but the repeat business from his customer mailing programme was excellent. The problem was that the number of people willing to risk ordering a dozen bottles of lesser known wines off-the-page was diminishing. Possibly, Bordeaux Direct had run out of readers who had a good knowledge of wines.

The solution I offered was akin to what happens when you go to a wine shipper who sells wine by the case. You are allowed to taste the wine first. So I stole the book club idea. Instead of sticking our new customers with a case of unknown wine, they could now take three bottles for a minimal price in exchange for their agreement to order some of the wine they liked best. Since Bordeaux Direct was already losing money on the first order—because the advertising cost exceeded the revenue generated—why not spend money to subsidise the product offer in order to save money on advertising?

The new offer worked and ran for quite a few years. It worked because it elevated the immediate benefit in responding above the risk of responding.

This proposition can be applied to any advertising which solicits a direct response. It does not, however, mean that the only way to secure a response is to pepper an ad with bargains, free offers, or the words 'new', 'now' or 'send no money'. Useful as these devices may often be, they are used when the perceived penalty in responding is unacceptably high when compared with the immediate benefit in responding. They are there to adjust the odds in favour of a response.

To illustrate this point, let us now assume we are launching a new luxury car and have made a video for prospective buyers. This offer is intrinsically very attractive and there is no apparent penalty in responding. The problem is the reverse of the wine shipper's problem: the offer is attractive to people including children, perhaps, who are not remotely likely to buy the car. In this case we have to raise the penalty in responding—for example, by declaring our intention to pass their name and telephone number to a dealer—in order to qualify the response. We may even require our respondents to send us their business cards. By keeping our simple proposition in mind and exercising our imagination in seeing who our offer may appeal to, we can most often avoid catastrophic errors. We can get the balance between reward and risk to the consumer more or less right.

Learning through observation

We can also learn more from our observation of other people's advertising. Instead of making superficial and, perhaps, arrogant judgements about book club, or any other, advertising we can learn more by assuming the advertiser has a pretty good idea of what he or she is doing. From our observation of what the advertiser is doing we can often gauge how difficult or costly it is to get a response and whether it is becoming more or less difficult over a period of time. We can see this by noting changes of offer and technique.

If you live in the UK you will have seen many ads just like Fig. 4.1. It may seem incomprehensible to you that the advertiser, who runs a mail order catalogue business, should devote an entire ad to depicting free gifts and a coupon. Here one must admit to sympathising with your point of view. Indeed it does seem that a pure recruitment vehicle like this ad can do nothing to expand the market because it assumes, on the part of the reader, total comprehension of what the catalogue is like and the benefits that catalogue shopping bestows upon the shopper.

Had you been watching this advertising over a period of ten years you would have seen the entire evolutionary process. Without making any value judgements, we can observe and explain this process. At first, about one-quarter of the ad was devoted to featuring a low-value gift which, the ad made clear, was available to the shopper who made at least £10 worth of purchases from the catalogue. Later, the majority of the ad was devoted to the gift. The value of the gift was then increased, and the £10 qualification was dropped. Then, more than one gift appeared until, eventually, the ad became crammed with gifts.

The first assumption we can make with complete conviction is that each change must have been productive in whatever terms the advertiser used to measure success. Secondly, from observation, we could note that competitors followed suit—some quickly, others after a considerable lapse of time. Thus, they were using common measures of effectiveness.

From the nature of the advertiser's business we could imagine two highly influential characteristics. The more

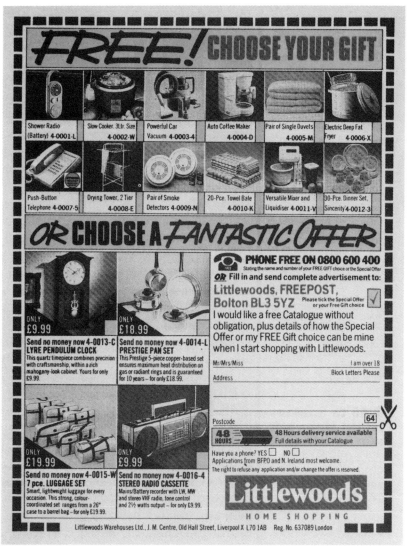

Figure 4.1 Littlewoods.
Gifts and a coupon. But where is the catalogue?

obvious of these would be the high cost of sending a large catalogue to an enquirer. Obviously, since we know the market to be large, the cost of fulfilment (sending the catalogue) is likely to be at least as much as, if not more than, the advertising cost of securing an enquirer. We can also guess that putting a free offer in the ad would have assisted response.

The second, less obvious, characteristic would be the creditworthiness of enquirers. Since the catalogue business is a credit trading business, we can assume that many enquirers will be rejected. Furthermore, that those most *likely* to be rejected are those most likely to respond—since they are finding it hard to get credit or are most in need of it. Such people would respond whether a gift were offered or not. There would be no need to offer them an additional inducement.

We can now make an educated guess that putting the offer of a gift in the ad increases overall response, increases response from creditworthy people disproportionately, and increases conversion rate. We can also assume that the gradual withdrawal of any copy or illustration of the catalogue did not show up as a disadvantage in any response data.

The later increased value of the gift suggests that the quality (measured by creditworthiness) of the enquirers kept increasing along with the quality of the gift. The dropping of the £10 purchase qualification suggests that it was depressing the value of the first orders. The multiplicity of gifts may still be a puzzle. Later you will discover that the more decisions you ask a reader to make, the less likely he or she is to respond. The explanation must lie in the often large number of competitive ads in one publication. The more choices one ad offers, the less likely the reader is to look for additional choices in other ads.

Everything that you have now read is capable of being deduced from observation by the experienced direct marketer. It explains the apparently strange behaviour of a particular advertiser in neglecting to say anything good about the catalogue on offer. You may think the long-term strategy of the advertiser is not very soundly based, but you can readily appreciate that the advertiser has responded logically to response and conversion data as they have been received. Depending on what view you take of the sophistication of the advertiser, you may also believe that leaving out any 'sell' for the catalogue and substituting 'bribes' for this sell, did not adversely affect the subsequent purchasing behaviour of the intake.

On the other hand, our knowledge of human nature and behaviour should lead us to the conclusion that the effective life-cycle of the recruits may well be reduced because, if they can get their account into fully paid-up status, they can now accept a 'bribe' to switch catalogues. The more creditworthy they are, the more likely they will be in a position to do this at frequent intervals. The effect of this kind of behaviour would take a long time to show up in the figures and by then the die would be cast, because competition would, by then, have copied the strategy and made it well nigh impossible to withdraw the benefit. This conclusion would be supported by the gradual appearance of ads for new catalogues which claimed points of distinction, better or more fashionable merchandise, better terms and so on. Such ads began to appear within a few years of the glut of 'gift' ads.

This rather long-term and complex example illustrates the principle of what may be deduced from observation. It is not often possible to read quite so much into an advertiser's behaviour but a great deal of information can be gained from observing tests and seeing which ads are repeated. It is generally more helpful to assume that an advertiser is behaving rationally than not. If behaviour is puzzling, it is more constructive to look for a logical explanation than to assume ignorance on the part of the advertiser. Why back your judgement against that of someone who can see all the figures? A sense of wonder is better than a sense of superiority.

Our examination of such advertising should not, however, lead us to the belief that it cannot be improved. Perhaps it can be made more modern, stylish, emotive. Perhaps it can add more value to the commodity being advertised. It is only necessary to observe any advertising over a period to see how it reflects changes of taste and sophistication. Such changes are continually occurring, and necessarily so. Yet the principles behind those items that make an advertisement provoke a response do not change. It is these principles that concern us now.

Separating style from principle

The principles are best observed in action by studying the behaviour of traditional direct response advertisers. This is because their concern is purely for the measurable effects of making changes and their survival depends upon getting it more or less right. We may not wish to undertake advertising that looks like theirs and, indeed, it might be quite inappropriate for it to do so. Nevertheless, appearance is superficial and principles are fundamental. It is not necessary that two ads should look the same to employ the same psychology.

The advertisers we have discussed have reduced advertising to a very simple formula. The book club does not attempt to enlarge the market for hardback books by extolling their virtues. The book club ad does not dwell on the pleasure of handling hardback books or of turning the crisp, white pages; not does it suggest what a bookcase full of beautiful books might do for your self-esteem. The ad does not even attempt a reasonable description of the contents of each book. Rather it decks itself out like a sweetshop would to tempt a child. It is saying, 'Look at all these beautiful books you can choose from—you can pick the three or four you like best and have them for next to nothing.'

By doing this, the book club has enlarged the market for hardback books. It has achieved what it appears to have made no direct attempt to achieve. In fact many hardback book publishers would be struggling to survive without book club sales. This puts the book club in a position of great power, enabling it to negotiate terms that are favourable enough for it to give good choice and value to members while retaining a healthy margin.

It rather goes against the grain for those of us brought up in the advertising business to accept that the most efficient way to expand a market might be such a simple appeal to acquisitiveness rather than any kind of argument, whether predominantly rational or emotional. What kind of account planner or marketing person would, on the basis of research, come up with the book club proposition as the main thought for a campaign to communicate? I suggest that the conventional method of arriving at an advertising proposition would make it impossible. The research would have told us of the tactile, sensuous pleasure of handling well-printed and bound books; the value of books in making a statement about their owner. There is not the slightest possibility research would have told us to forget all that and rely on the prospect's greed overcoming his caution.

Such an idea has to be invented and tested to ensure that the maths are correct. It is an entrepreneurial idea that is easier to understand if we think of the ad as a shop rather than as an ad. If bookshops displayed 40 books in their windows and made the same offer there would be a lot of window gazing going on.

Appealing to the predisposed

A study of hard-nosed direct response advertising makes it clear that the advertiser does not directly attempt to enlarge the market by including an educative element in the advertising unless the commodity is new or unknown. The ad appeals to those who are already predisposed; it appears not to swell the ranks of the predisposed. This is actually an over-simplification. Such advertising may increase the ranks of the predisposed but its sole objective is to generate orders or convertible response. The way to do that is to keep the proposition simple, not to crowd the ad with reasons why you should buy from a catalogue, read books, or take a language course.

The language course promoter assumes your interest in wishing to learn a second language. You may occasionally see a campaign, using large spaces, in which the language course promoter does not make this assumption, but attempts to jerk you out of your apathy and make you think seriously about it. Provided that his language courses are widely available in retail outlets, this could be a sensible strategy. As they are probably not, cynics among us may believe that such a campaign is the result of hiring a conventionally trained marketing director who will cost the company a great deal of money until the scales are removed from his eyes. No entrepreneur would make such a mistake.

The language course ad (Fig. 4.2) is a typical example of an ad which assumes your interest in learning another language. It does not waste a single word on why you should learn the language. It assumes you have your own good reasons. The example I have chosen appeared in a credit card magazine in 1987. I cannot remember when I first saw the headline, 'Which of these languages would you like to speak?' I am certain it was not later than the mid-1970s. We can, therefore, safely assume that this ad is one of the all-time winners and the headline may still be running ten years from now, as long as the courses are still available.

The fact that the ad does not sell the principle of learning a second language does not mean that it has done nothing to enlarge the market. Far more people would like to speak another language than will ever overcome their inertia to do something about it. The sole purpose of the ad is to overcome the reader's inertia. Our aforementioned conventionally trained marketing director, who thought that people had to be sold the *idea* of learning another language, had failed to define the problem. The problem is not a shortage of people who want to speak another language, it is a shortage of people who believe they can do so without excessive effort.

The purpose of the ad is to convince readers that it is quite easy, so that they will make an enquiry. That is why many language course ads will address the issue directly in the headline with words such as 'Speak French, German, Spanish or Russian in just 30 days'. Using a dramatically

Figure 4.2 Linguaphone.
Linguaphone assume your interest in speaking another language.

short period of time like this is the clearest way of suggesting that the language course is simple.

Since the Linguaphone course is fuller than competitive courses, it takes three months. The unusual feature of Linguaphone is that the range of languages offered is more comprehensive. The headline is an involvement headline, directing readers towards a list of over 30 languages. Readers are invited to get their pens out and tick the chosen language. The sub-head reads, 'Tick the one you want to speak in 3 months' time'. Some people tick more than one language. Notice that the work 'speak' is used in both the headline and the sub-head. Notice that the word 'learn' is used in neither. Speaking another language is the reward, learning it is the, possibly painful, process.

Even though Linguaphone is not able (or is too honest) to claim that you can speak another language in less than three months, the time taken is still stated. This is because even three months does not sound like an endless slog and is much shorter than most people would have thought—for example, from their experience at school. A side benefit is that three months may seem more credible than competitive claims.

Tough as it is to get people to enquire about a language course, it is tougher still to get them to take it. The ad therefore offers a free demonstration cassette so that the enquirer can discover how easy it is. This was the main offer for many years but, to overcome inertia, a free personal stereo is offered to buyers (not enquirers) of the course in the example shown.

Admittedly, the ad is not much to look at and it could, perhaps, be cleaned up to advantage. However, if you are still judging such ads so superficially, you are missing the point. The point is that the headline directing you to a check-list of alternative languages is a piece of brilliant psychology. I do not doubt that it has led to the sale of tens of thousands of language courses.

A peculiarity of the UK language course market is that the necessity to learn a second language does not exist. Therefore, total demand is small and it is fragmented over a number of languages. The most popular language, French, is learned by a minority of students. Minor languages, such as Serbo-Croat, sell in small quantities. However, they serve a useful purpose to Linguaphone. Most people who want to learn French will do so as a hobby or so that they can get more from their holidays. The expense and the effort involved put off many people whose interest is so casual. No one learns Serbo-Croat unless he is contemplating marriage to a Yugoslavian or intends to live there for a while. Such an enquirer is very valuable because he is much more likely to be converted into a buyer. As European harmonisation proceeds, there are likely to be more serious buyers but not necessarily for low-cost home study courses.

In contrast to the UK situation, a German language course promoter has a larger market to tap and could get by offering only one language—American English. Yet, the psychological insight which led to 'Which of these languages would you like to speak?' can be applied in Germany. Years ago I met the German distributor for Linguaphone courses.

He offered a choice of English courses. His reply device incorporated a questionnaire designed to test the enquirer's aptitude or, rather, motivation. If you were really keen, you would receive details of the more expensive Linguaphone business English course. If only averagely keen, you would receive details of the standard course. If you had filled in the questionnaire as a hoax, you would receive a polite letter asking you to desist from wasting the company's time. These ads were extremely successful, involving the reader just as the UK ad did. The device employed in Germany is an excellent example of an information providing response ad, a category we referred to in Chapter 3.

Lateral thinking

The Linguaphone company had never envisaged that their more expensive business course could be sold in this way. They had believed, because this course involved the purchaser in more expense and greater effort, that it could only be sold by a salesperson. But the use of the second course to increase involvement in the ad and to flatter the best motivated enquirers at fulfilment stage, proved the company wrong. The ingenuity of the distributor, in turning this dead duck (he had no intention of employing a sales team) into an opportunity, is a classic case of the entrepreneurial way of thinking, which is at the heart of direct marketing.

The ability to side-step obstacles and arrive at a solution which is so simple that it seems obvious afterwards is a theme that recurs in both direct marketing and advertising. The difference is simply that in advertising it is a way of communicating an idea so that it touches the right spots we seek out. In direct marketing the same creativity, the same insight into human psychology, is applied to framing an offer that is irresistible to the consumer, yet profitable to the company.

Many of the best direct marketing ideas have come from advertising people—most often from creative people. It is impossible to arrive at such ideas by following what most people would regard as a logical series of steps. This is because the logical series of steps follows a model based on something that worked before. It excludes interesting ways of arriving at the end result which are based on a superior understanding of human nature and the prevailing mood. Sequels to blockbusting feature films are a good, if rather literal, example of what happens when you copy a successful model. The second film is almost certain to make money because risk has been reduced. However, it will make less money than the original. And unless someone has the imagination and confidence to create originals, there can be no sequels.

It takes creative people, in the broadest sense, to produce originals. Of course, if we wish to be pedantic, there is no such thing as a totally original idea. What we think of as an original idea is one for which the parallel is not obvious, such as an idea for a film, which came from seeing a painting or a football game rather than another film or a book.

Finding out what works about it

You may wonder why, since I extol the virtue of originality, I counsel you to study other people's ads. There are two answers to this. Do you remember my offer of three bottles of wine at a nominal price? I have already admitted to you that it was not an original idea. I stole it from the book club business. But the point is, no one else had thought of doing that. Sometimes you can get by, just being fairly original.

The second answer is that I have not counselled you to study other people's ads just to see what works for them. I have counselled you to try to think out *why* it works. Unless you do this and avoid slavish plagiarism, you will be in for the occasional unpleasant surprise. In this chapter, I have quoted two examples of advertising which offers respondents an extensive choice—in one case of gifts, in the other of books at nominal prices. The literally minded may deduce that choice is what pulls response. Book club advertising depends upon an appeal to acquisitiveness. The array of books represents temptation. Actually, book club ads offering only one book have worked from time to time. But the book that has such wide appeal that it can carry a book club ad is rare. Such books are only published once in a decade. Most books appeal to minority tastes.

Our mail order catalogue advertiser competes for attention with others, often in the same publication. If competition is offering a gift that our ad does not, we may lose response to our competitor. The circumstance is peculiar to a particular market. We apply it to another market at our peril.

Response ads work by elevating the gain in responding above the risk and by making it easy to respond. Presenting the consumer with a difficult choice makes it more likely that the response decision will be postponed.

For several years, I worked on the direct mail new customer acquisition programme for a large mail order company. My client was a very trusting man with confidential marketing information but not at all trusting of my agency's abilities. In every campaign—there were two a year—my agency's mailings were split-run tested against those of new agencies that he would appoint provisionally, just to run tests. In fact, the way we started on the work was by being one of the new agencies. Before he finally gave up testing other agencies against us we had won 42 such tests. We did not invariably outpull the competition but we won on cost-per-customer obtained.

You may think the relationship was somewhat fraught by this stage, but my client and I were, and are, personal friends. He saw what he was doing as logical and, in view of the size of his investment, amounting to several million pounds a year, a rational way to proceed. For my part, I found the competition stimulating and I think he was quite shrewd enough to see this, believing it motivated me to do my best.

The reason we won so many tests was simple. The competitive agencies would run mailings obviously derived from what had worked before, what had worked for another client, or what they had stolen as an idea from the USA. Our mailings were based on working out *why* some of the previous mailings had pulled better, or converted better, than others. Thus we could test a new mailing, looking nothing like any previous mailing, with a reasonable expectation of success because it incorporated the winning psychological elements. We used tests to increase our understanding of the people we were mailing to, so that we could increase our efficiency in securing responses and subsequent sales.

I found it astonishing that competitors, who were given exactly the same mailing samples and back data, never tumbled to this. The one or two who produced an acceptable result and were retained for a further campaign almost invariably performed worse second time around. None survived a third term. They had not learned from their experience because they could not see, or did not try to see, what the results were telling them about the consumer. I suspected they thought that the mail order catalogue business was beneath them. In which case they lost an opportunity to learn something about a £2 billion business.

The lessons this work taught me were priceless. I should have been paying the client and I suppose, in a way, I was.

His response rates increased sevenfold in as many years. Such a result would be impossible if one merely copied a successful model, changing the odd element here or there. Allowance must be made for inspiration, for tests which appear quite radical but which are based on a knowledge of the psychology of the potential buyer. Not all such tests will work. But, without them, a geometric progression in response is impossible to achieve.

You will appreciate that a progression of this order cannot always be achieved. To increase response sevenfold, even over a long period, it is necessary to start from an inefficient base. The reason book club ads tended to get into a rut is that they were relatively efficient. It requires a monumental idea to move from what works well to what works superbly.

Advertising that informs

Not all response advertising, even that undertaken by traditional direct response advertisers, can assume knowledge of the product on the part of the reader. The examples we have thus far considered are familiar products—mail order catalogues, book clubs and language courses. But direct response advertising is often used to pioneer sales for new products, which may or may not become available through retail outlets. As we are looking at the traditional and least glamorous aspects of direct response, let us continue and consider the business of newsletter publishing.

Newsletter publishing is a wonderful business. It is a wonderful business because it is a way of adding an astonishing amount of value to a relatively small amount of paper. It requires scarcely any capital to become a newsletter publisher and, if you get it right, you can build up a small fortune in quite a short time. Looking back, I realise I must have missed an opportunity by failing to go into such a potentially lucrative business.

Like all lucrative businesses, it has a downside. The problem is that there are clever people in the business already—and they seem to be the only survivors. Many have tried and failed. You need good administration, an acceptable product, a brilliant product idea and a superlative ad. The ad is the most important ingredient. It will generally be a magazine or tabloid page ad and there will also be a mailing package. Once you have the skill to sell a newsletter you can apply it to selling other products or courses aimed at self-improvement. Figure 4.3 gives such an example for a diet programme.

Newsletters are sold to would-be-self-improvers, or dreamers. I always think of them as 'if only ...' people. People who believe they would be happier or richer if only ... The truth is that most of us are dreamers to a greater or lesser extent. However, newsletters perform better in the USA and certain other countries than in the UK. But the subjects that work, and the kind of ads that work, work everywhere. Winning subjects are how to start in business, how to make money in your spare time, how to make money on the stockmarket, or how to make money as a horse race punter.

The newsletter allows subscribers to dream about their secret ambitions—ambitions that will never be realised. This is not necessarily the newsletter proprietor's fault. The readers may have given a hundred sure-fire ways to make

Figure 4.3 Chartsearch Ltd.
An irresistible headline, editorial-style layout. A typical example of narrative copy.
Reproduced by permission of Chartsearch Ltd.

spare-time money. But they do not really want to make the effort or take the risk. What they want is to dream about it and so they carry on subscribing until they get another hundred ideas, then another hundred. The newsletter gives them all the satisfaction they want. They can dream of being rich and admired without their dream becoming tarnished by reality.

Story telling copy

There is only one way to sell a newsletter. It is with narrative (story telling) copy under a compelling headline. In direct mail it is likely to be fatal to send a free sample of the newsletter. The fantasy of what the newsletter could bring to the subscriber is so much more powerful than the real thing. The example of a newsletter style ad in Fig. 4.3 is typical, even though the ad is actually for a diet programme. The copy for such an ad is important and is protected by copyright, being reproduced in part here by kind permission of Chartsearch Ltd. 'My two skinny cousins had abandoned me ...', reads the heartrending headline above the author's name: 'By Sharon Meyer, R.N., M.S.N.'

> You and I have never met [begins Sharon]. But perhaps we share a common problem.
>
> When I was seven, my two cousins and I were playing in a nearby churchyard. Like kids do, we didn't realize how late it was. It was getting dark faster than we expected. In a panic, my two skinny cousins climbed over the wall that surrounded the churchyard. No problem. But I couldn't make it. I was too heavy. Too fat. I stood there crying for over an hour, until a neighbour crawled in and helped me over the fence. I've never forgotten that experience. Nor have I forgotten the two skinny cousins who abandoned me.
>
> For years I was teased about my weight. Even kids at school called me names. And the teasing persisted through school and even college. I vowed that some day I'd cease being the ugly duckling. But I was overweight and it seemed almost hopeless.
>
> Several years later, after I had completed my nurse's training I was working in a hospital overseas. Through a friend, I was introduced to Dr. J. Thomas Cooper, a doctor who specialized in helping people lose weight without being hungry or deprived.

We have now met our hero, Dr Cooper, whose Weight Loss Programme can be ours for £9.95 plus 75p for postage and packing. The writing style may not be the last word in elegance and Sharon's accent is distinctly American, but your heart goes out to her. The psychology is faultless. She can use words like 'fat' to describe herself which she could not use to describe her readers. I bet Sharon has the laugh on her two skinny cousins now. And she certainly gets around. Here is another example of her work: 'When I read his letter, I almost dropped my fruit juice,' reads her next headline. 'Hello, my name's Sharon Meyer,' reads the sub-head.

> Like most of us [says Sharon], I have to watch my eating habits. I seem to gain weight just by looking at food.
> So when I wrote to a friend of mine recently, I began the letter with my usual trite complaint about trying to lose weight. And failing.
> Within a week he answered my letter. That was a surprise in itself. But in it he told me about a special new weight loss programme developed by Dr. J. T. Cooper, a doctor who specialized in helping people lose weight without being hungry or feeling deprived. When I read about the results he was achieving, I almost dropped my glass of fruit juice.

It appears that Sharon loses more weight each time she meets up with the good Dr Cooper and she seems to be losing her American accent as well. Whatever you may think of such advertising, it runs because it brings results. It is not easy to find the winning formula and, when you have found it, you cannot be sure how long it will continue to be the winning formula it once was. This is why Sharon is such a busy lady, racing here, there and everywhere to meet up with Dr Cooper and find the answer to her problem.

Personally, I always enjoy reading these classic ads, challenging me with such headlines as 'Who says you can't make easy part-time profits', and 'How to get rich sooner than you think'. The style was adopted by Joe Sugarman for his JS & A mail order operation to sell merchandise. This is how Joe starts a sell for a pair of sunglasses, branded 'BluBlockers'. Under a colour shot of the sunglasses, which also displays the brand name, the cheeky caption reads, 'They look like sunglasses'. The headline reads 'Vision break-through', the sub-head, 'When I put on the pair of glasses what I saw I could not believe. Nor will you.' The ad is by-lined 'By Joseph Sugarman'.

'I am about to tell you a true story,' says Joe. 'If you believe me you will be well rewarded. If you don't believe me I will make it worth your while to change your mind. Let me explain.' Joe then tells us the story for several paragraphs before we get into the magical properties that distinguish BluBlockers from ordinary sunglasses.

This narrative copy style has been equally effective for selling 'idea' products of the type Joe Sugarman sells as for selling newsletters or diet plans. It probably originated with self-improvement courses to improve use of English, memory, public speaking skills and so on. Certainly, it was in use for such courses early in the twentieth century. A famous headline from the early days was, 'Do you make these mistakes in English?' There were many others which worked then but have since been outmoded by sociological and economic changes. 'Are you strangled by the old school tie?' was one little gem that was still running as late as the 1950s. It was a reference to the incredibly class-conscious British society of the first half of the century when a regional accent was a barrier to advancement, or at least perceived as such.

Since ads in this style survived for so many years and are used to sell speciality products delivering high profit mark-ups, they repay the modest effort required to study them. The most famous direct response ad of all time was a narrative style ad, 'They laughed when I sat down at the piano, but then I began to play ...' Naturally, it was a correspondence course.

The value of a headline

Leslie Goodwin, who was for many years at the publishers responsible for so many correspondence courses to improve memory, grammar and whatever else 'if only' people might want, and was also marketing director of Linguaphone for a while, believed his vast experience showed that 50 per cent of the success of an ad lay in the headline. Once he had a winning headline he might tinker with the copy and design endlessly, but the gains would generally be relatively slight compared with what he could get from the headline.

A feature of such advertising is that it does not rely on visual appeal, although the typographic layout is extremely important. Even Joe Sugarman's merchandise ads rely heavily on storytelling and argument, rather than pictures to make their point. The ads have an editorial appearance and you slide into the copy because the headline intrigued you, not really being conscious of reading an ad until you have been hooked. The ads are designed, like editorial, to appear easy to read, using narrow column body copy, sub-heads and panels.

When appearances count

Not all direct response ads for new or unknown products conform to this formula, which is suitable only for products whose appeal is not visual and which offer a solution to a perceived problem or need. However, if you can find a product this approach fits, you can do very well with it. Any pension, life insurance, permanent health insurance, or home insurance could be sold this way. The good insurance salesperson uses stories from personal experience to bring home the product benefits, to make them real. You could use the approach to sell personal loans or even finance for management buy-outs or business start-ups. You could use it to sell oil or gas to provide heating for poultry-rearing, under a headline reading, 'The night the power cables blew down ...' Story telling copy has more applications that it has been awarded. Such experienced direct response advertisers as the Franklin Mint or Time Life would at first sight find such an approach irrelevant although they, too, need to use relatively long copy. The role of the art director and the typographer is crucial in the creation of an ad or an insert for Franklin Mint. The value of what is on offer is largely visual, although it can be greatly enhanced by what is said about it.

But even in the field of selling collectables, a good story helps the sale along. In the case of the collection of porcelain plates depicting maritime subjects (Fig. 4.4) the visual appeal is so strong that the story can concentrate upon how

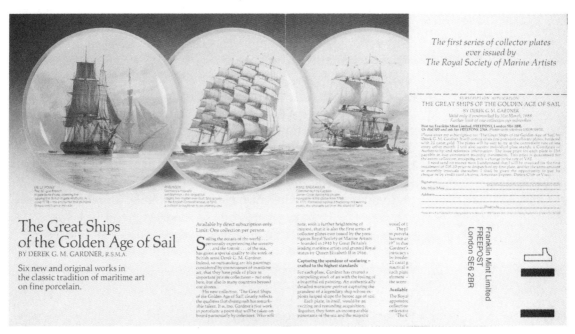

Figure 4.4 Franklin Mint.
A Franklin Mint insert. Here the story is everything.

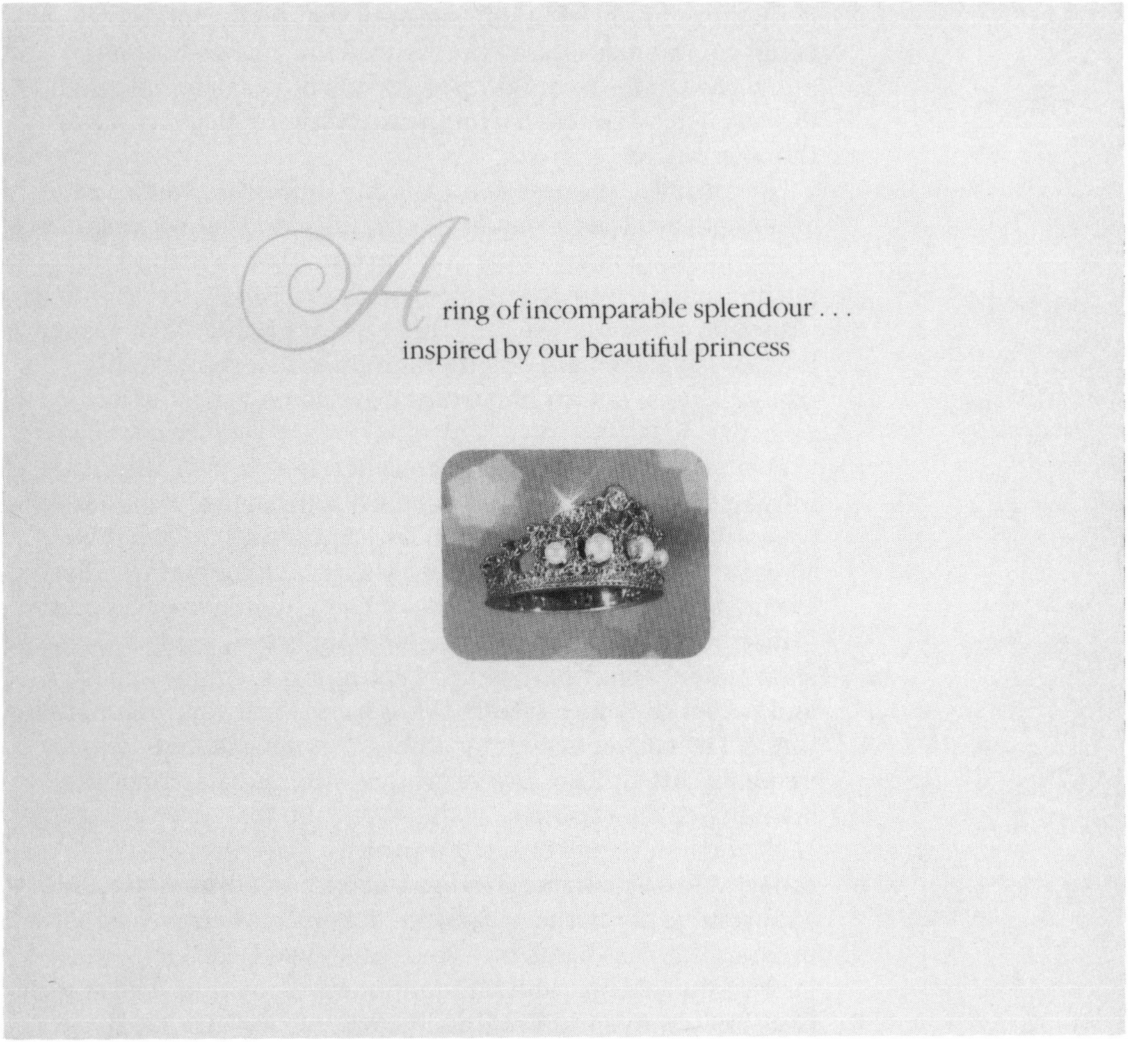

A ring of incomparable splendour . . .
inspired by our beautiful princess

Figure 4.5 Franklin Mint ring.
Selling on visual appeal. Another Franklin Mint insert.

the plates were created and the artist who was responsible. However, the product is not always so visually dramatic. From the same stable is another insert (Fig. 4.5) which offers a ring in the shape of a tiara. The words on the front of the insert are here as important as the small colour shot. 'A ring of incomparable splendour . . . inspired by our beautiful princess.' The approach is a little less direct, more dependent on the narrative. The advertiser is not relying upon the illustrative content to carry the main burden of the selling message.

The value of such offerings is generally enhanced by bearing some kind of third party endorsement—for example, from The Royal Society of Marine Artists. Less obviously, it is further enhanced by reference to the importance of what is being commemorated by the issue. This may sometimes allow the writer to build up the value of the original when the issue is a replica. By implication the replica's value is then increased.

Necessarily, the creative work for limited editions and other collective items must be carefully crafted because craftsmanship is an important part of what is being sold, authenticity being of great importance also. One reason why inserts are heavily used for this type of product is to ensure that illustrations are crisply reproduced on good quality paper. This is not an important criterion for most direct response ads.

It is widely believed that the collecting urge is almost universal, but that has not been my experience. I cannot remember a collect promotion which did well unless it was something as simple as trading stamps, or collecting halves of notes that would be valuable when a match was achieved. I imagine the problem may be that collectors tend to specialise. Franklin Mint are looking for magpie collectors and, when they have them, these people are very valuable to them. The cost of acquiring a new customer is high, which makes it difficult for new entrants to compete against the established operators.

Nevertheless, my study of Franklin Mint and other collectable advertising has been useful, enabling me to add apparent value to the occasional one-off replica or 'aesthetic' product that has come my way—and even to do some work for Franklin Mint, which I found most enjoyable. The study of work within specialised fields for such experienced operators as Franklin Mint and Time Life, is well rewarded. It tends to keep very much to a formula and, while I would not suggest that nothing else could work better, it is a formula that works. It is not difficult to pick up the bones of what works about it and flesh it out in quite a different way. Doing this, one can create something that appears fresh and different but exploits proven psychology and sequencing of any argument. There is no point in re-inventing the wheel, because you will not make it rounder.

What the old timers can teach us

You may consider that I have dwelt too long on traditional direct response advertising which forms the beginning of direct marketing as we know it today. What lessons can such advertising teach to the practitioner of advertising or the marketing person who expects to be around, doing good work in the twenty-first century? Yet it is true that most developments in marketing are really transferences of big ideas from one field to a number of others. Since man has been in the business of selling food longer than other commodities it is, perhaps, not surprising that the shape and psychology of a modern retail store was originated in the grocery business and a lot of people get rich by applying it to selling other items. Since the soap and detergent business was one of the fastest growing and most aggressively competitive businesses from the 1930s to the 1960s, it is not surprising that marketing departments in most large companies became based on the Procter & Gamble model of 1938.

The ability to see parallels that are not obvious to the less imaginative is the surest way to achieving success. It can only be done with a highly developed sense of curiosity. As human nature does not change, the appeals that have made traditional direct response advertising work for so many years are still valid today. They will remain valid in the twenty-first century. The point about such advertising is that there can be no doubt as to the objective. Therefore, we know exactly what the advertising is there to do and we know, equally well, that the paymaster is looking at the results to ensure he is getting value for money.

In these circumstances, we can be sure that an ad or a formula that keeps running, keeps working. In no other sphere of advertising can we be so certain that the model we are examining is a working model.

Nevertheless, the object of our examination is not to copy what we have seen. If we did that we could not advance. We would be applying something that would become outmoded and irrelevant to our situation. We would be replicating yesterday, tomorrow. The point is to gain an understanding of what works about the ideas we see. Because the insight into the human motivation and behaviour that make these ideas work is a true insight, one that we will do well to understand and exploit.

I am not making a reference to any of the companies mentioned in this chapter when I say that I have found it extraordinary that there are marketing people within experienced direct marketing companies who have absolutely no understanding of what works about their own advertising. It is this lack of understanding that creates stagnation. If you cannot grasp what makes an idea work, you have to keep on copying it slavishly. This is what establishes rigid formulae. Any advertising person old enough to remember the sixties will remember the dead hand misinterpretation of the USP (Unique Selling Proposition) philosophy placed on TV advertising. At the time I asked a product manager from Pedigree Petfoods to explain the point of having so many brands when they were all sold on the same pseudo-rational nutritional benefit claim. 'Why don't you exploit people's emotional attachment to their pets and segment the market between emotive brands and rational brands?' I asked. He looked at me pityingly, as one who did not understand his company's infallible formula. Within a few years all the brands were on an emotive appeal. It was the new formula.

This dogmatic attitude (if you will excuse the pun) is rife in many marketing departments. It stems, like other dogma, from ignorance. The ignorance is caused by ultra-rapid job movements, leaving marketing departments permanently staffed by transitory people. Fortunately, the nature of direct marketing is experimental, not dogmatic. Thus people are not under such pressure to defend the winning formula and, when tests are executed, they cannot help learning something from them. The difficulty lies more in their unwillingness to test any idea that smacks of adventure, because they lack the knowledge to assess whether it appears fundamentally sound. The best answer is to be patient and try to increase their understanding—and therefore their interest and curiosity—so that they are sufficiently educated to make bolder decisions. They then leave and double their salary!

Borrowing good ideas

Once we understand what works about a winning idea, we can not only develop it out of all recognition for the same product or within the same market, but we can transfer it to quite a different market. An idea that has worked for years in a direct marketing business can be exploited to equally good effect in across-the-line advertising for a commodity that sells through a dealer network.

Using a little imagination in this way can pay big dividends. Clive Ellings acquired direct marketing skills while working for Volvo Concessionaires. When he went to Multi Broadcast, a TV rental company, he exploited these skills to reduce the loss rate of customers. Then he used his direct marketing agency to execute the new business advertising. It was second nature to him and to the agency (MSW Rapp & Collins) to use a specific offer and measure the relative take-up of the offer in stores that received advertising support and in stores that did not. For the first time Multi Broadcast were able to get a direct measure of their advertising effectiveness. Furthermore, he staggered the use of press and radio so that he could assess the relative effectiveness of each medium. All this was done without using any redemption devices in the advertising. And Multi Broadcast knew exactly what a new customer was worth to them because they recorded the payment behaviour, loyalty, and willingness to uptrade of their customers. They knew the lifetime value of a customer in exactly the same way as a direct marketing business does. The sole difference was that they used shops to recruit new customers, collect payments and uptrade.

Bill Phelan, as marketing director of Renault (UK), applied direct marketing principles, which he learned at American Express, to selling cars. There are not many, but an increasing number, of examples of senior marketing people picking up broad principles learned from directly measurable advertising or direct marketing activity in one company and introducing them into an altogether different context in another company. Of course, neither Clive Ellings nor Bill Phelan would have been able to transfer any specific idea without adaptation even if they had wanted to. What they did was to apply working principles, established where they seemed obvious, in a context where their application was not obvious.

It may not be necessary to go to the extent of moving from one company to another to do this. The examples of working ideas are all around us if we have eyes to see them. David Ogilvy claimed that his early experience of direct response advertising was crucial to his development as a writer of great advertising. Who are we to doubt this?

The pay-off

Dedicated attenders of direct marketing seminars will have endured many presentations in which the experts would have us believe that the secrets of obtaining a positive response can be reduced to a check-list of miracle ingredients. I, for one, will be very pleased if I never again have to sit through, '14 ways to improve your response', '17 winning headlines', or '23 ways to advertise your agency under the guise of giving an educational presentation'. This kind of presentation does little to commend direct marketing to those who always believed it was so much hocus-pocus served up to the credulous punters by unprincipled charlatans.

Nothing that is worth doing well should be diminished by attaching big numbers of infallible rules to it. If I am wrong, why not '9 ways to write an all-time great symphony even if you're deaf'? The truth is that we can, and must, gain inspiration from big ideas that have worked, but we must avoid a literal transposition of them. We need to use our curiosity to see what these ideas are telling us about the people who respond to them.

The best source of this information is probably traditional direct response advertising. Not because the best brains are concentrated within this arena, but because the objective of the advertiser is crystal clear. There is no possibility that an idea which runs and runs is doing so for any reason other than its efficiency. There is no possibility that observation of an evolving strategy cannot teach us about what is working and what has been discarded. Such advertising provides us with a valuable insight into what it is that causes people to respond.

The only proposition that must remain in the forefront of our minds is: People respond to ads only when the immediate gain in responding *exceeds* the risk or cost of responding by an acceptable margin, *and* it appears easy to respond. The only additional point we must always remember is that we can increase response if we can convey urgency, by close-dating the offer, suggesting shortage, or in some other way. This is because it is difficult to overcome natural human inertia. Tasks put on one side, however simple, are most often left unperformed.

In studying the efforts of direct response advertisers, a sense of wonder is infinitely more valuable than a sense of superiority. Inelegant prose and low design quality may not be commendable. But if an ad continues to run, it is continuing to work. If it is overcoming the disadvantage of appearing to be thrown together, the idea behind it must have a powerful appeal. We can still borrow and adopt what makes the idea work without borrowing the treatment. To allow the execution to impede our judgement of the idea is a mistake.

The observation of other people's advertising should be in support of, not instead of, our observation of other people's behaviour, the way they talk and what seems to interest them.

We should now be in the right frame of mind to look at mechanics, such as close dates, coupon design and so on, because we appreciate that these are useful devices that can assist response, not infallible ways of securing it.

5 How to plan—enquiry generation

The proposition

The traditional direct marketer has a choice. To go one-step, that is to complete the sale off-the-page, or two-step. Going two-step implies securing an enquiry, or sales lead, for conversion to a sale later. Most direct response advertisers have no such choice. Their sales will be made at the dealer's showroom, in a store, or by a salesperson.

This chapter deals with the considerations that apply to two-step response advertising. It is an exacting area because it involves striving for the optimum balance between the quantity and quality of response. It is seldom right to maximise response, since each enquiry costs money to handle. An enquiry that is unlikely to be converted into a sale is an enquiry we may be better off without. It may even serve to lower the morale of a sales team or cause aggravation to dealers.

In a mail order environment it is not difficult to work out the optimum balance between quantity and quality entirely mathematically. But in a salesforce or dealer environment this is not so easy. There may be hidden costs caused by the effect that working unproductive sales leads has on the attitude of the salespeople.

The mail order, travel or financial services advertiser is most likely to use two-step advertising if its product needs more explanation, demonstration or illustration than is possible within an ad. In some cases—for example, investment products—it may not be practicable to include all the detail that the law requires within the confines of a newspaper page. Alternatively, the company may use two-step advertising if its 'product' is a catalogue or a credit account driven by a catalogue. Such a company is in the happy position of being able to test one-step ads against two-step ads and measuring the results, which is much better than guessing.

Most response advertisers are not in this position, yet they still have many options open to them—enough to keep them testing sizes, formats, response mechanisms, offers and media for ever more. At least 10 per cent, and up to 25 per cent, of the budget may be spent on such tests because what worked yesterday will not necessarily work tomorrow—and almost certainly will not work quite as well. It is most notable that traditional direct marketers, such as mail order companies, spend a higher percentage on testing than relative newcomers. The fact that they already have more knowledge (from previous tests) simply demonstrates to them the value of testing.

The more experience we have, the more fallible we know we are. Nothing that is likely to have a significant effect should be left to rational judgement when it could be put to empirical test. Out of the experience of many such tests over a long period we can make certain generalizations, but each individual case has its own peculiarities.

Our first plan will be nothing but a series of tests. After that our plan will include a core plan, virtually guaranteed to produce a certain volume of enquiries and business, plus a series of test programmes. The extent of testing will, of course, depend on the size of the budget. A small budget will include few tests representing, perhaps, 25 per cent of the total outlay. A very large budget will include many tests which nevertheless add up to, perhaps, only 15 per cent of the outlay.

This picture may be clouded by the use of tactical advertising booked at the last minute on a heavily discounted basis. Such advertising will generally be a part of the core plan using proved copy, offers and media.

We embark on two-step response advertising in a spirit of investigation, knowing that our ally will be our insatiable curiosity about people and what provokes them to respond. This ally is bound to lead us to the right answer—for now; because the right answer for now will probably not remain the right answer for long.

Two-step advertising

Two-step response advertising embraces a very wide range from hard-nosed direct response ads promoting mail order sales to ads that merely carry a discreet token coupon or telephone number. In this chapter we shall ignore the latter entirely, assuming that we are serious about wishing to provoke enquiries. Serious response advertisers now include such giants as General Foods and the Ford Motor Corporation. Ford undertake what they call 'curriculum marketing' in which they enter a dialogue with prospective buyers, which both educates the potential Ford owners and receives feedback from them. Even a large advertiser such as this does not wish to enter such an expensive conversation with someone who is never going to be in the market for what they sell. It is no easy matter to control this. Such a dialogue may be started by a TV commercial in which the 'image match' core message is 'wrapped' by a direct response message—the first part alerting the viewer to the possibility of responding, the second part containing the offer and telephone number.

Alternatively, the direct response element may be 'blended in' to the ad. It is particularly difficult in TV to control the quality of response except by slotting the commercial at times when the highest percentage of people within the target market are viewing. Fortunately, this is not a problem we need to deal with here because we are chiefly concerned with print advertising. A later book in this series covers the subject of direct response TV.

In Chapter 3 we saw that the quality versus quantity conundrum is best considered mathematically by comparison of the relative cost of securing a response with the cost of handling it. The latter cost may be a little or a lot, depending on whether we are undertaking a continuing dialogue (like Ford), using an expensive salesperson's time, or simply mailing a brochure. These are ways in which we can qualify response later, but it is best to aim for the right balance between quantity and quality in the advertising enquiry production process, and therefore our four major considerations are: targeting (media selection); copy (advertising content); format (the advertising vehicle); and offer (inducement to respond).

Whatever we do with our 'offer' or 'format' to increase the quantity of response will almost invariably reduce the quality of response. The only ways in which we can increase the quantity of response without reducing its quality are by improving our media selection and copy. Even in these areas there may be a trade off. The media which produce the lowest cost per response may not produce the lowest cost per sale. We may pull more enquiries with 'short' copy, but in doing so we may be producing less well-qualified enquiries.

Targeting

I am often asked to rank targeting, copy, offer and format in order of their significance. There is no definitive answer to the question because tests have shown that any of these variables can account for differences of 100 per cent or more in effectiveness. However, advertising badly to the right people is surely better than advertising well to the wrong people. It is hard to argue against targeting as the most important single variable after the product itself. Direct response advertising is a media planner's paradise, information hungry as good planners always are. However, it is also hard work involving analysing response data, interpreting it and using it to forecast the effects of future media decisions. The area merits a complete chapter and, in Chapter 9, it is covered in greater depth. For now it will be sufficient to look at the basic principles.

The planner's decision process starts with the objective. If the response element of the advertising is secondary to a primary purpose of establishing awareness and an image, then the plan will be affected by this as it will seek to produce an optimum balance of reach and frequency. The campaign, as a result, will be more concentrated than a campaign designed primarily to produce response. It will be more narrowly focused by the use of fewer media. It will use a higher frequency in each medium. It may be more concentrated in its time span. A plan constructed entirely or primarily to deliver response cost effectively may look quite different. Media will be selected on the basis of test insertion performance. Many media will be tested and the list of those that work best will contain some surprises. They will include media that would have been discarded without a second thought by a planner solely concerned with building coverage and frequency as efficiently as possible. The discovery that this is the case encourages the planner to start thinking in a rather different way. For example, more thought will be given to the psychographic profile of readers of a particular magazine than would have been done before, making connections between those people considered to be attracted by the editorial and those who are in the market for the product. This does not mean that the planner is no longer concerned with cost. Far from it. A planner may well experiment with media that gave spectacular deal rates on the basis that, at the price, they must be worth a try.

Frequency

The two key reasons why a planner's media schedule will be a lot longer are, firstly, that new media must continually be tested in case they work better than some of the staple media and, secondly, testing will have shown that there is an optimum frequency in the media being used. In some cases this may be quite low—some colour page advertisers start to experience diminishing returns from as few as four pages in a year. In other cases it may be quite high, though rarely more than one space every four weeks in any one newspaper. Such low frequencies as these would seem extraordinary to many media planners but, of course they are arrived at empirically through practical response experience, not theoretically. One advertiser in the UK has used more than 150 different publications in the space of a year. About 30 of these will be new media tests. But the others are all on the schedule because they worked in the past. The planner may also have to be content with the slotting of advertising within quite a narrow response window if demand for the product is sharply seasonal. All planners juggle with the elements of size, number of media and number of insertions in each, and will be asking questions such as: 'Will it be better to increase frequency beyond the optimum in the best medium in order to drop the worst?' 'Will it be better to upgrade the size in the best medium or bring in one or two extra media?' Planners will be providing their own answers through their response forecasts. Their learning rate is very rapid because they are continually in a position to compare forecasts with reality. One of the first things a planner will learn is that the first space he or she buys in a new publication (new to the schedule, that is) will generally be the most effective. So much for advertising theory about frequency build-up. The second ad will usually be almost as effective as the first. The third will be quite a bit less effective and the fourth will be slightly less effective than the third. It does not always work out like this, but it does more often than not. Response will follow a lazy-S curve, if you imagine the S lying on its back (Fig. 5.1). The only way to avoid this pattern is to space out insertions over a long period. Doing this will reduce the volume of response received from the medium within a given time frame but increase the response per insertion. If we need the volume of response within the time frame we must then increase the size of the space or introduce new media. If we are already using the optimum size, increasing it will only increase response by a little more than the square root of the increase in size. This will very possibly reduce cost effectiveness faster than increasing frequency or bringing in marginal media.

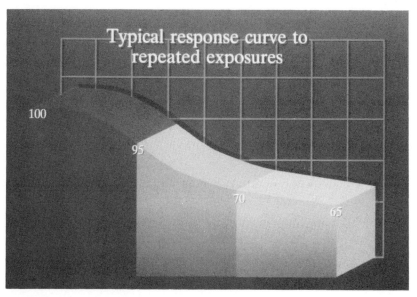

Figure 5.1 Regression curve.
The effect of a series of insertions. Diminishing returns may start from the second appearance.

Size and position

Another factor that the planner must contend with is position. This may affect the optimum size within any publication. If a front page solus position is most cost effective, and is only available as a 20-centimetre double column space, then that is what dictates the optimum size. Position is not simply a matter of solus or semi-solus ads on specified pages versus run of paper ads. Despite repeat evidence of readership studies, right-hand pages generally outpull left-hand pages. For smaller ads, outside edge positions outpull inside-edge (gutter) positions.

There considerations, which may seem complex enough, are not in isolation from creative considerations. The optimum size for an ad today may be less than the optimum size tomorrow, because we may hit on a creative solution that obtains more response but justifies a larger space. Direct response advertising does not lend itself to departmentalised thinking. Actually, no advertising does, but the need for integration of creative, media and marketing thinking is more apparent when it is possible to observe the effects that each has on the other.

The planner must keep abreast of opportunities to split-run alternative copy and offers. It is often difficult to find enough testing opportunities within the media that work most efficiently. One solution to this problem is to turn the test ads into loose inserts. In this way, they can be supplied to a magazine printer interleaved in an A, B, C, D sequence so that a four-way split-run test can be conducted. As many as eight different copy treatments are sometimes simultaneously tested in this way.

The value of testing

The value of such testing quickly becomes apparent when it is seen that a change of headline alone can make a difference of 30–50 per cent in the pulling power of an ad—which is enough to make the difference between profit and loss in many businesses. It is therefore incumbent upon the planner to allow for sufficient media tests. The creative test programme will quickly begin to show the degree of creative sensitivity to the product. Some products are rather insensitive to changes of creative treatment, others are highly sensitive. While it is rather difficult to generalise about this, commodity products such as motor insurance or clothing are fairly insensitive, while speciality products such as language courses or newsletters are highly sensitive. Clearly the number of creative tests should be determined by the size of the potential gain from an improvement. The more sensitive the product is to change of treatment, the more worthwhile it is to keep testing to find something that works better.

There is a lot of unnecessary mystique about creative work. There are pieces of folklore about how changing one word in an ad made a dramatic difference to response and so on. This is generally nonsense. It is possible to change response dramatically by changing one word, but only if the one word is in the headline, or if the one word is 'FREE' and had been omitted before. We shall deal with what makes a good ad later, but for now it is enough to list the staple ingredients, as our planned tests should only be concerned with major influences on response.

At least 50 per cent of the effectiveness of an ad depends upon the headline and main illustration. The headline and main illustration will generally work if they concentrate upon the major benefit and will generally not work if they do not. While it may appear that the major benefit is known beyond dispute, this is not necessarily the case. The major benefit could be the immediate benefit to be derived from responding. This may not be the same as the major product benefit. The major product benefit may be that our new car will take four adults in comfort for 70 miles on one gallon of petrol. The major response benefit may be to obtain a free brochure containing an interest-free finance voucher. It may not be possible to decide beyond reasonable doubt which of these two benefits will pull the best response when placed in the headline. We may have to test to find out.

If at least 50 per cent of the pulling power of the ad is determined by the headline and main illustration, it is clear that these are the features that should be the subject of most experimentation. The number of tests can be controlled by eliminating ideas that are 'clever'—that is, ideas which do not focus on a major benefit. Clever ideas do not pull response because they do not direct the right people, those in the target market, to read the ad. The only possible excuse for testing a clever idea is to educate its perpetrator or a client. There are always enough different ways to say or show something that it is never necessary to stray away from benefit led advertising.

It is rarely possible to change the headline or main illustration without changing something else in the ad as well. A new headline may involve changing the introductory copy. A new illustration may require a new layout. It is a mistake to be so rigorous about testing only one variable at a time that we should not make commonsense detail changes which are consequent upon a major change. If the body copy has to change as a result of a headline change, then so be it. The change is the consequence of the change of headline and is therefore a legitimate part of the same test.

Narrowly focused tests of this sort are essential, giving us the opportunity to increase our effectiveness systematically and progressively. However, we should leave room for more adventurous testing as well. Provided that a completely new idea is based on a sound understanding of the psychology of what has worked for us or someone else in the past, there is no reason why it should not work better than our current winner. It is seldom that progression in effectiveness follows a smooth path. Rather it appears to go in occasional big steps, more often than not.

Personality endorsements

An example may be the use of a personality endorsement. It is often supposed that the introduction of a personality into advertising works by increasing the credibility of the product or offer. I am very dubious about this, and with reason. Back in the early 1970s, when I was a consultant to

McCann Erickson, we tested the use of a personality for *Children's Britannica*. The test was by split-run in the *Radio Times*, in *The Observer Magazine* and in a solus cold mailing shot. The personality was Judith Chalmers, who was a well-known broadcaster with the BBC. Not surprisingly, she outpulled the no-personality ad by the biggest margin in the *Radio Times*. In fact, by well over 30 per cent. In *The Observer Magazine* she improved response by a little over 20 per cent. This was very gratifying but the surprise was provided by the mailing. In the mailing, the use of Judith Chalmers' endorsement had no effect whatsoever. We concluded that her value was not to increase the credibility of the product or offer, but to increase the attention value of the ads. She would do this most effectively where her face was best known. She had no effect in mailings because the mailing package was already achieving a 100 per cent noting score.

Clearly *Children's Britannica* was a reputable product from a renowned publisher. Nevertheless, my subsequent experience with other products supports the general conclusion that the main benefit to be derived from the use of a personality is not in the endorsement, but in the attention value of a known face. This is not to say that the relevance of the personality is unimportant. As with any attention device, relevance is always important. Only once have I had the experience of a personality reducing response. As I have no wish to enter tiresome litigation just for the sake of satisfying your curiosity, no name shall be mentioned. Nevertheless, the experience justified my predilection for split-run testing personalities, a practice regarded as mildly eccentric—by their agents. To date, no agent has refused a request for a split-run in my experience. A fee (equivalent to about six weeks' use) is paid. The results give a rational basis for evaluating the annual worth of the personality to the advertiser. If such a test is successful it is an example of one of the occasional large steps in effectiveness improvement to which I alluded earlier. It is not usual for such an improvement to come from experimentation with the reply device, yet I have known hardened direct response professionals to start with this and build the rest of the ad round it on the reasonable basis that the reply coupon is what the ad is about. While I do not share this rather mechanical notion of advertising design, I would concede the great importance of this functional part of the ad.

The attention value of reply devices

In Chapter 1 we observed that direct response ads attracted higher noting scores than non-response ads. The conclusion we must draw from this fact is that the reply device is of itself an attention-getter, signalling to the reader the presence of an offer to which he or she can respond. Since the people we most desire to read our ad are probably those most likely to be attracted by a direct response offer, the coupon (or other reply) device has particular value as an attention-getter. It should therefore be made as prominent as possible and be consistent with the message, the tone of voice in which it must be delivered and the style that befits the product. Creative people who have little direct response experience are inclined to consider the reply device as an after-thought to be allotted as little space and prominence as possible. This is a quite fundamental mistake.

Later we shall consider the relative values of alternative reply devices. A tip-on reply card will typically increase response to a magazine colour page ad by 150 per cent. A tip-on 'mini mailing package' may do better still. The use of a telephone response mechanism may increase response substantially. In some cases, it may be more important than the coupon. Whatever we decide to use, its design and content are likely to be significant factors in the success of the surrounding ad. The reply device is of fundamental importance and, next to the headline and main illustration, should receive most attention in testing. Perhaps it goes without saying that the coupon should both sell the benefits of responding and give the respondent sufficient room to write legibly his name, address and any other details we require. However, many coupons fail to do this.

The fact that a coupon should be given prominence does not excuse such self-indulgences as cleverly shaped coupons which do not look as if they are designed to be clipped. Many years ago I read in a book of David Ogilvy's that he had tried putting a coupon at the top of the ad with beneficial effects. It did not work for me. The reason, I presume, is that a coupon is the visual culmination of the ad; it is the close of the sale. To ask for the order first and explain why afterwards may occasionally work but the odds are against it. Not very long after this early experience I recall that an *Encyclopaedia Britannica* sales representative made the improbable statement that he had discovered a way in which the company could double its advertising response. He refused to part with the idea until a contract was drawn up that would reward him for his initiative. Sceptical as the managing director was, he felt he could not pass up what might just be a golden opportunity, so the contract was duly signed. The ceremony completed, the representative was asked to state his idea. To the horror of all concerned, it was to use a line drawing of a pair of scissors over the broken rule forming the edge of the coupon. While it was well known to the company that this would have little or no effect on response, it did not wish to be prevented (by the contract) from ever using such a device. The advertising department was despatched to search through the archives until an example of a their ad using a drawing of a pair of scissors could be found. Fortunately, an example was found and the representative was despatched to sell books, not ideas.

The message is that reply devices should be prominent, sell the reward for completion, give sufficient space for the respondent to supply information and not be crowded with gimmicks. If they contain an illustration of a free brochure, free cassette or other benefit, all the better. If they are postage paid, response will generally increase and conversion rate will drop a little. If you do not want minors to respond, it is as well to make this clear. If the ad is in colour the coupon may be made to contrast with the surrounding background, perhaps by overlaying it across a full colour illustration. In the case of a small space, e.g. a 15-centimetre double column ad, it may be a good idea to turn the entire ad into the coupon by surrounding it with a broken rule.

The body of the ad

I have suggested that the bulk of testing should be of headlines, main illustrations and reply devices. However, it generally does not take too long to achieve the winning formula for reply devices and, thereafter, occasional tests will be sufficient. While I have given a lower priority to body copy and supporting illustrations, these are still important. A small ad may consist of little other than a headline, an illustration, a few words of copy and a coupon. But a full-page ad is a different proposition and should be put together, more often than not, in such a way as to give the reader a number of start points at which he can begin reading the ad. These start points may be picture captions or they may be sub-heads. A good deal of tinkering may be required to craft the ad so that it is as appetising as a plate of *hors d'oeuvres* and so that the type is of readable size in every adaptation. Yet I believe that it should not be necessary to test every conceivable permutation of the various elements; rather it is generally sufficient to rely on good copy and design sense, and on experience. An exception to this is the design and copy for loose inserts of four pages or more where the creative team cannot so easily control the order in which the reader looks at the pages. So many alternatives are available to the reader that some experimentation is required to hit on the best way of sequencing the argument that the piece delivers.

Insert formats

This leads us into a consideration of the importance of format. An ad need not be a full page or even a part of a page. It may be a loose insert, a bound-in insert, or a page with a tipped-on card or leaflet. An insert may take many forms from a simple card to a miniature catalogue or mailing pack. It may incorporate involvement devices like scratch-off panels, pull-tabs or press-outs. It may be serially numbered. It may be 'personalised' to the publication in which it appears. It may double up as a package insert riding in the mail with a bank or credit card statement, with a mail order despatch or promotional mailing. It may even be used as 'take-one' leaflet in a retail outlet dispenser. Such alternative uses may constrain the size and shape of the piece and, once the requirements of alternative distribution vehicles start to become incompatible, it is best to purpose-design the piece for each vehicle, length of print run permitting.

Years ago, when it was generally possible to book a solus run in a magazine for a loose insert, one could generally rely on a pull of at least six times that produced by a full-page ad, even from a simple single sheet card format. In those days there was such prejudice against inserts, advertisers believing that they were invariably regarded as an irritant and shaken out onto the floor or rail station platform. Now that their value is widely recognised, there is more reason to fear that this will indeed be their fate. Readers have become much more selective in the attention they accord to inserts, especially when three, four, or more fall out of one magazine.

Nevertheless, for two-step advertising the attention value of an insert and the convenience of responding to it are still very advantageous. A pull of four or five times that of a full-page colour ad is still feasible. This advantage is generally offset by a considerable increase in cost-per-thousand circulation and a diminution of conversion rate. The easier you make it to respond on impulse, the lower the conversion rate will be. It is therefore necessary to test inserts against space ads to discover the winning formula, and this may not be the same in alternative media. Inserts may be at their most effective in low-circulation media where the space-cost-per-thousand is high and production costs loom large. They may also be particularly effective where there is a requirement for a great deal of 'legal' copy, as in the case of a credit card application or investment product. Such legal copy is likely to take up a good deal of valuable advertising space but adds little to the cost of an insert. Another advantage which inserts offer is the tight control the advertiser can exercise over the quality of reproduction of colour photography.

When to use inserts

Such considerations as these raise or lower the odds in favour of inserts in individual cases. The advertiser who habitually uses full-page ads is more likely to benefit from switching to inserts than an advertiser who uses small spaces. This is not invariably the case but is more likely to be the case. The advertiser who depends on attractive full-colour illustration may benefit from using inserts. The advertiser requiring long, or legal, copy may benefit more. The advertiser who uses a long list of low-circulation magazines and business-to-business publications is very likely to benefit more. The advertiser who can make good use of serial numbering, scratch-offs, pull-tabs and other gimmicks will almost certainly benefit most of all. The advertiser in a low interest product category, for example the financial advertiser, is likely to benefit from using inserts because of their high attention value and their relatively long life. Finally, the advertiser who is prepared to make exclusive offers to particular target groups, such as Diners Club Members or Chartered Surveyors, can personalise his inserts to these groups with great effect.

Rational considerations like these are important but, by now, we have recognised that there is no substitute for the empirical approach of testing and re-testing until we are satisfied that one format can or cannot perform better than another. Even when we have completed this process we must periodically re-test because, for no readily explicable reason, the relative pull of inserts against space ads varies quite significantly from time to time. If we can make inserts work we have a great advantage for two reasons. The first is that we now have a vehicle that can pull a high volume of response from a relatively low circulation. The second is that we have a vehicle for testing many new media (often on a part-circulation basis) without incurring excessive additional production costs.

Our high-pull vehicle may be particularly valuable should we have a relatively narrow response 'window' due to high seasonal demand. Against this it might be argued that inserts give a lower advertising value than space ads because they buy less circulation per pound spent. This is certainly true, but it is a disadvantage that may be offset to some extent by their enhanced attention value. I recall having such a discussion with a cruise operator. His advertising account was split between my direct marketing agency and a mainstream advertising agency which ran large, coupon-type, space ads promoting the joys of cruising in general and his cruises in particular. Our job was mainly to secure repeat business but we also ran new business inserts which produced a phenomenal response. Our cost-per-response was about one-twentieth of that of the other agency. With my best professional ethics I argued that the other agency was setting the scene for our harder-nosed response vehicles and was buying him relatively more coverage for his money. He responded that he could not believe that such an enormous response differential could be saying nothing about the relative attention and interest value of our inserts against the space ads. He was right, of course, so I changed the subject and he changed his advertising agency.

Bound-in inserts

Although loose inserts are subject to the criticism that they are often shaken out onto the floor, and although the magazine publisher's printer does not always insert them correctly, I have nevertheless to admit that I have not had much luck with bound-in inserts. Bound-in insert cards are an ideal vehicle for selling subscriptions to the magazine in which they are inserted, easily outpulling loose inserts used for the same purpose. For some reason, they appear less effective for other advertisers. Furthermore, it is less likely that a bound-in insert designed for a particular publication will be technically suitable for other publications or other uses. This is because not all magazines are bound in the same way and, in many cases, an eccentrically folded piece will be required which may be unsuitable for package inserts or take-ones.

With all the problems of proving that loose inserts were or were not inserted in accordance with the instructions on the order, they are nevertheless a better bet for most advertisers. Furthermore, they can be regionalised—often with no cost penalty. This facility may be particularly useful for test markets, regional advertisers and for markets where demand is disproportionally high in certain areas. They are also ideal for testing the copy or the offer because they can be supplied interleaved on pallets, so that they are in perfect random order.

Experimenting with formats

One thing that is not easy to test is alternative insert formats because it is not practicable to insert these on an A, B, A, B basis. However, this should not deter us from experimenting with formats until we have achieved what we believe to be the optimum mix of quantity and quality of response. The more elaborate and gimmicky the insert, the higher the response is likely to be. However, this incremental response is likely to be of lower quality than the base response. There is no limit, other than size or weight, to what we might do to increase involvement with the piece to improve its 'play value'. If the insert is on card it may feature scratch-off panels to reveal hidden messages, or press-out tokens. If it is on paper it may be folded and gummed in such a way as to allow pull-tabs to be used to reveal messages, symbols or, even, a unique serial number. Folding and gumming in this way may be used to provide a pre-paid reply envelope which, for some reason, is called a bang-tail. Naturally, such devices may greatly increase the production cost of the insert but they will make little and, in some cases, no difference to the media cost. It is like being offered a double-page spread for much the same cost as a single page.

This is not to imply that it is always correct to take advantage of flat rate insert changes and use the most elaborate format. Relatively simple formats are often the most cost effective and the majority of inserts are single sheet or four-page formats. Some single sheet inserts are L-shaped with the reply portion forming the base of the L.

The idea is that a reply card which is so obtrusive invites separation from the main part of the format. I thought I was the first to use this format in the late sixties only to discover someone else had thought of it five years earlier. And possibly, that was not the first, either. The wheel is often re-invented as ideas come in and out of fashion. The L-shaped is efficient in paper usage as, when printed four or eight up, the cards dovetail so that no precious board is wasted.

What is undoubtedly much newer than this simple idea—because it is based on a finishing process that had not yet been conceived in the sixties—is the 'mini-mailing package' in which the ends are gummed together and perforated. Once the perforations are torn, a single sheet of paper becomes three or four separate pieces, perhaps including a letter, a leaflet, a reply form and a reply envelope. Inserts of this sort are often used tipped-onto a space ad rather than loose. Complex inserts of this sort are often more appropriate to one-step advertising than to two-step, where the information content may be overkill.

It is not uncommon for 'gimmick' inserts to pull two or three times as much response as plain inserts. This does not indicate that they are always appropriate and a price for this enhanced response must generally be paid in the conversion rate. Sometimes, however, the gimmick is peculiarly appropriate to the message, enhancing the advertising value of the piece. Scratch-'n'-sniff cards promoting perfume fall into such a category, as would any insert used to carry a sample of the product in one form or another. Inserts used to carry a questionnaire, a prize draw, or a competition are also disproportionately more effective than taking space for the same purpose.

The reply portion

An important variable is the reply mechanism. An insert may feature a perforated reply-paid card. More simply still, the respondent may return the entire card. Alternatively, the piece may be folded up by the respondent to form an unsealed reply envelope. Then again it may offer gummed strips along the edges so that the envelope can be sealed. Finally, the envelope may be pre-formed as in the case of a bang-tail insert. Sometimes inserts are printed on thin paper but the end is folded over and gummed to form a reply card. There are two considerations to apply. The first is Post Office regulations. At the time of writing, in the UK, the Post Office has turned a blind eye to cards that fall below the minimum acceptable weight. However, if would be dangerous to size cards down to below the acceptable size. The second consideration is largely one of common sense. If the reply is confidential, as in the case of a credit card application, then a sealed format must be offered. If it is not, most sealed and preformed formats have to work hard to justify their additional cost. Preformed envelopes are generally, though not entirely, most appropriate to one-step advertising. Clearly, if a high percentage of response is expected by telephone, it is a waste of money to elaborate the postal reply mechanism. As with any other form of direct response advertising, the reply mechanism should be given prominence and even with a simple perforated card this can easily be done through colour contrast and, perhaps, a triangular cut at one end of the perforation.

Tip-ons

Tipped-on inserts were not made available in the UK until the late seventies, many years after they had been available in the United States and other major European markets. *The Observer Magazine* was first and my client, the publishers of *Encyclopaedia Britannica*, needed little persuading to book the first one, using a simple tipped-on reply card with a backing coupon as a saver in case there were any hiccoughs in attaching the cards. No tip-on has ever worked quite as well for me since. In increased our pull to five times what we would expect from a colour page. It was equivalent to a loose insert at about 60 per cent of the cost. However, as the novelty value declines, tip-ons settled for most clients to around two-and-a-quarter to two-and-a-half times the pull of a colour page. We had a brief golden era, lasting about two years, before the market woke up to the opportunity when, production problems permitting, we could scarcely fail. Of course, the conversion rate fell because we had a higher proportion of impulse response but our cost-per-sale dropped significantly.

Now that tip-ons are commonplace it may sometimes be necessary to be more creative in their use and today we see all kinds of vehicles tipped onto ads, even mini-mailing packs. Cards, too, have become more interesting, one example being the Carphone Group ad using a card in the shape of a mobile telephone referred to elsewhere in this book. In general, however, a tip-on falls midway between a colour page and a loose insert in both cost and pull. Generally, it will produce an inferior conversion rate to an ad and a superior conversion rate to a loose insert.

Offers

In many cases the main problem may not be to secure the maximum number of enquiries but to reduce the number of frivolous enquiries. In such a case you will not want to offer any inducement to respond beyond, perhaps, the facility of a toll-free or freefone telephone number or a freepost coupon. Your offer may be no more than a simple brochure. In other cases, a simple economic requirement to reduce cost per response may necessitate a freebie. In yet others, you may wish to feature an offer that is conditional on purchase; the offer is employed to improve conversion rate but it can double up as an incentive to respond. The offer, whatever it is, will work even better if it is close dated. However, this close date should be genuine if you wish to remain in good status with the various advertising controlling bodies.

In most cases it is necessary to give the respondent further information; that is why he is responding. The simplest thing to do therefore, is to turn this information into something more exciting. It might include a product sample. For example, language courses offer demonstration cassettes. It might include swatches of material. It may even be a video, although this will often be on loan. Air France, I think, were the first to offer a travel video in exchange for the respondent's credit card number. If the respondent did not return the video within a stipulated period they debited his or her account. When Ford in America offered a floppy disk, an idea they stole from Buick, they succeeded in getting respondents to pay for it. There are endless ways in which you can dress up an offer of information to make it more exciting, to give it enhanced value. However, you will not always want to do this. Some items, like horticultural catalogues and holiday brochures, have a strong editorial appeal in their own right. In such cases, the offer should be conditional on purchase. You may even want to impose a charge for the brochure, if you can get away with it, making this charge refundable against purchase.

Habitat introduced a charge for their catalogue many years ago as self-defence against people using it to collect design and furnishing ideas without ordering from it. Many people were quite willing to pay for it and, subsequently, Laura Ashley and Next launched catalogues for which they imposed a charge.

A charge is a rather crude but nevertheless effective way of qualifying respondents, but your offer can qualify them in many other ways. For example, the offer may require the respondent to send his business card, give you his telephone number or other personal information.

Fine tuning the offer

The offer can be varied from one medium to the next according to the enquiry cost and conversion rate, which is characteristic of each medium. The practice of varying the offer to attract the optimum mix of quantity and quality of response has been employed by the publishers of *Encyclopaedia Britannica* since 1973. This company has been the victim of some of my most costly mistakes over the years. Back in 1973, they were offering the 20-volume set of *Children's Britannica* on a conditional basis to buyers of the *Encyclopaedia Britannica*. Response to advertising was on a downturn that year and I recommended that we should feature the offer in the advertising and test giving away Volume 1 of the *Children's Britannica* to the ad respondents. Our split-run test result showed this produced an upturn in response of about 70 per cent and a sales increase of about 40 per cent.

Later we discovered we could offer a free book—which was not part of a set, but had a value in its own right—just to get a reply from the best converting media. We also discovered that the more closely this book was related to *Encyclopaedia Britannica*, the less damage it did to our conversion rate. Non-book premiums did not work as well. Fired with enthusiasm, I persuaded my client to commission Tony Buzan, an author well known for his works on improving learning rate and memory, to write a book called *How To Make The Most Of Your Mind*. We thought it would have an irresistible appeal to potential buyers of the *Encyclopaedia Britannica* and, to a few, it did. The problem was it also had an irresistible appeal to thousands of other people. One lecturer in the north-west thought the book was so good he insisted that all his students should send for it. Britannica were inundated with totally inconvertible response from the test ads and no amount of tinkering with the ads to qualify respondents better would correct the situation. *How To Make The Most Of Your Mind* was a disaster because the appeal was too strong. I learned two lessons from this. The first was that apparent relevance is not enough. An offer whose appeal goes away beyond that of the advertised product is generally a bad idea. The second lesson was that the offer is such a strong element it can outweigh every other variable.

You cannot fine tune to turn a badly conceived idea into a good idea.

Since the purpose of the offer is to increase sales and not simply to increase response, it is axiomatic that it should not disappoint the enquirer. Any incentive that is received by the respondent prior to purchase should have relevance not only to the nature of the product we wish to sell, but also to the quality of the product we wish to sell. One offer I have used, and which failed, was an audio cassette for a firm of financial advisers. The content of the cassette was simply not up to the task. Instead of raising expectations of professionalism, it reduced them.

Unless the advertiser is in the midst of an incentive war with competition it is not a good idea to keep chopping and changing incentives as this tends to encourage repeat response from freeloaders. For planning purposes, you may decide to test a conditional offer against an unconditional offer and, having ascertained their relative effect, you may then wish to test alternatives to the offer. A good offer will generally have quite a long life, sometimes five years or more, but it is always necessary to have something else in readiness in case response should start to dry up.

The main alternatives are:

1. *Offer on purchase* (it is nearly always right to promote this up front). This may be gift or a discount.
2. *Reply gift.* Low value gift to encourage response.
3. *Sample offer.*
4. *Conditional reply offer.* For example, the loan of a video cassette or a product sampler at a subsidised price.
5. *Combination offer.* A two-stage gift promotion with the first part of the gift on response and the second part on purchase.
6. *Competition or prize draw.* Usually in combination with a purchase incentive.

The decision whether to use a reply incentive in a two-step mail order operation is purely mathematical. Suppose our cost per response is £10 and the fulfilment cost (brochure, order form, postage, etc.) is £2. That means that the total cost of each response handled is £12 whether it leads to an order or not. If we assume, for the sake of example, that the conversion rate is 20 per cent we shall use up five responses for each order at a cost of £12 each, so our cost per order is £60. We test a reply incentive which doubles our response. However, the reply incentive costs us an additional £2 to purchase and despatch with the brochure. Our cost per response is now £5, plus £2 for fulfilment and another £2 for the incentive. That is a total cost of £9 for each response whether it leads to an order or not. Our reply incentive has brought in a proportion of extra replies from serious enquiries and a proportion from freeloaders who only wanted the incentive, with the result that our conversion rate slips to 15 per cent, so we are now using six and two-thirds responses for each order. So our cost per order remains exactly the same at £60 but we shall have 50 per cent more orders, making our incentive a good investment. In this case the decision to persist with the incentive is very simple.

But if the conversion rate had slipped to 12.5 per cent we would now need eight responses per order, and as each response will cost us £9, that is a total cost of £72 per order. This looks like bad busines but it is not necessarily bad business. We are still generating additional orders as we can see from the equations shown in Tables 5.1 and 5.2.

In effect, the additional 25 orders have cost us £3000, or £120 each. By extending our analysis to profit per order we may be able to justify this additional cost. Suppose, the incentive is shown to have no effect on order value. Suppose, also, the order value is such as to produce a profit greater than £120. Each additional order costing £120 will produce, therefore, an incremental profit. We may wish to extend the analysis beyond the first order. Suppose the anticipated lifetime value of a customer is £500 in profit, spread over an average of three years. Now additional new customers gained at a cost of £120 may look like very good business indeed, particularly if the use of an incentive has no adverse effect on their subsequent purchasing behaviour. The

Table 5.1   Control—no reply incentive

Advertising	Response	Fulfilment @ £2	Total cost	Orders	Cost per order
£5000	500	£1000	£6000	100	£60

Table 5.2   Test—reply incentive

Advertising	Response	Fulfilment @ £4	Total cost	Orders	Cost per order
£5000	1000	£4000	£9000	125	£72

problem we shall have with looking at subsequent purchasing behaviour is that it takes time. We shall nearly always have to make a decision in advance of having repeat purchase information. However, there are other ways in which we may wish to evaluate the benefit of our 25 extra orders. Suppose the only other ways in which we could get these orders would be either to use less efficient media, less efficient large spaces, or advertise in less productive weeks? Now we can compare the effect of increasing business from our best media, space sizes and period, by using an incentive, with the effect of increasing the business by using less efficient media, space sizes and periods. We can do this by using similar equations, as presented in Table 5.3.

Table 5.3 Comparison of plans without or with incentives

Plan	Advertising	Response	Fulfilment	Total cost	Orders	Cost per order
A (without incentive)	£100 000	10 000	£20 000	£120 000	2000	£60
B (with incentive)	£100 000	20 000	£80 000	£180 000	2500	£72
C (without incentive)	£180 000	12 500	£25 000	£205 000	2500	£82

In the case of Plan C, the same number of incremental orders (500) has been produced as Plan B at an additional cost of £85 000 instead of £60 000. So each extra order has cost £170. Clearly, Plan B is more cost efficient than Plan C.

From our test we can extrapolate and see what effect rolling out our incentive will have. In practice, planning is a little more complex than our simple equations may suggest. Different media will produce different reply costs and, in all probability, different conversion ratios. Although the incentive may have slightly differing effects in different media, if our test shows a 100 per cent uplift in response but only a 25 per cent uplift in sales, this should hold good, plus or minus a few per cent, when it is rolled out. Provided, of course, that our test was of a sufficient scale to produce results which are statistically significant with a high degree of probability. It is preferable also that our test result is based on insertions in several media.

A 100 per cent uplift in response and a 25 per cent uplift in sales may be a good proposition in one medium and a bad

Table 5.4   Costs without and with incentive

Publication	Advertising per reply	Fulfilment	Total	Conversion ratio	Cost per order
A (without incentive)	£10.00	£2.00	£12.00	20%	£ 60
B (without incentive)	£ 5.00	£2.00	£ 7.00	10%	£ 70
A (with incentive)	£ 5.00	£4.00	£ 9.00	12.5%	£ 72
B (with incentive)	£ 2.50	£4.00	£ 6.50	6.25%	£104

Table 5.5   Total costs of Publication B without and with incentive

Publication B	Advertising cost	Number of responses	Fulfilment cost	Total cost	Number of orders	Cost per order
Without incentive	£5 000	1000	£2 000	£ 7 000	100	£ 70
With incentive	£5 000	2000	£8 000	£13 000	125	£104

Additional cost with incentive	£6 000
Additional orders with incentive	25
Cost per additional order	£240

proposition in another. As is shown, for example, in Table 5.4, where it can be seen that, in the case of Publication A, the additional 25 per cent of orders have been gained for an additional average order cost of £12. In Publication B, the average order cost increases by £34. This is because the fulfilment cost of £4, including £2 for the incentive, remains the same but twice as many replies are needed to gain an order from Publication B. The addition of £2 for the incentive virtually cancels out the advantage of halving the reply cost in Publication B. All the incentive achieves is an extra 25 per cent of orders at an unacceptable marginal cost. Actually, in this example, the incremental orders cost £240 each as we can see if we look at the total cost, response and order figures in Table 5.5.

It is, of course fairly laborious to do such calculations manually when juggling with a number of variables and it is a good idea to model campaigns on a PC so that 'what if?' questions can be asked of it. However, it is a mistake to become so dependent on modelling that you lose sight of the odds. A number of ideas clearly do not make sense on the basis of mental arithmetic and it is a great advantage in response advertising to have some feel for the numbers. Apart from anything else, it enables one to spot obvious errors in response and order reports. Such errors do occur quite frequently because someone has forgotten to input a cost variable.

Planning variables

Each planning variable—media selection, creative treatment, format and offer—is susceptible to the type of analysis that we have seen in these simple examples and should be incorporated in a model that can be used to isolate the effect of each element in results analysis. The same model can be used for forecasting and setting parameters to cover the most and least profitable result of any change to the plan.

Such a plan invariably contains one fixed point, which may be: (1) the promotional budget, (2) breakeven, or (3) a fixed number of replies or orders. In the first case you will want to know how to spend the budget to the most profitable effect. In the second case you will want to know how much you can spend before you start bringing in orders at a loss. In the third case you will want to know how you can generate a given number of replies or orders most cheaply. Occasionally models may take in repeat purchase behaviour but the principles are exactly the same. There will always be at least one fixed point, sometimes there will be two: for example, there may be a budget constraint but also a breakeven constraint which makes is impossible to spend the entire budget until you have found a way of improving efficiency. Sometimes, it is difficult to track responses all the way through to purchase. An example where this difficulty might exist would be a durables manufacturer directing enquiries through to retail outlets. In such a case an attempt to quantify resulting sales must be made if efficiency is to be optimised. This can be done by running a purchase tracking study using telephone research on a one-in-n sample basis. In this way a true advertising contribution can be arrived at with greater precision than would be possible with an econometric model of the type often used to isolate advertising from other sales influences. Unlike such a model, your purchase tracking study will give you strong clues as to which media, treatments, formats and offers are most cost effective.

The pay-off

Planning a direct response campaign is like shooting a
moving target. The first problem is that altering one
variable affects all the others. The second problem is that,
however good our forecast, unexpected results and
opportunities will occur while the plan is running, and the
plan may need overhauling as the results come in—unless it
is so seasonal that nothing can be done until the next year.
The basis of a good plan is a good forecast. This will enable
you to evaluate late media deals and it will contain fewer
unpleasant surprises. Without accurate back data it is
impossible to make a good forecast. If the results come out
right and you did not base your forecast on past experience,
this does not mean you can see into the future, it means you
were lucky. Next time, on the law of averages, you will be
unlucky. This being the case, a plan for a new product, or a
product not using response advertising previously, will
consist of nothing but tests. It does not matter what anyone
else calls them, tests is what they will be. In the
circumstances it makes sense to test all the major variables,
budget permitting. Do not try to second guess the consumer
(or business buyer) when you can find out what he wants by
testing. Never try to rationalise away sensible alternatives
when you could easily find out their true value through
empirical evidence.

Your plan will be constrained by at least one fixed
instruction: this will be (a) to conform to a given budget, or
(b) to discontinue when breakeven (or minimum acceptable
profit) is reached, or (c) to produce a given volume of
enquiries or business. It may be further complicated by
subsidiary instructions, for example, to produce no more
than 20 per cent of the enquiries in any one month, to
produce a conversion ratio no lower than 10 per cent, etc.
The best way to handle these requirements and to isolate all
the variables that make up the campaign achievement is to
build a computer model that recognises each variable.
Alternatively, give your media planning work to someone
who has already developed a model that can readily be
adapted.

The major variables, other than the product, which will
contribute to the result are targeting/media buying, copy,
format and offer. It is really impossible to arrange these in
any firm order of priority but I must admit a tendency to
look first at the media and the offer when I am consulted on
a campaign that is under-producing. More often than not,

these ingredients are most influential. Copy is usually the least influential, yet even copy can create a difference of as much as 100 per cent. Since newspapers charge no more to run good copy than bad copy, it is worth taking some trouble to get it right. The difficulty is that everyone is an expert on copy and few are interested in media planning or dealing. Most campaigns feature too few media tests. Most would benefit from longer media schedules with more new media coming on and more old media dropping off the schedule as diminishing returns set in.

Designing a good offer is part of the creativity in direct response. Its status and value as an intrinsic part of the campaign should not be belittled. A good offer is one which reinforces the value of the product, not one which detracts from it. People are acquisitive and bargain conscious. What the offer does, particularly if it is close dated, is to turn their interest into action. It may also act as an attention device.

Format is also influential and the influence of any one format can wax and wane over a period. For reasons I have never been able to fathom, the relationship between the pull of, say, a colour page and the pull of a loose insert can change periodically. Nor is this relationship constant between media.

Anything we do with the offer or the format to improve response will almost invariably carry a penalty in lost conversion rate. It is therefore essential to track response through to orders or sales before becoming too excited about changes that reduce response cost.

If planning two-step response campaigns now seems complicated, I apologise. It is complicated but it is enormous fun and very satisfying when it comes out more or less right. The best/worst part is that results come in weekly or daily to confirm or confound out best predictions. There is never a dull moment and it has provided me with enough excitement to have kept me away from the bookmakers throughout my adult life.

6 How to plan—sell-off-the-page

The most exciting direct marketing activity is sell-off-the-page advertising. The excitement is doubtless similar to that experienced by a short odds gambler. Many have tried to make their fortune from this activity and almost none has succeeded. In this chapter we shall examine some of the reasons why this should be so and when it makes good sense to employ sell-off-the-page activity as part of a direct marketing strategy.

In principle, sell-off-the-page advertising cannot work. Like a bumble bee it is too heavy to fly. What it can do quite effectively is make short trips to bring pollen back to the nest. In direct marketing terms its use should be considered as a way of starting a customer relationship, as a means to an end, not as an end in itself. The reason why so many have failed at this activity is that they did not understand this and were insufficiently capitalised to make the correct use of it. As a result, the media have had to adopt codes of practice that protect their readers from the consequences of mailing off cheques to companies who then fail to meet their obligations. Before such voluntary regulations were introduced, sell-off-the-page represented an almost irresistible temptation to the back street operator who wanted to use customers' money to finance his business. While the income exceeded the outgoings, everyone could be satisfied. However, the odds are against this state of affairs continuing indefinitely. In the UK the Newspaper Publishers Association introduced a Reader's Account System in which consumers' money was held in a separately administered account until goods were despatched. This stopped the under-capitalised operator or fraudster getting his hands on the money until he had fulfilled his obligations.

No one should put more money into this activity than they can afford to lose and then it is necessary to maintain a high level of liquid capital in order to meet the consequences of the occasional disasters that inevitably occur. Providing these conditions are met and the business is geared to supplying, on a continuing basis, identified customers through catalogues or one-shot mailings, sell-off-the-page can be a cost effective way of growing a mail order business quite rapidly. There are six main types of operation:

1. *Credit mail order business* (mostly selling clothing through catalogues)
2. *Cash/credit mail order business* (selling through specialogues)
3. *Collectable business* (selling mainly through one-shot mailings)
4. *Service businesses* (selling mostly renewable insurance, other financial product, or travel)
5. *Subscription selling* (magazines, newsletters, etc.)
6. *Charities* (donation or membership)

Since the object of the exercise is to build long-term customer relationships, it is clear that the best type of operation offers either subscription-based products or a synergistic range of products targeted to people of a common lifestyle or set of attitudes. In earlier days, many sell-off-the-page operators sold what they could buy cheaply. While it is necessary to have an adequate margin, it is not usually sufficient because repeat purchase levels will be much lower from a disparate collection of products than from a coherent range. Few of the operations covered by the six main categories above expect to see much, if any, profit from sell-off-the-page. It is seen as a new business activity building lists of customers or trial lists on a cost-effective basis. As such it needs to perform and in this chapter we shall discuss ways in which it can be made to perform better.

Understanding the numbers

It is a good idea to have some grasp of the mathematics of sell-off-the-page and an understanding of advertisers' expectations. Typically, although there are wide variations, a simple cash/credit card offer is expected to produce, in net sales value, three to four times the advertising investment. Thus, as can be seen in Table 6.1, the margin on merchandise is high and customer returns for cash refunds are also high. These are the conditions that would prevail if we were selling clothing. For most consumer durables, the margin would be lower (perhaps a mark-up of 50–65 per cent) and returns would be much lower, say 5 per cent. For books, the margin would be even higher than for clothing (perhaps a mark-up of 200–300 per cent) and returns might be 10 per cent or so. However, in the case of books the selling (advertising) cost is high. I have simplified the example in Table 6.1 by leaving out tax and I have made no allowance for postage on returns.

Free approval

It is easy to see that things get a little more complicated if our offer is on free approval as we can see in Table 6.2. By introducing the idea of free approval (send no money) we can increase response because we are reducing the consumer's risk and may induce more impulse orders. The trade-off is that we shall almost certainly increase the returns rate, we shall incur some bad debt, we shall slow down cash flow and we shall incur collection costs. We may also, to contain bad debt, incur credit bureau costs and have to reject orders from people with an unsatisfactory credit history. In this case we shall need tighter and more expensive administration and it will not be so easy to contract out the work to a bureau or fulfilment house. Our operating costs will be much higher.

The table shows that, because we have not been careful to contain bad debt to a more reasonable 5–7 per cent, we have reduced our profit before operating and will incur higher operating costs. To compensate, we have 20 per cent more paying customers and these are people to whom we know it is pretty safe to make further free approval offers. This means that we should be able to increase their order value

Table 6.1 Cash with order

Gross order value	£50 000		
Less Cash refunds	£10 000	(returns rate 20%)	
Net sales value			£40 000
Less cost of merchandise	£22 500	Including non re-saleable returns)	
Less Advertising	£10 000		
Less Handling/despatch	—	(self liquidating)	
Less Credit card charges	£ 1 000		
Total Costs			£33 500
Profit before operating			£ 6 500

Table 6.2 Free approval

Gross order value	£75 000		
Less Bad debt	£ 7 500		
Less Returns	£17 500		
	———		
Net sales value			£50 000
Less Cost of merchandise	£34 375	(including supplying debtors and non-resaleable returns)	
Less advertising	£10 000		
Less Handling/despatch	—	(self-liquidating)	
Less Credit card charges	£ 1 250		
	———		
Total costs			£45 625
			———
Profit before operating			£ 4 375

from repeat sales because we can continue to make free approval offers to them, thus securing higher response than if we had to keep demanding cash up front. Long term, Table 6.2 shows more profit potential then Table 6.1. Remember, I have told you that the object of one-step advertising is not to make a profit in its own right, it is to start profitable customer relationships. We can now readily see that the decision to offer free approved terms depends on:

1. *The ratio of advertising cost to merchandise cost.* If the margin on merchandise is high and the selling costs are also high, free approval is likely to be more profitable than cash-with-order. The converse is also true.
2. *Potential returns and bad debt.* If the product is disproportionately likely to attract high levels of returns and bad debt (e.g. down-market clothing), it is unlikely that free approval will prove more profitable than cash-with-order.
3. *Capitalisation or maturity of business.* Even if free approval may produce more long-term profit a small business may not be able to stand the loss of cash flow and administration expense in the short term.
4. *Potential lifetime value of customer.* The greater the potential lifetime value of customers, the more effort should be made to get as many as possible and to encourage them to keep on ordering. Free approval is a good way of doing this. Free approval plus credit terms is even better.

Credit selling

If we decide to sell on credit, the situation is broadly similar to the free approval example but somewhat more complex. The first complication is that a number of orders, possibly 30 per cent, or even 50 per cent, will have to be rejected. The second is that, instead of having a clean break between 'pay' and 'don't pay' we now have a number of part payments. These may include deposits or, if we are offering free approval as well as credit, simple instalments. It is almost impossible to make any profit at all selling on free approval and credit from the first transaction. Mail order companies which offer these terms do so purely as a way of buying customers. Most of these companies also use two-step advertising, allocating their expenditures between one-step and two-step in a proportion determined by the vehicle that is working best at the time.

Charities and other users

Other operations which use sell-off-the-page methods are magazines and charities. Magazines are not big users of print media advertising, with the exception of subscription cards within the magazine itself, because it is usually more cost effective to rent lists of people who subscribe to other magazines. Charities are larger users, often canvassing donations when their cause is topical or pre-Christmas, sometimes selling membership on subscription. A charity or magazine may expect to pay 100 per cent of what it receives from a new customer or donor in advertising expense. It will recoup this from subscription renewals or later mailings. Unlike magazines, newsletters can often be promoted off-the-page at a profit. This is because the subscription is expensive and the newsletter cheap. However, they enjoy no benefit from advertising space sales and have a relatively poor renewal rate.

A profit is often taken at the front end by collectables companies, such as Franklin Mint. The margin on such merchandise is exceptionally high. It is common practice to bill customers after order but prior to despatch. This billing may be for the full cost of the item or it may be an instalment payment, depending on the price. If a reservation is taken for a series of items, the cost of each is generally billed prior to despatch. This is not the same as a book club where the billing is with each despatch. It has always surprised me that collectable promoters are not freer with credit and free approval, bearing in mind their high margins and the inertia value of billing with despatch. Perhaps they know something I do not about the people who are their customers and the general level of satisfaction with their merchandise. These characteristics can be significantly different between one product field and another. When *Children's Britannica*, a 20-volume encyclopaedia, was sold off-the-page on credit, returns were non-existent and bad debt negligible. This is not uncommon with serious good-value products that are marketed to mature up-scale consumers.

The dimensions of offer

In looking at the mathematics, we have started the subject of sell-off-the-page where we left the subject of two-step response; that is, with the offer. The offer is absolutely crucial in sell-off-the-page although the variables of media format and copy are also important. The offer is crucial because it has a number of dimensions to it, each of which is highly influential. The first of these dimensions is the terms of business, a subject we have already started discussing. The second is value. The third is additional incentives.

Terms of business

The terms of business are a trade-off between immediate profit and lifetime customer value. They can be used to adjust the lifetime customer value upwards. For example, a book club member agrees to buy a minimum number of books in exchange for accepting an introductory offer. Alternatively, a variable direct debit mandate or credit card continuous authority agreement may be signed. In this case we shall generally make a loss on the first transaction but we are prepared to pay this price in order to maximise the eventual worth of our new customer. Variable direct debit mandates and continuous authority credit card agreements are used to sell subscriptions, whether these be to magazines, such as *Which?*, or membership organisations, such as the AA or the RAC. They are extremely powerful devices as renewal becomes an inertial process. The member has to make a conscious effort to cancel. Because of this inertial aspect, the consumer is reluctant to enter such agreements, just as he or she is reluctant to join a book club.

To counter this reluctance it is necessary to add inducements in the form of gifts, discounts, or subsidised books. This brings in our third dimension, that of additional incentives. These are tactical and can be chopped and changed more or less at will. Our terms of business should be the subject of rigorous initial testing but, once we have discovered the optimum terms, we should be reluctant to change without a compelling reason because this will entail a major administrative upheaval and render customer's future behaviour less predictable. The terms of business shape our enterprise, determining whether it sacrifices long-term growth for delivering a fast return or investment, or whether it swallows up a great deal of capital in order to meet an ambitious growth target.

Adding value

Let us then assume we have settled our terms of business and go on to the important dimension of value. There are two ways in which a desirable commodity or service can be given enchanced value. One is through pricing, or under-pricing. The other is through scarcity. A dress from a top designer may have scarcity value. A near replica of the same dress from a mail order company may have a price value. There is more security in selling on scarcity value because margins are higher. The difficulty lies in keeping a desirable commodity scarce. This entails keeping one significant step ahead of competition or selling limited edition commemorative merchandise which competition has not time to copy. The problem then is that there is a constant launch expense, each launch representing quite a substantial commercial risk. Scarcity is only available to businesses that can originate product or source original product and keep on doing so with a high success rate. That is why mail order items are more often cheap than exclusive.

However, credit and subscription selling excepted, the best mail order business sells scarcity. This is often the specialogue business, which may use a combination of single item space ads and loose inserting of mini-catalogues. The mini-catalogues, when times are good, produce a profit from the first transaction. They also test inventory, so that the hottest items can be run in space ads. The life of such items is often incredibly short and the operator must, as his specialogue may proclaim, 'scour the world', or at least the Far East, for his next big winner. It is possible to grow such a business very fast and for it to collapse even more rapidly.

The business of staying in business demands dedicated professionalism in merchandise sourcing, negotiation and rigorous control of marketing and operating costs. When I was running a direct marketing agency I stayed well clear of any such client. If he is good enough to stay in business he does not really need you enough to pay you well and if he is not, you will be staring at a substantial unpaid account before too long. The best operator of all, if ability to trade profitably over a long period is anything to go by, is Joe Sugarman of JS & A in the USA. He even writes his own copy and his ads are an education in themselves.

Sell-off-the-page items have to offer enhanced value because, contrary to what any direct marketing evangelist may tell you, the vast majority of people prefer to buy things in shops. They prefer to touch, feel, smell, take apart and put back together whatever they are buying before they buy it. Even free approval cannot remove the inconvenience of having to return an unwanted item. If it has to be returned, most people would prefer to go back to the shop with it than entrust it to the mail. Almost the only commodity you can buy through mail order in the same way as in a store is perfume. If there is a scent strip on the loose insert, you can sample the product in the same way as in a shop.

Range selling

However, some items lend themselves better to catalogue browsing than to shopping for many people. Often hobbyists will gain more satisfaction from a mail order catalogue with a comprehensive inventory than from a shop with a limited inventory. Most often, however, such catalogues are promoted on a two-step basis. Women who take large dress sizes will often prefer to buy through a dedicated mail order catalogue than a shop. To many people, there is little difference between booking their holiday direct with a tour operator and booking it through a travel agency. Either way they will generally choose their holiday from a brochure or, if it is a late seasonal deal, off-the-page from an ad. In the fields I have quoted, enhanced value still prevails. The extensive hobby inventory has scarcity value, as does the comprehensive range of outsize fashions. The direct sell holiday operator either cuts prices below indirect sell operators, or he specialises in exotic locations, or specialised activity holidays, that have scarcity value.

Offers and margins

However solid the rest of your plan, if the perceived value of the offer is insufficient, your plan will fail. If, however, the perceived value is on the borderline you may be able to tip the balance in your favour by adding an extra inducement, possibly close-dated, to prompt the reader to respond. This will most probably be a gift, but it could be a quantity discount. It could even include a sweepstake entry if you are using loose inserts. If you do run a sweepstake the terms of your offer must include free approval (or deferred direct debit) and you must accept entries from non-orderers.

If you cannot afford to risk a substantial loss at the front end of a customer relationship, one thing you must not do is tinker too much with your selling margin. A mark-up of much less than 90 per cent is highly questionable on clothing because of high returns rates and a mark-up of much less than 45 per cent is questionable on the most reliable of durables. Most of the successful operators work on margins considerably higher than these. Some products, such as books, cost more to sell and may require mark-ups of at least 200 per cent. The same may apply to low ticket speciality merchandise or products with a substantial handling cost, such as personalised items. Any product which competition can easily source and sell competitively against you is vulnerable. Sooner or later the margin will be cut, rendering the product unprofitable to both suppliers.

Handling charges

For products which incur physical distribution costs, a handling charge is usually applied over and above the price. A common exception to this is magazines sold on subscription. If this additional charge is described as post and packing, then it should not exceed the cost of post and packing. It can, however, be described as handling and despatch, giving a margin for order processing. Sometimes the charge is subsidised if the true cost looks unreasonable. There is no reason why such charges cannot be built into the price. The reason why they are not is either to secure good price pointing or because one flat charge is applied irrespective of the number of items ordered. Some advertisers use handling and despatch charges as a form of quantity discount, waiving the charge altogether on orders over a certain value. Credit marketers usually build handling and despatch into the price.

Media and format testing

The principles of media and format testing are exactly the same as for two-step advertising. However, your options may be somewhat more restricted. It is unlikely that you will need less than a magazine page size ad unless you are selling a low-cost bargain space item. If you are selling cash with order, your insert options are restricted. You will need to run a mini-catalogue or a piece including a reply envelope more often than not. Inserts not offering the benefit of displaying more goods and not offering a reply envelope tend not to work too well. In two-step advertising, inserts easily outpull space ads, partly because of their increased attention value but partly because they pull more impulse response. This is less likely to be the case in one-step advertising because purchases are more considered. So your insert needs to have a lot going for it. One way of giving it more is to make it up into a small catalogue on lightweight paper. Another is to make it easier to order and enclose money.

If you are selling on free approval terms then you will be less constrained by format considerations. Collectables marketers, like Franklin Mint, are extensive users of inserts and there is no reason why you cannot tip-on an order card to a space ad provided you are not asking for confidential information. If you are—for example, a credit card number—then your tip-on device will have to fold and seal.

These considerations aside, media testing is just as rigorous and important as in two-step advertising, although your media schedule will often include larger ads in a shorter list of publications. Your frequency may, however, be much greater if you are rotating ads for a series of different products, so the effect will be to increase concentration in a smaller number of media.

Copy testing

The extra variable in the case of sell-off-the-page is product. Unlike most two-step advertisers, many one-step advertisers promote a multiplicity of products, some of which may have a very short life and many of which may be highly seasonal. This increases the element of gamble, particularly in long copy date media. It also has a pronounced effect on copy testing because there is often little time available to hone and polish creative treatments for products that have a short life-cycle. The main distinctions here are between topical advertisers and non-topical advertisers. Topical advertisers include mail order merchant businesses selling clothing or innovative merchandise, limited edition products, holidays, unit trust launches and famine relief charity appeals. Non-topical advertisers include other categories of financial advertising (for example, credit card offers), subscription sales and book clubs. Even book clubs change their 'lead' books frequently but work to a formula that has been polished up over a long period of time.

When there is little or no time to test creative treatments then it is foolish to take chances just to be different. That is why most sell-off-the-page advertising follows a sensible formula in which the product, including any variants, are depicted clearly, the offer sings out and the copy both sells positively and handles all the likely sales objections. There is no substitute for experience when there is no time for testing. However, this does not have to be your own experience as you can always borrow someone else's, either directly by hiring a good freelance writer or indirectly by close observation of what experienced operators do. The ads worth looking at are those that are continually repeated since, to be repeated, they must be paying for themselves either in direct profit or in list building. Your study of sell-off-the-page advertising will reveal that it has all the ingredients I have stated even when the copy is written in the less conventional narrative form used by JS & A for product ads in the USA. If your ad leaves important questions unanswered it will fail.

Carrying conviction

When we discussed two-step advertising I suggested that at least 50 per cent of its effectiveness would depend upon the headline and main illustration. I see no reason to downgrade their importance with sell-off-the-page but must draw your attention to the fact that you now have a lot more convincing to do. People will only respond when the benefit from responding exceeds the risk or penalty from responding. In the case of a simple cash-with-order offer this means that you have to convince the reader that you have under-priced the merchandise or given away too many freebies with it. Since you (or your client) cannot afford to under-price the merchandise then the work of the copy is to enhance its perceived value, albeit truthfully. If the product is susceptible to illustration, you will need highly descriptive photographs that highlight what is special about it. You will certainly need a convincing copy argument and you will probably need to summarise the main benefits in a panel, list all of the product's uses and, possibly, list all the people who could benefit from it—for example, fishermen, climbers, long-distance walkers, ramblers, outdoor workers, farmers, vets, etc. You will need to explain that there is no other source for the product, or that no other source can supply it on such advantageous terms, or offer such exceptional after sales service, or whatever. As your copy moves towards the reply device you will need to explain why it is advantageous to order now. Your ad is now beginning to look pretty well packed and you will need to use illustrations and sub-heads judiciously to make the ad look easier to read and to invite the readers to start at the place that most interests them. The headline will usually contain the main benefit and sub-heads will contain supporting benefits, leading the readers in a shorthand argument towards the order form.

Captions to photographs perform a similar task to sub-heads, sometimes even more effectively, because the eye is naturally drawn first to pictures and then to the words nearest them. Any colour options or design options should be featured in inset pictures, if at all possible. For clothing, these may be in the form of swatch illustrations rather than complete garment pictures if space is tight.

In the build up to the close, and before the order form, you must include whatever guarantees and endorsements can be mustered and are needed to reassure the prospective buyer. Finally, clear instructions on how to order must be contained above, alongside or within the order form.

Ordering should generally be by telephone and post. The order form should make any options and the terms of the offer very clear, and should have sufficient space to allow respondents to fill in their requirements, their credit card number, their signature, their name and address and any other detail you may require. You may also want phone callers to complete this detail before they call so that they can read it off rather than delay matters by searching for their credit card number.

These principles are illustrated by two ads picked more or less at random out of the *Telegraph Weekend Magazine*. The first ad (see Fig. 6.1), for Innovations, features a computer peripheral which turns an IBM compatible PC into a fax

A revolution in communications for all users of business and personal computers!

Add facsimile communications to your PC for just £399*

COMPUTAFAX is a major new development in computer communications which is guaranteed to save your business time and money. Whether fitted to your portable, stand-alone or part of a network, it enables you for the first time, to send and receive facsimile messages – direct to and from your PC to other computers and fax machines.

COMPUTAFAX is cheaper, quicker and more reliable than conventional electro-mechanical facsimile machines because it is built into your PC system. Without any moving parts, COMPUTAFAX transmits screen information straight down the phoneline to the receiving PC or fax machine, achieving high speed and top quality reproduction.

Easy to install. Simple to operate.

COMPUTAFAX hardware takes the form of a modem expansion card which you can install into your PC in a few minutes. Then load the software programme onto your hard disk, plug it into a standard BT socket and you're ready to go. All your telephone contact numbers are stored in an easy-access directory, so once your message is typed into your PC it takes only a few seconds to transmit.

Significant cost savings through lower phone usage.

COMPUTAFAX transmits at 9600 bits per second, which is four times faster than accepted data transfer standards. This means your phone call costs are cut dramatically, and because the message takes far less time to send, the chances of faulty transmission through line interference are considerably reduced. In addition, the queuing facility allows further cost-saving through automatic sending at off-peak times.

```
━━━━━━━━━ COMPUTAFAX ━━━━━━━━━

SEND A FAX          - PRESS F1
RECEIVE A FAX       - PRESS F2
PREPARE A FAX       - PRESS F3
INSPECT QUEUE       - PRESS F4
INSPECT LOG         - PRESS F5
EDIT DIRECTORY      - PRESS F6
PRINT/VIEW A FAX    - PRESS F7
SETUP               - PRESS F8
```

Top quality reproduction.

Unlike ordinary fax machines, COMPUTAFAX doesn't need to scan the page electronically before it sends – so reproduction at the other end is much better. And because it uses your PC printer to generate a hard copy, there's no expensive thermal paper to worry about. If you wish to send drawings and photographs which are not held in computer format, you will also need a scanner linked to your PC.

Time-saving features.

As well as minimising phone time, COMPUTAFAX cuts down on administrative time. Major documents and complex spreadsheets (up to 212 character width) don't need to be run off, then scanned, then sent. They can be sent straight off computer memory. COMPUTAFAX also includes these management control features:

- Queuing system (fax multiple destinations at preset time)
- Repeat dialling to engaged numbers
- Automatic re-send of rejected pages
- Off-peak sending
- Automatic remote polling (have you got something to send me?)
- Fax log (allows cost analysis of your fax traffic)
- Sophisticated directory facility (no wrong numbers dialled)

Completely confidential fax transmission.

COMPUTAFAX has the facility to send and receive messages in a coded form when communicating with another COMPUTAFAX PC. You can encode your message so that it can only be unscrambled if the recipient knows which

of 65,535 PIN code numbers to use. COMPUTAFAX users receiving transmissions from ordinary fax machines can read the facsimile straight from the PC screen: there's no need to print a hard copy unless you wish to.

Ideally priced for the home PC user – or the largest PC network.

At only £399* COMPUTAFAX makes high quality, low cost facsimile transmissions a realistic proposition for PC owners who require the facilities of a conventional fax machine that could cost several thousands of pounds. The home user or small business will discover a whole new method of efficient communication. The large office - with lengthening secretarial queues for its fax machine - will find it cheaper and easier to give each of their PC operators their own individual facsimile facility.

COMPUTAFAX is a major new British invention, exclusively available from Innovations. Just fill in the coupon or phone through your order today.

COMPUTAFAX is fully approved for use with BT lines, and can be installed in all IBM AT/XT† or compatible PCs, including:	
Amstrad	Opus
Apricot	IBM
Compaq	Toshiba
Olivetti	Zenith
And many others	

†IBM and AT/XT are trade marks of International Business Machines. All trade marks are acknowledged.

Our Guarantee

COMPUTAFAX is designed and manufactured in Britain, and is fully guaranteed for 12 months. The only customers we want are satisfied customers and that is why we will refund your money in full if the product is returned within 30 days. This guarantee is offered in addition to your statutory rights. We aim to despatch within 10 days of receiving your order, but please allow up to 28 days for delivery.

☏ Ordering by phone

Call (0793) 514666 day or night to place an order on your Access, Visa, American Express or Diners Club card account. Please have your card number to hand and quote the reference number TM08.

Innovations (Mail Order) Ltd., Euroway Business Park, Swindon SN5 8SN. Registered No. 1917662.

Send to: Innovations (Mail Order) Ltd., Euroway Business Park, Swindon, SN5 8SN. Registered No. 1917662

Name _____

Address _____

Postcode _____

Daytime Tel No. _____
Please debit my Access/Visa/American Express/Diners Club card account number

Credit card expiry date _____

Signature _____

Date _____

OR I enclose cheque/postal order for £ _____
Cheques/postal orders should be crossed and Co'and made payable to Innovations.

		Qty	Total Value £ p
H430 COMPUTAFAX	Item Price: £399.00		
	Plus Delivery and Insurance: £4.00		
	Plus VAT: £60.45		
	£463.45		

the grand total of £ _____

INNOVATIONS
THE SHAPE OF THINGS TO COME

Reference No. TM08

Select the message you wish to send.

Select the phone number of the fax machine or Computafax PC you wish to send to.

Transmit the message.

*Excludes VAT, delivery and insurance.

Figure 6.1 Innovations.
A logical sequence. Answers the reader's questions as they arise.

machine. In this case the company has had a bit of a struggle to achieve attractive price pointing and the all-in price including delivery and insurance is £463.45. This has been manipulated down to £399 by removing Value Added Tax, delivery and insurance from the displayed price in the headline. The headline reads: 'Add facsimile communications to your PC for just £399*.' No frills. The headline tells the reader exactly what is on offer at a low price. The overline targets potential buyers: 'A revolution in communications for all users of business and personal computers!' By reading only the words in panels and sub-heads we can find out what the product will do, what benefits it offers, what PCs it is compatible with, what consumer protection we are offered and how we can order. Furthermore, these are presented in a logical sequence, answering queries in the order they are most likely to occur to us. Incidentally, this ad is in black and white as colour is not required to emphasise the product benefits.

The John Harvey Collection space coat ad (Fig. 6.2) illustrates the same basic principles and demonstrates a method of handling colour options with six colours shown within a panel under the main garment shot. Five sizes are offered and this is suggested by showing a man and a woman wearing the coats in the main picture. An endorsement from Sir Ranulph Fiennes of the Transglobe Expedition is handled by using a small cut-out illustration over a signed quote.

There is nothing particularly clever about either of these ads, but they are highly professional. They exhibit the straightforward factual communication and attention to reassuring detail that is a prerequisite of successful selling off-the-page. It is worth taking considerable trouble to ensure that whatever guarantees, endorsements and options are likely to improve volume are costed and included.

Handling response

A particularly useful device is a live in-bound telemarketing facility allowing respondents to place orders by telephone. This, if skilfully manned, also allows queries to be handled and may suggest additional information which should be included in the copy. Tele-ordering will almost invariably increase business but, unless it is well managed, it can lead to clouding of the results as well as a failure to reassure potential customers. Clouding of results occurs when the source of order information is either not collected accurately or is not entered correctly. If an outside telemarketing bureau is used, it is essential to ensure that these demands are included in the contract. The same advice naturally applies to fulfilment houses also.

It is usual practice for a fulfilment house to submit daily batch reports detailing orders handled and a daily or weekly financial report showing cash banked and credit card payments. A daily, twice-weekly, or weekly report will be issued on source of orders, showing whatever detail is required. These analyses may no longer be on paper and may

SPACECOAT THERMAL THE CLOTHING INTRODUCE

"SPACE COAT"

From John Harvey

SPACECOAT GARMENTS Thermal Clothing introduce another addition to their unique range of thermal clothing: "THE SPACE COAT." A simply designed and well cut gilet with a tough, siliconed nylon showerproof outer and Aertex mesh inner, can be worn either as a lightweight gilet, or as a body warmer. "THE SPACE COAT" is fully interlined with Spacecoat SP27 thermal interlining, providing the wearer with unsurpassed, "State of the Art" thermal warmth.

WHAT IS SPACECOAT SP27 THERMAL INTERLINING?

THE CREATION and manufacture of Spacecoat SP27 thermal interlining is a direct "spin-off" from technology developed for the NASA Space Programme. The result of years of research and an investment of millions of dollars that sent man to the moon.

TECHNOLOGY FROM OUTER SPACE – TRIED, TESTED AND TRUSTED HERE ON EARTH

HERE ON EARTH many expeditions journeying to some of the coldest places in the world have recognised the unique body heat conservation properties of Spacecoat SP27.

Spacecoat SP27 was chosen by Sir Ranulph Fiennes as the thermal interlining for the clothing worn on the Transglobe Expedition in the first successful circumnavigation of the world.

"The lowest windchill factor we have so far experienced is minus 110°F... If we succeed in the first circumnavigation of the world it will largely be due to the excellence of our protective clothing"

Ranulph Fiennes
The Transglobe Expedition

LOOK FOR THE SILVER LINING

THE SPACECOAT SP27 spaceman label, with its unique roll number, is our guarantee that your "SPACE COAT" is interlined with genuine NASA "State of the Art" Spacecoat SP27 thermal interlining.

SPACECOAT SP27

STATE OF THE ART THERMAL INTERLINING

The John Harvey Collection

Harvey House, Tring, Herts HP23 4AJ.

THE SPACECOAT "SPACE COAT"

THE "SPACE COAT", fully interlined with Spacecoat SP27, has a full length zip, stud fastening and deep handwarmer pockets, small stand-up collar and adjustable hip fitting. Versatility makes The "SPACE COAT" a must for leisure, outdoor wear and for the golf course. Ideal for sportsmen the "SPACE COAT" makes a unique Christmas gift, warmly remembered long after the festivities are over.

Choose from: three plain colours, two tartans, and "golfer" grey, in sizes XS(36"), S(38"), M(40"), L(44"), XL(48"). *Price £39.95* (+£2.95 p&p)

Tartan Green   Sage Green   Tartan Red

Golfer Motif Grey   Dusty Pink   Petrol Blue

HOW TO ORDER YOUR "SPACE COAT" Simply fill in the coupon below, with the correct size, colour, and quantity you require. Allow 28 days for normal delivery from receipt of your order. Please send payment and coupon to: The "SPACE COAT" offer, The John Harvey Collection, Harvey House, Tring, Herts HP23 4AJ.

If you are not completely satisfied with your purchase please return it within 7 days for a full refund.

The John Harvey Collection, Harvey House, Tring, Herts HP23 4AJ.

Please send me:	REF	QTY	SIZE	PRICE (inc p&p) EACH
The "SPACE COAT"–Dusty Pink	52TA			£42.90
The "SPACE COAT"–Petrol Blue	52TB			£42.90
The "SPACE COAT"–Sage Green	52TC			£42.90
The "SPACE COAT"–Tartan Green	52TD			£42.90
The "SPACE COAT"–Tartan Red	52TE			£42.90
The "SPACE COAT"–"Golfer" Motif Grey	52TF			£42.90
TOTAL ORDER VALUE				

I enclose a cheque/PO in full payment, or debit my

(tick box) ☐ ACCESS ☐ VISA. Remittance should be made payable to The John Harvey Collection. CASH PAYMENT use Transcash – quote FREEPAY 2. (Details from your local Post Office.)

Card No: ☐☐☐☐ ☐☐☐☐ ☐☐☐☐ ☐☐☐☐

Signature

Name: (Mr/Mrs/Miss)
(Block letters)
Address:

Post Code

Regd. 1581341 Proprietors: John Harvey (Collection) Ltd. Please allow 21/28 days for normal delivery.

Figure 6.2 John Harvey Spacecoat.
Originally a colour ad. The coat is available in six colours, displayed in small illustrations next to the coupon.

be received on-line, in which case they may be constantly updated.

An unmanned answering system can be used but this is generally more satisfactory for receiving brochure requests than it is for receving orders, when the reassurance of a live answering facility assumes greater importance. A further advantage of telephone order handling is to alleviate perennial problems, in some types of mail order business, of out-of-stocks. Sometimes, substitute merchandise can be sourced and the customer can be switched on the telephone. It is also less irritating to the customer to be informed immediately of the problem in this way.

Clothing is particularly prone to out-of-stock situations because of the lack of opportunity to test market any garment prior to the short selling season. A cash-with-order business can quickly lose its acceptability as an advertiser with media owners if it runs into out-of-stock problems. An advertiser selling on free approval can escape such strictures but will still lose money and potential customers by failing to supply.

Continuing relationships

Fortunately, problems such as these do not apply to non-merchant businesses such as associations, magazine proprietors, newsletter publishers or charities. Here the big variable is the trade-off between the tightness of the new customer relationship and the cost of recruiting a new customer, subscriber or donor. The lower the commitment, or the shorter the subscribing term, the easier it is to get a new subscriber. The problem is that it is also easier to lose a short-term subscriber. Typically, a weekly magazine which offers 12 month and, as an alternative, 6-month trial subscription terms will get only 40–45 per cent renewals on the trial term if it gets 60–65 per cent renewals on the full term. This holds good even if the magazine offers a 'cancel at any time' option in which the unused portion of the subscription payment is refunded. Magazines that are sold primarily on subscription generally carry a somewhat artificially high news-stand price enabling them to offer big discounts for subscription terms. It is their equivalent of the tempting book club offer, although they will often provide a valuable gift in addition to the discount.

A problem I encountered when testing subscription sales for *Punch* was that the magazine was not artificially highly priced, yet I was aware that it would be difficult to sell subscriptions without a dramatic discount. They were prepared to drop 25 per cent for a 12-month subscription. I would not settle for anything less than 50 per cent discount but I was prepared to try something that had never been done before. That was to offer only one subscription term—two years. My little equations that convinced them I might be right are presented as Tables 6.3 and 6.4, detailing the subscription income from 1000 *Punch* subscribers over a four-year period.

You will see from the tables that there is little more than 5 per cent difference in cash receipts between offering a 25 per cent discount and finding a creative solution to offering a 50 per cent discount. This difference is countered by the superior cashflow generated by Table 6.4. However, the major benefit is that Table 6.4 leaves more than twice as many subscribers on board at the end of four years. In these examples, no assumption has been made that the half-price offer will attract more subscribers, nor has it been assumed that people signing up for two years will be more loyal than people signing up for one.

In the event, the loyalty rates were higher than anticipated and this enabled us to try renewing subscribers for an indefinite term. About two-thirds of renewed subscribers opted for 'till cancelled' subscription with regular billing. Incidentally, we did not offer the half-price deal within the magazine itself. We did not want to subsidise people who already bought the magazine regularly to such an extent.

Continuous authority

An even more effective way of getting subscribers, or members of an association, to stick with you is to enrol them

Table 6.3 25% discount for 12-month term (theoretical)[*]

Year 1		Year 2		Year 3		Year 4	
No. of new subscribers	Receipts @ £18.75	No. of renewals (60%)	Receipts @ £18.75	No. of renewals (65%)	Receipts @ £18.75	No. of renewals (70%)	Receipts @ £18.75
1000	£18 750	600	£11 250	390	£7 312	273	£5 119

[*] The cumulative cash receipts from this illustration total £42 431. The number of subscribers available to renew for year 5 is 273.

Table 6.4 Two years' subscription for the price of one (theoretical)[*]

Year 1		Year 2	Year 3		Year 4
No. of new subscribers	Receipts @ £25.00	Receipts	No. of Renewals (60%)	Receipts @ £25.00	Receipts
1000	£25 000	Nil	600	£15 000	Nil

[*] The cumulative cash receipts from this illustration total £40 000. The number of subscribers available to renew for year 5 is 600.

on a variable direct debit mandate or on continuous authority credit card payments. In this way they keep on paying without noticing it although you must inform them of any price rise and give them time to cancel. This can increase what would be a 65 per cent annual renewal rate to something like 85 per cent although, technically, there is no renewal with a direct debit or continuous authority payment. The cumulative benefit of securing such an agreement is enormous. It is not uncommon for associations to secure the equivalent of more than 90 per cent annual renewals in this way.

Table 6.5 shows a cumulative cash benefit of £20 150 over three years from continuous authority payment, or more than £20 per recruit. At the end of three years only 52.5 per cent of cash payers remain on board, while 82.8 per cent of continuous authority payers stay with the product. The administration charges for continuous authority payments are offset by savings on a number of renewal mailings that would have to be sent to cash payers each year to retain 70 per cent or more of them.

The price paid for this advantage is that it costs more to sign people up on a continuous authority basis than on a one-year commitment because more inducement is required. However, we can readily see from the table that, if it costs £15 in advertising to sign up a cash payer, it would still be good business to pay upwards of £25, even £30, to sign up a continuous authority payer. Alternatively, we might give the continuous authority payer a bigger discount or a better category of membership for the same money. We could solve the problem of differential pricing if we wished, by refusing to accept cash payers. However, I like the idea of a discount because it appeals to the bargain instinct.

Table 6.5 Membership organisation charging £50 annual membership (theoretical)

Payment Method	Recruits	Year 1 Revenue	Renewal	Year 2 Revenue	Renewal	Year 3 Revenue	Members
A. Cash	1000	£55 000*	70%	£35 000	75%	£26 250	525
B. Continuous authority	1000	£50 000	90%	£45 000	92%	£41 400	828
Difference (B minus A)		−£5,000		+£10,000		+£15,150	+303

* £5 joining fee charged to cash payers.

Continuity selling

The same basic principles apply to book and record clubs, to continuity series book publishing and to charity donations. It is worth a big inducement to secure a major commitment. A charity which receives, on average, a £15 donation may be fortunate to receive one-third as much again from the donor in the next two years, say a total of £20. The same charity offering membership for £10 can expect an 85 per cent renewal rate, obtaining £25.72 over the same period and carrying forward a much higher potential income. Furthermore, some members will make additional donations, others will buy from the charity's catalogue and a few will sell raffle tickets or go on sponsored walks. For tax reasons charities can do better still with covenanted or PAYE subscriptions.

One of the interesting features of continuity selling in the various guises we have looked at is that it can easily be applied to markets where it has not yet been applied. Earlier in this book I mentioned that I had stolen the book club principle and applied it to wines. Earlier it had been stolen for selling cosmetics and, in the USA, even for selling cheeses. While writing this chapter I came across an ad promoting a malt whisky club with subscribers receiving a collection of miniatures for £11.50 each month. There is a free book to join and there is also a post and packing charge. The idea is good in principle because there are more than 100 different single malts. The book club principle can only work if there is an appearance of extensive choice. A further advantage is that many people like to collect miniatures. However, the offer looks too low for such a large commitment. It seems insufficiently generous, the value does not look right and a shipment a month looks too much to me. By the time you read this the jury will have reached its verdict on this offer. My experience encourages me to recommend a high value front end offer in exchange for a reasonably substantial commitment.

The market for mail order continuity series books is not as buoyant as it once was and *Time Life* are left without any substantial competition in the UK at least. However, the principle of continuity series selling could be applied to any suitable product. The idea is to use the mechanism of free approval to allow a negative option distribution system to be applied. After the initial order and agreement is returned, the supplier can keep on sending monthly despatches accompanied by invoices until the subscriber cancels or stops paying. The subscriber can, of course, return any unwanted despatches. What happens is that there is generally quite a steep decline through the first two or three despatches and then this decline tapers off as the hard core of genuine subscribers is reached. The initial response and rate of decline can be modified by increasing or reducing the generosity of the front end offer. This system is not quite the same as a book club system, the latter being more complex. A book club will send a newsletter or magazine in advance of despatch, allowing the member the choice of accepting the recommended book, another book, or no book at all. A lack of response is interpreted as a request for the recommended book. The book club relationship is also open ended. Unless the member stops paying or cancels, membership will continue indefinitely. A continuity series offers no choice at all and the relationship is finite in duration because the series of books is 18, 20, 24 or whatever. The malt whisky example mentioned above appears to offer no choice but the relationship is of indefinite length, so it falls somewhere between a book club and a continuity series.

A continuity series works because it forms a definite collection with a common theme. Subscribers know at the outset exactly what they will get if they continue to subscribe. For this reason, a variation to continuity series selling is sometimes used. This has the merit of reducing shipment costs and increasing sales of complete sets. It works like this: after the second or third despatch, the subscriber is notified that the remainder of the set will be sent in one shipment. However, the subscriber may continue to pay for a book a month, that is on credit. The problem with this system, which in direct marketing jargon is called a 'load up system', is that it increases credit risk and provokes a large number of cancellations. Clearly, the further down the series it is applied, the lower the risk but the less the potential benefit.

Ingenious systems such as these have been applied to selling books because books are high margin products which are hard to sell. They can work equally well for other products, provided the product has collector appeal and the cost of the product does not make the inherent bad debt risk unaffordable.

One possible application would be in sales promotion where, instead of the consumer having to collect 10 pack tops to qualify for an offer, the consumer 'pays' for each monthly or quarterly freebie by sending back pack tops. When the consumer stops sending them back, their membership ceases and they get a re-solicitation mailing to tempt them back. Continuity devices of this type deserve more widespread usage since their effectiveness has already been demonstrated.

At the time of writing there has been a trend, most marked in the USA, towards continuity promotional programmes for fast-moving consumer goods. The reason for this is that cents off coupons have increasingly tended to cause little more than blips on sales graphs, while redemption rates on coupon distribution have fallen as the volume of distribution increases. These trends have encouraged producers to build customer databases, offering consumers the opportunity to receive benefits in exchange for repeated purchases. Since a database entails communicating by mail it is, in any event, necessary to make a mailing influence a number of purchases in order to recover its cost. Programmes of this type need not be discount based. They may offer other benefits, for example, babycare booklets in exchange for disposable nappy (diaper) purchases. Anything which the user wishes to collect, and is readily available, is appropriate.

The pay-off

Consider one-step advertising when what you have to sell can be explained satisfactorily in a page ad, or smaller, or in a loose insert. If you are willing to risk offering free approval terms, one-step advertising will almost always beat two-step advertising, because you are overcoming only one inertia stage instead of two. However, you should not generally expect to make money on a continuing basis from one-step advertising. It is best used to build a file of people who want to do business with you. You must then consider the compatibility of the first transaction with the remainder of what you have to offer. A disparate selection of merchandise does not induce continuity. If you are selling out of a catalogue, a page ad offering one item may initially be more cost effective than two-step catalogue request ads, but it is likely to produce customers of poorer quality. This is because the catalogue respondent was sold on the idea of shopping from the catalogue. The one-step ad respondent may never purchase from the catalogue. It is best to try both one-step and two-step advertising in this situation and, provided they come close in overall cost effectiveness, persist with both because their relative pulling power can switch around from one season to the next. It is axiomatic that a customer's purchasing performance must be measured continuously. If you measure the sales from one-step advertising and repeat purchasing separately, as if they were different businesses, you will not find the winning formula. One-step advertising is simply a means to an end.

There are businesses which do little else than insert mini-catalogues in magazines or as parcel stuffers and appear to do very nicely. Do not be tempted. Such businesses, to survive, must be continuously brilliant in scouring and negotiating advantageous terms on merchandise and print. The big opportunity lies in continuity promotion and a range of merchandise, or collector series, appealing to a specific lifestyle or set of attitudes. In such cases you may be able to induce your respondent to give you a forward commitment, such as club membership, a subscription, or a minimum purchase agreement.

A significant difference between planning one-step and two-step campaigns is that one-step is nearly always more topical, depending heavily on fashion, novelty, or seasonal demand. This reduces the opportunity to test and makes a campaign more of a gamble. It is best not to put too many eggs in one basket as the item that you were sure was going to pull like crazy may bomb out, while the one you were in two minds about could pull like a train. The very unpredictability of one-step makes stock problems come to the fore. This means juggling to ensure maximum back-up stock with minimum stock commitment.

While it is possible to move into one-step with fairly low capitalisation, this reduces the options and increases the risk. Asking the consumer to send money in advance, requires that you provide something utterly desirable, unique and with a high perceived value. It is not the best way to build a lasting customer relationship. To take the opposite route and launch collections, of the kind offered by Franklin Mint, requires considerable funding in product origination and a long wait for the pay-off, because profit is dependent on a large customer base. Yet the growth potential in continuity business is far greater than in the one-off product merchant business.

Advertising for one-step is akin to a sales presentation in which all of the potential sales objections must be anticipated. While the ad must lead with the major benefit, all the supporting benefits must be included. This is why most successful one-step ads follow a formula that is not difficult to study and to apply to other commodities or services.

Media spaces are likely to be bigger and inserts more expensive than in two-step response. There are also likely to be a number of product offers and, therefore, a higher frequency can often be used. This generally means a shorter media schedule, more money being spent in any one publication and, therefore, greater negotiating strength. In one-step it is almost invariably better to use this strength to deal short term. The last thing you may wish to saddle yourself with is an uncancellable volume discount deal when, as can all too easily happen, response may suddenly dry up.

One-step, then, should be considered as the beginning of a customer relationship. For this relationship to work it is necessary to have an inventory that is synergistic, or credit terms that foster re-purchasing. It is necessary to make ordering as simple as possible, by telephone and post, and to deliver all that you promised, when you promised it.

7 The great ad gallery

The proposition

Before we go on to discuss what makes a good response ad, which is the subject of the next chapter, I thought it would be amusing and instructive to ask some good friends in the business to contribute to a gallery of great response advertising.

Aside from their generosity, what the participants have in common is that all have achieved distinction in the world of direct marketing. Some are old enough to have done so in the advertising business before the growth of direct marketing demanded their full-time involvement. Each achieved distinction through his creative talent as a writer or art director before assuming the wider responsibilities of a creative director.

Distinguished as they are, my contributors would not claim to represent the whole cream of direct response talent. But it is beyond question that they represent a very significant part of it. In alphabetical order they are Chris Albert, Chris Barraclough, Drayton Bird, David Bull, Bruce Collins, Terry Hunt, Chris Jones, Roger Millington, Graeme Robertson, Chris Rudd and the inimitable George Smith.

Each contributor received the same brief. It was to lend to our gallery the direct response media ad that they would most liked to have done and explain why. Then to lend to our gallery the ad created, either by themselves or their agency, which they were most pleased to be associated with. Again, they have explained the reason for their choice. Their explanations are both entertaining and illuminating. Nothing teaches like example. I have learned a lot from these examples and I hope you will too.

You will notice that many of the ads, even allowing for the limitations of reproducing them in a book, are not necessarily aesthetic triumphs. But that is not the point. The point is that they worked, extraordinarily well, which reinforces my belief that the standards by which many advertising people judge creative work are irrelevant. They are not the standards that the ordinary reader applies.

Certainly not the standards of the reader who is within each advertiser's target market.

Often those with direct response experience have the clearest insight into what the consumer seeks. They have learned their craft with the experience of response—sometimes lack of response—from their readers. It is the consumer's vote that counts.

Brilliant isn't brilliant unless it sells. Brilliant advertising says something entirely relevant to the reader in a different and more persuasive way. It is nice to be creative. It is essential to be persuasive. The ads in our Great Ad Gallery are both.

When I asked our contributors for their offerings I imagined I might have a problem. I feared that two or more of them might select the same ad. I should not have worried. Creative people are both sharply observant and highly individualistic. While many of their choices feature intangible products—surely the ultimate challenge—they have each selected different ads, even omitting the one I would most liked to have written. This ad led off with one of the few truly great direct response headlines: 'Cash if you die. Cash if you don't.'

One contributor, Chris Albert, was associated with this all-time winner for Lloyds Life. Therefore, Chris—since he had not chosen this ad himself—received an additional brief. It was to feature the ad I would most like to have done. I am confident that the ad will still be the subject of discussion and admiration well into the twenty-first century. When a headline says it all in eight words, how could it be anything else?

Chris Albert

Chris Albert is executive creative director of Watson Ward Albert Varndell and is deputy chairman of the WWAV Group. He studied graphics at Kingston College of Art and has worked over 20 years in conventional advertising agencies, winning both DADA and Creative Circle awards. The last 12 years have been spent in direct marketing—first at Trenear Harvey Bird & Watson where he was responsible for the design of the majority of the award winning mailings, packages and ads of the agency.

In 1981 he helped set up WWAV, now Britain's largest direct marketing agency which, under his creative directorship, has established itself as the most creative in its field, winning nearly twice as many awards as any of its rivals.

Chris has been a judge three times on the BDMA awards and is active in promoting the improvement of creative standards in the industry.

'Our budget account . . . '
Mercantile Credit

" When I look at ads in newspapers, colour supplements and magazines, I must admit when it comes to ads that have a coupon or require the reader to actually buy something off the page, it makes me sad that I rarely feel 'boy, I wish I'd done that'.

And this tends to be specially true of the financial sectors. When you think of the growth in direct selling of financial products, it's depressing that so much of the work is so *safe* and *predictable*, and must be less effective in response terms, because it all looks alike—relying too much on illustrators and is bankrupt of good ideas that dramatise the offers or problem with originality.

And that's why I chose this advertisement for Mercantile Credit. Full page black-and-white ad in *TV Times* with a colour tip-on (Fig. 7.1).

Tip-ons in the colour supplements have been the single most effective development in response advertising over the last few years, and in this ad is a photo of a manilla envelope with address, etc. Often they are just a repeat of the ordering device in the form of a card, but this took the idea right through, by following the good rules (and had a coupon on the page as well if the tip-on failed to appear). When I flicked through our copy of the *TV Times* this ad hit me. Firstly, by

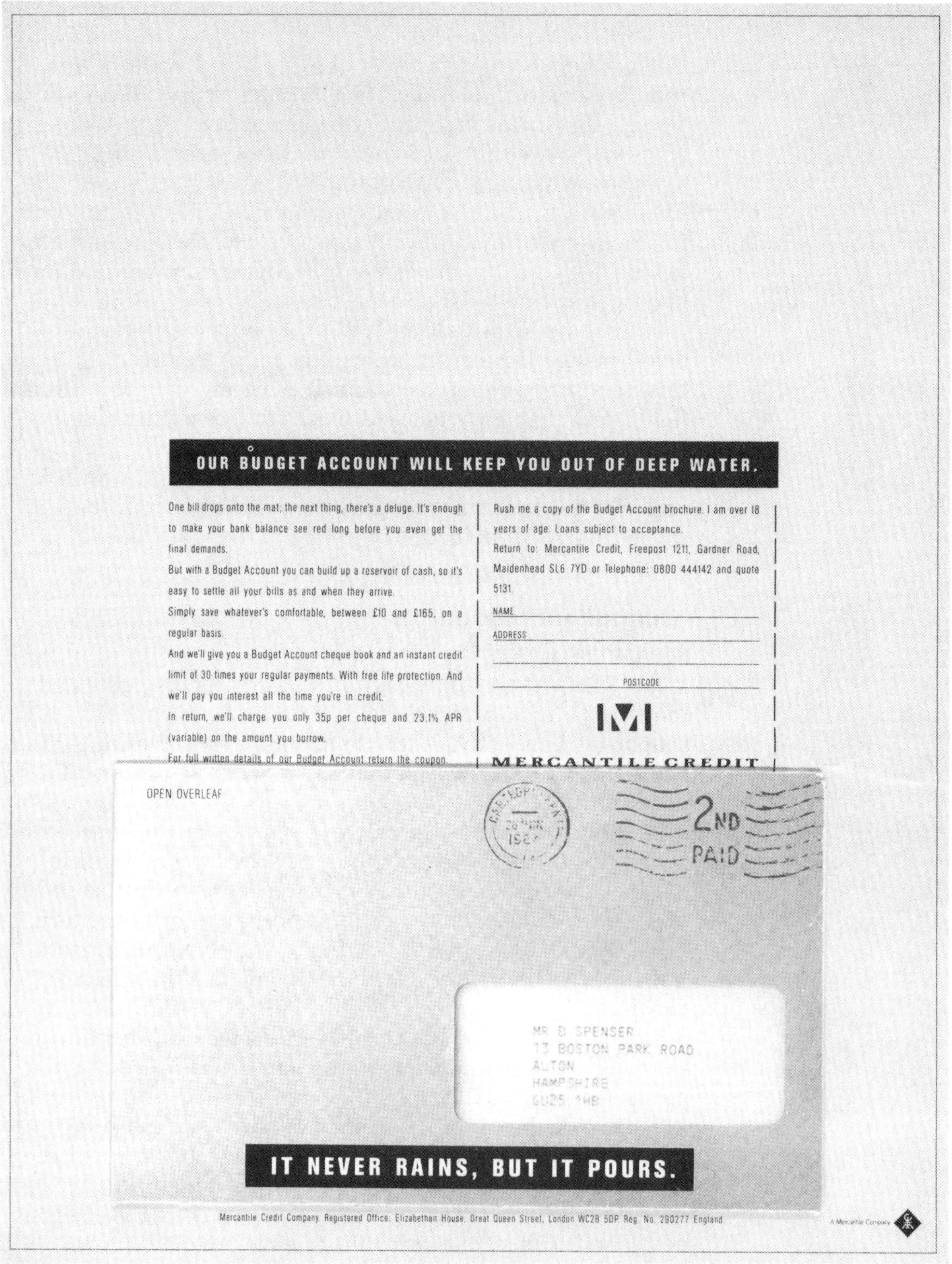

OUR BUDGET ACCOUNT WILL KEEP YOU OUT OF DEEP WATER.
One bill drops onto the mat; the next thing, there's a deluge. It's enough to make your bank balance see red long before you even get the final demands.
But with a Budget Account you can build up a reservoir of cash, so it's easy to settle all your bills as and when they arrive.
Simply save whatever's comfortable, between £10 and £165, on a regular basis.
And we'll give you a Budget Account cheque book and an instant credit limit of 30 times your regular payments. With free life protection. And we'll pay you interest all the time you're in credit.
In return, we'll charge you only 35p per cheque and 23.1% APR (variable) on the amount you borrow.
For full written details of our Budget Account return the coupon.
Rush me a copy of the Budget Account brochure. I am over 18 years of age. Loans subject to acceptance.
Return to: Mercantile Credit, Freepost 1211, Gardner Road, Maidenhead SL6 7YD or Telephone: 0800 444142 and quote 5131.
NAME
ADDRESS
POSTCODE
MERCANTILE CREDIT
OPEN OVERLEAF
2ND
PAID
MR B SPENSER
13 BOSTON PARK ROAD
ALTON
HAMPSHIRE
GU25 1HB
IT NEVER RAINS, BUT IT POURS.
Mercantile Credit Company. Registered Office: Elizabethan House, Great Queen Street, London WC2B 5DP. Reg. No. 290277 England.

Figure 7.1

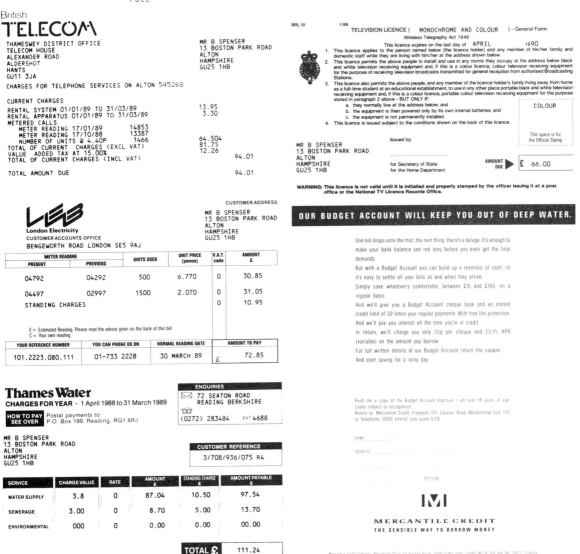

Figure 7.2

the sheer simplicity of the layout, it looked like a bill envelope stuck on the page, with a teasing headline: 'it never rains but it pours' on the envelope—now isn't that just what we all feel when the bills all roll in one after the other? I couldn't resist looking inside, which was only a simple sleeve. I was expecting the usual leaflet to drop out complete with standard headlines about having a loan for all the things you don't really want. So when what fell out was a concertina fold of facsimile bills, telephone, gas, rates, TV licence and at the end a very clear and easy to understand two-stage budget account brochure to be sent for, it all made sense (Fig. 7.2). A loan to tide me over the humps of all those bills especially as it's a budget account and I can pay what I can afford each month. What a marvellous, obvious way to dramatise the subject. The copy is sharp and to the point.

> One bill drops onto the mat; the next thing, there's enough to make your bank balance see red long before you even get the final demands, but with a budget account you can build up a reservoir of cash, so it's easy to settle all your bills as and when they arrive.
> Simply save whatever's comfortable, between £10 and £165, on a regular basis.
> We'll give you a budget account cheque book and an instant credit limit of 30 times your regular payments, with free life protection. And we'll charge you only 35p per cheque and 23.1 per cent APR (variable) on the amount you borrow.
> For full written details of our budget account return the coupon ...

The whole treatment said to me that Mercantile Credit understood my problem, didn't put pressure on me to purchase conservatories, motor boats, cars or holidays, and I'm afraid we're all responsible for following this formula—there is just one thing that could have made this into a great ad, after all those bills—what a pity there wasn't a reply device, i.e. self-seal envelope with free post—it would have increased response. But making it a little difficult can improve the quality of fulfilment. Perhaps they had their reasons.

I don't know whether it worked, I haven't seen it again yet. I hope it does. To see a major give a lead in this field, which has had a bad reputation, and to find good creative thought that is right on the button, uncluttered by secondary thoughts or fussy layout, was a joy to me.

Yes, I wished I'd done this ad. I'm jealous of who did it and, boy, I'll try harder because of it! **"**

'Visiting day'

Compton & Woodhouse

" It's always difficult to choose just one advertisement created by one's own agency. I have chosen an advertisement for Compton & Woodhouse, who sell limited edition figurines and plates in fine bone china by the famous pottery houses. The main reason for my choice is that the agency actually owns Compton & Woodhouse—now this puts a completely different complexion on things. If it doesn't work *we* actually lose money. *We* also have to understand all the problems a client has from first hand—will the factory deliver on time? Quality control—will the handpainting be consistent and to price fulfilment? Bad debt and the difficulty of staged payments and issuing the same edition number on collections, returns, product development, research. It's all our own money that's at risk—a very sobering position for an agency to be in and I can tell all you theorists, at times it hurts. It also changes other clients' attitudes to the agency, they know that you have experienced the sharp end.

This does not mean we produce stilted work on Compton & Woodhouse—far from it, we have won awards both in the UK, Europe and the States for our work.

Firstly, imagine the audience for the products. We describe them as fifty-five-year-old ladies (C2) living on a housing estate—very house proud especially about their front room—they like collecting but wouldn't have the courage to go into an antique shop to buy a figurine or plate. They would not be too sure of their own taste, or of the prices and, really, they prefer something new. Now all the creative work is based on making them feel justified in their choice—yes they are deliberately traditional in treatment—they must reflect the subject matter and it's pretty memories that motivate the customers most into buying. Now over the four years or so we have been operating Compton & Woodhouse there have been many different figurines, some linked to charities as this one I am showing, others as collections linked to museums, i.e. the V&A or National History Museum, all made by the famous china houses of Britain—Coalport, Royal Worcester, Wedgwood. The products are very different to Franklin Mint, who generally manufacture in the Far East in porcelain, which is easier to reproduce and generally a little cruder. Fine bone china is much more subtle, softer in colour and always very delicate—a real test for the art director and photographer, especially when we are mainly appearing in the colour supplements printing on very poor quality paper. Who knows what will happen to the colour?

With this figurine, 'Visiting Day' (Fig. 7.3), we decided to link it into the centenary of the Great Ormond Street hospital for sick children and for each figurine sold a contribution was made to the hospital.

The figurine of the little girl was extremely delicate of colouring, very soft tones which are the hallmark of Coalport work for Compton & Woodhouse. To create the feeling of the period, a sepia drawing of the hospital was drawn on the

COALPORT

Inspired by over 100 years of caring by
The Hospital for Sick Children, Great Ormond Street, London

"Visiting Day"

A numbered, limited edition in fine English bone china by Coalport.

Strictly limited to 9,500 figures only

Each figure individually numbered; accompanied by a signed Certificate of Authenticity

Designed by Elisabeth Woodhouse, sculpted by Sheila Mitchell

Available only by direct subscription from this advertisement. "Visiting Day" is not available from any shop

Send no money with your application

THROUGH the blustery April streets of Victorian London walks a pretty young girl – the freshening wind swirling out her petticoats in a froth of lace. She wears her best boots, her best pinafore, and wrapped around her is her best paisley shawl; a little threadbare, perhaps, but clean, neat, and proudly worn.

If you stop her as she hurries shyly across the cobbles, she might tell you, breathlessly, that she is "off visiting" her older sister who is in the new Hospital for Sick Children in Great Ormond Street.

"Visiting Day," from Coalport, perfectly captures this delicate scene. Inspired by the story of this now famous Hospital, designer Elisabeth Woodhouse and sculptor Sheila Mitchell have succeeded brilliantly in creating a beautiful figure, full of life and movement, which is available *only* by direct subscription.

Applications may now be made. And for each figure sold, a contribution will be made to the Great Ormond Street Children's Hospital.

Made and painted by hand

The Hospital for Sick Children at Great Ormond Street was founded by Dr. Charles West, in 1852. What moved him, and still moves people today, is the special care given by the Hospital to children. Little wonder that this touching subject should now inspire this Coalport figure "Visiting Day."

Created in fine bone china and exemplifying all the care and skill of Coalport, every detail of "Visiting Day" has been carefully and faithfully rendered.

Each figure is entirely hand made – even the flowers she carries and the ribbon that ties her

Each figure bears, on the base, the Coalport back-stamp, the number of the figure in the edition, and the initials of the designer, Elisabeth Woodhouse.

hair – and each is meticulously painted by hand in delicate fresh colours.

This unparalleled attention to detail, and the painstaking care revealed in every fluid line of "Visiting Day" recall the tradition of exquisite figure sculpture in the eighteenth and nineteenth centuries. Rarely, today, will you find a contemporary figure of such outstanding quality.

Strictly limited numbered edition

Only 9,500 examples of "Visiting Day" will ever be made by Coalport, and each figure will be numbered on the base. The figure will *only* be available by direct subscription from Compton & Woodhouse, dealers in fine English china.

The full price of "Visiting Day" is £97.50. You may choose to pay in five convenient monthly instalments of £19.50. No payment is required with your application, which can be posted or telephoned to us. Upon acceptance of your application, the figure will be sent to you for your approval.

If for any reason you are not absolutely delighted with the figure, you have our unconditional guarantee: simply return it in the security packaging provided, within 28 days, and your money will immediately be refunded in full.

Applications will be dealt with in strict rotation. Your application for "Visiting Day" should therefore be made as soon as possible.

ABOUT COALPORT
Part of the world-famous Wedgwood Group, Coalport is one of the most respected names in fine English Bone China, as well as one of the oldest names, with a history going back to 1750.   COALPORT

"Visiting Day" is shown here actual size of 7¾" high.
Note the painstaking care lavished on such details as the frothing petticoats and the untied bootlaces of this innocent young girl. Even the tulips she carries are hand made, and each beautiful figure is painted by hand.

Compton & Woodhouse Registered Office: 126 High Street, Billingshurst, West Sussex RH14 9EP.

Figure 7.3

144

background then the figurine was placed in front and photographed with the illustration slightly soft to create a feeling of depth.

The layout may seem traditional—it is not. The typography is classical book—but the use is very subtle. To make it clear that this is a direct selling advertisement for a product costing £97.50. The use of the 'Coalport logo' is of prime importance as is 'Bone China' and 'Made in England'—so here we used the stamp technique in the prime top right-hand corner. 'Visiting Day', the title, would seem to be the headline, but is it? This ad doesn't really have one, it has several key statements, all very important triggers. For example:—'Inspired by over 100 years of caring by the Hospital for Sick Children ...' 'A numbered, limited edition in fine English bone china by Coalport.' Then secondary triggers ... 'Strictly limited to 9,500 figures only, each figure individually numbered, accompanied by a signed 'Certificate of Authenticity.' 'Designed by Elisabeth Woodhouse, sculpted by Sheila Mitchell.' 'Available only by direct subscription from this advertisement. "Visiting Day" is not available from any shop.' 'Send no money with your application.'

So the importance of the origins of the figurine and the offer is set. Now the copywriter gets into his stride painting the picture.

> Through the blustery April streets of Victorian London walks a pretty young girl—the freshening wind swirling out her petticoats in a froth of lace. She wears her best boots, her best pinafore, and wrapped around her is her best paisley shawl; a little threadbare, perhaps, but clean, neat and proudly worn.
>
> If you stop her as she hurries shyly across the cobbles, she might tell you, breathlessly, that she is 'off visiting' her older sister who is in the new Hospital for Sick Children in Great Ormond Street.
>
> 'Visiting Day', from Coalport, perfectly captures this delicate scene. Inspired by the story of this now famous hospital, designer Elisabeth Woodhouse and sculptor Sheila Mitchell have suceeded brilliantly in creating a beautiful figure, full of life and movement, which is available *only* by direct subscription.

It may all look simple, and critics say it's all old hat—I can assure you it's not. The name of this game is crafting, crafting, crafting, plus a lot of psychology mixed in.

Crafting of the copy all written with our target audience in mind, written with sympathy and warmth—no pressure selling, no trendy style, just good writing.

The art of this achievement is that copy and art direction all blend together in a sympathetic whole, reassuring and persuading—it must work and create a sale—we can't send you to a shop to buy—it can only be bought from this advertisement and we need to tell you enough for you to justify that purchase.

As I said, owning the client makes it a different game for an agency—our money is where our mouth is. It's nice also that we were able to make a total donation of £18 000 to the Great Ormond Street Century Appeal at the end of the campaign.

"

Chris Barraclough

In 1981 Chris graduated from the University of Sussex with a degree in Law. Being unable to face a life confronted by conveyancing forms and wills, he quit Law School to sell advertising space.

After two years on the phone, Chris answered an ad for a junior writer at Smith Bundy, one of the country's more interesting direct marketing agencies. Working on practically every account within the agency, he picked up BDMA awards for his work on Linguaphone, Bradford and Bingley Building Society, Securicor Communications and Oxfam Trading.

After three happy years Chris felt the need for a change and was delighted to answer Graeme McCorkell's call to join MSW Rapp & Collins. There, he worked on a variety of accounts, winning both a BDMA and an EDMA award for some work selling carphones.

Graeme's departure coincided with an offer from DDM Advertising, one of the country's largest agencies, to become their creative director. After 18 months Chris's most memorable moment has been to produce a campaign for British Airways featuring a genuine French impressionist painting as a competition prize. This was one of the few UK entries to win a bronze 'Echo' in the 1989 American DMA awards.

For the marketing press, he's written various articles on the role of creativity and has a regular 'humorous' column in direct marketing's trade magazine *Precision Marketing*.

'Just another day at the office'

The Army

❝ My first real job was to sell recruitment advertising space for an ailing engineering magazine. Sadly it was at a time when UK engineering firms were laying off workers by the thousands, so no-one needed to advertise vacancies.

And I wasn't very good.

Apart from my lack of success, I became acutely aware of how sterile most recruitment advertising was. It all looked the same. Said the same things. In the same hyperbolic language. Whatever the job, whatever the company.

Which is why I was surprised when I first saw CDP's campaign for Army Officers (Fig. 7.4). They were brilliant pieces of work in their own right *and* they were recruitment ads!

Just another day at the office.

Your alarm buzzes for the second time. A freezing mist lies heavily over the camp. Your radiator is barely warm.

—6.15 am—

From the room next door a worn-out tape of Dire Straits shakes another young officer awake. On your left you can just hear Mozart's Flute and Harp decorating the morning. With close friends like this, who needs a radio?

Outside twenty-two bleary eyed soldiers await your arrival. What are you going to torture them with today?

They'd know if they'd bothered to look on the notice board: an eight mile run.

"Come on you lot, you know you can do it." And in fact they can. It's all part of being a professional.

Panting back, strung out like washing on a line, leading from the front one minute, urging from the back the next, you pass another platoon swimming across an icy river. Your men shout derisive encouragement.

—7.45 am—

A quick shower and change into uniform.

You walk past portraits of distinguished Generals and spruce Brigadiers to breakfast in the mess.

Most officers are on first name terms but somehow you always seek out friends of your own age and rank. Not that it matters much, hardly anyone talks at breakfast.

You could choose muesli and yoghurt (heaven knows you've vowed to often enough) but the smell of bacon and mushrooms overwhelms your best intentions.

—8.45 am—

Time to inspect your platoon not so much for bull but well being. You make eye-contact with each man. Is one still having trouble with his girlfriend? Is another's wife still fed up with married quarters? Has a third got over the flu bug?

A look can often tell you something you should follow up in private later.

You tell one of your Corporals to take them off on anti-tank weapon training leaving you to discuss the day's programme with your senior NCO.

He's a Sergeant six years older than you and whose knowledge and experience you've learned to respect greatly.

You tell him you've arranged a showing of a film about the Falklands war, what went right, what went wrong and why.

You check on one soldier whose sick leave has gone on suspiciously long, then on to preliminary planning for next Autumn's exercises in Cyprus.

—10.45 am—

During the coffee break you bump into an Army Air Corps Officer who's just flown in the Brigade Commander by helicopter.

He's hacked off that a unit he was due to do abseiling exercises with next week, has suddenly been re-deployed.

Your mind races. "Hang on."

You'll need an instructor and permission from your Commanding Officer, but your men will get a day's abseiling 90ft down from a hovering helicopter.

They're really knocked-out when you tell them after a radio codes lecture just before lunch.

—12.30 pm—

The light falls through large windows onto long, polished tables and finds reflections in illustrious regimental silver.

However often you walk into the dining room you always feel the tradition: the battle honours from wars you studied at school.

Sitting at the table are many of the colleagues who will become life-long friends. You find a place among them and chat.

'Soup or melon sir?' You serve yourself to the other two courses.

Afterwards there's just time to flick through a newspaper in an armchair built uncompromisingly for masculine comfort.

—2.00 pm—

You drop in on your platoon while an NCO is demonstrating the new SA80 rifle.

They are silent as he holds up its lethal, efficient lines for them to admire.

Like a car salesman he feeds them facts...'automatic fire...only two-thirds the weight, smaller calibre...'

Knowing you won't be needed, you leave. The men have to learn practical map reading. This afternoon you can plan a course.

—2.35 pm—

Armed with stopwatch, map, compass and notepad you drive in your third-hand Alfasud to some woods in the next county.

As you run through the empty landscape, it starts to rain and you step in a pool of liquid mud. Brambles tear at your tracksuit. Was this such a wonderful idea?

But in two hours you're back in the car with the heater full on, one trainer full of mud and a desperate need for a cup of tea.

Still, you've planned another day's training.

—6.00 pm—

Your bed has been made and your room cleaned but your dirty clothes are a matter for you and the regimental washing machine.

Exhausted but with a quiet mind you sit down to write a report on a Corporal who's asked permission to apply for a commission.

His career could depend on what you write. You're thinking deeply, pen poised, when there's a knock on the door. It's one of your brother officers looking disgustingly fresh.

"You haven't forgotten we're playing squash before supper?" he enquires. "Not tired are we?"

The Corporal's application will get better attention in the quietness of the evening.

Meanwhile, there's someone who deserves a good thrashing on court.

Please send me more information about life as an Army Officer.
Full name
Home address
Date of birth
Place of study
I have or expect to obtain □ O-levels (no.) □ A-levels (no.) □ degree or equivalents as applicable. Send to:
Major John Floyd, Army Officer Entry, Dept. A037, Empress State Building, London SW6 1TR.

The Armed Forces are Equal Opportunity Employers under the terms of the Race Relations Act 1976.

Figure 7.4

To some of us, finding recruits for the army may have seemed an unchallenging brief. So how do you bring that proposition to life? How do you make it interesting to read and understand? Make the reader *want* to find out more. It's that ability to turn a brief on its head, produce something creative, original *and* effective that distinguishes good work from the ordinary.

'Just another day at the office' achieves all this by taking us through the long and demanding day of a typical officer. But before we study the copy we should look at the ad as a whole. For me, it shows how much a great piece of advertising relies on superb art direction. Not just to make it look pretty, which it does, but so that the ad's message comes from the visual elements as much as the words.

The photograph is beautifully shot. It gives us a feeling of wide open space. Of freedom. Of excitement with a hint of danger. The image relates specifically to a section of the copy, but the elements within the picture also say 'if you're thinking of becoming an officer your stamina, health, intellect and your motivation are vital to your success'.

Not only that, great care has been taken with the grid and with the typography. There is a harmony between the copy and the design. The clean lines of the copy are elegantly broken up. Not by sub-heads, but by time-checks that help you through the ad and through the officer's day. I bet the art director and the copywriter worked closely together to ensure the copy fitted format, and the advert is much stronger for that.

The headline bears relevance to the visual as well as the body copy. It's short, sweet and to the point. The irony is nicely understated and carefully aimed at anyone who's looking for something more challenging. The aim of the ad is to deliver an alternative to commuter tedium. Not an alternative that appears unachievable, but one that appears exciting, stimulating and realistic.

The length and message of the copy are effective ways of screening suitable prospects. It's like the first stage interview. If you can't face a day like this, don't apply!

The copy puts you in the officer's shoes. It relays your thoughts. Your experiences. It's as if you were there in person. 'You' or 'Yours' appears 23 times before the end of the second column of type!

This is an ad in which you take part.

And it's not just descriptive of the product. Real thought has gone into creating an empathy with the mind of the reader. What shines through the copy is that this ad has been thoroughly researched. All good advertising is. Not just the product facts, but the attitudes and expectations of the most likely prospects.

'You could choose muesli and yoghurt (heaven knows you've vowed to often enough) but the smell of bacon and mushrooms overwhelms your best intentions.' That's empathy. It strikes a chord with all of us.

The career itself is unusual in that an officer's responsibilities and duties are very broad. Some of us when asked to describe the breadth of those duties would have written exactly that. But you make the point much more effectively by posing authentic questions like 'Is one still having trouble with his girlfriend? Is another's wife still fed up with married quarters? Has a third got over the flu bug?' And you may have noticed the reportage is all in the present tense, which adds to the involvement and the impact.

Although the energy of the copy never falters, the writer has employed subtle changes in style to change the pace—as and when appropriate. While some passages are staccato. Like this. Others are quite lengthy and literate—'The light falls through large windows onto long, polished tables and finds reflections in illustrious regimental silver.'

And the ad doesn't finish with the expected 'for further

details, etc., etc.' which could only be an anti-climax, but with a neat little vignette about a forgotten game of squash. 'Meanwhile there's someone who deserves a good thrashing on court.'

Then the coupon. Short and to the point. But it's worth remembering that this is far more than a recruitment ad. It does a great PR job for the army, making *all of us* aware of what life in the army is really like. And like much direct marketing, prospects will not only respond via the coupon but through other channels—high street offices, exhibitions, university 'milk rounds', etc.

'Just another day at the office' achieves so much. Above all, it slots comfortably into a superb campaign that's been running for years. At first sight, it's not what some would term a traditional direct response advertisement. But I'm convinced anyone who starts to read the copy will be utterly captivated and *at the very least* be tempted to consider responding. And that *must* be classic direct marketing. **"**

'Grand-mummy' and 'Fine art'
The Crown Suppliers

" Business to business advertising has a reputation as a creative graveyard. For some reason, even the best creative teams are overcome by mental paralysis when asked to sell something to a businessman. Products end up displayed in the most lifeless manner, with copy a turgid recitation of features.

Which is why DDM's work for the Crown Suppliers (for which I can personally claim little credit) is such a breath of fresh air. Even when dealing with the most day-to-day products, the work rises above the brief and displays remarkable creative flair.

For example, what could be more everyday than a bench or a display case?

'The fine art of contract furnishing' and 'Mummy' centre on precisely those two products (Fig. 7.5). Yet both executions elevate those products beyond their day-to-day functions.

Before we go any further, I ought to explain who The Crown Suppliers are. For over 600 years they've been supplying furniture and furnishings to the public sector—government departments, museums, art galleries, local authorities, fire stations, etc.

They don't just supply desks and chairs, but every single fitting from a conference table to a fire bucket.

When DDM started working with The Crown Suppliers our research indicated that they had little or no awareness. Even within the relatively small public sector market. They did have a memorable logo; a known name (once prompted); and a reputation for quality—especially as many of their products are designed to a particular project's specifications. It became clear that these were the key strengths that the advertising should stress—through the tone of the copy, the quality of photography and typography, and the subject matter featured.

Awareness was important. But we were talking to a relatively small marketplace. So it made sense to find out who our customers were so that we could tailor future communications more specifically to their needs. One method was to ask people to respond to an offer of a free copy of The Crown Supplier's catalogue.

That meant the brief was a double-edged sword. Awareness and response. How do you start? There's only one way. To immerse yourself in the subject.

We visited sites furnished by the client. Not just once, we've continued to do so every year that the campaign's been running. We've visited places like the Tate Gallery in Liverpool for the 'fine art' advert. Or the British Museum for the Ikon Showcase.

Taking the time and trouble to research a project helps you find the creative hook. For example, in the British Museum we noticed how sad and tired many of the mummies looked in the old wooden cases. Therefore, we felt it was vital that the new Ikon Showcase System showed the mummy 'alive and well'.

Similarly, when seeing the visitors' bench at the Tate *in situ*, it became obvious that it naturally fitted into its surroundings. Photographed in isolation, the strength of its design would have been totally lost. With two modern paintings as a backdrop, a simple wooden bench suddenly betrays a new quality.

Both photographs are expertly composed and art directed. As are the advertisements themselves.

Look at how the ad is balanced. The size of the image, the position of the headline, the weight of the typography, the strength of the logo. The shape of the coupon. Everything is neatly ordered, achieving a balance to satisfy the harshest aesthete.

The mummy itself is a memorable image. Especially when you bear in mind that it appeared in such worthy publications as *Local Government News* and the *British*

In here, he'll last to be a grand-mummy.

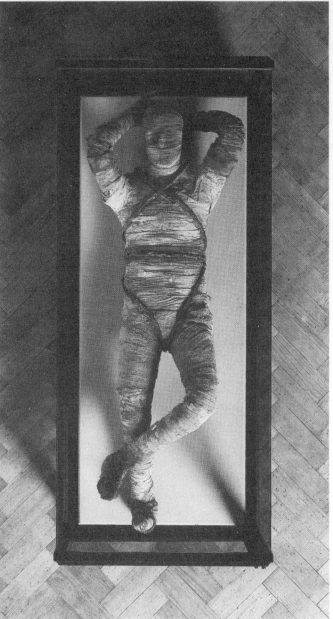

Because he's relaxing in a new Ikon showcase, from The Crown Suppliers.

The Ikon system was developed from extensive discussions with museum staff about their needs for the 1990s and beyond.

The result was a showcase system far more advanced than any of its competitors.

Nowhere is this advancement more obvious than in Ikon's conservation features. Sophisticated air management lets you control both air temperature *and* humidity. So exhibits stay in peak condition.

Ikon also sets new standards in security and flexibility.

There are two types of locking—mechanical and electronic. And the system can be easily dismantled and reassembled by the museum's own technical staff.

Of course, this kind of innovation is typical of The Crown Suppliers.

We've been supplying the public sector for over 600 years. With anything from office furniture to fire fighting equipment, fabrics to electrical generators.

What's more, all our 7000 products are subject to the most stringent tests. Not just for quality but for safety, too.

And if we can't find one to satisfy us, we'll design it ourselves or have it designed.

All this results in quality products that are excellent value. Like Ikon, for example.

To receive a free brochure on Ikon or a copy of our free, two-volume, 1988 catalogue, just complete and return the coupon.

Or phone 01-922 2449.

THE CROWN
SUPPLIERS
YOUR PARTNER IN THE PUBLIC SECTOR

Figure 7.5 (and opposite)

The fine art of contract furnishing.

This magnificent piece of contemporary furniture can be seen in the Tate Gallery Liverpool. But you may be surprised to learn it is not an exhibit.

It is a visitors' bench.

Designed to our specifications by Architects Michael Wilford & Associates, it was modelled on ancient Egyptian footstools and ottomans and crafted by John Corlyon.

It is just part of the refurbishment we undertook for this Grade I listed building, supplying office furniture, audio-visual aids, cafeteria and cloakroom facilities and bespoke carpeting.

Managing complicated projects is nothing new for us. We have a 600 year history of servicing the public sector. Expertise and experience that is now available to the private sector.

As experts in the art of contract furnishing, we are skilled in weighing up aesthetics, practicality and cost-effectiveness, not to mention delivering on time and within budget.

Often we have an advantage because we can draw from our own range of over 5000 superbly designed products.

And as the largest contract furnishers in the UK, with a purchasing power of £100 million, we can buy in bulk and offer you competitive prices.

For more information send for your free catalogue today. Post the coupon below or phone 01-922-2449 to order your catalogue direct and for details of your local showroom.

THE CROWN
SUPPLIERS
AT WORK FOR YOU

To: The Crown Suppliers, FREEPOST,
Marketing Services Group, London SE1 8YZ.

Please send me my free copy of your new catalogue.

Name

Position

Organisation

Address

Postcode

Telephone Number

BR/10/89

153

Association of Friends of Museums Yearbook. And although the product is basically a box (albeit a very sophisticated one), its benefits come to life thanks to the understated humour.

'The fine art' belongs to the following year. But however comfortable one feels with a particular campaign, especially one that has run for several years, you can't afford to get complacent. 'Mummy' and other executions had proved their success. But we still looked hard for ways to improve our client's advertising while retaining its underlying strengths.

I hope that if first you read 'Mummy', then 'The fine art' you'll detect an improvement in the style of the copy. There are more changes of pace giving it a little more life. Other factual snippets show that the writer's done even more homework to produce a more interesting ad.

The copy sells The Crown Suppliers and the breadth of its services via the excellence of the bench. But watch how it skilfully develops its themes moving from the very specific '(the bench) was modelled on ancient Egyptian footstools and ottomans and crafted by John Corlyon', to the very abstract 'aesthetics, practicality and cost-effectiveness'.

Within all this we also address a new marketplace 'Expertise and experience that is now available to the private sector', before establishing the client's credentials 'the largest contract furnishers in the UK, with a purchasing power of £100 million', to climax with a call to action.

All in 200 words.

'Mummy' and 'The fine art' are driven by exceptional art direction. A talent that's alien to me. They are carefully crafted pieces of work following the guiding principles of good advertising—showing and explaining the product and the service in a creative way. Much credit must go to the client too, for actively encouraging and supporting work that wasn't ever a 'safe bet'. **"**

Drayton Bird

Drayton Bird is vice chairman and creative director of Ogilvy & Mather Direct Worldwide—the world's largest direct marketing network—and a board director of Ogilvy & Mather Worldwide.

Based in London, he has been a copywriter since 1957—and continues to write copy. His current clients include: American Express, British Telecom, Lever Brothers, Xerox, Reader's Digest, Save the Children, Shell and The British Royal Mint.

His book, *Commonsense Direct Marketing* (1982), was the first on this subject in the United Kingdom. Leading US educator, Dick Hodgson, acclaimed it as 'One of the finest books ever written on the subject of direct marketing'. The second, completely rewritten and much expanded edition is now available from the publishers, Kogan Page, London. 'Everything the testimonials say, and a bargain at any price,' commented Robert Heller, Britain's leading business writer.

A well-known speaker, he has entertained audiences from virtually every significant market in the world—including China, the US, Japan, and every major European country.

'Hot home-baked rolls'

White Horse Hotel

" Every time I wonder whether I'm a good writer—which is frequently—I take comfort from two qualities I have in common with writers I know *are* good.

First, I admire and study good work. Second, I always change the brief. I have, therefore, taken the liberty of exceeding what you asked for. As requested, I've written about two ads I admire, one from our agency and one not. And I have also mentioned some other pieces of work I wish I'd written, which were not ads. Unfortunately, I can't think of anything I've written myself which I find particularly admirable.

I wish I had written just about anything David Ogilvy wrote. His gift for words is astonishing. I particularly enjoyed his description in an article a while ago of a certain type of creative person as: 'Callow boobies.'

I wish I had written my ex-partner John Watson's headline for an insurance product: 'Cash if you die. Cash if you don't.'

I wish I had written Ed McLean's: 'If the list upon which I

found your name is anything to go by, this is not the first, nor will it be the last invitation you receive to subscribe to a magazine.'

I wish I had written my New York colleague Bill Trembath's letter: 'Quite frankly, the American Express Card is not for everyone.'

And you may be surprised to know that one piece of writing I have always admired immensely was a direct mail shot that you yourself wrote for your agency 10 years ago. It was original, provocative, and wonderfully appropriate for somebody selling a direct marketing agency. (Please don't allow false modesty to cut this out.)

The letter began, as I recall, telling the reader that you knew in advance how many people out of every 100 receiving it would start to read; how many would read all the way through; and how many would reply. And it explained that you only knew this because you measured everything and, therefore, you knew exactly what was going to happen from experience—then going on to point out what a wonderful form of advertising direct mail is, especially when carried out through your agency. This letter impressed me enormously at the time, and still does.

Having managed to evade your brief so far, I will now meet it.

There is one campaign, and one particular ad which I really wish I'd written. The campaign was written by professionals in our New York office. The ad was written by amateurs. But it was so good, I was convinced they must be professionals. I was wrong.

It was for a small hotel near me in the West Country. It was a very small ad, selling a product in a very competitive market. There was no picture. Here's the copy:

HOT HOME-BAKED ROLLS

Wine-laced dishes with freshly picked herbs. Scrumptious puddings with thick local cream are served in the beamed restaurant of our small Georgian Hotel. 2 miles Exmoor and coast. Phone owner-chef Dick or Kay Smith, WHITE HOUSE HOTEL, Williton, Somerset TA4 4QW 0984 32306.
Try a 4-day

BARGAIN BREAK
& save £30 per couple

This advertisement is a gem. It does *everything* an enquiry advertisement should do in few words. First, it *positions* the hotel. You can immediately see it's not one of those nasty plastic modern hotels but a cosy traditional establishment. It paints a word picture of the hotel, too—demonstrates the product as it were.

It is personal, giving the names of the owners, and explaining they do not merely own the hotel but do the cooking. They must care. And, finally, it makes an offer.

Brilliant!

I rang the owners of the hotel to ask them whether the advertisement was successful. They said: 'Well, it doesn't do as well as it used to.' I asked them how long they'd been running it 'Seventeen years' came the reply.

"

'Hemingway'

Quality Paperback Book Club

" The campaign which I wish I'd written was produced by our New York office for the Quality Paperback Book Club (Fig. 7.6). Much of the credit for this campaign must go to a copywriter called Niall Kelly and an art director called Michael Rosenbaum. It won lots of awards, including our US agency's award for the best work of the year—direct or any other kind. Equally important, it got lots of sales.

Why do I admire it so much? Because the book club is an exceedingly difficult product category. The concept was invented nearly 60 years ago by Maxwell Sackheim and Harry Sherman and has not really changed since. The same approach remains favoured: you can buy three or four books very cheaply, if you then agree to buy a certain number each year at a higher price. And, of course, you get a regular stream of monthly selections which you have to act to refuse.

But this campaign takes this book club concept and manages to do something different. Something with character, wit and relevance.

The idea is simple. This is a book club for intelligent people. The proposition is equally simple. You don't have to buy a certain number of books each year. The way in which proposition and positioning are exploited to create splendid advertisements is remarkable. The proposition is explained pithily and idiomatically: '3 books. 3 bucks. No commitment. No kidding.'

One ad has a cartoon showing a devil prodding someone towards two doors—one labelled 'Damned if you do', the other labelled 'Damned if you don't'. Another shows a man sitting in bed reading a book entitled 'All things cold and slimy'. The line is: 'The book club for people who are tired of reading what other people read.'

One advertisement I particularly admired had the usual

Figure 7.6

'3 books for 3 bucks' with a picture of Edgar Allan Poe and the line: 'And a fourth book free if you recognise me.'

But to me, the campaign reaches its peak in a series of advertisements featuring famous literary or intellectual personalities. For instance, one ad features the Russian writer Vladimir Nabokov with the headline written in Russian. Under the picture of the writer is the English headline: 'Translation: Three books. Three bucks. No commitment. No kidding.' And in the coupon the line: 'OK. Send me 3 books for 3 bucks. Nyet commitment. Nyet kidding.'

In another advertisement the proposition is expressed as a mathematical formula with a picture of Albert Einstein. And in yet another—the one I like, I think, most of all—Hemingway is featured. The headline runs: 'Tres Libros por Tres Dólares and a Farewell to Commitment. No Bull.'

This campaign manages to be witty in the same way that someone else I admire greatly, Bill Jayme, is witty in his mailings. (I also wish I'd written 'How much should you tip when you're planning to steal the ash tray?', not to mention 'Do you lock the bathroom door behind you, even when there's no one else in the house?')

And just as Bill Jayme's mailings are not only witty but very successful, this campaign was. Previously the account had been handled by two very famous American agencies, one of which has become even more famous as a result of financial shenanigans. That is Lord, Einstein, Geller, Federico. The other was the Della Femina agency, which held it before we did. This campaign produced results almost twice as successful as those produced by Della Femina's agency. **"**

David Bull

David Bull has been writing copy since 1957, which must make him one of the most experienced copywriters around. He didn't enter direct marketing, however, until 1985.

By far the greatest part of his career to date was spent at Foote, Cone & Belding, where he became an associate creative director. Here he was responsible, over an 11 year period, for some of the agency's best-known work for BOAC and British Airways.

David Bull has also held senior creative positions at Mallerman Summerfield, FCB Direct, Geers Gross and MSW Rapp & Collins. He is now joint creative director of Payne Stacey Partners.

'Answer these ten questions'

Albany Life

❝ *But the headline doesn't contain a promise.*
But there are no sub-heads to break up the main copy.
But there's no offer, except for a brochure.
But the coupon's not very prominent. And where are the scissors?
But there's a shadow intruding into the coupon.
But the reader isn't left with a copy of the address once the coupon is removed.

Well, yes, I know all that. And I realise this advertisement (Fig. 7.7) would be unlikely to find much favour among direct-response advertising purists.

So why have I chosen it?

The answer is simply that despite all the shortcomings which, with a decade's hindsight, we might be able to ascribe to it, I believe it has a very great deal to teach those of us who now create direct-response advertisements.

It was produced by a team who have gained a deserved reputation for producing great advertising: Tony Brignull and Neil Godfrey. When they created this ad in 1980, they had never heard of 'Direct Response Advertising'. (Who had?) I'm sure they simply set out to produce a campaign to raise people's awareness of an insurance company called Albany Life.

They succeeded in projecting for Albany an image of a company which was helpful, friendly, approachable, thoroughly trustworthy, and endowed with great financial expertise.

Answer these ten questions and work out the date of your own death.

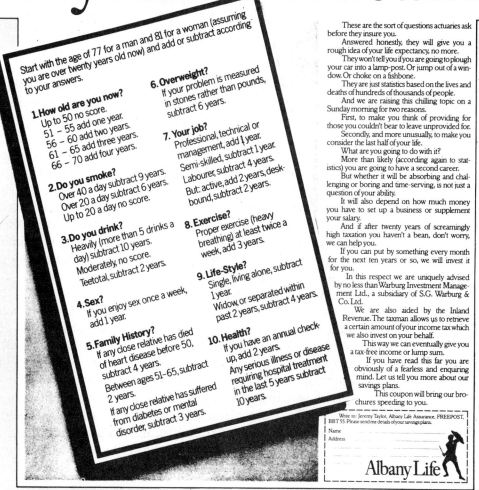

Start with the age of 77 for a man and 81 for a woman (assuming you are over twenty years old now) and add or subtract according to your answers.

1. How old are you now?
Up to 50 no score.
51 – 55 add one year.
56 – 60 add two years.
61 – 65 add three years.
66 – 70 add four years.

2. Do you smoke?
Over 40 a day subtract 9 years.
Over 20 a day subtract 6 years.
Up to 20 a day no score.

3. Do you drink?
Heavily (more than 5 drinks a day) subtract 10 years.
Moderately, no score.
Teetotal, subtract 2 years.

4. Sex?
If you enjoy sex once a week, add 1 year.

5. Family History?
If any close relative has died of heart disease before 50, subtract 4 years.
Between ages 51–65, subtract 2 years.
If any close relative has suffered from diabetes or mental disorder, subtract 3 years.

6. Overweight?
If your problem is measured in stones rather than pounds, subtract 6 years.

7. Your job?
Professional, technical or management, add 1 year.
Semi-skilled, subtract 1 year.
Labourer, subtract 4 years.
But: active, add 2 years, desk-bound, subtract 2 years.

8. Exercise?
Proper exercise (heavy breathing) at least twice a week, add 3 years.

9. Life-Style?
Single, living alone, subtract 1 year.
Widow, or separated within past 2 years, subtract 4 years.

10. Health?
If you have an annual check-up, add 2 years.
Any serious illness or disease requiring hospital treatment in the last 5 years subtract 10 years.

These are the sort of questions actuaries ask before they insure you.

Answered honestly, they will give you a rough idea of your life expectancy, no more.

They won't tell you if you are going to plough your car into a lamp-post. Or jump out of a window. Or choke on a fishbone.

They are just statistics based on the lives and deaths of hundreds of thousands of people.

And we are raising this chilling topic on a Sunday morning for two reasons.

First, to make you think of providing for those you couldn't bear to leave unprovided for.

Secondly, and more unusually, to make you consider the last half of your life.

What are you going to do with it?

More than likely (according again to statistics) you are going to have a second career.

But whether it will be absorbing and challenging or boring and time-serving, is not just a question of your ability.

It will also depend on how much money you have to set up a business or supplement your salary.

And if after twenty years of screamingly high taxation you haven't a bean, don't worry, we can help you.

If you can put by something every month for the next ten years or so, we will invest it for you.

In this respect we are uniquely advised by no less than Warburg Investment Management Ltd., a subsidiary of S.G. Warburg & Co. Ltd.

We are also aided by the Inland Revenue. The taxman allows us to retrieve a certain amount of your income tax which we also invest on your behalf.

This way we can eventually give you a tax-free income or lump sum.

If you have read this far you are obviously of a fearless and enquiring mind. Let us tell you more about our savings plans.

This coupon will bring our brochures speeding to you.

Write to: Jeremy Taylor, Albany Life Assurance, FREEPOST, BBT 55. Please send me details of your savings plans.
Name
Address

Albany Life

Figure 7.7

I don't know how many people they persuaded to clip the coupon. I suspect that, in any case, the advertising was not judged solely on the immediate response it generated. It was almost certainly judged on the results of research that would have discovered whether people's knowledge and image of Albany was better after the campaign appeared than it had been before.

Which brings me to what I believe the advertisement has to teach us.

First it teaches us that in our anxiety to generate the greatest possible response to each individual advertisement, we should not lose sight of the need to protect and enhance the image of the advertiser or his brands.

In the short term, getting response at the expense of image may seem justified. After all, brand images are rarely changed overnight. But in the long term, with consumers becoming increasingly aware of all the methods that are employed to persuade them to respond, it will prove to be short-sighted. Intrusive, ugly, patronising and offensive advertising will inevitably undermine an advertiser's image, erode his credibility and lose him business.

Further, the more we give consumer groups just cause for complaint about the work we produce, the more likely we are to bring government interference down on our heads.

Secondly, it teaches us that if you are going to sell something to somebody, you have got to get their attention first. Get their attention, that is, in a way which makes them want to read on. A picture of a scantily-clad girl is known to achieve a certain degree of success in attracting the eye of the average male reader. It is not, however, renowned for its ability to tempt him to read any of the copy.

In the case of the Albany Life ad, it is almost inconceivable to me that anyone could fail to be arrested by the headline. And having been drawn to the ten questions, how could anyone fail to be tempted to look for their own age, their own smoking, drinking and sex habits, their own family history, weight, job, exercise, life style and health? And having allowed their attention to be focused on the advertisement for the time it took to tot up their own personal score, who could fail to want to find out what Albany were offering in connection with what the copy describes as 'this chilling topic'?

In other words, it is a classic example of 'reader-involvement' advertising—luring the reader into becoming mentally involved with the advertisement and, consequently, much more receptive to its message.

Thirdly, it is a lesson to all copywriters on how to write copy. It succeeds in making an intrinsically boring financial subject into something immensely interesting. Most people who start reading this advertisement will find they are compelled to read right to the end.

The copy talks to you as an intelligent individual, instead of shouting at you as if you were part of a crowd. It is friendly and chatty. It is witty without being corny. It is refreshingly free from financial cliches. It is simple to understand without being patronising. And it is broken up into short, easily-digested paragraphs.

So that's why I wish I had written it.

Bear in mind, too, that the advertisement was written in 1980. If I had possessed that kind of writing ability then, and added it to all I have since learned about direct-response techniques, there is no knowing what fame and fortune I could have acquired by now!
"

'Wates homes at Sunninghill'
Wates

" Figure 7.8 is part of a campaign for Wates, art directed by Mick Kirby, which I wrote in 1985. I include it here not because I think it is the best thing I ever wrote, but because it enables me to continue with the theme of 'image'.

It proves that you can achieve a high rate of response without sacrificing an advertiser's image—that, indeed, you can actually use that image to achieve even greater response.

The campaign's main objective was to increase the number of people visiting Wates sites. High frequency was achieved by the use of small spaces. The one shown, for instance, was a mere 5 inches deep.

But at the same time we strove to maintain Wates's image of a friendly, thoroughly trustworthy builder—one that not only offered home-seekers a very well-constructed roof over their heads, but also promised them a better standard of living.

The headlines, while endeavouring to exhibit a certain amount of wit, always contrived to include 'Wates' and the town or village where the homes were to be found.

The body copy was written in a chatty style, and always included the main features of the properties, how easy they were to heat and maintain, where they were in relation to schools and shops, and how close they were to road and rail links.

Wates homes at Sunninghill are few and far between.

Large discount for fast exchange.

Not surprisingly, nearly all these distinctive new homes, set amidst the beautiful Berkshire countryside near Ascot, have already been snapped up.

We therefore recommend immediate viewing.

With just 45 of them spread across a wooded site of more than 13 acres, each offers you the sort of space you'll rarely find with a new property these days.

Accommodation and gardens are of generous dimensions, with kitchen and bathrooms closely resembling the kind you see in house-and-garden magazines.

Construction and building materials are of the highest standard, to give you easy maintenance and low heating costs.

Despite the semi-rural environment you'll find several schools (both state and private) close at hand, and shops within walking distance.

Waterloo is a mere 30 minutes from Sunningdale by rail, and you'll have easy access to the M4, M3, M25 and Heathrow airport.

See the show homes quickly. Or get more details by phoning (0990)28104.

Cumberland Hill, Cavendish Meads, Bagshot Rd, Sunninghill, Berks.

4 bed detached houses, 1 bath, 1 cloakroom shower from £107,000.
4 bed detached house, 1 bath, 1 en suite shower from £127,000.

Mortgages available. Prices and availability correct at time of going to press.
Fully-furnished show homes open 7 days a week, 10am–6pm.

Wates.
Improve your standard of living.

Figure 7.8

Every possible step was taken to help ensure that the decision to visit the site was not shelved and then forgotten.

A flash across the top right-hand corner offers a large discount for acting quickly. A map, plus a very full address, makes it very easy to locate the site. And even if you can't get to the site right away, there is a phone number for you to ring for more details.

Finally, the advertisement makes it quite clear what kind of price bracket the homes are in.

The results?

In very round (but not exaggerated) figures, the response from this campaign was double the response of the previous year's campaign. And that previous year's campaign had doubled response compared with the one before that—a campaign which, while seeking the highest possible response, had been designed to raise the awareness and improve the image of Wates.

Advertising budgets for the three campaigns were similar.

But it seems we did rather too well. Since so many homes were sold, the client was able to slash his advertising budget. You can't win!

Bruce Collins

Bruce Collins is creative management director of the MSW Rapp & Collins Group. He was born on 15 July 1937 and was educated at Kingsbury Secondary Modern, Harrow School of Art and The London School of Printing & Graphic Art. This is what he tells us:

'I gave up being an art director at Freeman, Mathes & Milne, a main line London agency in 1963, to start my own design company. Influenced by an American direct mail pioneer, Richard Browner, eight years later I became a creative specialist in supplying a wide spectrum of top English and European direct marketing agencies with a full creative serice. These accounts included La Mondadori (a Milan publishing company), Marion Edwards Ltd (an English company that supplied work for the German market) and Intermail (a Parisian agency that we worked with constantly for over a decade). I joined MSW Rapp & Collins when they acquired my company C+C Design Ltd in April 1984, where I had the privilege of working with the author of this book.'

'Government to condemn <u>80,000</u> more dogs'
RSPCA

❝ Before discussing this paragon of excellence (Fig. 7.9), I had better declare an interest. For fifteen years now, I have been the proud owner of a magnificent West Highland Terrier, and, on top of that, a soft touch for all things canine!

That said, this particular advertisement doesn't really need any special pleading.

The work of writer Kate Woodford and art director Nick Thomas at Chapter One Direct, it is a fine example of a powerful headline wired up to an arresting visual. The page crackles with vitality.

Look at those elements separately and you get a better idea of why they work so well together. The image plays on all our sympathies for 'The Victim' by putting the fate of an animal into poignantly human terms: destroying a dog, says the photograph, is just like putting a human being in front of a firing squad. Sure, it's the good old pathetic fallacy—but this time, it's got real bite.

When I first saw the ad as a double-page spread, it had a total of seven or eight dogs lined up for execution. Imagine the grab that photograph had as I flicked through the magazine!

GOVERNMENT TO CONDEMN 80,000 MORE DOGS.

According to the latest figures, an estimated 200,000 dogs are registered as strays each year; over 40% are destroyed. So, lack of Government action, will condemn to death another 80,000 unwanted dogs in the next 12 months.

Now the Government intends to abolish the dog licence as part of new legislation currently going through Parliament.

Don't let the Government turn its back on the stray dog problem. Support the RSPCA's Charter for Responsible Dog Ownership. For your free Information Pack, simply fill in the coupon and return it to: RSPCA, FREEPOST, Northampton, NN4 0BR. Or better still, telephone (0604) 767676 now.

RSPCA

RT3

I want to know more about the RSPCA's Charter for Responsible Dog Ownership. Please send me my free Information Pack.

Name: _____

Address: _____

_____ Postcode _____

RSPCA, FREEPOST, Northampton, NN4 0BR. Freepost means we pay the postage but if you could use a stamp it will save our precious funds for preventing cruelty to animals

Figure 7.9

The emotional grip is tightened by the copy.

Look at the vocabulary: *condemn, strays, destroyed, condemn to death, unwanted*: you're barraged with impressions and messages designed to arouse pity, sympathy, anger.

But it's not just the emotions that are manipulated here: the appeal is to the head as well as the heart.

The headline, for example, is very specific about the facts of the matter: 80 000 it specifies. Fact. More facts in the opening paragraph: 200 000 strays each year, 40 per cent destroyed, 80 000 will be destroyed in the next 12 months alone.

Notice, though, that in going from head to heart the ad isn't automatically *en route* for the wallet.

Instead of being asked to dig into our pockets, we're to send for an Information Pack giving details of the RSPCA's *Charter for Responsible Dog Ownership*.

It's an excellent offer.

Even if the Society doesn't ultimately coax some cash from respondents, it will certainly succeed in disseminating information, in spreading facts about the problem of strays.

And giving out the facts, defining the reality of a specific problem, is the first step in winning public opinion.

Just as significantly, the Society is reinforcing its own branding as the major player in its particular market: informative, compassionate, authoritative. In the long run, that's got to pull in more pounds than the predictable 'Send £5 today' approach.

That's a fact (or, at least, a strong probability) which illustrates the main reason for my admiration of this ad (apart from the aforementioned special interest!).

Envy.

It's one of those ads which, as soon as it's seen, you know you would have liked to have done yourself....

Well, I would.

"

'I'd like to come and talk to you ... '
Business

" Back in the 1950s, Bill Bernbach laid the groundwork for a fresh approach to advertising. Under its terms, the product was to be sold with panache. Fun, wit and memorability became at least equal partners to Benefits and the Unique Selling Proposition.

It's that approach to the craft of advertising which underlies this particularly successful advertisement (Fig. 7.10). *Business* magazine was the brainchild of Irish publisher Kevin Kelly. Kevin brought together his partner on *Interiors* magazine—publisher Condé Nast—and the *Financial Times* and the idea of a well-produced, investigative business monthly was born. The question was, how best to launch it.

What was the best way to persuade a busy, highly selective audience that *Business* would make a significant contribution to their understanding of the marketplace?

And the answer was, to be fresh, witty and memorable.

A pilot launch was put together in October '85 (a full five months before the actual launch) and the selected advertisement was designed to sell subscriptions on the basis of that pilot. Instead of a discount subscription offer up front, this advertisement took the increasingly rare liberty of telling prospects more about the product. And it did that in an attractive, friendly manner. By clipping the coupon or making a call, prospects in central London could have a personal presentation explaining what the magazine was all about, how it would help them and the high standards it would profess and maintain.

Figure 7.10

This presentation would be given by one of our team of smart, business-like young ladies who would instantly give the magazine a charm and personality to differentiate it from the competition.

The freshness of this approach was matched by its efficiency. The presenters carried with them specially designed 'Charter Subscription' forms which offered the prospect 15 issues of the magazine for the price of 12—an offer which gained power and persuasiveness from the fact that the product and its benefits had been explained in detail, face to face.

So did it work? There's no doubt it did. The pilot issue campaign put the magazine well on the way to its target circulation of 40 000–50 000 subscriptions. A few months after this initial campaign, publisher Keven Kelly could say in *Campaign*, 'The subscriptions we're getting are the top of the top.'

Here, then, you have a campaign that has undoubtedly proved its worth.

Amidst the clutter of lazy, stupid or boring off-the-page work, this piece stands out as a genuine advertisement. It mocks the existence of a hypothetical 'line' between image advertising and direct response by admirably doing the job of both disciplines. How? By combining that rare entity—an idea—with a powerful request for interaction.

It is, dare we say it, the way advertising *should* be done ... 🟥🟥

Terry Hunt

After a spell in publishing and promotions with Macmillan, Terry Hunt joined direct marketing agency Smith Bundy, learning the copy craft under the wise tutelage of George Smith. Left there to be creative director of DDM Advertising, where he worked with David Evans and Ken Scott.

Evans Hunt Scott was established in December 1986 and has progressed to become one of the top direct marketing agencies in the UK, employing over 50 people and working for such clients as Commodore Computers, RAC, Barclaycard, British Telecom, Sun Alliance, Johnson Wax, and the Sunday Times Wine Club.

'To get to the top'

ManuLife

" Is smiling allowed? Direct response advertising does seem to be a stout champion of the po-faced school of copywriting. Whenever mainstream direct marketers have a stab at humour, it tends to come out tortuously self-conscious, rather like a starchy headmaster trying to pep up school assembly. Being funny in direct marketing invariably involves sentences ending with exclamation marks (the more, the merrier), followed by a litany of product benefits; an unsaid 'no, but seriously ... '.

The maxim that response is no laughing matter is, I agree, wise. Nine times out of ten, a punning headline or even a wry aside is just so much excess baggage getting in the way of the call to action. But because we hard-headed direct marketers are not in the habit of using humour we also miss out on those rare chances to be relevantly witty.

This little gem (Fig. 7.11) by Axel Chaldecott and Steve Henry, produced in 1988 for ManuLife, shows how arresting and appropriate wit can be, even in that most unpromising of sectors—financial recruitment. The confident cheek of this ad reminds me of the ballsy, New York style that George Lois pioneered in the sixties. Lois's best ads were a heady cocktail of newsworthiness, irreverence and enthusiasm. They were sharply defined one-offs. For me, this recruitment ad for financial consultants is of that breed.

In design and content it is almost minimalist. A stock shot, a headline and a coupon. But what else does it need?

The coupon copy is simple and explanatory. The headline contains the offer of increased status and self-esteem. And

TO GET TO THE TOP IN MANULIFE, YOU'VE
GOT TO BE BRIGHT, HONEST AND WELL-INFORMED.
SO NOT EVERYBODY NEED APPLY.

I'm interested in being a financial consultant for ManuLife, dealing with life insurance, pensions, investments, mortgages and savings. I realise that ManuLife has an outstanding financial record and that their reputation rests on only accepting the very best people for training.

Please send me further details.

NAME:

ADDRESS:

Jean Wood, ManuLife House, St George's Way, Stevenage SG1 1HP. Telephone: 0438-356101.

ManuLife

BE HONEST.
ARE YOU GOOD ENOUGH FOR MANULIFE?

Figure 7.11

the picture is more than a thousand words' worth (why is this trio of former world leaders inherently rib-tickling?).

I know that this sort of lead generating direct response advertising is so much easier to produce than a money-off-the-page offer. I acknowledge that this particular example could have done with a bit of direct marketer's good housekeeping (Job title? Telephone number? Postcode?). I also haven't got a clue if it recruited a single new financial consultant.

What I admire about it is its conciseness, relevance and confidence. But most of all, its wit. Why shouldn't we aim to get response with a smile?

"

'How to harvest £8000'
The Daily Telegraph

" British broadsheet newspapers are peculiar institutions, quite apart from the megalomania of their proprietors. The editorial staff rule the roost, quite rightly. Unfortunately, editorial staff seem to hate the necessity to sell newspapers. Or at least they hate the methods one might 'stoop to' in pursuit of sales.

My own experience, working with *The Daily Telegraph*, was both enlightening and frustrating. For example, when we were producing a thankfully successful direct mail campaign to convert younger readers I was summoned by the editor, Max Hastings, to go through the copy; particularly the text of the letter he was to sign. As soon as I entered his study, this towering gentleman addressed the blank wall with a brief lecture on the poisonous influence of junk mail and the illiteracy of all advertising. Barely acknowledging my presence in the room he dismissed my well-honed letter written on his behalf, and replaced it with his own idiosyncratic version. What was most galling to my copywriter's pride was that his was an excellent, hard-selling direct mail letter.

Part of our direct marketing strategy for the paper was to collect names and addresses of existing readers for loyalty activity. One obvious method of name gathering was the use of in-paper competitions devoted to specific areas of interest.

This competition ad ran to coincide with the Chelsea Flower Show and *The Daily Telegraph*'s special gardening supplement.

True to form, the paper's gardening editor insisted on providing the competition questions.

Judging by their obscurity, he was presumably aiming at a

How to harvest £8,000 to landscape your garden

Fig 1. Put on your favourite gardeners' thinking cap.

Fig 2. Using your fertile mind, fill in the coupon.

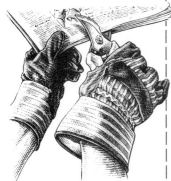

Fig 3. Neatly clip the coupon.

To win £8,000 worth of landscaping for your garden, answer the following questions. Then post this coupon to: The Daily Telegraph "Gardeners' Questions", PO Box 9B, East Molesey, Surrey KT8 0PE, to arrive on or before 10 June 1988.

1. Can you give the common name for the seed vessel of the following trees? (eg: Drupe, plum).
Thorn .... Oak ....
Ash .... Rose ....

2. Give the botanical name for the following flowers (eg: pampas grass, Cortaderia). Swiss cheese plant ....
African violet ....
Hibiscus .... Dumb cane ....

3. Which fruit carries its seeds on the surface? ....

4. What are the following?
Duke of Devonshire .... Duke of York ....
Lord Lambourne ....
Lord Derby ....
Which is the odd one out? ....

5. Put the following botanical group terms in order of precedence.
Genus .... Cultivar .... Family .... Species ....

6. What type of weedkillers are the following, residual, contact or translocated?
Glysophate (Tumbleweed) ....
Paraquat (Weedol) ....
Simazine (Weedex) ....
Sodium chlorate ....

7. What are the main countries of origin of the following?
Fuchsia .... Eucalyptus ....
Forsythia .... Tulip ....
Tomato ....

8. Which is the true one amongst these "roses"?
Sun rose ☐ Rock Rose ☐ Rose of Sharon ☐
Rosemary Rose ☐ Christmas Rose ☐

9. How many species of rhododendron are there?
10 ☐ 100 ☐ 1,000 ☐ 10,000 ☐

10. Identify the lime-hater(s) among these shrubs.
Arbutus unedo ☐ Erica erigena ☐ Kalmia latifolia ☐
Rhododendron ☐ Ferrugineum ☐

11. Which of the following is the odd one out?
Lady Belper ☐ Lady Betty Balfour ☐
Lady Hillingdon ☐ Empress Josephine ☐

Mr ☐ Mrs ☐ Miss ☐ Ms ☐ Initials ....

Surname ....

Address ....

.... Town/City ....

.... Postcode ....

Telephone Number ....

Fig 4. Post the coupon in a suitable receptacle.

Fig 5. Assuming you have done all this correctly, you could win £8,000 to spread liberally around your garden.

Win £8,000 worth of landscaping expertise and you could make your garden quite spectacular. You decide what you want . . . mature trees . . . rock or water garden . . . patio . . . pond . . . arbour . . . summer house . . . and it will be designed, constructed and planted by Waterers

The Daily Telegraph
Gardeners'
—QUESTIONS—

Landscape, the UK's longest established, award-winning landscape experts. And as one of five runners-up, you could have a £100 voucher to spend at any B & Q Garden Centre.

The Daily Telegraph "Gardeners' Questions" Competition Rules 1. Entry open to UK residents aged 18 or over. 2. Employees of The Daily Telegraph plc and their families, agencies and anyone else directly connected with the competition are not eligible. 3. Entry must be made on the official entry form, no photocopies will be accepted. 4. The first correct entry drawn will receive the first prize of £8,000 worth of garden landscaping by Waterers. 5. The next 5 correct entries drawn will each receive a voucher to the value of £100. 6. All winners will be notified by post or phone. 7. The draw for the 1st, and the 5 runners-up prizes will be drawn on 13 June 1988. 8. The complete list of questions and correct answers will be available from the competition address after the winners have been drawn. 9. There is no cash alternative to any part of the prizes. 10. Winners must be willing to participate in publicity accruing from the competition. 11. The judges' decision is final and no correspondence will be entered into.

Figure 7.12

limitless readership of horticulturalists with PhDs in biochemistry. No amount of argument would persuade him that questions on translocated Glysophite weedkiller might be a little too esoteric. Our job then was to water this arid examination paper, and make it flourish as an attractive, productive ad.

Written by Simon Kershaw and designed by Steve Stretton, with a bit of help from yours truly, this modest space, black and white ad (Fig. 7.12) pulled victory from yawning jaws.

Using the Gardener's Question Time theme, with appropriately arts and crafts style woodcut illustrations, it must boast the most inventive and amusing call to action in the history of direct response (well, maybe).

Fig 1.   Put on your favourite gardeners' thinking cap.
Fig 2.   Using your fertile mind, fill in the coupon.
Fig 3.   Neatly clip the coupon.
Fig 4.   Post the coupon in a suitable receptacle.
Fig 5.   Assuming you have done all this correctly, you could win £8,000 to spread liberally around your garden.

I'm proud of this ad not only because it worked well beyond expectation, but that it did so in a way that perfectly fitted the personality of the brand. A certain quiet charm and English dottiness are important characteristics of *The Daily Telegraph*, and I believe this ad managed to capture that spirit and make it work in direct response terms.   "

Chris Jones

An honours graduate of the Chelsea School of Art, Chris Jones has worked as an art director for the past ten years. He joined the board of Ogilvy & Mather Direct Worldwide, London, in 1984 as creative director. His work has been recognised in British, European and US awards. His wife Kay is also an art director specialising in direct marketing. They have a daughter, Kate.

'How it took me just one day'
Epson

"There can't be many direct response ads that actually make you laugh out loud—for the right reasons—but that's exactly what I, and my colleagues in the creative department, found ourselves doing, when we first read this one for Epson portable computers (Fig. 7.13).

And now that David Ogilvy and Drayton Bird both agree that humour can work in advertising, I'm willing to confess that this is one ad I wish I had done.

At first glance, it looks like one of those finely crafted ads of old, with its long, long copy and familiar, busy layout. But once you see the picture of the cross-eyed gent *not quite* staring out from the page at you, and read the headline with ... well, almost a benefit in it, you start to suspect all is not what it should be.

In fact, it turns out to be a very witty pastiche of the whole direct response advertising genre. But it's not a malicious attack—more a fond tribute to that golden era of wordsmiths we all hark back to.

And the wonderful thing is, it works. The device of an-over-the top salesman in conversation with his prospect (a man with an appalling memory and someone with whom I closely identify) allows the ad to make every selling point the client would want to make, without the reader feeling he is being sold anything. Outrageous claims that would normally offend any sensible prospect:

'The PC AC40/80 can ALSO make you FABULOUSLY POPULAR and SUCCESSFUL at work!' he went on.

leave you smiling and practically nodding with approval. Even the use of computer jargon seems to make sense:

The door to DYNAMIC GROWTH is WIDE OPEN, with NINE expansion slots, an extra 360K FLOPPY disk drive available and a MAXIMUM POSSIBLE RAM OF 15.5 MEGABYTES.

as well as adding to the humour.

Figure 7.13

The art director, too, had fun: with various boxes, bullet points and reversed-out panels (although I'm relieved he drew the line at starbursts).

All in all, it's a witty, well-written ad that works extremely hard. But if the truth be told, it's probably intended to increase Epson's awareness and establish a positioning for them, rather than actually generate a high volume of leads.

However, I did fill in the coupon for more information and was still chuckling to myself even after the ink had dried. I hope Epson are laughing all the way to the bank. **"**

'Secretaries able to write this sentence'
Rank Xerox

" In contrast, Fig. 7.14 is an ad our Frankfurt office produced for Rank Xerox. To sell their 'Ladylike' typewriters, Rank Xerox knew they had to reach the real decision makers: the executive secretaries.

Research had revealed that they were responsible for 95 per cent of all typewriter sales in small to medium-sized companies. As well as generating highly qualified leads, the ad's secondary objective was to increase the dismally low awareness of Rank Xerox as a typewriter manufacturer.

However, as no personalised list of executive secretaries existed, the agency realised they would only be able to use the relatively untargeted medium of press. And, no matter

Figure 7.14

how precise a media-strategy is, there is always a high element of wastage. So reducing the number of unwanted, unqualified leads was one of the creative department's priorities.

Fortunately, their research had also told them that the more sophisticated secretarial skills of shorthand and good grammar were generally exclusive to executive secretaries (common sense and personal experience had probably told them that already).

And it was this fact that helped them develop an ingenious mechanism to exclude all those unwanted responses. They devised a competition, with a holiday to New York, as an incentive to respond. Roughly translated, the headline read: 'Secretaries able to write this sentence including the words ballet dancer, rhubarb and hieroglyphics without a mistake, won't fly to Liechtenstein, but may fly to New York.' (Presumably, Liechtenstein is the teutonic equivalent of Blackpool or Coney Island.)

The secretaries had to use their superior skills to identify a number of spelling and punctuation mistakes on the headline.

But to further qualify the response, the copy then proceeded to explain the competition rules and described the fabulous prize in ... shorthand. Not only did this help to make the ad, visually, very interesting—you don't see many ads set in shorthand—it also effectively excluded all those secretaries who were not in the target market, as defined by research.

Despite this, the agency had perhaps underestimated the ingenuity of the more junior secretaries. It was discovered later, that many of them had simply asked their senior colleagues to read the ad to them, and then entered, anyway.

However, with a further qualification mailing, the ad did pull in approximately 4100 highly qualified leads. Spontaneous awareness for the 'Ladylike' line increased to over 50 per cent. And happily, the ad also won an Echo at the Direct Marketing Association awards.

"

Roger Millington

Roger Millington opened Millington's Direct Marketing in 1983. Previously he had been one of the small team that started the London operation of Ogilvy & Mather Direct ... then creative director of Wunderman International ... and then creative director of HLY.

Roger is a familiar speaker at conferences and seminars. Recently, he has made presentations in Hong Kong, Australia, New Zealand and the USA.

In his spare time he is a prolific writer, producing articles for computing magazines, medical journals and direct marketing magazines. He has seven books to his credit, published in the UK, the USA and Japan.

Roger claims several 'firsts'—including the first edible mailshot, the first pictorial cheques and, in the 1960s, the first radio commercials for condoms!

'Send for your free Eagle shirtkerchief'
Eagle shirtmakers

" I started my copywriting career in a provincial agency in the early 60s. As luck would have it, they gave me a subscription to the *New Yorker* just as the 'creative revolution' started. Soon my walls were covered with Bill Bernbach's ads for Volkswagen and Avis. It wasn't long before I spotted several London agencies successfully copying his style.

But it was a San Francisco copywriter whose work gave me most pleasure. Howard Gossage had a tongue-in-cheek approach no-one has ever matched.

Figure 7.15 is the second ad in a long series he wrote for Eagle Shirts. (Founded in 1867, the shirt company hadn't advertised for 40 years!) A black-and-white picture shows a shirt and instructs you to turn the page. Overleaf (Fig. 7.16), you are invited to suggest a use for the square of cloth attached to the shirt.

Just look at Gossage's copy. That one-word sentence. Good. The notion that Eagle have a department called Pockets. And the 'no matter what' ending to Pockets' request.

The last-minute doubling of the offer of six shirts: Make it a dozen. And the delightful coupon instruction: Please send me whatever it is.

From that one ad in the *New Yorker* they received over 11 000 replies. In a follow-up ad, he explained what happened. One person in 14 suggested the Shirtkerchief is

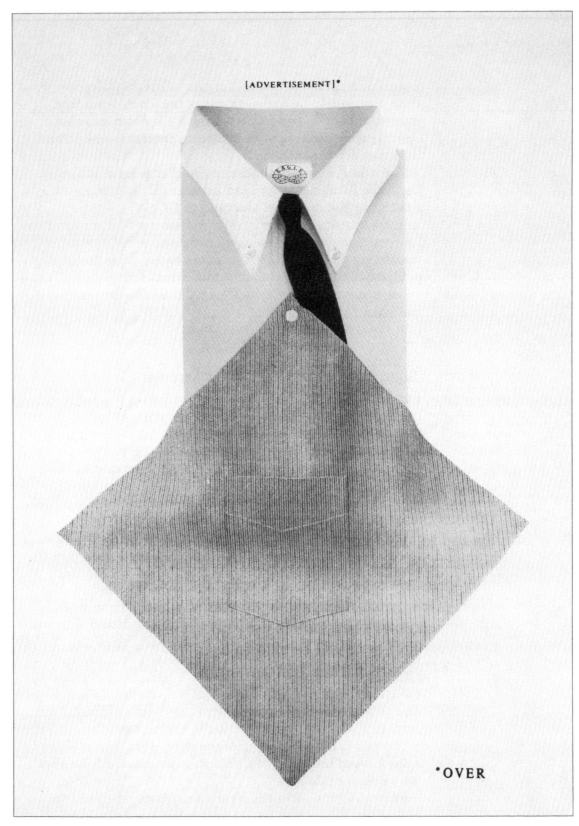

Figure 7.15

[cont. from preceding page]

SEND FOR YOUR FREE EAGLE SHIRTKERCHIEF (SHIRTKIN?) (NAPCHIEF?)

AS far as we know this is a brand new invention. Perhaps you will be able to figure out how to realize its full potential. ★ It all started when we tried to devise something to send you—short of an actual shirt—to illustrate a few of the fine points of fine shirt making. A sample to take with you when you go shirt shopping. ★ So first we hemmed a piece of fine shirting; *20 stitches to the inch*, just like in our shirts. At this point you could still call it a handkerchief. ★ But it did seem a shame not to show one of our threadchecked buttonholes, so we did. It makes a pretty good shirt protector: just whip it out of your breast pocket and button it on the second from the top to avoid gravy spots. Good. And tuck your tie in behind it. ★ But then somebody in Pockets said, "Look, if you let us sew a pocket on it, it will show how we make the pattern match right across, no matter what." ★ So if anyone knows what you can use a pocket in a handkerchief/napkin for we will be glad to hear. We will give a half-dozen shirts for the best answer. Make it a dozen.

Eagle Shirtmakers, Quakertown, Pa.

Gentlemen :

Please send me whatever it is. (Signed)_____

Address_____City_____State_____

Figure 7.16

ideal for keeping toothpicks. 'Hundreds recommend it for storing eye-patches' ... poking gentle fun at David Ogilvy's ads for Hathaway Shirts. Macmillan actually published a book of the best Shirtkerchief letters.

I'm supposed to describe one ad here, but I can't resist quoting from the follow-up. Here he tells you about the material:

> It is a two-ply broadcloth first used for shirts 40 years ago when we ordered some sight unseen from England, not knowing that up to then it—the English called it 'double poplin'—had never been used for anything but top quality umbrellas. Delighted anyway (we had to be, we had tons of it) we changed the name to Snowsheen; and what fine shirts it does make.

In a subsequent ad, Eagle ran a colour-naming contest—the prize was a 'glamorous weekend at Quakertown, Pa, our HQ, with a free sightseeing trip into romantic Philadelphia'. Among the thousands of names submitted were: Gar Beige, Shan Franshishco Beige, How Now Cow Brown, Wernervon Brown, Unforeseeable Fuchsia, Hill Mob Lavender, 'Enry 'Iggins Just You White, Franklloyd White, White Urp, and Follow The Brick Road Yellow.

For Washington's birthday, Gossage celebrated British catastrophes—with shirts in Of-Their-Eyes White, Saratochre, and Wallis Corn. To make amends he marked Nelson's birthday with a gingham range called the Trafalgar Squares.

Howard Gossage was a gifted writer. But more important, a generator of ideas. He printed a coupon worth 3 cents when you bought a $7.50 shirt. (You had to post it to the Prompt Accurate Payment Department.) He struck a Golden Jubilee medal in honour of Miss Revera Afflerbach who had been Forelady at the factory for 50 years. One of his ads for Irish Whiskey stopped halfway through a sentence and continued next week.

Gossage set a record for coupon responses in the *New Yorker*. And he got you searching for the latest Eagle ad every time the magazine arrived. We'll never see his like again. **"**

'12 reasons why'

Jiffi

" The Jiffi account got off to a quick start, back in the early 70s when I was at a small agency in Soho. Jiffi was a new company, selling pub-catering systems. The pitch for the business involved presenting a complete house style: logo,

12 reasons why Jiffi is the most exciting new idea in pub catering

1 Profitability
Jiffi is a completely new system of pub catering that assures steady profits. A Jiffi cheese snack costs you only 7d to produce . . . a ham snack 7d . . . egg and bacon 7d . . . beef curry 8d . . . a beans snack only 5d.
You sell Jiffi snacks at prices from 1/6 to 3/-. And that's real profit!'

2 Speed & ease of preparation
To make Jiffi snacks you need a Jiffi Grill – a compact machine that stands easily on a bar top. Using ordinary sliced bread and savoury or sweet ingredients you can make a succulent snack in only 70 seconds. A highly enjoyable dish without the need for a chef or kitchen staff.
You don't even need to keep an eye on the machine. It switches itself off when the snack is ready.

3 No cooking smells
The Jiffi Grill is a pleasure to use. No smells or smoke. And just a wipe is needed to keep it clean.

4 Low cost
The Jiffi Grill pays for itself very very quickly. You can pay over a period if you wish – so you make a profit right from the first day.
Incidentally, you get Jiffi's unmatched support services without paying a penny extra.

5 End kitchen drudgery
Why should your wife be stuck with pots and pans in the kitchen? If your wife looks after the catering she can make Jiffi snacks at the same time as she promotes goodwill at your side.

6 Variety
There's no limit to the snack ideas you can make. You'll find yourself experimenting with new tastes, using foods from your local shops or – like most of our customers – using the superb range of ingredients specially prepared by Jiffi.

7 Personal service
A Jiffi Customer Relations Officer calls to see you regularly. She takes the details from your shoulders . . . advises on menus, prices, publicity and staff education. Make no mistake, she's a trained expert who can promote your profits.

8 Brings new customers
In pub after pub, licensees tell us that Jiffi brings in new customers. It not only increases food sales but helps increase drink sales.

9 Fast food delivery
When you need new food stocks just phone your nearest Jiffi Branch Office. Or send us an order form . . . we supply the forms and pay the postage. A Jiffi van brings the food right to your door. By the way, we're constantly adding exciting new lines. Beef Italienne and Chicken Savoury have been two highly successful newcomers.

10 Guaranteed maintenance
It's exceedingly rare for anything to go wrong with a Jiffi Grill. But if it does, you have a cast-iron Guarantee. Just pick up your phone and a factory-trained engineer will be there within 48 hours.

11 Sales promotion backing
We supply you with as much advertising material as you want. Posters, menus, table cards. Bright, colourful and attention-getting, they are a reminder to your customers that yours is one of the best eating places in town.

12 Proof of Success
From the smallest pubs to the swish new London International Hotel, Jiffi is proving itself as one of the brightest ideas to have been offered to the Licensed Trade in many years – backed by a service that is remarkably comprehensive.
In the relatively short time since we launched this idea, we have received a long list of genuine testimonials from satisfied public house licensees. A selection of these testimonials can be seen at any of our Branch Offices.

I would like to know more about the Jiffi System. I understand that sending this coupon places me under no obligation of any kind.

NAME (PLEASE PRINT)

ADDRESS AND NAME OF LICENSED PREMISES

TELEPHONE NUMBER

POST TO: FAST FOODS LTD, 25 MARLOW RD., MAIDENHEAD, BERKS. OR PHONE: MAIDENHEAD 32244/5/6

FAST FOODS LTD, 25 MARLOW RD., MAIDENHEAD, BERKS. MAIDENHEAD 32244/5/6

Figure 7.17

stationery, van delivery, the lot. The pitch took place at the client's office in the evening and it was after nine when I was told: 'We like everything. You've won the account; start producing artwork tomorrow.'

Next morning everyone at the agency was delighted with the good news. Not so pleased when I revealed that my journey home last night had required three separate trains. Tired and emotional after the presentation, I had left the layouts on one of the trains.

Luckily, the art director was able to re-create everything from memory.

A few weeks later I had a call from the *Morning Advertiser*, a daily paper produced for the licensed trade. An advertiser had pulled out and we could have a full page at a remarkably low price ... if we could deliver artwork later in the day.

The snag was that we hadn't even started thinking about press ads. The first priority had been to produce sales-folders for the Reps.

Could we create and get the artwork ready in time? Fortunately, we had just completed a set of illustrations for the sales folders.

Allowing the time I would need to take the ad to Maidenhead and show it to the client, plus the time for typesetting and paste-up, this gave 90 minutes to write the ad and create a layout.

Generously, I allocated 15 of these minutes to the art director and told him to sharpen his pencils while I began typing.

Figure 7.17 shows the 90-minute ad. It drew nearly 200 enquiries, most of which were converted to sales. The paper didn't publish its circulation figures but we judged it to be a satisfying response from a trade press ad. The paper sent me a congratulatory bottle of Scotch.

Later with more time at our disposal, we created much more carefully written and glamorously presented ads. None of them drew comparable response rates.

There seems to be a lesson here, one I have re-learned on subsequent occasions: if you want good results, an urgent deadline may be the answer. Remember what Dr Johnson said: 'Depend upon it, Sir, when a man knows he is to be hanged in a fortnight, it concentrates his mind wonderfully.'

There are a couple of conclusions to the Jiffi story. After its initial successes, the company expanded too rapidly and went bust a few months later. So did the agency.

"

Graeme Robertson

Graeme Robertson is vice-chairman and creative director of Christian Brann Limited, the only international direct marketing agency to be based in the heart of the English Cotswolds.

With over 50 writers, art directors and finished artists, Christian Brann Limited's creative department is the largest in Europe. Its work for clients such as Barclays Bank and the Ford Motor Company is known and respected the world over.

Graeme attributes the agency's creative success to the unique atmosphere he has been able to create in his department. 'We have an excellent balance of youth and experience here,' he says, 'and this generates just the sort of friendly and supportive environment in which genuine creativity can thrive.'

'Six questions to ask'

Benton & Bowles

" The ads I most admire—the ones that I believe are most *creative* in the truest sense—are those written by people who transcend the rule book, who obey the spirit of the direct response code but are not bound by its every letter. You look at their work, and you instantly know that though they've probably read all the books and digested all the theory, their understanding of direct response is instinctive.

Figure 7.18—a self-promotional piece by Benton & Bowles—appeared as a DPS in American marketing journals. It's the perfect demonstration of the sort of thing I mean, and I envy the talent of the individual who wrote it.

I admire the way the whole ad is subtly—almost intuitively—targeted towards the prospects. The headline instantly selects the ad's audience: marketing managers with responsibility for commissioning advertising campaigns. But it also *primes* the audience—the readers immediately know that they're about to be given some useful information—information that may well help them to do their jobs better. So there's a real benefit right up there in the headline, even though it's communicated in the sort of restrained way that's just right for the target market.

Putting a number in your headline (like 'Five Good Reasons For Using The Acme Mousetrap') is often a recipe for disaster. By the time your readers get round to the fifth 'good reason', their credulity has usually been stretched to the limit. Not so here. The choice of the 'question' format obviously helps, yet the simple truth is that the sixth question is just as valid—and the copy just as meaty—as the first. So for once, here is a 'numbers' headline that doesn't create an unfulfilled expectation.

The body copy itself is calm and unsensational. The grammar and the punctuation are both precise and conventional. There isn't a single exclamation mark. There's a point to all this—it isn't just fashionable understatement. The aim throughout the ad is to create an illusion of complete impartiality. The message is credible because you hear it intoned in a steady, clear, open and honest way. The tone of voice is confident and self-assured: the writer clearly *believes* in the product that is being sold, and so there's no reason to make exaggerated and unsubstantiated claims. This is the language of Mount Olympus, not the loud hucksterish babble of an account executive on the make.

Six questions to ask before you approve an advertisement.

1. Is there a big idea?

Nothing else is so important to the success of an advertisement. A genuine selling idea transcends execution. Before you approve an advertisement, ask yourself if it really has a big idea and if that idea emerges clearly, emphatically, and single-mindedly. Ask yourself: Is it an important idea – such as Scope's "medicine breath", the positioning of Pledge furniture polish as a dusting aid, or AMF's "We make weekends"?

2. Is there a theme line?

A theme line that presents your selling idea in a memorable set of words can be worth millions of dollars of extra mileage to your advertising. Provocative lines like "When E.F. Hutton talks, people listen", "Please don't squeeze the Charmin", "We really move our tail for you" (Continental Airlines) make it easier for the customer to remember your selling message. Incidentally, when you get a great one, treasure it and use it prominently in every print ad and television commercial you run.

3. Is it relevant?

If your advertising is remembered but your product forgotten, you might as well run "compliments of a friend". Jokes that steal attention from your selling idea, inappropriate entertainment devices, celebrities who have no logical connection with your product, and other irrelevances can be devastating. Look for relevance in every advertising execution.

4. Is it hackneyed?

Is the advertisement fresh, innovative and original or is it merely a pale carbon copy of somebody else's advertising? Too much advertising is look-alike, sound-alike advertising. These advertisements are often costly failures. Don't run the risk of being mistaken for your competitor. Demand an execution that is all your own.

5. Does it demonstrate?

Nothing works harder or sells better than a demonstration of your product's superiority, especially in television. Look for every opportunity to demonstrate. If you can't demonstrate, at least show the product in use. Demonstrations – such as simple exposition of how the Trac II razor works or the coating action of Pepto-Bismol – are convincing ways to sell.

6. Is it believable?

Does the advertising overpromise? Does the selling idea sound a false note? An advertisement can be totally truthful, yet sound unbelievable. Better to underpromise and be believable than to overpromise and lose credibility.

We know that great advertising is not made by rules nor created by guidelines. It comes from creative people. However, we also know from experience that most successful advertising has certain readily identifiable and wholly predictable qualities. We have listed six. There are others. We would like nothing better than to show you some of the advertising that illustrates these points.

Please call or write to Jack Bowen, President, Benton and Bowles Inc., 909 Third Avenue, New York, N.Y. 10022. Telephone (212) 758-6200

Benton and Bowles

New York, Chicago, Los Angeles, and other major cities worldwide

It's not creative unless it sells.

Figure 7.18

Notice the glorious lack of technical jargon. An intelligent general reader could understand—and probably draw benefit from—this copy. Okay, so the ad appeared in a trade journal, packed from cover to cover with talk of 'demographic profiles' and 'lifestyle analyses'. But surely that's all the more reason for choosing to communicate in plain language: coming across just two pages of straightforward prose in one of those magazines is almost as refreshing as breakfast in a Jacuzzi with two Swedish air hostesses.

The effect generated by the copy is enhanced by equally sensitive and skilful design. The choice of typeface adds to the general credibility of the ad by giving the text an editorial feel. It also makes the voice in which the copy is spoken seem perfectly calm and restrained. Every design feature is in there for a reason. Even the thin key line above the agency's name serves a useful purpose by separating the 'impartial advice' above from the credentials of the message's sponsors below.

Central to an ad's credibility is its level of internal consistency. This ad, though it traverses some pretty treacherous ground, doesn't come a cropper once. By inviting its readers to criticise advertisements, this ad is in effect holding itself up for criticism. But even the most cynical reader has to concede that the writer meets each of the ad's own six criteria of excellence.

This ad *never* contradicts itself—not even in the closing section where the writer admits that 'great advertising is not made by rules nor created by guidelines'. The phrase leads into a very neat and entirely characteristic call to action, in which the reader is invited to find out more about the 'certain ... predictable qualities' of successful advertising.

And speaking of the call to action, I applaud the decision *not* to put a coupon on this ad. When you're sitting in a plush office with a pile of correspondence on your desk and a secretary in the room next door, a coupon clipped from a magazine isn't the most obvious way of starting a dialogue with a senior manager in another company. So instead of a coupon, this ad carries a response mechanism that's true to the target market: the promise of a *personal* contact with none other than the president of the agency.

Lastly, we come to by far the best feature of this truly outstanding ad—the brilliant strapline: 'It's not creative unless it sells.' (How I wish I'd written that!)

Straplines are often written to sound important and impressive, yet they rarely stand up to more than a second of intellectual examination. This strapline is written using straightforward language—but the sentiment it conveys is both potent and memorable. It fires your imagination, leaving you with one last morsel to savour as you walk away, duly humbled, from the table of a master. **"**

'17.5% guaranteed ... '
Hambro Guardian

" I've chosen our June Bond ad (Fig. 7.19) for Hambro Guardian Assurance plc, written by creative director Tim Ferguson and designed by senior art director Helen Olsen. At first sight, it doesn't look particularly *creative*—there are no fancy graphics and no clever puns—but that's not the real measure of creative excellence. As my favourite ever strapline says, 'It's not creative unless it sells'—and this ad does an outstanding job of selling a complicated, high-ticket product straight off the page.

Once again, the most impressive thing about this ad is its instinctive feel for the psychology of the target market. The product—a guaranteed safe 12-month investment bond—was launched at a time when investors were still mindful of the Stock Market crash of October 1987. The cautious money had long since moved out of the equities market and into the building societies. Hambro knew that if they could only offer a guaranteed investment with an interest rate higher than that of the building societies they would be on to a winner.

But the job wasn't as easy as it sounds. For a start, a really attractive guaranteed interest rate could only be provided for those willing to make a *minimum* investment of £5000. To make matters worse, many investors were steering well clear of direct-sell investment products after the collapse of the investment house Barlow Clowes. (Hambro Guardian, although very well respected in the financial world, is a new company which hasn't yet enjoyed the same level of confidence-building exposure as the big High Street names.)

The obvious risk was that the proposition would come across sounding something like: 'Write a cheque for at least £5000, put it in an envelope, and send it to someone you've never even heard of.' So in order to sell an excellent product effectively, the creative team had to build credibility and trustworthiness into the ad as part and parcel of the selling message.

The headline is a straight promise—a simple statement of fact—completely free of superfluous hype. (When the product is so right for the times, why let anything spurious get in the way to confuse the message?) 'Guaranteed' was a stunningly

HAMBRO GUARDIAN ANNOUNCE JUNE BOND
THE SAFE HIGH RETURN 12-MONTH INVESTMENT

11.75% GUARANTEED
N E T
NO IFS, NO BUTS, NO RISKS

Put in £10,000 now.
Receive £11,175 in 12 months

£1,175 in interest in just 12 months! That's just one example of how 11.75% net of basic rate tax adds up. And we guarantee to hold this rate over the whole year. So you run no risks. And your money isn't tied up for any long period.

This is the new June Bond from Hambro Guardian. It's a 1-year investment – and there's nothing else like it. You can put in any amount between £5,000 and £50,000 – as long as you move fast…

First come, First served

The guaranteed-growth June Bond offer will close as soon as it is fully subscribed. A maximum limit has been set for the total amount we can accept for investment at this exceptional interest rate - so Bonds will be issued strictly on a first-come, first-served basis. We guarantee the interest rate - but you need to apply in time to qualify for it! If your application is unsuccessful your cheque will be returned to you promptly.

You invest	We pay you in 12 months	Interest guaranteed
£5,000 (min)	£5,587.50	£587.50
£7,500	£8,381.25	£881.25
£10,000	£11,175.00	£1,175.00
£15,000	£16,762.50	£1,762.50
£25,000	£27,937.50	£2,937.50
£50,000 (max)	£55,875.00	£5,875.00

JUNE BOND

Guaranteed by Hambro Guardian

The June Bond is guaranteed by Hambro Guardian Assurance plc. The company is backed by the strength, experience and resources of two of Britain's most respected financial names – the long-established Hambros plc and Guardian Royal Exchange. Between them they manage over £12 billion of policyholders' money.

HAMBRO GUARDIAN
A member of LAUTRO
Reg. Office: 41 Tower Hill, London EC3N 4HA
Reg. in England No 2261746

The small print

This plan is invested in fixed interest deposits and there is no risk of losing money. Your capital is secure, and the interest rate is guaranteed for the entire period.

Life assurance included
Every penny you invest is covered by life assurance, so in the event of your death during the 12 months of the Bond, your initial investment will be returned in full. Interest is paid only on maturity after 12 months. You can buy June Bond on a single or joint life basis.

Your tax position
There is no liability to Capital Gains Tax and the interest quoted is paid net of basic rate income tax. There is no further tax to pay unless you are a higher rate taxpayer. In this case you will be liable for the difference between the higher and lower rates of tax, currently 15%. Tax deducted is not reclaimable by non-taxpayers. Tax rules may of course change in the future.

Cancellation
Once your investment has been accepted, you cannot withdraw it before your June Bond matures one year after the day it was issued.

Ages
You must be a UK citizen aged between 18 and 75 when you apply. A copy of the terms and conditions is available on request.

Figure 7.19

potent word in the investment business even before Black Monday, and only rarely does the law allow writers the opportunity to use it. The numerical promise of the headline is made still more real by the first sub-head, which boldly translates the percentage into real money figures: 'Put in £10,000 now. Receive £11,175 in 12 months.'

We hear a lot these days about the need to work image-building into direct response—and many people seem to think it's just a matter of making the client's logo bigger and wearing a bow tie to the presentation. But the best way to communicate image messages in direct response ads is to build them in at a subliminal level. *Every element* of this ad works hard to create a powerful image of security and stability for Hambro Guardian.

There's a copy block all about Hambro Guardian, yet it's there for a reason—it's not just an exercise in corporate puffery. There's a real benefit in it for the reader: the confidence-building news that Hambro Guardian is part of a group which already manages over £12 billion of policyholders' money.

And there's more—much more. All the way through the ad the tone of voice is consistently calm and reassuring. The writer has nothing to hide. He even has such confidence in his product that he's prepared to make the small print part of the selling copy—complete with its own sub-head.

Of course, the writer also knows the direct response rules, and so there's a closing date—and a 'first come, first served' stipulation. But the way in which these facts are presented is entirely in keeping with the prevailing image of financial probity: 'Please be Prompt: A strict limit has been set on the total which can be invested in this Bond.' There's no risk that readers will think they're being pressured into a hasty decision.

The coupon is perfectly simple and easy to fill in. It doesn't ask any unnecessary questions, and there's a free phone number with a real live person at the other end. (That in itself is a powerful confidence builder, even if you don't happen to have any queries yourself.)

Like every masterpiece, this ad has its flaws. The central block extends too far down the page, and I'm still not sure about that arrowhead graphic on the coupon. When you strive for perfection, such details can be very annoying— yet the results more than compensated for the minor quibbles.

Tim and Helen's ad broke all the records. It ran in the national press on 3 June 1989 and pulled £10 million with just one insertion. The June Bond itself was fully subscribed within a mere six days.

For a total spend of under £26 000, this one creative treatment generated over *£42 million* of business for Hambro Guardian—and for every marketing pound spent, the client received *£1149.20* return on his investment.

At first glance, few people would call this ad 'creative'. Yet to me, it's a work of art. **"**

Chris Rudd, FInstD, FInstSMM, MInstM, MIPA, MCAM, is the creative director of CAS Ltd. Having trained as an archaeologist and worked for two years as a hospital theatre technician, Chris Rudd cut his direct response teeth writing mail order ads for GUS at Osborne Peacock (now McCann Erickson, Manchester), where he worked with Graeme McCorkell, Drayton Bird, Rod Allen and Peter Marsh. In 1979 he joined ABM as a creative director and helped create The Listening Bank, The Guinnless, Harp Stays Sharp, Gotta Lotta Bottle and The Age of The Train. After being creative planning director of Christian Brann Ltd, he re-joined CAS in 1988, where he'd begun his advertising career in 1957.

'Could you turn the other cheek?'
Metropolitan Police

" Most of the direct response advertisers that I know are always aiming for the largest quantity of coupons to be clipped. 'Fret not, Chris, we'll worry about the quality later. Just get as many enquiries as you can. Our salesmen will sort out the time-wasters later.'

So it was with considerable joy that I came across this recruitment ad (Fig. 7.20) for the Metropolitan Police in *The Independent Magazine*, 7 January 1989. I wish I'd written it because it's a masterpiece of what I call CQC—Coupon Quality Control. Most direct response advertisers have never even thought about Coupon Quality Control, let alone practised it. They would do well to study this restrained double-page spread in detail, and its precursor which was headlined *Could you disarm him?* The credit for this ad must go to copywriter Indra Sinha and art director Neil Godfrey.

If you want to know how to persuade precisely the right people to phone you or write to you, please examine this ad meticulously. Firstly, please note that it doesn't look like an ad; it wears all the clothes of a colour supplement feature article. Secondly, look at that photograph by Don McCullin and be aware that it was this amazing picture that pulled your attention to the page in the first place. Thirdly, feel the challenge of that headline, which was printed in blood red. Now read every word of the copy and see how cunningly the writer sucks you in, knocks you down, picks you up, knocks you down again, picks you up again and drags you staggering to that quiet little coupon, at which point you will know with stunning certainty whether or not you wish to be a Metropolitan policeman. That's Coupon Quality Control, that is. **"**

'100 years ago it was a brilliant idea'
Reed Business Call

" In 1988 Reed International Plc asked CAS, the business-to-business agency, to help them launch a new telephone marketing company, Reed Business Call. A key feature of the launch strategy was to highlight the high-tech computerised facilities of this new service, which was away ahead (and still is) of anything else available in Europe.

'We want to get as many top people as possible watching us at work,' said managing director, Tanya Pearson. 'To see us, is to believe us.'

CAS were given two tasks: firstly, to build rapid awareness of Reed Business Call among the marketing directors of Britain's largest companies; secondly, to persuade their senior management to visit Brighton in person for a live demonstration.

CAS proposed a two-part campaign: full-page ads in the marketing press, followed immediately by a mailing to the directors of Britain's blue-est blue-chip firms (see Fig. 7.21).

The first press ad showed an antique phone and said, '100 years ago it was a brilliant idea. Now we've had a better one.' The second ad showed a modern phone and said, 'In this country it's a phone. In America it's the most powerful marketing tool available. Why?' Both ads asked readers to phone Suzanne Russell, the general manager of Reed Business Call. The copywriter was Paul Burns and the art director was Colin Eckersley.

After running these two press ads, CAS sent a large box by overnight courier to a very selective list of top directors, supplied by Reed Database. The box said, 'Until you call us you'll only have half the story on telephone marketing.' Inside the box was the first half of a free gift—the base of a real £90 cordless phone, minus the handset. To get their handset, directors had to phone Reed Business Call and pick it up in Brighton, where they would also receive a personal demonstration of Reed's service.

Those directors who didn't respond to the mailing within three days were phoned by Reed Business Call and invited to visit Brighton.

The response to this launch campaign surprised both agency and client.

COULD YOU TURN

COOL CUSTOMER, are you? Okay, let's see how far you can get before you blow your stack.

You are walking down a street. Some youths start jeering at you: "'Ello, 'ello, 'ello." Smile. You've heard it all before, every name a copper can be called: rozzer, old bill, pig, fuzz, peeler, flatfoot, the filth. And some less complimentary. Shrug it off.

You're out in the patrol car when you see a car without lights weaving through the traffic. You flash your headlights at him to stop. Instead, he accelerates away.

Siren on. Ahead your target, still without lights, narrowly misses a woman on a pedestrian crossing and then goes the wrong way round a roundabout, while a youth leaning out of the passenger window showers you with empty beer cans and two-finger salutes.

"You can't go on the attack, whatever the provocation."

The car skids round another corner and slides into a brick wall, but the youths inside are out and running. You chase, abandoning your car with its engine still on and door left wide open. As you grab the driver, he mouths obscenities at you.

Still in control of your temper? Okay, try this.

A demonstration is turning into a riot. You're bussed in, nervous and not sure what to expect. It's frightening. The crowd, in ugly mood, surges against the frail police line.

Suddenly a lone voice calls your number "EF203, EF203." The others take it up. "EF203, EF203." They're all staring at you, trying to psyche you out. Why you?

It gets worse. Bottles arc down and burst in showers of flame. Stones and half bricks drop out of the air and threaten to brain you. You cannot leave the line.

At last the crowd starts drifting away. As the tension ebbs, you see a man step forward and deliberately stub out his cigarette on the flank of a police horse.

This all sounds a bit melodramatic, but we've made none of it up. Each of the details we've described really happened.

How would you have reacted?

Strangely, people often find that in a real emergency they stay icily calm. But stress builds up in the body like static

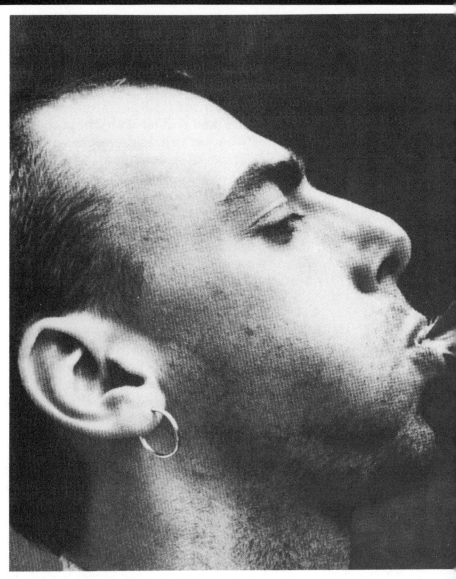

As a police officer, sooner or later you're bound to encounter abuse, threat, provocation, even physical violence. Be careful how you respond. Lose your temper and you could lose your job. **Photograph by Don McCullin**

and can earth itself without warning.

Three days after a riot like the one above you may arrest a well dressed drunk. "Look here," he drawls, "do you realise who you're talking to?" And jabs you in the chest.

Careful. This trivial annoyance may become the lightning rod for all that

pent up stress and rage. If, in any of the situations we have described above, you were to lose your temper, you might also lose your job.

It doesn't seem fair, does it? But then being a police officer is no ordinary job. As someone sworn to uphold the law, you of all people cannot break it.

And the law says that you may use no more than reasonable force. You can't go on the attack. No matter what the provocation.

So what should you do? Should you say: "Are you going to come quietly or do I have to use earplugs?" In fact, a bit of humour can often defuse a potential

HE OTHER CHEEK?

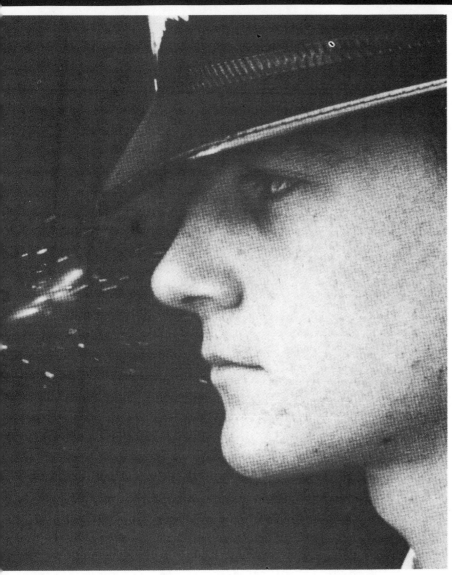

cope with the reality. And we need people who can cope. People who are tough, tender, sensitive, strong and disciplined, all at the same time.

People like this aren't easy to find. At present we take only one in five applicants. We'd rather look at fewer, better candidates.

Seeing you've got this far, we'll now admit that a career in the Met isn't all grief. Few jobs are as rewarding.

Ask the much loved Streatham home beat officer who, helmet under arm,

"It gets worse. Bottles arc down and burst in showers of flame."

cigar stuck firmly in mouth in flagrant disregard of regulations, can tell you the name of every child in his manor.

Ask the constable who, while patiently unravelling the intricacies of gang warfare in, of all unlikely places, Southall, has been invited to six Indian weddings in the last year.

Ask the sergeant who now runs what is virtually a Bengali advice centre in Whitechapel.

We can offer 28,000 more examples. If you don't believe us, stop any police officer in the street and ask.

When you've learned what they get out of the job, ask how they got in.

They'll tell you about our twenty week basic training course at Hendon. And life on the beat at one of London's 187 police stations where, under the tutelage of a sergeant, you will learn the art of handling people. And yourself.

Right now, your next step is to fill in and post the coupon below.

We're looking for mature, fit people aged between 18½ and 45, especially from the ethnic minorities. You should be at least 172cms tall if you're a man, 162cms if you're a woman.

Ideally, you'll have some 'O' level passes or their equivalents, but we value your personal qualities more.

ly situation. As can tact, restraint and od common sense.

Of course, it's a strain being on best haviour 24 hours a day. Never switching . With the very highest standards to and live up to. Sometimes, all that ttled up stress can make us difficult to e with.

An officer on motorway patrol raced an accident. A car was on fire. The heat s ferocious. He had to watch, helpless, a child the same age as his own daughter rned to death before his eyes.

When he got home, his wife produced supper. Without a word, he picked up his plate of food and flung it through the window. Until then he had kept control of his emotions. But that night of all nights he could not face a cooked meal.

As a police officer you will inevitably endure your share of unpleasantness and you'll have to evolve your own way of dealing with it.

But why are we dwelling on these traumatic subjects?

Isn't this supposed to be a recruitment

advertisement? Are we trying to put you off? Actually, yes. If you're put off by an advertisement, you'd never be able to

To find out more please telephone: 01-725 4492 (Ansaphone: 01-725 4575) or fill in the coupon or write to: The Recruiting Officer, The Metropolitan Police Selection Centre, Department MD423, Freepost, London W2 1BR.

Name

Address

Postcode   Age

Figure 7.21

Fifty per cent of the directors phoned for their handsets and, after follow-up phone calls, a total of 66 per cent agreed to a presentation by Reed Business Call. Of these respondents, 83 per cent are currently 'active'. They have either used Reed Business Call's service or are still talking about doing it.

'We knew we had a good service , a good offer and a good agency,' says Suzanne Russell, 'but none of us guessed we'd get a 66 per cent response.'

"

George Smith

George Smith is chairman of the Smith Bundy Group of companies. The parent company is one of the largest independent direct marketing agencies in the country and was formed in 1973. George is a writer, as much celebrated for his column in *Direct Response* magazine as he is for his many award-winning campaigns. He has spoken on direct marketing platforms throughout the world, is a former council member of the British Direct Marketing Association, a former borough councillor in London and author of various trivia quiz books.

'Sell-out'

Sterling House

" The precise wording of the request puts me in something of a quandary. Ask me if I really want to write ads for the likes of Sterling House and honesty demands a negative—if only because I've written lots for clients like this. Ask me if I admire this sort of stuff and the anwer is objectively positive. I guess I'm saying that these ads are terrific but that other people should have to write them.

Terrific? I honestly mean it. Ads like Fig. 7.22 never win awards but you see them week after week, doing the business. A selling message has been constructed here from all the eternal verities of direct marketing. In my lifetime, it is a tradition that goes back to Headquarters and General in the fifties, John Bloom's Rolls Razor in the early sixties and various direct-selling exercises out of Essex ever since. An advertising agency may be hovering around the production of this ad but they won't have been very central to its creation: one senses that the guvnor wrote it himself. In half an hour.

To celebrate it is not to be sentimental on behalf of the crude and untutored school of direct marketing. It is to observe, quite genuinely, the professional sophistication of what's going on here. It reminds me, to be slightly pompous, of someone like Vaughan Williams who started collecting folk songs because they were interesting and discovered in doing so that the songs were in fact melodies of extraordinary sophistication and power: he turned it on symphonically with things like 'Greensleeves' and 'Dives and Lazarus', but the tune and the basic harmonics make these pieces work.

Enough of this culture. What makes this ad work?

Stocks Delayed by Pre-Xmas Post Strike Offered Now in January

SELL-OUT

SEND NO MONEY NOW See Below

YOU LUCKY PEOPLE! Everybody loves a **JANUARY SALE BARGAIN** and **THIS MONTH** you can secure one of the **most practical and versatile bicycles** ever designed at a **LOW PRICE** that defies competition! Made especially for a major mail order company, who was left sitting on large stocks as a result of the Autumn postal strike. This identical machine was selling on the pages of those glossy mail order catalogues at £97. **NOW**, readers of this newspaper can profit handsomely and secure one (or more) at **UNDER HALF THEIR £79.95 LIST PRICE! BUT PLEASE REMEMBER** – this sensational price is **STRICTLY LIMITED** to this one strike hit consignment and can in no way be repeated!

The **complete family cycle** for all ages from teenager to grandma, this **20″ wheel folding bicycle** is ideal for around town commuting, shopping, travelling to school or college, holidays. Quality specifications to **BS standards** include **20″ wheels, twin caliper brakes, safety reflectors** that glow like cats eyes in the dark, **rear luggage rack**. Can be **adapted on-the-spot** for any member of the family to ride . . . from a **10 year old tearaway** to a **nimble 90 year old** – male or female. Quickly, easily, compactly folds to carry in car boot or hatchback – and can be stored in any spare corner around the house. The lightweight frame is finished in tough, scratch resistant enamel **SKY BLUE** or **PEARLISED WHITE**. Includes **10 YEAR FRAME GUARANTEE** plus comprehensive guarantee of all parts and labour. Exceptional value at this **WINTER SALE PRICE** of **£38.95 + £4.95 p&p.**

Also available **SUPER DE-LUXE MODEL** features the same superb specifications as above model **PLUS** the addition of a **3 speed gear, bell, prop stand, tools,** etc. List Price £89.95 NOW £48.95 + £4.95 p&p. **RESERVE EITHER MODEL NOW** by sending just £4.95 carr – pay balance on delivery. Offer applies to U.K. including N. Ireland. Despatch 7-14 days unless advised otherwise.

PUBLISHED LIST PRICE £79.95

SALE PRICE THIS MONTH £38.95 +p&p

IMPORTANT – If like our many regular customers you prefer to send **FULL REMITTANCE NOW WITH ORDER** we will include a **SUPER ELECTRONIC WATCH ABSOLUTELY FREE!**

CREDIT CARD HOLDERS CAN ORDER NOW ☎ ON **0702 331411** (24 HOURS)

STERLING HOUSE (DEPT IN 1FC)
507-511 LONDON ROAD, WESTCLIFF, ESSEX SS0 9LF
CALLERS WELCOME AT OUR SHOWROOMS -
★ 507-511 London Road, Westcliff, Essex ★ 15 East Square, Basildon, Essex

Figure 7.22

First, it makes an offer. A bike at half-price. If you don't believe me, go and find another bike at this price. Second, it turns it into an event. The ad appeared a few weeks after Christmas, 1988. So it becomes a January sales offer. Third, it becomes a story. The postal strike the previous autumn left these bikes unsold and on the books of a major mail order company. Fourth, it knocks the competition. The bike was selling in a 'glossy' mail order catalogue (I love the implicit sneer) at £97. I happen to know that this is true. Fifth, it qualifies the offer. Stock is strictly limited. The offer cannot be repeated. Rush now, to use the old phrase, while stocks last.

I sense that the audience may be sneering at this point. You've seen all these tactics before and you may be forgiven for not attaching 100 per cent credence to them in every part. That's your privilege and all I can say is that the ASA have given it the nod. And what's good enough for the ASA is good enough for me.

Move on through the benefits. That whole, long, second paragraph is crammed full of them, pulled out in bold. We slip into bold caps with the colours, the guarantee and the repeated price.

We offer three ways to procure the bike. Send no money and you've 'reserved' your bike. Send cash with order and you get a freebie. Use your credit card and you can phone your order through. Want to see the thing? Try your chances at the listed showrooms.

Two pieces of photography sustain this breathless offer. The leggy lady is probably inevitable but she does give some idea of scale and shape of the product. The inset squared up shot demonstrates what is almost certainly its secondary selling feature—the ability to fold into a car boot.

The headlines wrote themselves and the price is as bold as it should be. Which leaves me with one quibble. The coupon is physically inadequate, almost certainly because the ad artwork has been reduced down from a larger space to fill a space booked at short notice.

So I'm also guessing that the advertiser has got his space cheap as well as his message virile. All in all, you are witnessing selling technology in this ad as much as direct marketing technology. Here's a trader who knows what his product margin is, therefore how many he has to sell to make sense of the advertising investment, therefore how much he's prepared to spend on media and, very lastly, how he should deploy message to get the financial equation right. I'm guessing that he succeeded, probably massively.

I know people who would take the same product, book a full colour page, commission lots of expensive photography, bang the price back up and spend weeks in refining the ad so that it coincides with their own cultural norms and sense of corporate dignity. The typography would by stylised, sub-heads would creep in and so would a degree of verbal pomposity. The ad would be extremely unlikely to start with 'You lucky people!' and any copywriter hapless enough to have suggested it could be asked to demonstrate the relevance of Tommy Trinder to the target audience.

I think the Sterling House ad cost a few hundred quid and I think it likely that it shipped quite a few hundred units within the following two weeks. It demonstrates with whatever banality, the nature of direct selling. And, if it does so in tones that remind you of a street trader, I shall sharply rebuke you by explaining the uncanny congruence of selling from a barrow and selling from an ad.

So, do you want to win an award or do you want to sell product at a cost-effective margin? You don't have to be crude to achieve the latter, any more than you have to be clever to achieve the former. But you should always worry about the difference. Because, at the time of writing, the difference is growing apace.

"

'The magical new Silver Solution'

Innovations

" The ad shown as Fig. 7.23 created huge sales and also won an award. It also warped a few textbook lessons. At the time of producing it, it was conventional wisdom that you could not sustain the high promotional costs of colour magazine advertising with a product price as low as £12.95. Which is undoubtedly true most of the time. Until you bump into the exception that always lurks after any direct marketing rule.

For Silver Solution was a massive mail order success for about six months until the direct-selling market was saturated and the retail trade caught up with it. I do know the gross sales of this product but I'm not going to tell you; suffice to say that you will have seen this ad a great number of times and an ad like this is not repeated by accident.

It was one of the first ads we did for Innovations, who specialise in state-of-the-art high-tech sorts of products. Up to now, there had been a very successful catalogue used as a loose insert and an increasing urge to go off the page with the right product. Co-proprietor, Nigel Swabey, applied his

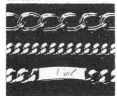

Figure 7.23

usual prescience and guessed that Silver Solution was the right product. I know Nigel too well to have argued.

The product is now ubiquitous and it is therefore difficult to explain in arrears that it was actually revolutionary. Before the Silver Solution, you had silver polish. What the new product did was to re-plate your silver with silver particles in solution form, the transference being a molecular function and the application a mere matter of wiping with a cloth. In other words, it was a genuine silver-plating process that you could do yourself in the comfort of your own home without baths, tanks, electricity or toxic chemicals.

A good and unique product, in other words, with enormous benefits for anyone who's ever stared wanly at the fading face of the family silver. But it ran the risk of sounding a bit gimcrack, a bit iffy, a bit too good to be true.

We could have gone two routes.

The first would be the demonstration route. We could do a 'before' and 'after' sequence showing Silver Solution effecting the difference in the happy hands of Joe Public. We reasoned that the available standards of colour magazine reproduction might betray us.

The second, and the one we adopted, was the authoritative route. What better means with which to defuse cynicism that good old-fashioned testimonials?

We had lots. The product had been tested, had been exhibited, and been the subject of a highly effective PR launch. And very many people had said how good it was and how genuinely it worked. We took some testimonials from the national press, some from the public and some, very importantly, from the jewellery trade who might reasonably have been expected to have been waspish. I have no doubts that these testimonials are the essence of the ad, far more valuable than anything I could have written in the space.

What I did write was the sort of narrative simplicity that looks an easy task after the seventh draft. There was a lot to say—the history of the product's development would have made an interesting full-page ad in itself. So, you are looking at highly compressed copy—summarising the offer in the first bold para, proceeding through usage and efficacy to a paragraph genuinely summarising the range of its application. I was determined to say what Silver Solution did *not* do and I honestly think that that strangely negative sentence helped Innovations portray themselves as honest reporters and not mere promise-the-earth merchants.

For the rest, equally simple facts about delivery and guarantees. Even these functional necessities can be turned into selling points—I'm particularly proud of the construction ' ... The only customers we want are satisfied customers so ... ' which we use to this day.

I wanted a simple statement for the headline and not a clever-dick advertising construct. I deliberately used the most succinct of the press testimonials over the headline (guess which paper we launched it in?).

Art direction was by Robert Green, a man who does brilliant things without any sense of performance. The Innovations typography has always been slightly distinctive. The insert shots come in very tight on the subjects so that we allayed the danger of bad colour reproduction. And we were always going to be stuck with a pack shot, though it took Robert to use the product on a clutch of ball bearings and stick them in front to give the shot a touch of class.

I've written more sophisticated ads but I've rarely written one that made as much money for the client. The product was probably always going to be a winner but the ad certainly pressed the buying pulses of the British public with clinical efficiency. The BDMA award a year later was a nice bonus.

I'll tell you two things about how Nigel briefed it. He gave me a huge file of technical information of the product and even left me a tape with lots of anecdotal banter about it. For once, I actually saw the product.

And, then, of course he gave me a couple of days in which to make the copy date.

All of which says that you don't need vast amounts of time to write a successful ad. You just need the information and a touch of excitement. Plus, of course, a sense of urgency! **"**

So there you have it: the Great Ad Gallery. But one ad is still missing from our collection. I mentioned at the beginning of this chapter that 'Cash if you die. Cash if you don't' is the headline I would most like to have written. Alas, I did not. But John Watson did. Thanks to his great friend and partner, Chris Albert, we are able to include this masterpiece of concision in our gallery (Fig. 7.24).

Like all the really gifted writers, John Watson can turn his hand to anything. He does not stop at eight-word headlines. I once read an eight-page direct mail letter that he wrote. It was riveting. Not a word was wasted in that, either. The most difficult job I could imagine would be to edit his copy. It would be impossible to paraphrase a single sentence for the sake of brevity without losing some of its clarity or power.

The headline, 'Cash if you die. Cash if you don't' is elegant only in its extreme simplicity. It is not witty or stylish in the superficial way that pulls in the advertising awards. It is entirely functional. It appeals, not to the advertising pundits, but to the people it targets: the great uninsured.

It is a fine example of the art concealing the art. A truly great headline does not make us think how clever the writer is. It makes us think that at last someone has invented the insurance policy we have been waiting for. That is why very few of the best direct marketing writers will ever have their talent recognised outside their own business. But it is also why they are among the very best salespeople in print. There's no tougher discipline than writing or designing to pull response. I cannot imagine anyone without that discipline writing a headline of such directness as John Watson's now famous headline for Link Plan.

'Cash if you die. Cash if you don't'
Lloyds Life

❝ There are many examples of an advertisement going down in the annals of time as a classic. But not many in direct response. '3 books for £1' was first written in the 1930s. Everyone quotes John Caples 'They laughed when I sat down at the piano ...'. my contender produced by our agency and written by John Watson is 'Cash if you die. Cash if you don't.'

The product was a life insurance policy with term savings, which we renamed 'Link Plan' and before had only been sold

Figure 7.24

by brokers and was sitting around on a shelf, gathering dust, not going anywhere.

We were asked to compete in a split-run test against a traditional financial copy headline written by the client to sell the plan direct off-the-page. Tabloid media were chosen as it was a very simple product with down-market appeal.

What John did was to simplify the message right down to basic key words *'Cash if you die. Cash if you don't'*, which are very strong, powerful words. So powerful we didn't think we'd get them past the actuary, or the account group, but the fact that it was a split-run test gives clients courage. Also if they are testing an agency, it's only right that they must not water down its work.

'Cash if you die. Cash if you don't.' These simple words satisfy the need and the greed in human nature. They talk in a language the target audience understands. 'CASH', 'DIE'.

Most financial ads at the time talked in couched terms like 'Financial security for your loves ones when you are no longer there' ... 'when you've gone what will you leave behind', etc. 'CASH' says loud and clear *No Tax*—another benefit of the plan. 'DIE', everyone knows it will happen some time—plain, simple talk. 'Cash if you *don't*' says there's something in it for you.

The underline asks 'Should you choose between life insurance and savings—with Link Plan you can have both' (your cake and eat it, you might say). The rest of the copy talks in a very easy way, explaining everything in plain language. So that by the end you are able to understand the whole plan, and therefore make a decision, and hopefully apply.

As well as having to get responses from the advertisement, because Lloyds Life was a direct selling operation, we also wanted to build brand values, with a friendly unpompous image that our target market would be comfortable with.

Building response and creating an image is what any good direct marketing agency should do as a matter of course.

Let's look at the layout design and typography of this advertisement, all very clean even though there is a lot of copy. It's also important to note that it's not trendy in any way. Insurance is all about confidence—if you feel it's a dodgy company you won't invest—being part of Lloyds was an important reassurance to the customer.

Key elements within the layout were the benefit tables, showing the values of the Plan at both death and the savings element.

In addition we added an example text to position the Plan

clearly in the eyes of the target market, i.e. people like you. And all importantly made the application form clear and easy to understand and easy to fill in. In every sense we tried to be open and honest with our readers.

This was also one of the first insurance ads to offer a free gift (you don't see many now without an offer of some sort!). It doesn't seem to be logical that a free gift would affect such an important and long-term commitment as life insurance—but think about it, you have to wait a long time to benefit from the saving or you even have to die—not much of a benefit, so why not choose a Plan that gives you something now for yourself, a reward for doing the right thing?

Free gifts can give an uplift of 10 per cent on average. You know it makes sense.

'Cash if you die. Cash if you don't.' This simple statement ran for well over three years, only stopped by the Finance Act, making the product less attractive than it was originally.

In that time we tried other approaches and adaptations, changing the type style to block/sans to suit the more down-market media like *The Sun* and *The Star*. We tested black headlines against reversed white out of black—the books tell you reversed headlines don't read as well!—in this case they worked better!

We tried a full colour cartoon ad as a complete contrast. It pulled in more responses—but converted less well. It did, however, allow us to increase our penetration in the key media which helped to keep the competition out. The campaign expanded into mailings, inserts and even on to television.

This campaign never won any awards; it did, however, make a lot of money for the client and was one of the reasons Royal bought Lloyds Life—and, incidentally, at the time, if you entered any creative department of an advertising agency with financial accounts they would be trying to better it. But they couldn't, and neither could we.

Classics are hard to come by and even harder to beat. **99**

8 What makes a good ad?

The proposition

'You can't teach a duck to catch mice,' explained the hard-bitten South African sales director of a life assurance company to me one day. To be a successful salesperson you need the killer instinct. Closing a sale requires the willpower of the salesperson to be stronger than that of the prospect. Selling is full of words and imagery, which suggest sporting or military combat and victory.

What distinguishes the direct marketing professional from many of his general advertising colleagues is this killer instinct. He or she is unashamedly a salesperson. There is little room for subtlety in selling. It is a black-and-white business. You made a sale or you didn't. You pulled the required response or you didn't. There is little else to be said about the result except to answer the question 'Why?'

Of course there are different styles employed in selling. Charm is a legitimate device. Excitement can be infectious. Yet all successful sales presentations follow a carefully planned structure, finishing with a powerful close. My first boss in advertising, a man called Godfrey Hope, was a brilliant salesman. He traded on the personal image of being a bluff, no-nonsense Northerner, a man who said what he thought and said it straight from the shoulder. Behind this image was a man of immense cunning, a brilliant psychologist who played on prospects' emotions with the practised skill of a maestro. Yet he never varied his close, which began with the words 'I'm old-fashioned enough, Mr Prospect, to say *I want* your business ...'. He had discovered that using those words smoothed the edge of his hard sell. The formula worked so he never varied it. I did not realise it at the time, but I had just received my first lesson in direct response.

But to be in a position to close the sale we must first gain the attention of the prospect. My second, more painful, lesson in direct response was given to me by another clever salesman, Peter Donoghue. He and I were sitting for the finals of the Advertising Association exams. Three weeks before the exams he confessed to me that he was concerned about the market research paper. He knew nothing of the subject. Would I teach him what I knew? I did what I could for him but I was not optimistic as to his chances. He won the National Prize. I failed. He was kind enough to explain why. He suggested that I might have been foolish enough to query the premise of the first question. He was right. He then told me that his answer to the question began 'When the tramp of the Roman Legions had died away ...'. When I asked him what connection this opening had with market research he admitted that it was somewhat tenuous. What he said was, 'Imagine you are an examiner. You have struggled to read over one hundred papers, most in spidery or indecipherable handwriting. Almost all are boring and conventional answers. Then along comes mine. What a relief! Peter had put himself in the examiner's shoes and won the reward which his intelligence and thoughtfulness deserved. You cannot sell unless you understand the point of view of the person you are selling to. How can you move him from point A (his viewpoint) to point B (your viewpoint) if you do not bother to find out where point A is?

These stories may seem to be a little removed from our subject. They are not. The classic AIDA formula of Attention, Interest, Desire, Action is based upon a simplified sales presentation. Direct response advertising is selling. Advertising is selling. We who undertake direct response, or any other kind of advertising, are salespeople. That is what we are for and we shall rue the day it slips our minds.

Creative people

Sometimes I get the impression that Britain is a club of which I am the only non-member. We human beings are a cliquey lot and like to group ourselves into cosy little societies designed to insulate ourselves from exposure to anyone who may not share our preconceived ideas, attitudes and prejudices. These societies are sometimes quite formally constituted. Masonic lodges, golf clubs, cricket clubs, tennis clubs and public schools are examples. Often they are not so formal and the qualifications for membership are more subtle. Formal or informal, their purpose is the same ... it is to create a comfortable little world in which we can exist uninfected by ideas from elsewhere, untroubled by thoughts of how things might be different. We live ignorant of how others live and are uncaring of their needs and desires. It is a recipe for misunderstanding and lack of communication. It is especially pervasive in England.

The creative person is an outcast from such groups because he is an observer more than a participant. His curiosity prevents him from identifying with any particular group because he is equally interested in all the groups. It is a paradox of advertising that the most cliquey people in the whole business are those who work in creative departments. They appear to flourish in a hothouse environment into which others must enter warily, particularly if they are called account executives. The hothouse certainly produces some wonderfully stylish and witty work which is targeted to identikit consumers whom the creatives have been told about by people called account planners. It strikes me as an odd way to carry on and it still amazes me that so much of what is produced is truly inventive. In describing it I find words like stylish, witty and inventive springing more readily to mind than words like well directed, emotive and convincing. However, it is not for me to criticise such gifted practitioners of the art of giving brands a personality. I would hate to work the same way as they do, and I have never known anyone with a track record of producing effective direct response ads who did work that way. To be a salesperson you must gain first-hand experience of what makes customers tick.

The big thing in creative departments now is the sub-clique, the team of a writer and a designer working together in splendid isolation. These teams are often more enduring than marriages and they move from agency to agency at a rate determined by the less stable or adaptable partner. It is a neat trick which has done much to hike the going rate for creative people. Agency managements have only themselves to blame for allowing this practice to foster for it is bad for the creative people concerned to work only with one partner. It is unnecessary to the execution of good work and it eventually cramps the imagination to be exposed to such a limited source of inspiration. This, together with the adoption of a lifestyle in which the creatives are limited to contact only with people much like themselves, may explain why the effective working life of so many is so short. Much shorter than that of journalists or designers in fields other than advertising.

Frustration with advertising people who are isolated and 'out of touch' has led many of the more entrepreneurial clients to keep a firm rein on their advertising. Bernard Matthews, the turkey producer, is an example. His advertising may be corny but it is effective. A former client of mine, Bob Johnson, who is chairman of the Farepak Hamper Group, maintains that corn sells. He has always been exceptionally fussy about how his food is photographed but detests irrelevant 'creativity' in the design of his ads or his catalogue. He sees these as vehicles for portraying the benefits instantly and clearly in a way that the most ignorant consumer can understand. Since most of his customers would identify anything smacking of good taste as 'not for them' and expensive, I would not doubt that he is right. After all, he has talked to more of his customers than any creative person. He knows what they are like.

As I write, support for my point of view is dwindling in the world of direct marketing as bright young things entering the business tell us that we should aim to raise our standards to those of the general advertising people. What they mean is that we should replace directness, conviction and sincerity with style, wit and elegance. What poppycock such pretentious nonsense is. It encourages me that the best advertising creatives do not kid themselves that they are there for any purpose other than to change attitudes and move merchandise. I well remember a telephone conversation with Tony Brignull, who has done so much to establish CDP in the forefront of creative agencies. In describing what went into a sell-off-the-page ad which required long copy I mistakenly used the word 'sell' instead of the phrase 'complete the sale'. He gained the impression that I believed his ads were not written to sell. I was glad we were not face-to-face because I had inadvertently delivered a most damaging insult. He is not renowned for his calm, self-control on meeting such foolish provocation.

Much of my early education was at the hands of Rod Allen—the Allen of Allen, Brady & Marsh. His work established ABM as the agency with the common touch, because their beer commercials appealed to the people who drank the stuff, not to the Old Etonians on the Board, or the creatives in the wine bar. Rod never ran an unsound, ill-directed campaign in his life. His ads sold soap, lemonade, carpet cleaner and chocolate to real people and in quantity. Listen to Jeff Stark, then creative director of Saatchi and Saatchi Compton, New York: 'UK creatives are producing work for their friends in the Zanzibar. They're coy and they don't care if their work actually sells anything. In the USA people are much hungrier for information and the one and only purpose of advertising is to flog things.' With support from such as these it does not concern me that my views are unpopular with so many in our business. Neither should it concern you if what you want to do is to write, design or commission good direct response advertising.

The essence of effectiveness

Because those creative people who are experienced at producing direct response ads are constantly confronted with evidence of their success or failure, they quickly get to grips with what works about it. That is why they are interested in the offer. They know that how you say it is important. But they know that what you say is more important than how you say it. They know that what you offer is usually even more important than what you say—and that to whom you offer it is probably most important of all. They therefore seek to extend their influence beyond writing words or designing ads, unless they have total confidence that the offer is compelling and the targeting accurate. When they see that an ad with the headline 'School fees made possible by C. Howard' keeps running month after month, year after year, they do not doubt that this 20 cm × 2 column ad is working. They quickly deduce that the idea of making an insurance policy provide for private education is a good one and that the advertiser sees no point in obscuring the message. It even brands the insurance provider strongly, so that those not yet in the market will recall the name. What else could you want from six words and one initial? The trouble is that there is nothing clever about it. All it does is flag the target market, address the problem, present a solution and identify the company. It is simple and effective. It will never win an award. It will never make anyone's reputation except the advertiser's.

Not every business idea is as simple and as sharply focused as making an insurance policy provide for school fees. When the product is less distinctive and the target market less definable, more ingenuity may be required to sell it. But the principles that this headline demonstrate are sound. Say who it's for, how they benefit and what it is.

Advertising is essentially a simple business and it remains simple as long as we do not lose sight of its objective.

Simple as it is, this does not make it any easier to describe what makes a good ad. Certainly it cannot be boiled down to a list of necessary ingredients, although such a list can be helpful to the writer and designer. I was reminded of this on receiving a questionnaire from the British Direct Marketing

Association. The questionnaire was part of an attempt to consult members on the formulation of objective standards for judging creative work submitted for awards. One question I found impossible to answer. It listed eight ingredients of successful creative work and asked me to allocate a percentage of the available marks to each. I cannot sympathise with such a mechanical approach to judgement. Surely there can be only two questions to answer:

Is it a good idea?

Has the idea been well executed?

Even these questions can pose problems. There is surely no such thing as a totally original idea. The ideas we call original are stolen from a less obvious source than the ideas we call derivative. If we can get an idea for an ad from a book or play, it is 'original'. If we steal it from a competitor, it is clearly not original.

Then again, what do we mean by 'well executed'? Do we mean well written and designed by professional standards? Or do we mean convincing? An ad can be appallingly badly written and designed, yet be utterly convincing. Its sincerity can shine through. When writing direct mail letters I try to make them read as if written by the proprietor of a business, rather than by a professional copywriter.

Some of my less kind colleagues feel I start with an advantage here. Yet all of us respond more readily to sincerity than to slickness. What must temper our approach in any specific case is the prospect's expectations of the advertiser. We expect a BMW ad to be smooth and sophisticated because that matches our expectations of the car. But we may be turned off by a smooth, sophisticated ad from someone who is trying to sell a fishing holiday in the west of Ireland.

Our ad forms a link between a business and its prospects. It must be based on the expectations of the prospect while remaining true to the character of the business. You will not find many award winning ads that do this if what happens to award winning agencies is anything to go by. David Ogilvy has quoted research which shows that out of 83 commercials that won Clio awards in the States, 36 of the agencies involved either lost the account or went out of business. In Australia, two of the 1988 FACTS award winning agencies lost the accounts within a year. Another lost the account before winning. A fourth had the ads pulled by the client because they were not working.

Below are listed a few simple notions of features shared by the majority of effective direct response ads. Even when our expectations may deliberately appear amateurish, it is dangerous to make the structure amateurish. A sales presentation has a beginning, a middle and an end, the close. The beginning secures attention and gains interest; the middle adds subsidiary benefits and answers sales objectives; and the end asks for the order. This formula is logical and has worked throughout the long history of selling. It is the basis for successful direct response advertising.

Flag the target market

Ads are not read simply because they are clever. Some people like clever ads, to be sure, but these people are not necessarily in your target market. It follows that it is more efficient to engage the interest of those who are within the target market at the price of excluding those who are not.

We buy newspapers and magazines to read editorial that we expect to be of interest. We do not generally read all of the editorial because not all of it engages our interest. Although we did not buy the magazine to read ads (unless it is a classified ad publication, like *Exchange & Mart* or *Dalton's Weekly*, or contains dream property ads, like *Country Life*) we shall nevertheless read some ads because they interest us. Being selfish creatures we shall mainly be interested in ads that seem relevant to our own self-interest. If we are suffering from back pain we shall almost certainly read an ad with the headline, 'Back Sufferers'. We shall do so even if the headline does not offer a benefit. It may be legitimate to leave the benefit out of the headline in order to give prominence to the words which flag the market. Our ad may not be big enough to give prominence to more than a couple of words. If it is bigger, it may be more powerful to add the sentence, 'Relief at last'.

We may decide, as an experiment, to test narrative copy using an editorial style layout. We shall then want to run a story-telling headline but, if it is to work, it must still flag the target market. For example, 'My back was killing me until a friend let me in on her secret.'

Not every target market can be defined as easily as those unfortunates who suffer from back pain. Yet the principle still applies. For example, the headline 'Tune into the world' above or beneath a shot of a high performance radio, clearly flags a target market. A photograph or illustration—which may be of some health fanatic pumping away at an exercise machine—can flag a target market as well as, if not better than, mere words. If the photograph is doing the job for you,

you may be able to use the words to develop the thought further, sticking closely to the main benefit. For example, 'A complete home fitness centre for only £39.95'. The main benefit is to become fit, but the supporting benefit of a low price is also indicated.

Lead with the main benefit

It is not axiomatic that the main benefit should feature in a headline. There may not be room to include it and flag the target market at the same time. In a narrative style ad, giving away the main benefit in the headline may detract from its intrigue. However, it is more often a mistake to leave the main benefit out than it is to include it. As a general rule one should include the main benefit in the headline unless there is a telling reason not to do so. The reader will only spare you a second or two to get to the point. He or she has a need or want and you have the solution. The longer it takes you to produce the solution, the more likely it is that the door will be closed in your face, or that the page will be turned, without your proposition being read.

The main benefit may emerge from a headline without being directly stated as in 'They laughed when I sat down at the piano, but then I began to play ...'. Disciplining yourself to include the main benefit, unless you have a compelling reason to do otherwise, is not a severe restriction on creativity. All creative processes follow disciplines. I can think of no circumstances in which featuring the main benefit should not at least be tested in the headline or main illustration.

One virtue of leading with the main benefit is that you are forced to decide what it is. This information may come to you from research or it may not. It may or may not be obvious. You may have to talk to some users of the product, people who use similar products, or people who are in the target market to help you decide. You may even have to feature alternative benefits to discover which one is most important to most people.

It will probably be necessary to test, for example, when you have the combination of a strong product benefit and a powerful offer. Should the headline be product benefit-led or offer-led? It may be better to run the headline, 'Speak French, German or Spanish in just 30 days', featuring a free demonstration cassette in the sub-head. Or it may be better to run the headline, 'Free language lesson on cassette', featuring the product claim in the sub-head. It would be difficult to be sure without testing.

If you decide to lead with the main benefit, then you must also consider all the other benefits in order to be sure you have made the right choice. Your list of supporting benefits will be important later, particularly if you are planning a one-step ad.

Having made your choice, that is not the end of the matter. You should never satisfy yourself with merely stating a main benefit if you could dramatise it. Sometimes space will prevent this. More often it will not. If you can use illustration as well as words to dramatise the main benefit, the attention will be increased dramatically, for pictures communicate faster than words and more often powerfully. A picture can demonstrate. It can portray emotion. It can do either of these things in the blinking of an eye; or at least between blinkings of eyes. 'They laughed when I sat down . . .' is a dramatisation. The writer of this headline did not rely solely on words to convey his dramatic idea. He did not just tell the story. He showed the scene.

It will not always be possible to do this. Sometimes a dramatic idea is conveyed better by words alone. Joe Karbo's famous headline 'The lazy man's way to riches' would not have been helped by a picture of an idling millionaire. This is because a picture would detract from the dramatic quality of the headline rather than add anything to it. But, more often than not, a big, dramatic idea can be conveyed with greater speed, clarity and emotional force by the combination of words and pictures. Actually, we have two brains—a right brain and a left brain. Only one of these brains, the left brain, can read. This brain deals with matters of logic, numbers, and so on. The right brain likes pictures. It deals with matters of the imagination and flights of fancy. A big idea appeals to our sense of logic and to our imagination. It will do so more strongly if it uses both words and pictures.

There are many ways of dramatising a benefit, and of turning it into a big idea. You will see examples in this book and more, many more, in newspapers and magazines. You will see examples that personalise the benefit by relating it to an individual user. This idea has been used to sell insurance and to raise money for charities. You will see other examples that use an evocative analogy. I have just seen a trade press ad selling airtime for 3AW, 'The thinking person's radio station', in Australia. The headline reads: 'Just because people hear you, doesn't mean they think about what you say.' The headline runs as a caption to a huge double-page spread colour photograph. The photograph is of a Nazi rally in pre-war Germany. The dramatic quality of an idea can be raised by the person stating or illustrating the benefit. For example, the publishers of *Encyclopaedia Britannica* have used the distinguished botanist (and contributor to *Britannica*) Dr David Bellamy. He says, 'I was a bit of a drop-out at school. But what I learnt at home from *Britannica* more than made up for it.' A benefit may be dramatised by comparison. For example, if a high-performance car will go from 0 to 60 mph in five and a half seconds we could think about what else could happen in that amount of time. Perhaps an Olympic sprinter might have covered 60 metres from a standing start. How far would our car have done in that time! Could we show a picture of the sprinter trailing our car by a respectable quarter of a mile? No? Well, how fast does a plane accelerate from a standing start? In half an hour we could have half a dozen potentially dramatic ideas. And if none of them works out well we could turn to other ways to dramatise acceleration or speed.

Many big ideas arise out of talking with consumers, some of them from qualitative research. Another example from Australia is Meadowlea margarine. The agency, Mojo, discovered that women were saying that the two words they heard least often in the kitchen were 'thank you'. They came up with the line 'You ought to be congratulated'. Not very clever, perhaps, but good enough to run for 12 years. Incidentally, the same agency has the good sense to discourage its clients from pre-testing ads using the specious 'research' referred to earlier in this book.

With so many possible ideas there can only be one excuse for merely stating the main benefit instead of dramatising it. That excuse is absence of space.

Make personal contact

To develop your ad from the main benefit you must establish contact with your readers immediately or you will lose them. Take our back-pain example. The first sentence of body copy should sympathise with the sufferer's predicament. The reader should feel the writer knows just how he or she feels. And you better know. Nothing sells like sincerity. The converse is that nothing unsells faster than the lack of sincerity. To accomplish this contact you must show understanding and, I shall not labour the point further, interest in other people is an essential ingredient in the ad-maker's constitution. It is not difficult if the interest is there to start with. In my own case I suspect it is not, so I have to work at it. The difficult part is that you then have to boil your collective readership down to one person. The single person may then be a mix of male and female, young and not so young, wealthy and less well off. You cannot write to the world at large. You have to have a specific reader in your mind. I am not sure that many writers are fully conscious of this but I am sure that successful copywriters all address their copy to one person. The funny thing is that when you read their copy you think that the one person is you. I have referred to writers to make my point. Yet I think it is equally valid for the designer.

This book is about media advertising. Yet the finest training for establishing contact is direct mail. The first sentence of a letter is crucial. The best practical lessons I received in writing ads were through writing direct mail letters. Actually, the first sentence is different because, in direct mail, you have to answer the question uppermost in the reader's mind, which is how you picked him or her to write to. But it is a good training because that first sentence should not only answer that question but establish contact at the same time. Words cannot be made to work harder than that.

The reader has started to read your ad because he or she thinks the main benefit applies to his or her circumstance. Unless the body copy immediately reinforces this view your reader will turn over the page. Once this first contact is established you can go on to re-state, in a different way, the main benefit before going on to the supporting benefits. If your ad is designed only to get enquiries, the supporting benefits may scarcely be featured, or perhaps not featured at all.

You will see many generally competent ads which do not seek to establish personal contact with the reader in the way that I have suggested they should. Many sell-off-the-page ads state a main benefit in the headline, state a supporting benefit in a sub-head or overline and go straight into developing the main benefit in the body copy. Yet I feel that these ads would be more emotive and powerful if they were as I suggest they should be. It is perfectly correct to pepper sell-off-the-page ads with factual information, yet relating these facts to the reader's own situation can scarcely make the copy weaker. In Chapter 2 we referred to image matching and the fact that this process is undertaken before fact matching. In sell-off-the-page advertising it is necessary to truncate this process, with one ad explaining, for example, what kind of statement about yourself a product is making while also explaining its practical benefits. If the ad merely explains the practical benefits, then it leaves the image-matching process entirely to the reader's imagination. There is a danger that the reader will turn over the page without having related the benefits of product ownership to his or her situation. An opportunity to reassure this reader that the product will be good for his or her personal image, solve his or her personal problem, develop his or her particular personality, or further his or her individual career prospects will have been lost. A good ad surely appeals to both the head and the heart. Since readers are interested mostly in themselves, it is missing a trick not to talk about them. Incidentally, the same principle does apply to appeals ads although it is applied indirectly. The charity appeal that explains how your individual donation will benefit an individual victim will almost always outpull an ad that describes a macro-scale problem. The only exception is with highly topical disasters such as earthquakes and droughts. Many of the most powerful examples of establishing immediate contact can be seen in appeals ads.

Make pictures count

Photographs and illustrations communicate more rapidly than words. They are powerful attention grabbers, which is why the words in a caption are very important. Often these words are read before the headline. Two points follow from this. First, it is a criminal waste not to caption pictures. Second, the major picture should support the main benefit.

There may be a good reason why the main illustration should be a cut-out rather than squared up. By cut-out I mean, of course, with no background to the subject other than white paper. There would need to be a good reason to use a cut-out illustration because squared off type, justified at each side of the column, is easier to read than type shaped to fit round a cut-out illustration. If you do use a cut-out illustration you may take advantage of 'call-outs' instead of a caption. Call-outs draw attention to details in the picture and are usually set in small italic type with a rule directing attention to the feature in the illustration which they describe. They may be used when the main illustration is of the product.

Pictures are not simply attention grabbers. They can often show more effectively than words can tell. They can lend authenticity to a description. You should never choose to use drawn illustrations in preference to photographs if photographs will do the job. Photographs are authentic. The camera cannot lie but it can be used to show the truth in the best possible light. Photographs are trustworthy, illustrations may not be. Photographs say, 'This is how it is'. Drawn illustrations say, 'Imagine how it could be'. The latter is sometimes appropriate. It is also appropriate to use an illustration to do something a photograph cannot do, such as to show an exploded view of a piece of engineering or architecture.

Because pictures are attention grabbers, they can be used judiciously to give readers several start points at which they can become involved with the ad. Small, single-column width, pictures are often used to this end and they will generally be captioned or will refer directly to the body copy set immediately beneath them. Ads that do not show people tend to be rather cold. Often the main shot will have to show the product in a fairly clinical way so that the reader can see all necessary detail. In such a case supporting shots may be used showing the product in use. People increase the attention value of pictures and it is hard to resist looking in the same direction as a model in a photograph. That is why you will see models looking into an ad rather than towards the facing page. It follows also that a well-known personality in a picture will increase attention value further.

Where it is not practicable to show people (or parts of people) it may be necessary to show the product next to a familiar object or objects in order to give it scale.

We are often suspicious of mail order goods when this is not done. It is often difficult to visualise the size of an object from quoted measurements. Sometimes it is possible to show the object actual size, and this adds to the authenticity of a photograph.

When an item is being sold off-the-page, that is in a one-step ad, it is always a mistake to go for mood rather than detail in a photograph. The ad has to come as close as possible to allowing readers to examine the product in minute detail, just as they would in a shop. Keep soft focus, or high key, shots for conveying an atmosphere. This is not to belittle the thought that has to go into successful photography for sell-off-the-page advertising. It is much more than a matter of plonking an item down in a studio and lighting it to show off the detail. However, the imagination that should be applied is the imagination to step into the prospective buyer's shoes. If you were examining the item in a shop, what would you look at first? What would you want to examine in minute detail? Are inset close-ups of individual features needed to substitute for this process of examination? Do the photographs highlight the key benefits featured in the copy? Can you use props to accentuate the product's value or status? Perhaps the same props can be used to convey the size of the product.

If, for example, you are selling a desk diary your main shot may be an open spread showing the working features of the diary. These may include week-at-a-glance format, space for notes, a calendar across the bottom of the pages and a silk ribbon book-mark. Appointments will be written into the dates to show the diary in use and the extent of space available for entries. Yet the picture can do more than this. The diary can be on a desk that is accessorised so as to convey the status of the owner. And you will need supporting pictures. You will need to show the diary closed. You will need close-up shots of gold-blocked initials, of the texture of the binding and of the gilt metal-reinforced corners. You will need another shot showing the atlas section of the diary, perhaps, and another showing a year planner or editorial information. These features must be given correct priorities. It will not always be possible to include all the shots you would like to use and, in any event, you will not wish to give each feature equal emphasis. Sometimes you will have to use 'call-outs' to indicate features that you have no room to show in inset close-ups.

What you will be attempting to do is to make the diary almost tangible. You will be trying to get as close as you can to making the reader feel he or she has seen and touched the diary, flicked over the pages and is satisfied that it is just what is wanted. You will, if you are successful, have done everything short of making the reader feel the weight of the diary and sniff the aroma of the luxurious leather binding. The writer's job (or part of it) is to help the reader to imagine those features that you cannot demonstrate pictorially.

From this example, you can readily see that a soft focus shot of the diary against an elegant background could not possibly do the job. Neither is it necessary to resort to such a technique to convey status or elegance. Beautifully lit and reproduced shots will convey these features as well as showing detail with great clarity. This is really a matter of common sense and it should not be necessary to have to debate the issue. What is of much greater practical difficulty is the optimisation of the limited space available to the writer and designer.

A good deal of juggling is often required to get the balance right between words and pictures. Too often we see ads in which the writer has been greedy and the designer has let him get away with it. The result is copy set too small to be easily read, pictures too small to show off the features to the best advantage, and a generally cramped appearance. It must be decided which benefits are best shown and which are best described in detail. It must be decided how large an illustration must be to do the job. It must be decided which benefits must be relegated to listing in a benefit summary panel. No direct response writer worthy of the name is so rigid that he or she will be unwilling to edit copy when it makes sense to reduce the space allocated to it. Editing copy that is already tightly written is a painful process because it inevitably loses something of its persuasive power as a result. However, we must understand that one-step advertising is always a compromise. We must do the best we can to simulate a sales presentation, using an inadequate medium with insufficient space. Most one-step ads start life over-written and over-illustrated. It is important to allow enough time for ruthless editing, because this will often take longer than the origination of the copy and design.

The most common mistake is to reduce the size of the coupon (or flagging of the telephone response mechanism). The reason this mistake is made so often is that it is the easy way out. It is fatal.

Earlier in this book you read that direct response ads attract higher noting scores than non-response ads. By reducing the prominence of the response mechanism we would be discarding our principal advantage. In the case of the coupon-type ad we may also be making it difficult for our customer to write a decipherable order.

Make copy easy to read

Just as illustrations that are too small to portray benefits clearly are not worth including, copy that is too long to be set in a readable size must be edited. If you give a salesperson five minutes to sell you something, you will be more likely to buy it if he says 600 words rather than 900. You cannot take in what someone is telling you if he gabbles away at the rate of 180 words a minute. You will switch off after the first minute because it is too much of an effort to listen.

The advertising equivalent is to jam copy in so that the ad is uninviting to read and, if you start reading, requires a great effort to continue. It is better to say too little clearly than the right amount unreadably. Indeed, the copy should be short enough to punctuate with sub-heads, giving readers the chance to skim over the ad, stopping at headers which gain their attention. This also serves the functions of emphasising key benefits, making the ad appear more inviting and making it seem easier to read.

I have met few designers or typographers who appear to know *how* people read. We cannot read anything with our eyes in motion. The eyes must be stationary. We cannot read words that are just within our peripheral vision. We can only read words that we can see in sharp focus. The main implication of this is that the copy should be set in relatively narrow columns. These columns should never be more than about 110 mm wide, otherwise the eyes will have to move to focus on the end of the line, then move back again to focus on the beginning of the next line. Although this book is set in a relatively narrow column, you can use what you are reading now to prove my point. Book text is set in wide columns because book text has always been set in wide columns. There is no good reason for this except that book printing pre-dates knowledge of how we read.

I prefer not to stretch copy as wide as the 110 mm I have mentioned. If you read a newspaper you will see how effortless the process is. It is effortless even though the paper quality may be poor so that the type does not appear very black on the page. It is effortless because the columns are only 40 or 50 mm wide. This means that you can read the whole of one line of text and go on to read several more lines without having to move your eyes.

The primary function of display type is to help the words make the ad inviting to read. The primary purpose of body type is to make the ad easy to read. The selection of a typeface must never be allowed to interfere with these priorities. The selection of a typeface may also suggest a certain style or quality of the product, but never at the expense of readership.

For this reason sans serif type should never be used for long body copy except in countries where people habitually read sans serif type. It has been said that serifs help to keep your eyes focused on a particular line rather than straying down the page. I am not sure whether this is true or not. It does not matter. For whatever reason, we find it easier to read serifed type. We may wish to use a sans serif to give a headline a bold, urgent quality. We should never use sans serif in long body copy.

We also find italicised copy hard to read except in small doses. The type may be quite legible but we are not used to it, so reading it seems an effort. A well-chosen typeface is like a good accompanist. We are not conscious of the art because its function is supportive. If it is conspicuous it is not doing its job. The same principle that applies to the selection of a typeface applies equally to the way in which it is used. Excessive leading between lines of body copy and unnatural spacing between letters or words makes it hard to read. We are not used to it. And why should we make the effort to satisfy the whim of some trendy art director who has not troubled to learn his craft? An ad is there to entice us. It cannot do that if the typography makes it forbidding.

A less common fault is to change typefaces within an ad. It is legitimate to pick one display face and one body copy face. It is legitimate to use a bold face version of the body copy face for introductory copy or copy set in a benefit panel. Italics can be used for call-outs, captions or panels. But greater elaboration than this simply interrupts the flow. It is like changing the tone of voice halfway through the copy. It makes typography intrusive instead of supportive.

Reversed out type, even white out of black, is much harder to read than black on white. Incidentally, only black on yellow is as legible (actually, slightly more legible) as black on white. It may sometimes be a good idea to reverse out displayed copy. Body copy should never be reversed out unless it is very short and there is an overwhelming design argument for taking such a risk. Reversing out of a plain colour background is a sin. Reversing out of a graduated tone background is a cardinal sin. Reversing out type over an illustration is worthy of excommunication from this profession. It is a designer's cop out of a space problem. The designer should be sent back to his desk to come up with a more creative solution to the problem.

Use the right tone

The style of copy depends not simply on who you are making a sale to but also on what you are selling. A product or a company has a personality just as the prospective buyer has a personality. It may be legitimate for a tabloid Sunday newspaper to scream superlatives at you in promoting the contents of tomorrow's newspaper.

You would not expect Mercedes-Benz to do so in extolling

the virtues of a new model. While this is obvious enough, it is actually quite difficult to get exactly right. It is possible to establish a very sharply defined personality even for a mail order company, an example being JS & A, referred to elsewhere in this book. However, it is essential that this personality is a true one, not a false one. If it is false, the customers' first experience of dealing with the company will be the last. Their transaction experience will contradict the image that attracted them.

The task of hitting the right note in copy is one of marrying the consumers' expectations to the reality of what the product or company can offer. A certain degree of idealisation is legitimate. You must tell the truth and nothing but the truth, though, not necessarily, the whole truth. The way you tell the truth establishes the personality of the company or the product. You may do so in a way that agreeably surprises the prospect but it must still be credible; you must not strike a jangling note. A bank can appear friendly but it should not lapse into over-familiarity. Once the tone of voice is established it must remain consistent.

This tone can and does reflect many different personalities for different companies or brands. It should, because, ideally, each personality should be distinctive, though widely acceptable. It may reflect breathless excitement, it may reek with distinction, it may exude warmth, it may convey utter trustworthiness—but, whatever it does, it must be consistent to ensure credibility over time and to shape a clear identity.

It may help to think of the company or the product as a person and to think of the kind of person the product would be. Now, since we have already singularised a whole target market of consumers into one person, our problem is to introduce the person we want to sell to the person we want to buy. How can we get the person we want to sell say the right things in the right way so that our introduction is successful?

Many would-be creative people never make the grade because they are unable to shed their own personal style and to adopt the imaginary personal style of a product. Their copy or design work keeps coming out the same because they cannot shake off their own style. They speak in the same tone of voice whatever they are selling, whoever they are selling to. They are unteachable because they lack sensitivity and imagination. They do not pick up vibrations. They hear only their own voices. They are too self-interested, too unaware, too dull to make the grade. It is a kindness to tell them so before they waste valuable years failing at one occupation when they might succeed in another.

The reverse of this coin is that if you are commissioning creative work from a good creative person or team, you should be very reluctant to demand any change which they say will strike the wrong note.

They are more likely to 'hear' a discordant note than you are because that is their training, their expertise. If they want to bury the offer halfway down the body copy, you stamp your foot down hard. But, if they tell you the prospect will be jarred by re-phrasing the terms of the offer in the way you want, think very carefully before you insist on the change. And what you should think about is how you would feel if you were a prospect. This may mean changing your personality temporarily because you may be quite different from your prospects. Be ready to accept that the creative people are probably more able to undertake this personality shift than you are. After all, they have to do it every working day of their lives.

Use panels

Do you ever go into a restaurant and find the appetisers more appetising than the main course? Keith Wride, a former chairman and a most perceptive creative director of what is now McCann Erickson Manchester, once referred to the style of good one-step ads as *hors d'oeuvres* copy. *Hors d'oeuvres* copy gives the reader a choice of places to start reading the ad. The text is broken up with sub-heads, captioned pictures and panels to make it more appetising.

Panels can help the *hors d'oeuvres* effect and can add a dash of colour. It is legitimate to set panel copy against a pale tint background or even quite a strong yellow, because yellow and black are a highly legible combination. Panels serve more than one function. They help create the impression that the ad will be easy to read. They can also help, in association with sub-heads and captions, give readers a shorthand route through the ad which they can use before deciding to read the body copy. Finally, they can be used to feature important points which, if they were included in body copy, would interrupt the flow.

There are probably four classic uses of panels. The first is to include a benefit summary. The main benefit will probably be in the headline. A panel allows the advertiser to list the supporting benefits underneath the main benefit. If the ad justifies the use of only one panel, more often than not it should be used for a benefit summary.

The second classic use of a panel is to feature a testimonial or testimonials. It is almost impossible to work these into body copy without disturbing the flow.

The third use is to feature a guarantee. This does much the same job as a testimonial. One of reassurance. It may be that a money-back offer is included in the headline. On the other hand, there may also be a product performance guarantee that extends beyond the trial period.

The fourth classic use of a panel is to flag different target markets by listing alternative uses of the product, or simply listing occupations or hobbies of people who the product would benefit.

What the panel is used for may suggest where it is placed. For example, if it is used for reassurance it might go near the response device. If it is used to flag target markets its natural place is near the headline and main picture. I have not seen evidence that one should worry too much about this. People tend to look at pictures first and displayed copy second, wherever the displayed copy may be. Panels should be placed where they will do most to make the ad look easy to read.

Position attention devices correctly

In many ads the most important attention device is the main illustration. The best place to put it is just above the optical centre of the ad. The optical centre of an ad is about 40 per cent of the way down from the top of the page. Even though you have placed the picture above the optical centre readers will look at it first, particularly if you have been careful to ensure that support pictures are small enough not to compete with it.

The reason you should place the main picture above the optical centre is so that you can place the caption in the optical centre of the ad. Usually, the words in the caption will be the first words of the ad which the reader will read. For that reason it is ideal if the picture caption is the headline. The headline may not literally be a caption. That does not matter as long as it is immediately below the picture. The headline may extend the whole width of the ad and the picture may not. That does not matter either.

In his excellent book, *Commonsense Direct Marketing*, Drayton Bird refers to testing undertaken by Ogilvy & Mather Direct Worldwide that proved conclusively the value of placing the headline, below the main picture, near the optical centre of the ad. In a series of four tests response increased between 27 and 105 per cent by moving the headline from above the main picture to below the main picture. The agency's founder, David Ogilvy, clearly knew a thing or two. He, more than anyone, set the fashion in the 1950s of placing headlines below large squared-up photographs. He also did not waste space by setting headlines in unnecessarily large type. Looking at the best O & M and DDB ads from those days and from the early sixties is an education. O & M's Rolls-Royce ads and DDB's Volkswagen ads do not look dated. They are classically designed, using correct positioning of headlines with typography that is unobtrusive, but which subtly suggests quality.

It is, of course, not always practicable to follow this formula. If you have a full-length dress to sell, the natural shape of a picture is long and thin. Since the picture is by far the most important element, you will want it to stretch from the top to the bottom of the ad. This means you cannot put the headline under the picture. You must put it alongside. Nevertheless, you can still set it in the optical centre, running body copy above and below it.

Earlier, we established that the response device is a powerful attention-getter. However, if it is a coupon the natural place for it is the bottom outside edge of the ad (right-hand side for a right-hand page and left-hand side for a left-hand page). This is the natural place because the sales 'close' should lead into the coupon, which should appear accessible to cut out or tear off. It may sometimes be justifiable to place the response device elsewhere. For example, when the Automobile Association launched 'Homesure', a home contents insurance policy, it was decided to allow only telephone response because this would produce a much higher conversion rate on enquiries. A sales talk over the telephone was more effective and helped to resolve queries more efficiently than correspondence. Because, at that time, people were not used to the idea of non-couponed direct response ads in the UK, or of buying home contents policies from ads, it was decided to make a telephone the main illustration in the ad. This was correctly placed above the optical centre of the ad with the headline underneath. It worked very well.

Make copy flow

If a salesperson's presentation were disjointed you would be less likely to buy than if it flowed smoothly to the sales close. The same applies to copy and, more critically, because the reader can simply stop reading.

Depending on the length of the sales penetration the salesperson may or may not use a number of trial closes before getting to the real close. The purpose of a trial close is to raise the tension, secure a point of agreement, and to allow the tension to evaporate. This has the effect of reducing tension by the time the salesperson has arrived at the real close. It is possible to use the same technique in long copy. For example, it is commonplace for a trial close to be used early on in a long direct mail letter. It would be unusual, however, for more than one trial close to be used. A trial close can be used in an ad just as it can be used in a direct mail letter. It gives the more impulsive reader, who does not want to read all the reassurance copy, a short cut. It allows the more careful reader to read the reassurance copy in a more positive frame of mind.

The trial close allows readers to agree that, were it not for a number of sales objections, they would really like to have the product. The subsequent copy can then pick off each sales objection in turn. At the same time it can pile on the supporting benefits. Using a trial close in this way does not interrupt the flow of long copy; it simply reaches a climax before building towards another climax. However, a trial close is irrelevant in short copy unless it is in the headline, for example, as an injunction: 'Speak French, German, Spanish, or Italian in 30 days or your money back.'

Copy flows better when it flows quickly. You can increase the rate of flow with the use of short sentences. Paradoxically, copy which consists of nothing but short sentences does not flow. It is merely breathless. A mixture of short and longer sentences is more natural and relaxing to read, being more like the way we talk. On the whole, it is not advisable to use many sentences of more than 15 or 16 words. A literate readership can cope with up to 32 words but sentences of such a length should be used very sparingly.

Inject warmth

Which of these two salespeople would be most likely to make a sale to you? Salesperson A is domineering, aggressive, hard sell. Salesperson B is likeable, shows understanding, cosies you along. For every order salesperson A gets, salesperson B will get three.

Not always correctly, we trust the people we like. And the more human they appear to us, the more it is we shall like them. Humanity can be suggested by the tone of the copy, by using photographs or drawings of people (especially children) and animals, by the use of testimonials and, when appropriate, by the use of narrative copy. It may be suggested by a sense of humour. However, humour must be used with care. Few people regard parting with a large sum of money as a laughing matter. They would like to think their order will be handled with care and treated as important.

The most significant way in which warmth can be injected into an ad is by identifying with the reader. Showing understanding of the reader's problem. Or congratulating him on his status. There is no limit to our capacity to wallow in sympathy or to respond to flattery.

Overwhelm inertia

There are five ways to do this. Inertia is the greatest enemy to response. Far more people will consider responding to your ad than will actually do so. We have already stated in an earlier chapter that the offer is the most important device for overcoming inertia. So the first of the five ways to overwhelm inertia is to ensure you have a powerful offer, whether it is an offer to respond or an offer that is conditional on purchase.

The second way to overcome inertia is to knock aside all the reasons for not responding. We have already made passing reference to reassurance. It is important, particularly in one-step ads, to imagine all the sales objections and to remove them in turn. There are even sales objections to overcome in two-step ads. For example, will my response provoke an unexpected sales call? Will I incur any expense if I do not wish to buy? Think of the ways in which you can give reassurance: testimonials, statistical information, case histories, true life stories, guarantees. Remember, an ad will work if the benefit of responding clearly outweighs the risk or penalty in responding.

The third way to beat inertia is to inject urgency into the copy. The offer may help you to do this. If not, a significant proportion of many target markets want to be among the first with a new product. Others may not want to be the only ones without a particular product. Others may want it in time for Christmas or their holidays. It is essential that *now* is made to appear to be the right time to buy or to enquire.

The fourth way to beat inertia is to threaten the withdrawal of a benefit. Ideally, an offer should be for a limited period. If this is not practicable you may be able to add a second 'early bird' incentive, available only to people responding by a stated close date (preferably) or within a set number of days if a fixed close date is not feasible.

The final way to beat inertia is to make it easy to respond. This leads us into a discussion of one of the most crucial elements of a good response ad: the response device.

Make the response device work harder

Some designers like to start by allocating the correct space to the response device. They are wise to do so for, if the coupon receives less space, the ad will suffer in more than one way. The ad will lose the full power of an attention grabber and it will be harder for the reader to respond. Starting by allocating the correct space to the response device makes it inviolate. It is just as logical as beginning by drawing in outline the type area of the space.

Allocating the correct space to a coupon entails a thorough examination of its content. This will consist of copy, probably an illustrative element and of sufficient space for readers to write in the information you require. The illustrative element may well include credit card logos as these signal availability. If so, there will have to be sufficient space for a normal signature and boxes of adequate size to write in the credit card number.

The coupon has a threefold purpose: (1) to draw attention to the ad by signalling that it is a response ad; (2) to sell, which it can do with words and illustration—for example, a free catalogue; and (3) to make it easy for the reader to respond accurately with the information you need.

A telephone response mechanism is easier. Because you do not require the respondent to write anything, it is less inflexible. However, it must still be prominent and it must prepare the respondent to provide the information your telemarketing team will need—for example, the credit card number and expiry date.

More commonly a telephone response mechanism is used in conjunction with a coupon. In this case you must allocate priorities. Does experience suggest that the majority of people will prefer to use the coupon or the telephone? What are the relative values of coupon and telephone responders?

Give greater prominence to the more important response device. Do not let two response devices fight it out by giving them equal prominence. Give the reader a clear recommendation. Doing this will not deter response. If you have given more prominence to the coupon, telephone freaks and the madly impulsive will still use the telephone. So will anybody who needs the product urgently or has an unanswered query. Equal prominence given to both devices does deter response because it provokes indecision. If you do not know how you wish people to respond, how are they to know?

The two worst mistakes in coupon design are easily dealt with. The first is to conceal it. We know better than to do this by now, but many creatives in general advertising agencies do not. They do not want to spoil the look of their pristine ad. They are too ignorant to know that a coupon will increase the noting score and too precious to concern themselves with response.

The second mistake arises through size adaptations. Non-response ads can be increased or reduced in size and in proportion photographically to fit the space required. Mostly there is little copy and it will remain quite legible in an ad occupying half the area. Some ads are actually improved by size reduction. A direct response ad is different. To start with it is probably busy and exploits the space it occupies for all it is worth. Secondly, it probably has a coupon. This coupon was the correct size for the original space and will cease to be the correct size if the ad is enlarged or reduced in proportion. There is no way round this problem except by re-designing the ad. This usually means editing the copy as well.

One final point. A response device will work harder if it costs nothing to respond. An 800 telephone number or Freepost service will increase response. It will increase response significantly for two-step ads. We may not always wish to increase response in this way (see Chapter 5 on Two-step advertising) but that will be the effect. A discussion of alternative response devices (tip-ons, inserts, etc.) appears in that chapter and it would be repetitious to cover the same ground here.

The pay-off

In this chapter we have examined the principal features that distinguish a good response ad from a bad response ad. We have listed some features that are shared by many effective ads. I hesitate to elevate these features to the status of rules because I am not convinced that any of the principles on which most successful ads are based should be treated as inviolate. Every now and then some genius will create something that breaks all the 'rules' and yet pulls response by the sackload.

However, the few people who may do this will usually have a good understanding of the psychology and the mechanics on which the principles are based. People who break the 'rules' successfully usually know what the rules are and why they are being broken. So let us re-state them now.

- Flag the target market
- Lead with the main benefit
- Make personal contact
- Make pictures count
- Make copy easy to read
- Use the right tone
- Use panels
- Position attention devices correctly
- Make copy flow
- Inject warmth
- Overwhelm inertia
- Make the response device work harder

Looking down the list, you can see that these principles are not restrictive. There are many alternative ways you can write or design an ad that follows them. An ad that does follow them can scarcely fail to be a good ad—that is, an effective ad. It will not necessarily be a brilliant ad. But there is no guiding principle for writing or designing a brilliant ad. That's magic.

9 Media planning and buying

The proposition

My first experience of advertising was gained in a media department in a Manchester agency. Later I progressed to being allowed to carry parcels to the Post Office. But it was the experience of the media department that convinced me I had made the right decision in choosing advertising as a career. I loved every minute of it, probably because the department head, Eric Simpson, was so patient with me and was a great teacher.

While I have forgotten a lot of what Eric taught me, I have not forgotten that the decision of where to advertise is probably more important than any other. Since those days I have been fortunate enough to work with, and be helped by, many clear-sighted media people. One of them, Ian Prager of CIA Direct, has given me much help with this chapter.

Many advertising people find the subject of media somewhat tedious. This is like wishing to be a surgeon without troubling to understand anatomy. Here again, those experienced in direct response work are at an enormous advantage. Firstly, they know how crucial media planning and buying are. Secondly, in the context of advertising that produces measurable results, media planning is positively exciting. Every selection, every buying price can be proved right or wrong, sometimes within a matter of days. Results add a new dimension, proving again and again that there is more to selecting media than doing a computer run against a target market.

Some media outpull other media that have similar readership profiles and deliver equal opportunities-to-see against a theoretical target market. Anyone who ever thought that qualitative factors—such as editorial stance, layout and the relationship between a publication and its readers—ought to enter the equation, is proved right again and again when results are analysed.

To media people direct response is very hard work, but very rewarding. They can bring to bear all their analytical skills, test and prove their more intuitive judgements and satisfy their bargain hunting instincts. Better still, they can assuage their hunger for facts by looking at results. There is something at the end of the day to show for a lot of endeavour. Best of all, nobody goes to sleep when they present the results. Direct response media analysis presentations receive rapt attention. Everyone knows how crucial the media person's role is.

At any one time the media person is looking at results of past decisions, is planning 'banker' spaces some distance ahead and is making decisions on late deal tactical spaces for tomorrow. Always, the media person is living in the past, present and future simultaneously. Calmness is a great attribute in this situation.

The direct response media person works both with readership research data and with clients' results data. These are the tools of the trade and we shall now take a look at them.

Media research

Although many direct marketers believe media research is of secondary importance for direct response media planning, the fact is that it is a logical starting place. If we have no back data, in the form of response, we have to start somewhere. We may have no back data because the product is new, the company is new (or has not used direct response before) or it may simply be that the media we are considering are new to our schedule. There will always be more media available than we could conceivably test. So informed judgement will be required before a publication can be included as a candidate for testing. Furthermore, response may not be the sole consideration. Our advertising may serve a dual purpose, direct response being no more than a useful by-product. In such a case, we may be just as interested in what a publication does for our market coverage as we are in what it does for our response. Finally, media research may be used as a basis for negotiation when we lack results data.

There are many aids to media research but the most important of these are the regularly issued industry-wide standard research reports and statistics. I shall list only those which apply to the UK.

National Readership Survey

The Joint Industry Committee for National Readership Surveys (JICNARS) is responsible for the NRS. NRS readership data are collected on a rolling sample basis, interviews being conducted at the rate of just over 2000 a month. This sample accumulates to 28 500 adults over the age of 14 in the course of a full year. The readership information gathered covers about 200 different newspapers and magazines. Respondents indicate whether or not they have read or looked at an average issue of any title for at least a couple of minutes. As you will see, this is a fairly loose definition of readership. Information on the ownership of some other products is also covered. For example, owners of washing machines or people who travel abroad. This makes it possible to establish which media are most efficient for covering certain specified target markets.

The NRS also provides information on respondents' exposure to television, radio and cinema, classifying them as light, medium, or heavy users of these media. Because the NRS sample is stratified it is possible to look at readership of any publication not simply against the whole population, or against ownership of washing machines, but against age groups, socio-economic groups, demographic information and region. The survey is cross tabulated with geo-demographic data so that it is possible to describe the readership of a publication, for example, in terms of its penetration of each of the 11 Acorn groups or 38 Acorn types. Acorn is an acronym for A Classification Of Residential Neighbourhoods.

Through cluster analysis of census data it groups similar types of neighbourhood together. This facility of the NRS is of special importance to direct response advertisers or any company that maintains a customer list. This is because it is a simple matter to attach an Acorn Neighbourhood Type code to any fully post-coded address. This enables the profile of a publication's readership to be compared with a profile of a company's customers. Or, better still, a profile of recently acquired customers. One limitation of this is sample size. Although the NRS sample is very large, the sub-sample of readers of any one publication may be quite small. By the time this is sub-divided into 11 Acorn groups, some of the sub-samples could well be too small to be statistically reliable.

Using NRS data it is possible to establish the coverage a media schedule gives of a selected target group, taking into account the duplication that exists between the readers of one publication and another (or several others). It is standard practice for non-response media planners to put in hand file runs to compare the relative efficiency of alternative solutions to a planning problem. The result will show which alternative builds up coverage most efficiently, that is, contains the least duplication of readership. It will also show which schedule produces the most opportunities to see and which gives the highest average frequency, that is, most duplication of readership. The governing parameter for such runs may be a sum of money or it may be a minimum acceptable coverage figure. Such data may seem academic to many direct response people yet I would submit that there are few large advertisers who should not be interested in the market coverage they are getting and few who should not be interested in avoiding excessive duplication of readership. Direct response advertisers often look closely at optimum frequency in any one publication, forgetting that this can be disturbed by insertions in another publication with a high cross-over readership. For example, 40 per cent of *Sunday Telegraph* readers may also read *The Sunday Times*. In which case, spacing of insertions in the *Sunday Telegraph* should take *The Sunday Times* insertions into account.

The NRS is an absolute essential for planning campaigns in larger circulation consumer media.

Target Group Index

The Target Group Index is produced by the British Market Research Bureau. In this annual survey among 24 000 adults, the focus is on product purchases. However, the information is cross-tabulated against readership of about 150 newspapers and magazines. It is also possible to measure purchasing habits against geo-demographic profiles. In fact, it was the TGI which first demonstrated the discriminatory power of Acorn as a target market descriptor before Acorn was ever used in direct marketing. The research is conducted by means of self-completion questionnaires of near book length.

Some 1400 brands are covered. Some difficulty may be encountered with sub-sample sizes when looking at one brand against individual Acorn groups or the readership of individual publications. However, the sample is of sufficient size for product group purchase data to be meaningful against virtually any other factor which can be cross-tabulated against it. An especially useful feature of this survey is that it includes lifestyle questions. Clearly, it may be more important to discover that health conscious people read *The Guardian* than that socio-economic groups A and B read *The Guardian*. TGI's ability to show the lifestyle attributes of readers of specific publications makes it particularly appropriate to the needs of the direct response media planner.

Audit Bureau of Circulations Data

The direct response media planner is vitally concerned with primary readership. That is, readership by the person who buys or receives the publication. Interesting as it may be to know how many people spend at least two minutes looking at a publication, the direct response specialist knows that more time will generally be needed before we can expect a response to a single ad. Furthermore, our ad may have only one coupon. Or it may be a loose insert, in which case it is unlikely to be seen by more than the primary reader and, perhaps, one secondary reader. From NRS we can see how many readers see one copy of any of the 200 or so publications it covers. The direct response planner will be more interested in a magazine that covers three million readers, having only three readers per copy, than one that covers three million readers by virtue of having six readers per copy. The number of readers is the same. But the primary readership of the second magazine is only half that of the first. Given similar readership profiles, the first magazine should outpull the second very comfortably indeed.

A limitation of both NRS and TGI is that they cannot cover more than a small number of the thousands of publications on the market. For this reason, as well as for information on primary readership, Audit Bureau of Circulations figures are vital. The Bureau receives average issue circulation sales figures from the auditors of most of the larger publishers. It has the right to investigate and random checks are made. The Bureau then issues an ABC certificate, which gives the average circulation and publishes a list of certified figures for national morning, national Sunday and London evening newspapers. It gives average circulation for each title in these categories for each of the preceding six months, plus the six-month average. Every six months the Bureau issues its circulation review covering magazines as well as newspapers. This review includes business magazines and local newspapers and shows the six-month average circulation in each case.

These figures are also published in British Rates and Data
(BRAD) which, of course, also gives rate card costs of all
available spaces, indicates whether inserts are accepted, and
gives the necessary mechanical data.

The Business Media Research Committee Report

The Businessman Readership Survey (which sounds
somewhat sexist) is conducted with a sample of just over
2000 businessmen. A businessman is defined as a man or
woman whose occupation implies the exercise of significant
managerial, executive, technical or advisory functions; and
who works in an organisation eligible on grounds of size.

The survey records the readership of national newspapers
and business orientated magazines among the sample.
Readership profiles are extensive. They include age,
socio-economic grouping, education, income, occupation,
industry, financial investments and employment status.

Media policy

With our information sources at our fingertips, we need to
decide on our media policy. This is worth considering in
general advertising terms before taking into account the
special circumstances of direct response. A policy, of course,
is a set of guidelines that make subsequent decision making
much easier. It is not the same as a strategy, which is a
method of achieving our desired objective. Most media
policies revolve around one or more of five selection criteria.
These are:

1. Creative suitability

To a direct marketing person, well schooled in the disciplines
of targeted marketing, it is well nigh incomprehensible that
media should be selected on grounds other than efficiency in
reaching a specified target market. But the purpose of
advertising is not simply to make known, it is also to
persuade. It is therefore quite legitimate to place ads in a
context in which they will be most persuasive. A product
may require demonstration and it is easier to demonstrate
with moving pictures than still ones. Part of the
demonstration may be how it sounds, certainly if the product
is a record album. It may, as in the case of fragrance
advertising, be a question of what the produce smells

like—in which case we shall need a scratch 'n' sniff insert card. These examples are clearly specialised, but they are chosen to establish that the principle of selecting a medium on the basis of what an advertising message can *do* is just as sound as the principle of selecting a medium on the basis that *the right people see it*.

Some of the most brilliant media selections of all time have been based on creative ideas. I can think of two originated by a British 'creative' agency (KMP), which was the most fashionable boutique back in the 1960s. One was to test market the J-Cloth in Northern Ireland. This is an impregnated disposable, wipe-clean cloth. An actual sample of the product was carried as an insert in a British newspaper. The other was a campaign to generate test market business for one of the outlying ITV companies. Research revealed that about a dozen marketing decision-makers had more than 50 per cent of all test market budgets within their grasp. Most of us would think of a creative way to send a memorable series of mailings to these people. Not KMP. They plotted each target's drive to work and booked a 48-sheet poster site on the way. Each poster carried a message personalised to that individual. More subtly, the context in which an ad appears affects our perception of it. If it is surrounded by compatible editorial, that will help to generate a receptive mood. If it is printed on nice paper, that may help, too. A cosmetic ad is more at home in a glossy monthly than in a daily newspaper.

2. Proven effectiveness

To quote Simon Broadbent's thoughtful work, *Spending Advertising Money*: 'The best predictor of an advertising schedule is the schedule of the previous year.' To change a schedule dramatically for the sake of change places the advertiser at an unnecessary and considerable risk. A profitable schedule should be continued until a convincing case is made for a new one. In other words, 'if it ain't broke, don't fix it'. Much advertising depends upon continuity to establish a clear-cut personality for a brand. It is easier to build such a personality if the media selection policy remains consistent. While this may be a less important factor in direct response advertising, few advertisers would be so foolhardy as to ignore the proven track record of their banker media, even though they would allocate some money to experimentation.

3. Availability and timing

The case for retaining flexibility may outweigh the case for individual media that cannot deliver flexibility. A retailer often requires topicality and may wish to change promotions at short notice. The decision to promote specific items may be driven by a stock situation or it may be driven by competitive action. The later these decisions can be left, the better are their chances of being the right ones. A one-step direct response advertiser may wish to pull an ad out of the press because he under-forecast demand and is running out of stock. Alternatively, the advertised item may have suddenly stopped pulling orders. However strong the media audience claims for media with long copy or cancellation deadlines, it simply does not make good business sense to use them in many retail or mail order situations. A multiple food retailer, such as Sainsbury's, may use colour magazines to run a campaign in support of a high quality image but also run promotional ads in national or local daily newspapers.

4. Regionality

The overriding consideration may be lack of national distribution. A product may be distributed only in one part of the country. A retail chain may be regional. A sales team may be restricted to one area. Selection of media will now be constrained. Only regional media, or media with regional editions, can be considered. This still leaves a wide choice but some media are more economical to use regionally than others. For example, we could use door-to-door distribution or loose inserts without any cost penalty at all. We might be able to use TV or radio at low local advertiser or test market rates. We may even be able to pick up northern edition deal rate space in national newspapers at well below rate card cost. But, on the whole, we shall have to pay well over the odds if we wish to use colour space in magazines.

5. Competition

There are two ways of reacting to competition. One is to match it. The other is to avoid it. While the latter course of action is superficially the more attractive, it is seldom employed. There are more established products than new products. A media policy for an established product will be defensive. It will seek to protect the product's franchise and will give up the high media ground to competition only when the product nears the end of its life-cycle.

A new product may be the subject of a heavyweight launch to steal the high ground, taking on the brand leader in a blood and guts head-on clash. In this case it will challenge the brand leader within the same media, more often than not.

On the other hand a new product may be launched into a specific market niche. In this case the media used may well 'choose themselves' on grounds of targeting. If not, the media used may be picked quite deliberately to avoid being swamped by heavier spending competition. In one or two extreme cases a 'sore thumb' media policy has been adopted. This is where advertising is deliberately placed in media that offer an inappropriate editorial environment. 'Sore thumb' advertising can work very well—for example, holiday advertising in trade union journals—but almost the only people who know this are direct response advertisers. I have often wondered why ad sales departments do not seem to have tumbled to this opportunity. To expand on my last example, a number of direct response advertisers have found that loose inserts pull exceptionally well in trade union magazines. There are probably two reasons for this. The first is that the magazines are generally distributed quite efficiently. The second is that they are extremely boring. An advertiser's insert is a welcome relief from the grey substance of union matters. Perhaps it goes against the grain to sell space to advertisers on the grounds that the surrounding editorial will seem tedious in comparison with the ads. Or perhaps the space salespeople know from bitter experience that most media people lack the imagination, or nerve, to present such an unexpected solution to their clients.

My favourite 'sore thumb' example was the idea of a supplier of equipment for oil rigs. During the North Sea boom he approached my friend, Piers Hartley, who makes TV commercials and videos. He asked Piers to make a commercial for his equipment, but Piers accused him of being out of his mind. After all, each sale was worth hundreds of thousands of pounds and only a handful of people could be expected to have that kind of decision power. 'Listen,' said the client, 'the guys in the market are all American. They are stuck here in hotels over Christmas. I can't reach them by mail. But I know they have nothing to do except watch TV.' Piers made the commercial and it was shown, once only, on Boxing Day. It pulled three enquiries and one sale. The sale re-paid the cost of the 'campaign' many times over.

All of these policy considerations may apply to a direct response advertiser in the same measure as they do to any other advertiser. Equally, while it is obvious that a conventional advertiser will need a media strategy, so does the direct response advertiser. If the direct response advertiser bases his plan on nothing more than a consideration of past results, diminishing returns will inevitably take their toll sooner or later.

A strategy for response

Many advertisers receive a positive benefit from consistency. If it takes time to build an influential brand identity it makes no sense to chop and change either the message or the medium. However, a campaign driven by the sole consideration of response effectiveness is not constrained by such a policy consideration. There is still nothing to be gained by changing what works best. But the direct response advertiser is in a position to isolate each part of his plan and examine its contribution in minute detail. Like the curate's egg, his campaign will be good in parts, but seldom good in its entirety.

The temptation, then, is to sacrifice all the less good parts and replace them with something new, hopefully better. There are two problems with this. The first, obvious, problem is that some of what is new will be even worse than some of what it has replaced. The second, less obvious, problem is that some of what did not work in the last campaign will start working in the next campaign. The consumer has a nasty habit of changing the rules every so often. No one knows why. Where and when the consumer will make the next change is unpredictable. What is predictable is that change will occur.

For this reason, the most experienced large direct response advertisers employ a broad media strategy which involves retaining some money in each media group, even though money may be withdrawn from individual media. For example, major mail order companies generally maintain some kind of balance between alternative ways of recruiting new customers. They may use direct mail to cold prospects, mailings to lapsed customers, mailings to unconverted enquiries, a salesforce, door-to-door distribution, loose inserts and space advertising.

However badly one of these activities is performing, it will not be dropped altogether unless the performance becomes progressively worse over several years. Within a broad category of this sort there will be major sub-divisions. For example, within space advertising, some money will go into general magazines, some into women's magazines and some into newspapers. Only with great reluctance will the advertiser pull all his money out of one of these media groupings. An individual magazine may be chopped but the media group it represents will not be chopped. Some investment will remain to give trend information or signal a reversal of the trend.

Such large advertisers do not readily panic. They have seen it all before and will not be hustled into ill-considered investments in speculative media beyond a set test budget. This test budget may represent 5–15 per cent of the total spend. That is, on pure media tests. As much again may go on offer, creative and timing tests.

A strategy of this sort is a protective framework. It is designed to achieve a specified result but also to contain risk. It recognises the inevitability of change and the unpredictability of where and when change will occur. The planner is free to chop and change tactically and to engage in distress buying within a broad framework. But the planner must recognise the existence of the framework and accept its constraints. It is there to prevent the logic of back data causing a future débâcle. However solid results information may be, however soundly based a response forecast may be, there is no such thing as a future certainty. Favourites do not always win.

Every aspect of a plan will be subjected to the same strategic considerations. It is predictable that the weeks before Christmas will be generally poor response weeks. That is because there is a logical reason why they should be, although for certain products they are very good. It is not predictable that because, say, last July was a disaster next July will be equally bad. Maybe the sun was shining last July and maybe we shall get four solid weeks of rain next July. Unless some money is retained in this month the advertiser cannot know whether the plan is soundly based or based, incorrectly, on one bad experience.

The media of direct response

At the time of writing there are some direct marketers who would have us believe that the days of media advertising in present-day volume are numbered. They believe that it is all too unscientific, not sufficiently targeted to work as efficiently as locating and nurturing prospects on a marketing database. They are wrong.

Their misconception is based upon a convenient lack of consideration of relative costs and upon ignorance of the power of media to discriminate between people of differing lifestyles. The fact is that space advertising is a very cheap way of reaching a great many people; and that even inserts and door-to-door distribution are much cheaper than direct mail. They will not always be more cost efficient, but that will depend upon the targeting possibilities in a particular case.

Any experienced user of 'cold' direct mail lists will testify to the considerable value of one solid piece of behavioural information about a prospect relative to the value of a whole mass of lifestyles data. It is commonplace for, say, a credit card company to discover that a list of wine buyers will outpull a carefully constructed list of people sharing a number of relevant attitudinal and lifestyle characteristics. What the most ardent mailing enthusiast should recognise is that the purchase of a magazine *is* a piece of behavioural information. If it is a special interest magazine it is highly descriptive of the buyer. If it is sold almost entirely on subscription, like *Reader's Digest*, it is highly descriptive of the buyer. The direct response media planner, like the direct mail planner, is acutely aware of the importance of psychographics in determining response levels. Many magazines are bought as aids to dreaming of a better life: perhaps in the countryside as a 'squire', or as the proud owner of a vintage sports car. Many mail order products are bought by dreamers, too. People's purchasing behaviour is as much influenced by the lifestyle they aspire to as by the lifestyle they enjoy at present.

Direct marketing technocrats who believe everything and everyone can be reduced to numbers are every bit as wrong as the media planner who relies solely on readership or audience statistics. If it could be boiled down to that we could pass the whole problem over to a computer and do something sensible for a living. I have never met an entrepreneur who had made a fortune out of direct marketing who was not either highly intuitive or at least devious.

No one will ever devise a system for picking up every single potential buyer for a product and for discriminating accurately between each potential buyer and each non-prospect. There is no technological reason why this is impossible. What makes it impossible is that computer systems depend on logic. The person who should logically buy (because he or she is just like the others who have bought before) will not always buy. The person who should not buy, because he or she is different, will sometimes buy. That is because people are not always logical. They are people.

Typically, it will cost 20 to 30 times as much to mail to someone as it does to advertise to them through a colour page. Clearly, although the mailing offers more scope for flattery, involvement and persuasion than a space ad, it will need to be much more precisely targeted to pay back equally well. Sometimes it can be so targeted. Often it cannot. It often pays better to trawl for prospects than it does to try to hook them with a rod and line.

The Sunday Times reaches almost 40 per cent of all UK 'businessmen'. To reach the same audience through direct mail would involve using many list sources and an expensive de-duplication exercise. There are times—for example, when promoting car rental—when it is not so easy to discriminate between the value of one 'businessman' target and another. Part of the market can be isolated through business travel magazine circulation lists and promotion to airline users. But this will still leave a valuable residue, which it is most economical to sweep up with wide coverage media.

Combe International, the makers of Odor Eaters, use direct marketing methods to gauge the potential of new products. A direct response ad is inserted, usually in a high circulation national newspaper, because the information on which to base a highly targeted promotion does not yet exist. The buyer of a new product is still an unknown quantity.

Newspapers

National newspapers lend varying degrees of authority and topicality to a message. Advertisers sometimes make the mistake of attributing their own attitudes to a publication (which they do not read) to the people who do. Any national newspaper carries some authority with the people who read it. Readers, on the whole, trust the newspaper not to accept ads from people selling worthless rubbish or people taking readers' money and disappearing to the Caribbean, leaving the offer unfulfilled.

Regional and local newspapers, whether free or paid for, do not on the whole work for direct response. They may work with a local telephone response mechanism. They do work as a vehicle for carrying loose inserts.

Magazines

Magazines depend even more strongly than newspapers on their relationship with readers. However, magazines that come free with newspapers often work as well as magazines that are bought. This may be because of their dual male/female readership and their 'cut-ability'. People do not like to deface expensive glossies that can lie on the coffee table. They do not mind clipping coupons from throwaway Sunday magazines. To prove it, if you wish, try placing loose inserts in each. You will find that inserts give you a bigger response uplift, compared with space advertising, in glossies than they do in weekend magazines. Better still, the publishers charge more (per thousand circulation) for space in glossies and often charge less per thousand inserts. This is because advertisement rates reflect production costs and demand for space. They have no direct relevance to value. Even free magazines have a longer life than newspapers. About half of the response will be received in the first full week from most ads, with the balance coming in over the next five or six weeks. In the case of paid-for magazines, particularly monthlies, the response 'tail' will be much longer. In the case of the *Reader's Digest*, for 'week' read 'month'. You could still be getting response in ones or twos per month three *years* afterwards.

As a general rule, the glossier the magazine, or the more specialised its appeal, or the smaller its circulation, the more likely it is that inserts will be a better bargain than space advertising. Furthermore, inserts can be tested in part runs in most magazines and, by the same token, can be regionalised.

Business media

Business and professional media are not, in principle, different from other magazines. They are, however, much more likely to be received at work. They are more likely to be delivered free as controlled circulation journals. However, there is no discernible difference between the pulling power of a requested copy-controlled circulation journal and a paid-for journal. Inserts nearly always perform well relatively to space advertising in business and professional media, presumably because there is always insufficient time or inclination to read the magazine from cover to cover.

Unfortunately, insert costs tend to be high (although there are some bargains) and your insert may be competing for attention with a handful of others.

Door-to-door distribution

Often using the same pieces as are used as inserts in magazines, door-to-door distribution is a highly efficient way of getting a response mechanism into the hands of a target market. The reason it is efficient is that it offers unduplicated coverage. Obtaining a similar coverage from inserts in magazines might involve twice as many pieces because of overlapping circulations. Door-to-door distribution can be targeted on a postal sector ranking basis. Using a ready-made geo-demographic targeting system, such as Mosaic, Pinpoint, Superprofiles, or Acorn, postal sectors can be ranked in order of their capacity to deliver to homes in the target market without excessive waste coverage.

The same procedure can be followed using any combination of census characteristics or other known data which are particularly effective in discriminating between users and non-users of a given product. A particular advantage is that distribution can be limited to the catchment areas of specific stores or shopping centres, these areas being defined by drive time.

For less selective distributions a saving can be made by using shared 'drops' with other advertisers. The most selective and expensive method is to use a solus drop conducted by the Post Office Household Delivery Service in the UK. This will generally outpull other solus drops (currently by, perhaps, 60 per cent) but will cost proportionately more.

Magazine inserts will more often than not outpull distributions for nationally promoted products. However, they do not give unduplicated coverage so that this advantage is eroded as a schedule gets bigger.

Package inserts

Package inserts, statement stuffers and other bill stuffers often outpull magazine inserts. Package inserts will normally travel with mail order product despatches and these will usually pull high response rates for other mail order offers. Statement stuffers riding with credit card statements will similarly be effective when making offers obtainable through the card.

Other media

We must leave aside consideration of other media because they either have a fairly limited relevance to direct response or because, like broadcast media, electronic media and direct mail, the subjects are covered comprehensively in companion books to this one. A brief reference to direct mail lists will be found in the next chapter, but anyone seriously engaged, or simply interested, in direct marketing must read John Fraser-Robinson's, *The Secrets of Effective Direct Mail*. This entertaining and simple-to-understand guide gives an excellent grounding in the most important direct response medium of all, direct mail. It is full of the wit and perception of a man who is in love with a subject he knows inside out.

Having established our media policy and our strategy, giving consideration to each broad media group available to us, the work has little more than begun. We now need to consider the issues of how much money to set aside for distress buying (late dealing) and how much we must commit to banker spaces or inserts, which we know from past experience are likely to be needed as the mainstays of our schedule.

We shall be guided in this decision making by the scarcity of specific media space, which we know to be generally effective. This may depend on how important specified positions are to us. For some reason, certain products perform better in small spaces in good positions (such as front and back page newspaper spaces) than do others.

Positions

Where ads appear in a newspaper or magazine is an emotive subject with most advertisers. Nothing ruins a Sunday morning like seeing your ad in what you believe is a poor position, especially if a competitive ad is apparently better placed. Yet it is important to keep a sense of perspective. The additional price paid by the competitor to guarantee a better position may well have exceeded its incremental value. It is comparatively rare for high-cost premiums for positions to be justified in the response improvement they bring. Booking on a run-of-paper basis enables the buyer to allocate a higher proportion of the budget to distress buying and, in fact, he or she will generally know exactly where the ad will appear at the time of booking. Taking into account distress buying discounts and the fact that a proportion of such ads will appear in good positions in any event, it is hard to justify the uplift in cost incurred by guaranteeing the position.

So what is a good position? Spaces on early pages nearly always outpull spaces on later pages in either a magazine or a newspaper. The few exceptions to this general rule are connected with relevant or strong appeal features in particular publications. For example, holiday ads positioned alongside competitive ads in holiday features are likely to out-perform holiday ads positioned earlier in the same newspaper. Front and back page positions more often justify the uplift in advertising rate than any other special position. A common exception to this is outside back positions in magazines.

Reading and noting studies often show that there is little or no difference between left- and right-hand pages. However, response experience points to the opposite conclusion. Right-hand page positions usually outpull left-hand page positions. Most often, direct response ads are designed for right-hand page positions with the reply device at bottom right. This may help to bias results in favour of right-hand pages. An ad designed for a right-hand page will have the reply coupon in a 'gutter' position if it appears on a left-hand page. A gutter position is the inside edge of the page. This makes the coupon appear difficult to cut out. However, the fact is that bottom right is the natural place for a designer to place a coupon. It is the culmination of the ad and we have learned to read from left to right and top to bottom.

For ads that are smaller than a whole page, a gutter position will be outpulled by an outside edge position, other things being equal. Readers' letters pages, horoscope pages and TV programmes pages attract high readership and ads appearing on such pages will almost always perform better than ads appearing on other inside pages.

These generalisations are useful but it requires a more intimate knowledge of each publication on a media schedule to weigh up the value of specific positions. Some publishers are more helpful than others in revealing their own research findings. One magazine that is forthcoming is *Radio Times*. A study undertaken for *Radio Times* by Gallup revealed that, while there was comparatively little difference between the page traffic on late feature pages compared with early feature pages, the late features attracted a much higher proportion of women readers. Naturally, spreads featuring TV programme details attracted higher readership than editorial features: 17 per cent of readers looked only at the programme details; 80 per cent read at least one editorial feature.

Research of this sort helps us to draw inferences that can be applied to other similar publications. With a little common sense it is often possible to deduce which pages are likely to attract high readership and who is most likely to read them. Nevertheless, an ad can do well on a low traffic page if it is surrounded by relevant editorial.

Negotiation

A knowledge of the value of alternative positions assists the buyer's preparation for negotiating space. He or she should also understand that ads appearing on Monday or Tuesday will generally outpull ads appearing later in the week. Wednesday is average. Thursday and Friday are poor and, with certain exceptions (for example, *Financial Times*), Saturday tends to be disastrous. This knowledge, as it applies to a specific advertiser, will be encapsulated in previous response history. This history is essential if the buyer is to negotiate with 100 per cent efficiency and we shall be covering what must be contained within it shortly.

For now, we shall assume the buyer has all the backdata needed to begin negotiating. This process always starts from the same premise—the sales representative wants more for the space than the buyer is prepared to pay for it. Furthermore, each may have a different notion of what constitutes a bargain because the seller's point of reference is full rate. To the buyer a bargain is a rate which, if his response forecast is correct, will make for his client a high contribution to profit.

To achieve this may only require a 30 per cent discount in one publication but a 60 per cent discount in another. It is generally possible to get this message through to a salesperson eventually. By this time the sale representative is promoted or changes jobs and the buyer must start all over again. Let us, therefore, assume that the sales representative is ignorant of the economics of direct response. This is the advice of an experienced and successful direct response media professional, Ian Prager of CIA Direct:

1. *Assemble the facts.* Know the response figures and targets before you begin any negotiation. Be prepared to discuss these on an index basis so that you do not have to disclose confidential data. Where no hard response data exist, use cost rankings based on TGI or NRS.
2. *Be economical with the truth.* Never lie. A buyer who is caught out because he has not told the truth has destroyed the basis of trust between his agency and the ad sales department. This basis of trust is crucial. However, it is a mistake to show all your cards at once.
3. *Involve the representative.* Tell him enough of the marketing strategy to make him feel he is on the team. If he feels that, through his efforts, the client has been successful, he will think of your client first when he has distress space to sell.
4. *Be sparing with aggression.* Assertive buying is crucial, but save anger for when it is truly justified. Irritable buyers don't get offers. Neither do they get help when they really need it.
5. *Listen for 'selling signals'.* These may include dropping the rate slightly, or a direct sales close such as : 'Shall I option a right-hand page or the outside edge position?' You have just won a concession because the sales representative thinks he is on the brink of a sale. Go for another concession.
6. *Remember the bottom line.* The difference between paying full rate and a discount rate is the difference between profit and loss to many, probably most, direct response advertisers. The client depends on your efforts to stay in business. It is not a responsibility to accept lightly.

Those tips are borne of successful experience. They need no elaboration. Years ago, when I was handling a portfolio of direct response clients at a major international agency, the media department did not heed this advice. To retain one client's business I found it necessary to set up my own direct dialogue with national newspaper ad departments. For another client, I took over the annual volume discount dealing. These moves did little to improve my relations with the media department but no one was prepared to make an issue of it. After some months, one sales representative told me I was getting their lowest rates. I had no way of knowing whether this was true but was suitably flattered.

I asked why this was so. I was hoping to hear about my business acumen and shrewd negotiating ability. No such luck. 'We can be sure you will be in when the others are in the pub,' she said. The fact is that the biggest discounts are available when time to sell the space is running out. To buy well, you must be available and in a position to make an immediate decision. You can acquire a reputation for these attributes very quickly as long as your work habits permit and are known always to have copy ready to run. You will also need a response code (key number) system that is foolproof, so that you can quote the correct response code over the phone. The clients who buy best are those who agree target buying prices and expenditures with their agencies and let them get on with it. Second best are clients who are equally disciplined about working late and make instant decisions. All other clients pay too much for their advertising.

The level of trust between client, agency and media owner can rise to an extraordinary level. Once, when I could not be contacted, a national newspaper made the decision to run a full page for one of my clients. They telephoned me in the morning to ask me what, if anything, I would be prepared to pay for it. I settled for a 75 per cent discount. If I had paid nothing, the offers might not have dried up but, then again, they might have.

Since that time the principle of standby discounts, allowing publishers to drop in a client's ad when they have space free, has become more established. The problem is that it makes control of response flow more difficult but, of course, the benefit is a considerable cash saving.

Leaving a high proportion of a budget unspent until the last moment can be nerve wracking, especially if the advertising is seasonal. It is a war of nerves in which the buyer does not reveal his desperate need for space and the seller does not reveal the number of unsold pages his ad director has just drawn, with considerable force, to his attention. The usual alternative is simply to pay too much.

A more sensible alternative is to negotiate annual expenditure contracts. However, these reduce flexibility, particularly if restricted to one publication rather than a group of publications that are under common ownership. Annual expenditure contracts diminish freedom to react quickly to unexpected trends and can easily become a millstone. What may seem a good deal can easily turn out to be not such a good idea. Such contracts are to be avoided by all except clients who have a need to generate high volume response on a virtually year round basis. It is generally more appropriate to undertake forward commitments only for space which is crucial to success and hard to obtain at short notice. This must be supplemented by doing battle with competitors to out-negotiate them in short-term dealing.

To enter this fray it is essential to know what must be achieved in response and sales, and to know the maximum permissible expenditure to chalk up the achievement.

Response analysis

Media expenditure occupies a massive part of most marketing budgets and it is vital that a thorough and precise evaluation of media performance is made on a continuous basis. The data produced by such an evaluation is a necessary prerequisite for forecasting the return from future expenditure.

Some clients and agencies have set up response analysis programmes that are capable of showing a great deal more than simply what happened. Thus they are able to compare, over a chosen period, full pages with half pages, inserts with colour pages, magazines with newspapers, and so on.

To illustrate what data are captured in order to do this, it is best to take an agency system because it has to cope with the needs of a variety of clients. One such system is CIA Direct's CARCIA system. An inventory of what the CARCIA system can contain is given in Table 9.1.

This system covers the needs of most clients, although one or two clients like to record the weather. This has some effect on newspaper advertising response but, of course, is not necessarily the same throughout a newspaper's circulation area.

From this information, which can be produced for any given period, it is possible to analyse the raw data to find out, for example:

- What copy to run in which titles?
- What are the trends in response—by medium, media group, period, offer, size, or copy?
- Which days of week work best in newspapers?
- How do front page positions compare with inside pages?

- How do competitive ads in the same medium affect the results?
- What is the most efficient space size by media group?
- How much did media, copy, offer and size tests cost in loss of efficiency?
- What is the margin between best, average and worst offer in cost per sale?

Clearly, the list of questions that can be asked is almost endless. The information, because it is organised to be easily accessible, is invaluable for forecasting. The forecast will include a required achievement and a budget. It may be driven by the achievement or it may be driven by the budget. To put it another way, the brief may require the planner to generate 50 000 sales at the lowest possible cost or it may require the planner to generate the maximum possible sales revenue from an expenditure not exceeding £500 000. More rarely, it may require the planner to generate the maximum possible sales at a cost per sale of no more than £10 per sale from the least efficient ad.

The starting point for such a forecast is to plan an 'ideal' schedule, assuming that what happened before will happen again. In effect, this means cutting out the bad bits from last season's plan. What is left will be insufficient to meet the sales target. Therefore, the planner must now look at what can be added to the best performing media before results are killed off by diminishing returns. To calculate this the planner will again use historical data to look at the effects of

Table 9.1   The CARCIA system

- Product	- Copy
- Medium	- Ad position
- Circulation	- Response by post
- Date	- Response by telephone
- Key number	- Response by other means
- Conversion stage	- Total response
- Rate card cost	- Response % of circulation
- Actual rate	- Cost per response
- Discount	- Total sales
- Production cost	- Cost per sale
- Fulfilment cost	- Conversion %
- Total advertising cost	- Sales value
- Space size	- Performance target
- Last year's response	- Performance index
- Last year's position	- Incentive index
- Response forecasts	- Competitive activity

increasing size or frequency. The odds are that the additions that are made will be insufficient to meet the target. Now it is necessary to look at new media opportunities, and look again at poorly performing media, to see if any can be 'rescued' by buying at a deeper discount.

Having covered all this, there is still juggling to be done. It is necessary to look at the forecast achievement for individual ads to see if we may have been misled by the back data. Did our last ad in this publication suffer because it appeared just before a Bank Holiday? Could we improve the results if we shuffled the dates around so that more of our biggest pulling media appeared in the best response weeks?

Even now, the whole forecast schedule is based on target buying prices. More work needs to be done to decide on what must be booked well in advance (because of its scarcity and value to us) and what must be left until the last moment because it will not give a pay back unless we get a 40 per cent discount.

The computer program is an invaluable aid to the planner but there is no substitute for the planner's experience, common sense and imagination in the actual planning process. It is always possible to get a freak result. The ability to be sceptical about such results and knock 30 per cent off the forecast comes from experience.

A computer cannot do this because it accepts all correctly input figures as equally valid.

Earlier in this book I referred to generally experienced effects of increasing size above the optimum, or running insertions at a level in excess of optimum frequency. However, to apply such generalisations it is necessary to know both the optimum size and the optimum frequency. To know these things it is necessary to have a working response analysis system, because the optimum size or frequency for one advertiser will not be the same as for another.

The response analysis system enables the planner to substitute specific data for generalisations, being careful to ensure that there are sufficient back data to act as a reliable indicator. To be statistically significant to an acceptable degree (which may be defined as anything between a probability of 70 and 95 per cent—there is no such thing as a statistical certainty), the numbers of responses or sales from past ads have to be sufficient. Less obviously, the number of instances of a variable occurring have to be sufficient. This means if we have tested a half page against a full page we cannot be confident that the same result would be repeated unless the sales generated were quite high. For example, if the full page pulled 20 sales and the half page pulled 15 sales this does not mean that half pages pull 75 per cent of the volume of full pages. If the full page pulled 200 sales and the half page 150 sales, we could be confident that a half page pulls more than 50 per cent of the volume of a full page. The likely range, if repeated, may be somewhere between 120 and 180 sales for the half page and somewhere between 170 and 230 sales for the full page. However, if this finding is the result of one test in one magazine it is still unsafe to assume that it will apply generally. Unless we have at least two or three instances of a half page pulling about 75 per cent of the volume of a full page, we cannot be too confident that the result will be repeated. Many mistakes are made in direct response planning because a planner or marketing manager has gone too quickly from the particular to the general. The same principle applies, though with less force, to split-run copy or offer tests. Do not make optimistic assumptions on the result of a one-off test, however big the numbers it produces may be. With media tests—such as space size, colour or position—what is true of one publication may not necessarily be true of another. Factors such as time spent reading the publication, its effective life and the number of ads contained within it, are all influences that are difficult to quantify or make good rational judgements about.

Planning a schedule for loose inserts is, in theory at least, much easier. Most publications with circulations of 50 000 or more will accept part runs. It is therefore possible to build a schedule through trial and error at fairly low risk. However, forecasting roll-out returns from a test experience is still not straightforward. Tests are invariably regional tests. No publisher can be expected to slow down his print schedule in order to have your piece manually inserted in, say, every tenth copy. Even if the publisher agreed to such a proposition there would be no guarantee that it would be carried out accurately.

The only way a part run can take place is to restrict it to an area or restrict it to subscription copies (as opposed to news-stand copies). Either way the result will be biased and your roll-out forecast must reflect the probable bias. If in doubt, reduce it by at least 20 per cent.

Furthermore, insert schedules are plagued by production problems. There is no way of being absolutely certain that all the inserts you booked were correctly placed on a one-per-copy basis. Every now and again you will know from the result that something went wrong and it is in just such a circumstance that the mutual trust you have established will come into play. The only way to arrive at a sensible figure for compensation is by agreement as to what is fair and reasonable.

Before signing off this chapter I should, perhaps, make a more philosophical point about the qualities of a good media planner. We have established that the planner must be numerate, inquisitive, imaginative and hard to ruffle. Beyond this it has been my experience that the very best media people, whether engaged in direct response work or not, seem to have an insatiable curiosity about both marketing and advertising. Their interest extends far beyond their immediate role and they are, as a result, equipped to produce unexpected solutions to media problems. These solutions are based on a logic that is superior to the logic of someone who is obsessed with his or her own specialisation and is content to let everyone else get on with the other bits.

Years ago, when Mike Yershon was media director of McCann Erickson, it was said he spent as much time on the third floor with the creatives as he did in his own department. Whether this was true or not, the creative people believed it. What he was doing, of course, was establishing the use that would be made of media so that media decisions could be made in their correct context. At the same time he broke down departmental barriers and established the mutual respect and admiration on which the best teamwork is built. When he left the agency the creative people were among the saddest to see him go.

It is equally important to understand what the marketing director is attempting to achieve and what factors are decisive in determining whether the marketing effort will succeed or fail. The numeracy and logical abilities of media people stand them in good stead to build up a rapport with anyone who has bottom line profit responsibility. Some agencies are inclined to hide their media people away from clients, believing that the client will be bored by their interest in detail. I sometimes wonder if the growth of media independents may have been fuelled by this. Certainly, I believe it is essential for marketing people to be generous with the time it takes to satisfy the media planner's curiosity.

The pay-off

The key to successful media planning and buying for direct response is to have response and sales data on tap so that they can be served up, without effort, to produce an analysis across any dimension. This dimension may be:

1. Magazines versus newspapers
2. Sundays versus dailies
3. Monthlies versus weeklies
4. Professional press versus national press
5. Day-of-week
6. Special feature versus other positions
7. Guaranteed positions versus run-of-paper
8. Half pages versus full pages
9. Colour pages versus mono pages
10. Inserts versus colour pages
11. Tip-ons versus loose inserts
12. July versus August
13. Reply incentive versus purchase incentive
14. Short copy versus long copy
15. Telephone response versus coupon response
16. Freepost versus paid postage

The analysis across any of these dimensions must be capable of comparing the effect of decisions on cost of response, conversion rate and cost-of-sale.

For two-step advertising it will save laborious and unnecessary work if all the costs are built in: advertising production cost, incentive cost and fulfilment cost. Saving labour in this way not only saves time costs but, even more importantly, ensures that analysis work which might otherwise be neglected is actually produced.

This sort of analysis is essential if forecast results are to be soundly based. In forecasting, common sense must be applied where previous results data are insufficient or may have been biased by some outside circumstance. It is vitally important to check that figures look as if they are in character. It is worth re-checking anything that looks odd. It may simply be an input error into the computer.

The sharpest distinction between direct response work and other advertising is that it is possible to isolate each specific area of strength and weakness. It is imperative to have this information to prepare oneself for negotiation. The media person who knows, plus or minus a few per cent, what a space is likely to be worth is in a much stronger negotiating position than one who does not.

After that, it is largely a matter of establishing a trusting dialogue between advertiser, media department, creative people, client service people and the media themselves. Departmental attitudes and territorial claims have no role to play in this. For the client, it is necessary to decide whether to employ a full service agency with a great deal of specialised expertise but with liaison problems to match, or to short-circuit the process and either buy direct or use a media independent. There is no general rule as to which may be the right decision. Factors such as expenditure level and sophistication of a business affect this.

What is essential is to gear up to ensure that sound decisions can be made instantly without going through a long chain of command. Media do not make short-term offers to people who cannot give them immediate decisions.

10 'Non-media' media

The successful response advertiser is nothing if not open minded. Aside from a willingness to invest good money in credit card magazine advertising and special interest publication space, the response advertiser is alive to opportunities that will be beyond the pale to the conventional advertiser or media planner. If inserts in credit card statement envelopes pull better then advertising in the credit card magazine (which they do), why not use them? If a good way of targeting prospects is to enclose a leaflet with another company's mail order despatch, why not test to see if it works? If mailing to people who entertain or buy wine direct is more efficient than advertising in the glossies, then why waste money on insufficiently targeted advertising?

The key advantages enjoyed by response advertisers are, firstly, that they are not concerned with building up a good frequency distribution of advertising impacts and, secondly, they can test at low cost to see if an idea works. They are less interested in where their advertising appears than in how well it works. They are not prejudiced in favour of any particular medium because their decisions are rational, not emotional. True, the decision to test or not to test may not be entirely rational. But the decision to continue to use a tested vehicle for advertising is entirely related to the projected cost—benefit equation. It is necessary for anyone who joins the marketing department of a direct marketing company, or who transfers to direct response media planning, to clear out a lumber room of preconceptions and prejudices and start to think clearly and opportunistically. Since the evidence in favour of doing this is readily available, the process is usually brief, though not entirely painless.

A problem that can face the new direct response advertiser may be a lack of unbiased advice. Unfortunately, while media departments and media independents abound and list brokers and, even, insert brokers are to be found relatively easily, there are few people who really understand both 'media' media and 'non-media' media. Direct marketing agencies are often the best bet in this situation, provided that they have sufficient real business through the spectrum of media and non-media opportunities. Media independents with a large stake in direct response will generally have a fair knowledge of inserts, but not of mailing lists.

The experienced response advertiser is less concerned with having all services under one roof and will tend to pick whoever is perceived as being best in their own specialisation. In these circumstances there is still some tendency towards perpetuation of particular budget splits and a slowness to react to switches in effectiveness between space, inserts and mailing. For reasons mentioned in Chapter 9, it is important to keep a stake in all media groups, using 'media' in its broadest sense, but it is also important to juggle the investments to obtain the optimum result.

In this chapter we shall examine 'non-media' opportunities and we shall now stop referring to them in this way. Any vehicle that can carry an advertising or promotional message is a medium, whether it is conventionally considered as such or not.

Direct mail

We are not concerned with customer mailings or mailings to identified prospects on a company's own file or database. We are here concerned with direct mail only as a potential advertising medium in competition for a budget with press advertising, broadcast media, door-to-door distribution, or package inserts.

Since the unit cost of reaching anyone by direct mail is relatively high, it is axiomatic that the targeting has to be more precise than that which is acceptable in lower cost media. If a magazine insert costs four times as much as a colour page, then a delivered mailing package will cost about six to eight times as much as the insert. Putting it another way, 24 to 32 times as much as a colour page. Clearly, the package has not only to be well targeted but must also be very powerful to overcome such a cost penalty. In many cases, this is almost impossible. In a sizeable minority of cases it is not only possible, but also likely.

Now that I am getting older and more crotchety I find it profoundly irritating when self-styled 'experts' drone on about a mythical 2 per cent response from mailings, invariably following this unjustifiable generalisation with an expression of concern for the effect the mailing had on the remaining 98 per cent. Where do they get this figure from? If 2 per cent is the limit of what they have achieved, or even their general expectation, why do they not spend more time learning their craft and less time pontificating?

The highest response I have experienced from a 'cold' mailing (i.e. one not aimed at established customers, lapsed customers, or identified prospects) is 41 per cent. The mailing consisted of a two-page letter, containing a cunning offer, a reply card and an outer envelope. It was to head teachers offering a trial subscription to a magazine normally read by people in local authority education departments. It was a piece of inspired targeting by my client.

The highest response I have received from a mass consumer cold mailing is 22 per cent. But I have also received a response rate of just over one per thousand—and the mailing was profitable. There is no sensible generalisation one can make about mailing response. It all depends on who is in the target market and what you want them to do. The only sensible criteria for evaluating whether the activity is successful are profitability in absolute terms and profitability relative to other ways of spending the money. The key factor is how well you can define the market in direct mail terms. This question is not always straightforward to answer. For example, in business-to-business activity, mailing may seem a most attractive alternative to specialist or up-market general media. The first step, in exploring this thought, is to discover how many, and which, companies are in the market. Sometimes, the answer is only a few thousand, or maybe less than a thousand. Sometimes it is possible to identify, with a fair degree of accuracy, which companies they are.

It should also be possible to overlay existing customer companies and delete them from the mailing file. This still leaves one major question: 'Can we identify the key decision makers and decision influencers?'

This is often the most difficult part. An industrial product may have specifiers and users. It may be bought by a purchasing officer. Its acquisition may involve a board level approval. All of these people may be in a position to stop our product being purchased, even though some of them will not be in a position to advocate its purchase. In a large company, they are probably not all in the head office building. They may even be hundreds of miles apart. By now our target 1000 companies may have expanded into a target of 10 000 individuals in 3000 locations. Identifying these people and locating where they are will require us to undertake telephone research at a cost of, perhaps, £5 per successful contact. We may be well advised to undertake this research but you can readily appreciate that building and maintaining an up-to-date contact list, which is the prerequisite of a successful mailing programme, is neither cheap nor simple. The money spent on file building has to be committed in advance of knowing how successful the programme will be.

Business-to-business lists

Many business-to-business mailings are less selective than this and will generally go out to rented lists. These may be directory based, giving size of company, standard industrial classification, and names of directors. Such lists are good for securing complete coverage (theoretically) of a specific business target market. The difficulty is that they tell you little or nothing about the decision makers in a company and will generally give you head office addresses only.

Usually, 'live' lists of people with known job titles pull better. A 'live' list is a list of people known to have responded to some other offer. They may be subscribers to a requested copy controlled circulation journal, subscribers to a service, or members of a professional association. If they read a controlled circulation magazine, why mail them instead of advertising? The answer is that you can generally select only those you want—for example, you may only want certain job titles. Instead of making a vertical selection between a number of magazines, you can make a horizontal selection between alternative status levels, or departmental responsibilities.

Many business-to-business magazines are specific to an industry. You may wish to reach design engineers irrespective of industry. And, of course, you may need to secure a higher response rate from your target market than you could achieve from space advertising or, even, inserts.

You can also use mailing for list building. Recently, I had to find the directors who were most interested in management development in the top UK public companies. They have all sorts of titles. Some have no title other than 'director'. In some cases, the chief executive is the prime mover on management development issues. A letter to the unnamed PA of the named chief executive produced a 24 per cent response, giving me the names I needed. The list was, of course, superbly accurate because I had explained exactly who I wanted in plain English. I know it was accurate because 11 per cent of the people on the list accepted an invitation to attend a director level seminar and agreed to pay the fee—a further 20 per cent pleaded another commitment and asked to be invited to a second seminar, and a further 22 per cent were kind enough to reply, refusing our invitation. In all, 53 per cent.

The number of 'yes' replies alone was equivalent to 2.6 per cent of the original list of companies. Had I attempted to guess whom to send the invitation to, I would have got it hopelessly wrong and would have failed to achieve anything like the same response rate. Business-to-business mailing is very interesting. I keep promising myself I shall learn about it one day.

Consumer lists

I am more at home with consumer mailing where the issues are simpler. There are several ways one could classify consumer lists but these four classifications will suffice:

1. Lists which there is a statutory duty to publish. These are the electoral roll and shareholder lists.
2. Other official or semi-official lists, usually contained within a directory, e.g. *Who's Who*.
3. Lifestyle 'databases'.
4. Lists which are a by-product of someone else's business.

All of these four, with the possible exception of the second, are important but they may be so for different purposes.

The electoral roll

Our first category is dominated by the electoral roll in the UK. This has assumed enormous importance for two reasons. The first reason comes about because of its value for credit checking and the subsequent development of credit scoring systems. The pioneers of credit scoring technique were Fair Isaacs in the United States. Their technique was quickly adapted and developed in the UK by the major credit mail order companies. Eventually, those companies made available their editions of the electoral roll and their credit scoring and processing expertise to other users, such as banks, building societies, credit card companies, retail stores and, even, competing mail order companies.

Mail order and credit card companies gain much from using the electoral roll as a single data source for direct mail rather than renting miscellaneous lists. The advantage is that it is possible, at the crudest level, to exclude names who have county court judgements against them, names of previously known bad debtors and names of existing or lapsed customers. At its most sophisticated level, it is possible to pre-score names for creditworthiness, mailing only those that are above the threshold. More than that, it is possible, by overlaying response and customer data, to attach response scores or sales scores to candidate names for mailing. This is done by discovering the recognisable characteristics of 'good' names and replicating these characteristics among 'unknown' names. Those that match 'good' characteristics best are mailed. This technique can work even if there is no serious credit risk. *Reader's Digest* have, over many years, proved its validity for subscription mailing and mail order book sales.

The second reason for the enormously increased importance of the electoral roll has been the introduction of geo-demographic targeting systems such as Acorn, Mosaic, Pinpoint and Super Profiles. Mail order operators, notably Littlewoods and the Reader's Digest, overlaid census data onto the electoral roll long before Acorn was invented. They used census data to discriminate (at ward level) between one area and another, employing the regression analysis technique. But Acorn and successive systems, constructed using the cluster analysis technique, made selectivity available to every direct mail user. Now it was possible to profile customers and replicate this profile among 'suspects' on the electoral roll.

This changed the electoral roll from a huge, largely unstructured, list into a file offering a number of interesting selection possibilities. It clearly offers massive advantages to branch-based businesses such as building societies or multiple store groups.

Businesses such as these require to achieve a high penetration of, often quite small, catchment areas. Other list sources are useless to them and even local media may be wasteful.

Geo-demographic information for local marketing, even for shop siting, extends far beyond direct mail in its usefulness. But the fact that direct mail employs the same data as those used for measuring branch performance gives it an advantage. It is possible to apply direct mail very accurately to correct weaknesses in penetration or to play to the strengths of the business.

Geo-demographic targeting systems are no longer based purely on census data. In the case of Mosaic, only 49 per cent of the weighting in the clustering is attributable to census data. The remaining 51 per cent depends on financial data, demographic data derived directly from the electoral roll and housing data.

One disadvantage of census data is that, in Britain, there is only one full census every ten years. Before the 1981 census, a large new town—Milton Keynes—was simply a black hole in the 1971 census. Reducing reliance on census data is therefore a welcome step. A further problem is that the data are only available by enumeration districts or wards. Enumeration districts, which represent populations of about 150 households on average, do not match up perfectly with post codes. This causes location difficulties.

Some demographic and housing characteristics from the electoral role, which are naturally available for individual households, recur so frequently that they can be used to describe individual post codes (roughly 14 households). Thus a system such as Mosaic is not tied to enumeration districts. There may be several Mosaic neighbourhood types within one enumeration district, particularly in large cities. And since electoral roll data change each year, as do financial data, there is a possibility of redistributing Mosaic neighbourhood types several times between each census, although it is not done every year.

The electoral roll is capable of being enhanced almost on a continuous basis. It is simply a question of whether bureaux find further investments in doing so pay off. This depends on all the uses that can be made of the data, not simply on direct mail. A relatively recent step is to add lifestyle and other data, specifically in relation to financial attitudes and activity. The collection of lifestyle data depends on individual questionnaire responses and does not, therefore, describe a market universe. But, cluster analysis-constructed geo-demographic databases are based on the proposition that birds of a feather flock together. It may therefore be assumed that this will also apply to aspects of their behaviour which are not described by the census. On this basis, it may be assumed that a financially active person is more likely to have financially active neighbours than a non-financially active person. With enough data, one can see that the penetration of known financially active people is much higher in one post code sector than another. It is, then, reasonable to deduce that there will be, in total, more financially active people in the first post code sector than the second. This is borne out by the experience of early direct mail uses of the electoral roll. When there was little else to go on except information about where your customers were, you mailed their neighbours, or you mailed streets with high customer penetration. It worked. Even mailing to addresses that were formerly occupied by customers worked. The same sort of people live in the same sort of houses, broadly speaking.

One of the great values of the electoral roll (or a good edition of it) is that it tells us about the composition of a household and how long the household has been there. With the gradual breakdown of the nuclear family, it has become increasingly important to know this. Mailing results show that single occupants (roughly 25 per cent of all households) do not react in the same way to a given mailing as family occupants.

Pseudo families (adults of different sexes and surnames) also react differently. The most responsive people are new occupants. They respond better to most offers. New voters (18 year olds) may be a strong target market for some products. They are a prime target for banks. How else could banks reach this group so efficiently?

Shareholder and directory lists

The other source of lists, which there is a statutory duty to publish, is Companies House. Shareholder registers are, of course, a target for investment products. More interestingly, it is possible to merge:purge shareholder lists from different companies and discover who the multiple shareholders are. In this way it is possible to discover people of very high potential net worth. Whether such activity becomes a target for 'an unfair processing' challenge under the Data Protection Act remains to be seen at present.

Directory lists are also available subject to copyright. Some directory publishers may make their lists available on magnetic tape or disk. Directory based lists of professionals are most interesting as the year of qualification is usually known. In this way it has been possible to build files of heavily demanded target groups, such as over-55s, based on year of qualification. This is a feature of direct mail to which I made reference earlier in the brief discussion of business-to-business mailing. In direct mail it is possible to make horizontal selections. Thus, segments of lists of doctors, dentists, vets, lawyers and accountants become one list of professionals aged over 55. It is impossible to replicate this type of selection through other media.

Lifestyle databases

Like most ideas that are new in direct marketing, the idea for lifestyle databases originated from the USA. In the USA there has been somewhat less emphasis on geo-demographic databases because less people qualified to vote can be found on voters' rolls. On the other hand, because zip codes have been around longer than post codes, the Americans long ago learned to run regression analysis against zips to take the most responsive segments of rented lists. Since there is an abundance of lists available for rental and many of them are very large, this clearly made great sense. Lists are not just tested and discarded or rolled out in the USA. Even if list A outpulls list B, there will be segments of list B which are better than segments of list A. Zip-code analysis is a good way of finding these segments. This enables the mailer to make a geometric leap in progress between test and roll out. Almost no list that is tested performs so poorly that it contains no usable zips; while even the best list's performance can be enhanced by discarding the least productive zips. Progress in this direction in the UK has been hampered by incompletely post-coded lists, the small size of many lists and, most importantly, by the fact that list rental is a seller's market not, as in the USA, a buyer's market. There are fewer lists than mailers willing to use them. This enables list owners to dictate terms.

An abundance of lists there may be in the USA, but lifestyle databases have still found a ready market. They offer a number of advantages. For a start, they can be built up to a very large size. Then again, used correctly, they may be more descriptive of a potential prospect or buyer than any other source of information.

Such databases are built from questionnaire responses to lengthy questionnaires completed by respondents and posted to the research company in exchange for some benefit, such as participation in a prize draw, or money-off coupons redeemable in foodstores. Questionnaires may be distributed in a variety of ways. They may accompany guarantee cards in packages containing consumer durables, such as electrical appliances. On the other hand they may be distributed as door-to-door leaflets or be inserted in magazines.

A well-organised database from such sources, such as the NDL database, will offer sophisticated selection possibilities and these are what makes it work. Suppose the user is an environmental charity. The charity might get an acceptable result by mailing all charity donors on the file. But, if the charity mails only charity donors who also (in answer to a separate question) revealed that they are interested in environmental issues, the response rate will be much higher. It may even be desirable to refine selection still further by taking only those with high incomes, only those with a credit card, or only those who are older. There is almost no end to the selection possibilities but, the more refined the selection, the smaller the resulting list will be. Each additional selection factor also increases the cost-per-thousand names slightly. Because selections may be of very small percentages of the file, it is clearly important that the overall number of responders is very large. At the time of writing, the growth of these databases shows little sign of running out of steam. However, there is clearly a finite limit to the number of people willing to fill in the lengthy questionnaires and to allow their names to be passed on to direct mail users. A critical point will be reached when the effect of duplicated coverage of potential respondents will slow down the response rate and may decrease the proportion of respondents allowing their personal data to be used. In the meantime, the growth of these databases gives the direct marketer a welcome addition to his armoury.

Rented lists

Lifestyle database names are responders' names. They are therefore more likely to respond to mailings than people, say, from the electoral roll, who are not known to have responded to anything. What is true of lifestyle database names is equally true of names on buyers' and enquirers' lists which are available for rental.

Perhaps, more so. Because, instead of responding to a questionnaire, they have demonstrated their susceptibility to promotion by responding to an ad or a mailing. It is not uncommon for lists of enquirers to outpull lists of buyers, though they may not convert so well. Enquirers may be enquirers because they like responding to offers. Buyers may only be interested in the product they bought and may not be generally interested in anything that comes through the mail. What rented lists of buyers or enquirers do is to describe one piece of behaviour and tell you (roughly) how recently it occurred. This may not seem much to go on and, indeed, there may be other descriptive details as well. Yet behavioural data are so very much more important than demographic or socio-economic data, one piece of behavioural information can outweigh everything else in its significance. A good many years ago I was doing some work for a small chain of up-market shoe shops, called Elliotts. Adrian Elliott had a customer file that was years ahead of its time. One selection factor was age. 'How do you know their ages?' I asked, naively. 'From the shoes they buy, of course,' said Adrian. 'I don't care if they are 15 or 50. If they buy teenage shoes, they are teenagers to me. That is how they want to appear.' The obvious sense of this is inescapable. People buy things that match their self-image. It makes sense to mail them, offering other things that will enhance that image. The fact that their self-image may be divorced from reality is of no concern to us. In fact, it is none of our business.

The art of taking one piece of behaviour and making accurate inferences from it is not vouchsafed to everyone. 'Art' probably describes it. If it is related to any science, that science must be psychology. I first heard the word 'psychographic' in 1969, at least ten years before it entered the general language of marketing. I heard it from a young man who was explaining to me how he went about picking mailing lists. At that time there was a specialist mail order company called Leisure Arts. One of its products was a classical record club. Another was vitamin pills. The record club was the best source of buyers of the vitamin pills. When I asked why, he told me it was obvious. 'Who do you think wants someone else to choose their records for them?' he asked. 'Why, the under-confident, of course,' I said, the light dawning. 'The same people who would believe they needed vitamin pills.' From that moment I decided direct mail was for me and within two years I was in the list broking business. I have been in it, part time, ever since. A list broker looks at lists at least as much from a psychographic point of view as anything else. List selection depends on making connections that are not obvious superficially. Not many people are good at it. However, that is not the main problem. The main problem in the UK is a paucity of good lists. At the time of writing, interpretation of the relevant part of the Data Protection Act 1984 has yet to be clarified by a test case and this is scarcely an encouragement to list owners to put their lists on the market.

Affinity group mailings

One solution may well be to make greater use of affinity group mailings where, in exchange for sales commission, or rental, the list owner makes available the mailer's product to his list. The mailing goes out with a covering letter by the list owner and is paid for by the user. We have already discussed affinity groups and it will suffice to say here that affinity group mailings, which answer the question 'Where did they get my name from?' comfortably outpull mailings that arrive without the list owner's identification. There are, however, two problems with substituting such mailings for conventionally rented list mailings. The first is that they require negotiation. It would be difficult to negotiate an affinity group deal for a test mailing of, say, only 5000 names. The second is that the list owner may be willing to rent names to a respectable user but may not be willing to endorse his product.

An affinity group mailing implies an endorsement even if it does not directly volunteer one. There are also certain legal complications posed by the Financial Services Act in undertaking affinity group mailings for investment products.

Testing lists and offers

Consumer mailing for any one user often involves using lists from more than one of the sources we have discussed. In general terms, geo-demographic or other selections from the electoral roll are distinct from the other sources. It is rare for any selection from the electoral roll (save new voters or new occupants) to match other lists for pulling power. However, the advantage of a single market universe data source is so overwhelming for some companies, there is little point in using anything else except as a way of enhancing electoral roll selections

Selection of other lists is primarily through short-listing and testing. For a large potential user, some list owners are willing to pass across tapes of small samples of their list in advance of testing. This enables the potential user to make some mathematical evaluations of the file. For example, he may wish to credit score or response score the names and addresses. More commonly, a duplication analysis can be made. A list that contains a high proportion of current customers for the advertiser's product will almost certainly pull well. It demonstrates a strong affinity between the user's customers and the list owner's customers. It also indicates that, once the list owner's list is 'netted down', by merge:purging (de-duplicating) it against the user's list, the final mailing quantity will be much lower than the total number of names available.

Most list owners will agree to a 'net names' rental charge, subject to a guaranteed minimum. When a number of rented lists are used they will also have to be 'netted down' against each other. This is done simultaneously so that no list is unfairly treated by being placed last in line for netting down.

Most often test quantities of each promising candidate are rented on a one-time-use basis. Direct mail is a tester's paradise because tests are highly controllable. It is possible to test lists, copy and offer simultaneously without running each copy and offer permutation against every list. For this purpose a test matrix is devised, allowing the maximum possible number of tests to be made from the minimum possible mailing quantity. The test quantities will depend on the expected response level and the expected difference in response between, say, offer A and offer B. Alternatively, the quantity chosen may reflect the necessary response increase required for the more expensive offer B to be justified. Whatever the basis, it is the level of response that determines statistical significance, not the mailing quantity. In order to minimise mailing quantity, therefore risk, the matrix will most often be devised so that all the offer tests are carried out against only one or two lists. Copy tests may be carried out against more, if they are expected to produce a small response differential.

Thus it may be possible to carry out a list test on a quantity of only 5000, an offer test on 10 000, but a copy test on 15 000. Our matrix may take the form shown in Table 10.1.

In this test, we have given a 5000 quantity test to each of three lists. We have given a 10 000 quantity test to a new offer. We have given a 15 000 quantity test to new copy. The only quantities we have used over and above what we require for statistical analysis are to the control list (15 000) and the control offer (20 000). Some people find it worrying that not every test is conducted against each list but, in reality, this does not matter. If we want to know how well test list 3 would have pulled using 'control copy', we simply need to multiply the actual result by the differential between 'test copy' and 'control copy'.

A slight complication is that the results require weighting. It is insufficient to, say, merely add up the response from

Table 10.1 Test matrix

List	Control copy		Test copy	Total
	Control offer	Test offer	Control offer	
Control	5 000	5 000	5 000	15 000
Test 1	—	2 500	2 500	5 000
Test 2	—	2 500	2 500	5 000
Test 3	—	—	5 000	5 000
Total	5 000	10 000	15 000	30 000

'test copy' and compare it with 'control copy' even though the mailing quantities are the same. The fact is that the 'test copy' result may have been dragged down by a poor performance from list test 3, which was not used for 'control copy'. Then again, 'control copy' was split between two offers and this may have affected its performance.

Nevertheless, the simple calculations we shall now need to make (or get our PC to make) are a small price to pay for the number of tests we have managed to conduct within 30 000 mailings. Had we insisted on 5000 tests of each variable within each other variable we would have needed a mailing quantity of 80 000. And, whereas with our test matrix, we were risking only half the mailing on untried lists and a third of it on untried copy, three-quarters of our 80 000 mailings would be pure tests. The formula for calculating the mailing sample required to produce a result in which we can have 95 per cent confidence is:

$$\text{Sample} = \frac{3.8416 \times R(100-R)}{E^2}$$

R stands for response rate (that is, the anticipated response rate in percentage terms) and E stands for error (that is the margin of error that is tolerable). For example, we may expect 5 per cent response but our breakeven may depend on achieving 4 per cent response. In this case we must be sure a 5 per cent response from a test will not be worse than 4 per cent when we come to roll out. Of course, we cannot be absolutely sure. There is no such thing as a statistical certainty. Using this formula, we shall be right 19 times out of 20. That is where the 3.8416 comes in. If we adjust this number we adjust the odds against achieving the same result (plus or minus tolerable error) on roll out. In most business-to-business mailing activity we shall need to work on a much lower degree of confidence because it is not practicable to mount such large tests. On the other hand, the risks involved are usually lower.

A more comprehensive description of testing for direct mail and the formulae for determining sample size and significance can be found in our companion volume, *The Secrets of Effective Direct Mail*, by John Fraser-Robinson, the editor of this series.

Offers and copy

Solus direct mail is, of course, suited to two-step response programmes for those advertisers who can target potential buyers accurately enough to justify the relatively high cost per contact involved. However, because of the lack of restriction imposed by space and format, mailings really come into their own in one-step programmes. What other medium gives you absolutely no restriction on space or number of pieces, beyond that imposed by postage weight price breaks? You can put together a very impressive multi-piece mailing within the minimum postal rate band in the UK and you can even mail out a small catalogue without increasing your postal cost.

Because it is possible to make a mailing more involving than an ad, it is possible to convey a great deal of information and, less obviously, to request a great deal of information. Furthermore, it is the only medium in which you can personalise the offer. That is one reason why prize draws are popular in mailings. The facility to give each recipient not just one, but a whole series of unique numbers, increases the impact, involvement and sense of optimism required to get a high entry level. The personal nature of the medium enables flattery to be employed very successfully. However, mailing does not invest purchase of a product with the same approval of a peer group as does public advertising. Advertising which says distinguished people buy product X is seen by millions and reassures the buyer that his purchase is likely to win the approval of peers. He is able to make a statement about himself through acquisition of the advertised product.

Bus mailings

Co-operative or bus mailing opportunities are promoted by a number of companies. These may go to the promoter's own customer list—for example, Christmas offers to a credit card list—but, more often, go to other specified target groups, such as investors or business equipment buyers. Often the format will be severely circumscribed, the most popular being a standard postcard size. Each advertiser pays a charge, comparable to any other insert charge, to ride with anything from 12 to 50 other advertisers. Surprisingly enough, in view of the total lack of editorial content, these mailings often work quite well.

There is something to be said for the 'sore thumb' media buying approach to these opportunities. Consumer offers may pull quite well when almost entirely surrounded by business-to-business propositions. Because of format restrictions, co-operative mailings are best suited to two-step advertisers.

Telemarketing

I am filled with enthusiasm for inbound telemarketing, but it is a way of handling response, not a medium. Inbound telemarketing is an alternative to postal response handling—often a better alternative. However, we are here concerned only with outbound telemarketing. Furthermore, we are not concerned with outbound telemarketing to established customers, but only to the marketplace at large.

The first question that must concern us is the intrusive nature of the medium. This is both its strength and its weakness. People often complain of direct mail as intrusive, as an invasion of their privacy. This is not really the case. It is possible to discard a direct mail package unopened, just as it is possible to ignore a TV commercial, zap it, or walk out of the room. The one is no more intrusive than the other. The reason why direct mail is accused of invading privacy is purely because it is personalised.

The logic in favour of protecting people from receiving direct mail advertising is little stronger than the logic in favour of protecting them from receiving television advertising. The only difference is that they chose to buy a TV set and watch commercial channels. They did not, in theory, choose to receive direct mail though, as we are aware, those who respond to direct mail receive many more mailings than those who do not.

Telemarketing is quite different in substance from direct mail or TV. If the telephone rings, you answer it. Thus telemarketing is intrusive and can breach privacy. For this reason, its use in consumer marketing is not something I would advocate. Yet, its value in business-to-business marketing is undeniable, particularly when it is used in conjunction with direct mail. It offers exactly the same testing opportunities as direct mail and, because it generally produces a higher response rate, tests can be more confined.

It also has two magic ingredients which direct mail lacks. The first is that a test can be mounted without the high origination costs and long lead time associated with other media, but particularly with direct mail. The second is that it can be used to find out *why* people are responding positively or responding negatively. A script can often be modified with advantage from this information while the test is still going on. It is therefore possible to achieve a degree of precision in framing a contact list, the offer and the copy which is well nigh impossible to match with any other medium. This, alone, can justify the high cost per contact involved.

However, because the telephone is not, as yet, a visual medium and will never be a tactile medium (textures and involvement devices are an important feature of direct mail and inserts), it may often be best used for non-visual subjects, or used in conjunction with mailings. For a full discussion of telemarketing, the reader cannot do better than turn to another excellent book in this series, *The Telephone Book*, by Robert Leiderman, who has made an enormous contribution to the rapid development of telemarketing in the UK.

Bill and statement enclosures

The bits of paper that drop out when you open your credit card statement envelope, are statement enclosures or stuffers. Years ago we had to sweat blood to get any of the banks to accept them, long after American Express statement envelopes were positively bulging with goodies. There is a double benefit to the bank in accepting credit card statement enclosures. Firstly, they can charge a stiff inserting charge because their lists pull well. Secondly, offers which are paid for by consumers with their credit card, stimulate account activity and give the banks a margin on the sales value. They really can't lose, providing the customer's tolerance of the enclosures is not pushed beyond the limit.

The double benefit also applies to the user, because the means to pay for the offer are available through the card and this acts as an implied endorsement of the offer. Statement enclosures pull exceptionally well for many offers. We touched on this important medium in our last chapter, but it deserves a little more elaboration here.

The most effective use of this vehicle is when the offer is well targeted and is exclusive. It is not difficult to tailor affinity group deals to a particular cardholder list. Doing this also helps to get your insert accepted. There is more demand for such enclosures than there is availability.

One might think that the bad news represented by a statement is a discouragement to further purchases. This is simply not the case as advertisers in credit card magazines know full well. A well-targeted offer can outpull a magazine insert by two or three times. Possibly, the recipient finds the advertising content of the statement a welcome relief from the editorial content of the statement itself.

The same principle applies to other bill stuffers, such as water rates demands. However, because the double benefit no longer applies and because it is harder to get the targeting just right, they tend to pull less well than credit and statement enclosures. Increasingly, we may see statement lists netted down because modern technology permits selective statement runs, using bar-coded statements. Thus bank customers or credit cardholders who do not wish to receive advertising material can be excluded. This will diminish audiences without necessarily reducing response proportionately.

The reverse of the same coin may be the offer of high spending selections of the file. I shall believe that banks will offer this when I see it happen.

Package inserts

Package inserts, also touched upon in our last chapter, are not the same thing as statement enclosures. These are items inserted within product packages. There is no reason, in theory, why these product packages need be mail order despatches rather than goods sold in stores. However, they nearly always are mail order despatches. One problem with inserting in shop distributed merchandise is the possible conflict with items sold by retail stockists. Another is that mail order buyers are better responders than shop buyers. A third is that it is sometimes more difficult to enclose items within a retail package and certainly more difficult to control the timing.

Film-processing envelopes are a common vehicle for package inserts, partly because margins on film processing are narrow, making any incremental income relatively attractive. Unfortunately, mail order film processing is a declining market segment.

Package insert opportunities also exist to target mail order book buyers, continuity card series collectors (e.g. cookery cards) and mail order durable goods buyers. Often, swops are negotiated, as also occurs with mailing lists.

These opportunities have not shown the same growth as statement enclosures, partly because mail order has not grown at the same rate as credit card ownership, and partly because package inserts are less attractive to many advertisers. It is mainly solus mailing users of rented lists who are able to target effectively on the basis of a known piece of purchase behaviour. Other advertisers are not familiar with the art of targeting in this way.

Yet the response rates from package inserts are generally higher than those yielded by magazine inserts. Some of this advantage, for two-step advertisers, may be lost through a generally poorer conversion rate.

Take-ones

'Take-one' dispensers in retail establishments, such as restaurants, shops and post offices, are a familiar sight to most people. These house inserts, often for credit cards, are usually placed by a representative of the company whose 'take-one' box is accepted. A commission is paid to the restaurant or shop when a sale results. This is classic 'PI' (per inquiry) advertising.

In the case of the Post Office, the procedure has been different and inserts have been sold in conjunction with QTV, when commercials for the same products have been shown to the assembled ranks of senior citizens and office juniors patiently awaiting service. There is a captive audience and it has worked for a number of advertisers.

There are, however, two major snags with take-ones. The first is that they require maintenance. An untended take-one box empties or disappears. They are best used by advertisers with sales staff calling on the outlets in which they are exhibited.

The second snag is that the cumulative audience may build up very quickly and then there may be a great deal of repeat exposure. This is not good news for the direct response advertiser. Diminishing returns can be expected to set in quickly except, perhaps, in restaurants or hotels with a high proportion of casual trade.

Not surprisingly, travel and entertainment card companies are the most successful users. The context is right and they have the means to keep the boxes clean and topped up.

Advertorials and PR

Unlike our other 'non-media media', advertorials and PR are really a non-advertising use of media. They represent the ultimate use of affinity group marketing, borrowing the goodwill enjoyed by a magazine or newspaper.

Advertorials are straightforward deals in which a competition is sponsored by an advertiser or the advertiser's product is offered on exclusive terms to the readers. Holidays are often promoted in this way. Advertorial offers comfortably outpull conventionally paid for ads, because they receive editorial treatment and are 'part of the newspaper'.

PR coverage is harder to obtain because it involves making the product or company newsworthy. It is not possible to be newsworthy in a positive sense unless the company is new and different, the product is new and different, or the product has become an overnight sensation. Even when coverage is secured, it is a neat trick if the editor is persuaded to include the name and address of the company. It does happen, however, and media appear to be more willing to avoid frustrating their readers (not to mention the company) than they once were, when they were reluctant to give a plug that readers could act upon. Nevertheless, it is much easier to get editorial for products that fall within a category that receives regular featuring. Examples are clothes, travel and financial products. A five-centimetre single column feature can pull as much as a full page ad. Most often, such featuring comes from direct contact between the company and a journalist. I would not recommend the employment of a PR company just for this purpose. I shall elaborate no further.

Broadcast media

I have touched on this subject in an earlier chapter, in the context of the relatively low frequency required by a direct response advertiser. It is not appropriate to discuss broadcast media at any length because a later book in this series will examine the subject in some depth.

From a media planning viewpoint, TV and radio are most

interesting when an audience segment delivered at a specific time of day (or night) is 'peculiarly appropriate' or when a telephone response is more beneficial than coupon response. An example of a peculiarly appropriate audience segment may be a 'drive time' commercial radio slot aimed at car phone users. One that I have exploited on TV is a children's programme slot for a commercial targeted to young mothers.

An example of the appropriateness of telephone response is the sale of motor insurance or personal loans. The enquirer's need is generally urgent and a quote can be given on the basis of the enquirer's personal details over the telephone. This might save frustrating correspondence and delay. It improves customer service.

Then again, a product may best be demonstrated on TV or on radio. For example, a record album. Or it may be available locally. Radio is a local medium.

The way rate cards are constructed in the UK, an advertiser needs to be able to exploit one or more of the benefits I have mentioned to make an investment in broadcast media pay off. One hopes that additional channels will help to improve the advertiser's situation. The widespread use of credit cards and almost universal ownership of telephones leave the door wide open. The interactive possibilities opened up by modern technology make TV potentially the prime direct response medium.

The pay-off

It behoves the direct response advertiser to be opportunistic in media planning and buying. The best bargains can often be found among those media that other advertisers neglect. This approach to media is best suited to the advertiser who cares little for coverage or frequency and everything for quantifiable results. The across-the-line advertiser, for whom direct response is a by-product of advertising, not its *raison d'être*, should not be tempted to fritter away his budget in niche media unless they are peculiarly apposite.

Many of the 'non-media' media opportunities we have discussed in this chapter can be tested relatively cheaply and vehicles such as package inserts, bus mailings or statement enclosures will never be more than a supplement to a schedule. Solus direct mail is a different proposition, as are broadcast media. Direct mail represents about half of all direct response activity, although that includes customer mailings, and it may sometimes be quick and cheap to test, although more often it is not. Most direct mail work involves considerable origination cost and longer lead times than most media advertising. It offers the powerful advantage of achieving an exceptionally high response penetration of a target market. Response rates may often be 20 to 40 times as high as response from colour pages. However, the cost of covering a market is also much higher.

In making cost-of-coverage comparisons it is important to remember that coverage, of itself, is of no significance. What are important are response and recall. The recall of one mailing may exceed that of a whole press campaign. In this chapter I mentioned Elliotts Shoes. My former partner, Bob Wright, designed a mailing for Elliott in the format of a pack of cards, illustrating each shoe style. Three years after the mailing went out, the mailing was spontaneously recalled by a number of recipients. They referred to it as, 'that pack of cards mailing you sent out a few months ago', and words to that effect. Note, ' . . . a few months ago'.

Clearly, if a mailing achieves 10 per cent response, it will also achieve very high recall. Thus its pure advertising value should not be measured in coverage alone. Nothing, apart from telemarketing, makes such an impact on a target group or causes attrition to set in so fast. The fall off in response from repeat mailings to the same list will be far more rapid than the fall off from ads, or even inserts, repeated at similar intervals. Mailing is like taking a sledgehammer to crack a nut. Space advertising is like taking an icepick to open a coconut. The one is a slower process than the other but, unless the targeting is precise, it is difficult to produce a comparable response cost from mailing. It is often best employed for one-step selling, in which long copy and detail-revealing pictures are particularly advantageous. The media owner, the Post Office, charges the same rate for a large space as for a small space. No other medium offers such flexibility. However, the Post Office does not endorse a product in the way another media owner gives an implied endorsement by accepting an advertisement for it.

A product advertised in an up-market glossy is receiving an endorsement from the magazine. The implication is that the sort of people who buy this magazine buy this sort of product. It is a form of reassurance and gives the product a status which the readers believe will win the approval of their peer group.

The great virtue of response advertising is that we can stop theorising like this and get on with some testing. Generalisations are never as valuable as specific experience.

11 Finding and using a good response agency

What makes a good direct response agency? Marketing know-how? Media buying *par excellence*? Direct marketing technical skill? Analytical skill? Down-to-earth creative people? Strong account handling? Or just the people in it?

I think it is all of these things, yet more besides. When I was commissioned to write a brochure for an agency, I wrote: 'No agency is merely as good as the people who work in it. It is either a little better or it is a little worse. It is a little better when it has a worthy ideal. An ideal which is shared by those who work in it.'

All good agencies are built around a strong central idea. It is contained in their philosophy, their policy, or their mission statement. A good agency has a core belief which sustains its staff when they are under pressure and keeps office politics at bay. If this belief is compatible with the way you see things, the agency will be a good agency for you. If it does not fit with your beliefs then the relationship cannot work. No agency can be all things to all people. Those that try end up as nothing to anyone, and go out of business.

This belief, if it is to work for you as a direct response advertiser, better not prevent the agency from being adaptable, quick to react to results and changed circumstances. It better not cause it to be opinionated. Dogmatic agencies sometimes produce stunning creative work but they are inflexible, slow moving and utterly unsuited to providing for the needs of the response advertiser.

It has been my fortunate experience that client–agency relationships have generally been extraordinarily good in direct response. Neither the client nor the agency can readily be dogmatic when it is so easy to be proved wrong. And so often. The fact that everyone's survival depends on the results helps create a bond between the client and agency teams so that they become almost inseparable. Yet this happy circumstance is not invariably the case. It depends upon commitment by both the senior partner, the client, and the junior partner, the agency. When this mutual commitment is there, the relationship is generally long and fruitful. When it is not, it is brief, acrimonious and unprofitable.

It follows that an agency must be chosen with some care. An employer, contemplating hiring a top manager at a salary of £100 000, with responsibility for a budget of ten times that amount, would receive the most careful vetting. The agency deserves at least equal attention. It must be chosen for its capability, its management, the people who will work on the business and for its philosophy.

The people who will work on the business must be compatible and committed. However, the agency's capability and philosophy are more enduring. People come and go. Will the relationship be based on qualities that will remain valid even if those people have gone?

It is a difficult decision. I am glad that I have never had to make it.

Getting it wrong

At the end of 1976, in collaboration with two partners, I started an agency. From the outset absolutely nothing went according to plan except that we kept on meeting our profit forecasts. In the 11 years I was there it grew from three people to one hundred and three, still producing the same profit per employee. Almost nothing else went the way we meant it to go. This must suggest that survival in business is not as difficult as is often made out. I had lost count of the number of mistakes I had made before we reached the end of the third year.

The agency became one of the largest direct marketing agencies in the UK. It was never intended to be any such thing. The idea was to create an all-purpose agency. One partner was a sales promotion professional who had been a director of three advertising agencies. A second had been creative director of an advertising agency. The third was a direct marketing consultant. That was me. I had also worked in advertising agencies. The sales promotion professional had proved his business acumen and sales ability by starting up and running a profitable sales promotion agency. The creative director was not only an extremely talented designer but knew agency administration inside out. I had an established reputation within my marketing specialisation and could also, *in extremis*, write copy. With such a range of skills between only three people how could we go wrong? The answer was: *all too easily*. Nobody wanted to know about an all-purpose agency, at least not one with only three people in it. We picked up a bit of non-response business, certainly. Our most prestigious job in the first year was to create the first ever tetrapak for a branded fruit juice. Until then, fruit juice came in glass jars. 'Our' fruit juice was called, 'Just Juice' and it became brand leader inside six months. But the business that rolled in and stuck was direct marketing business.

Within a few months my two partners who, otherwise, remain on good terms decided they could not work in the same business together. So we lost our only salesman and our main source of business know-how. Since he was also, in effect, the boss I had to step into his shoes. Eight months after being one of three partners in an all-purpose agency, I was running a direct marketing agency. The only thread of continuity was that we had been determined to be accountable and to grow our business on the back of our client's success from the outset. Since I was a rotten salesman and my remaining partner was worse, the business had to be grown on increasing budgets and recommendations. Fortunately, the recommendations kept on coming and we survived to make many more mistakes.

The purpose of this autobiographical interlude is to establish that I have come to the conclusion that it is possible to start and to develop a successful agency without a strategy. It is probably impossible to do so without a policy. Our policy was to do our utmost to bring success to our clients in anticipation of their rewarding us accordingly. It may seem a pretty lame policy but our clients did not let us down. They rewarded us by spending more with us, by paying us more and by recommending us to others. In my new business credentials presentations I finished with a list of clients. I would invite the prospect to pick any three of, say, 20 clients and to telephone each of them. I guaranteed that they would express complete satisfaction with my agency. Not many called my bluff, but one or two did and our clients did not fail me. I have never known another agency have the nerve to do this before or since.

Having a policy

When we sold our business on a five-year earn-out deal in 1983, I was able to influence the policy or, in American, mission statement of the group of direct marketing agencies that we had joined. It was: To be the best direct marketing agency in the world, to become recognised as the best and to seek the rewards of being the best. I do not believe that all of my overseas colleagues were as determined as I was to make this the truth. We enjoyed a more consistent rate of income and profit growth than any of the others yet, I believe, we were the least concerned with our own profitability and the most concerned with our clients' profitability. By now we had, at the request of our new owners, a development strategy as well. However, this was never of equal value and I departed from it whenever opportunism dictated. Strategies are more relevant to large companies with many small customers than they are to small companies with few large customers. Small 'know-how' businesses must remain flexible enough to adapt quickly to new circumstances. The policy that we adopted worked for us but it is only one of dozens of different, perfectly reasonable possibilities. The point is not our particular choice of policy. The point is that establishing a clear policy makes other decision making easy. The test of a decision is, 'Is it compatible with our policy?' Even if the decision is the wrong one, provided it is compatible with the policy, it will not seriously damage the business. The policy helped us to keep good clients and talented, productive staff. It helped to create a good working environment, relatively free of office politics, in which people generally knew how their performance would be judged.

I have never had to choose an agency and seldom, I am glad to say, have I been asked to recommend one. If I were in such a position my experience suggests that it would be a good idea to find out the policy that makes an agency tick. This is not necessarily contained within their statement of philosophy. That statement may have been designed purely for its supposed effect on prospects. It is easy to find out whether a statement of philosophy is real or not simply by asking several different people in the agency what it is. If you get different or fudged answers you will know that the agency's policy, if it exists, has not been communicated to the people who work there. They can, therefore, scarcely be expected to support it.

The only other feature, apart from a clear and sensible policy, that is critical to an agency is sound administration, particularly of finances. A business that pays out only a percentage of what it has got in cannot go bankrupt. It is very simple in principle, but gets harder as a business grows and has to make investments in anticipation of future profit.

From a business viewpoint, the clear-cut nature of any

agency's policy is more important than the choice of policy. From a client's viewpoint, the choice of policy is important. Clearly, no one but a fool would entrust his account to an agency whose policy is to maximise the profit it can make out of the business from day one. However, there are fools who do this, presumably because they are unaware of their agency's policy. A direct response advertiser should be wary of any agency whose stated aim is to create great advertising. Agencies of this sort are run for the benefit of someone's ego, not for the benefit of the client's bottom line. In some circumstances these two desirable objectives will not clash. The advertising really will be great and the bottom line will grow healthily as a consequence. Alas, this is all too seldom the response advertiser's experience. As we have seen, great direct response advertising is seldom of the sort that will carry off awards and win the plaudits of the creatives in the wine bar. An agency in the business of creating great advertising will want to make your advertising conform to their notion of what greatness is. You will realise what a disaster this may be when you ask them to show you some great advertising.

It does not matter whether a policy is attainable. If we had succeeded in becoming the best direct marketing agency in the world we would not have known. The point is that the policy should help to make the agency strive to be better. It should help to generate the right attitudes among the people who work there. In this way an agency can, perhaps, become greater than the sum of the individual abilities it contains. An agency with a worthy aim and sound financial management will generally develop and keep talented staff for longer than one in which these attributes are lacking.

If you, as a potential client or as a potential employee, wish to enjoy a long and fruitful relationship with an agency, it is ordinary prudence to discover what its policy or beliefs are and to decide whether they are compatible with your own. As a potential client you are betting on its learning rate, which will depend on its ability to deliver continuity of service from talented and committed people. If you are thinking of working there you will want to know if it will provide an environment that will stretch you and make you reach new heights of achievement.

Keeping in touch

I maintain that you can find out more about an agency by walking round it, talking to the staff, than you can by asking it to pitch for your business. If the agency is a hive of activity, that is a good sign. If the boss is visible, that is another. In many agencies, the boss is hidden deep within an inner office, protected from intruders by one or more secretaries. It is a sure sign of weak management. Once, I called on Boase Massimi Pollitt to discuss a presentation I was making at the Advertising Association Conference. On reaching reception, I was astonished to see the founder, Martin Boase, working in a glass-walled office in clear view of every visitor. He was doubtless already a multi-millionaire at the time. Had I been a client with a bone to pick, I would have walked in and accosted him. That is a sign of superior management. No wonder he has been so successful.

You can find out as much again by talking to an agency's clients. A hot agency has a buzz to it, which you can feel in the atmosphere of the place. Its clients will go out of their way to support it because they want the agency to be successful. Unfortunately, the more successful it is, the more it will have to change to support its growth. That is what tests the inner strength that its policy provides. Too many agency managements forget what made them successful. They became less involved with their clients and more interested in the business of playing with organisation charts, money and acquisitions. It is the kiss of death unless they have a solid succession strategy. Many agencies complain of the fickleness of their clients. Yet, in my experience, unless the client has made a grave selection error, clients are lost for one of only two major reasons. One is a change of client management. The other is that the agency has changed so that it is no longer the agency the client 'bought' at the last review.

I have worked at two agencies which became, briefly, the largest in the UK then went rapidly downhill. Along with many other people, I left at the right time.

In each case, the fall was triggered by the current management discounting the value of what caused the agency's climb to the top. Instead of playing to their strengths they devoted all their energies to correcting weaknesses that had not prevented the agency's rise. This preoccupation upset the clients and encouraged people who had contributed to the agency's success to market their talents elsewhere. In effect, management had lost confidence in the agency's policy. An agency cannot be all things to all of its clients. It must set its stall out to ensure it is best at something. I was lucky to learn this lesson less painfully in my own agency. The agency was perceived as being best at direct marketing by its clients and it was useless to fight this perception. It was more sensible to try to make the perception a reality. Accordingly, when my sales promotion partner left he was, after a brief interval, replaced with a new partner who was a skilful and experienced direct marketer.

A specialist or general agency?

I have dwelt on philosophy for so long because of its fundamental importance. Good direct response advertising is not the prerogative of direct marketing agencies. Indeed, good direct response advertising long pre-dated any direct marketing agency. Yet many general agencies appear incapable of creating effective direct response work and their brief forays into this area have proved costly to their unfortunate clients. The explanation for this is not a lack of talent or intelligence. It is an excess of arrogance. They start from the presumption that direct response advertising is poorly designed and written, that it lacks imagination, because no one as talented as they have tackled it before. They will teach their client and the direct marketing world how it should be done. They have forgotten how they learned the advertising business. They have discarded the habit of learning through acute observation and drawing inferences from other people's work. It is a terrible thing to say, but it is nearly always fatal to give direct response work to a creatively dominated agency. It appears to work only when the creative director takes a personal interest in it. Some of the best direct response campaigns ever have come from big-name creative people, including David Abbott and Tony Brignull. Realistically, the chances of securing the personal interest of a top writer/designer team are low in most 'creative' agencies. It is better to go to an agency where the person responsible for developing your business has some real clout internally.

As a client, you should bear in mind what the priorities are in securing success. Much will depend on whether your advertising's prime task is to produce response or whether response is a second feature. If the former, you can be sure that media planning and buying, over the longer term, will make a bigger contribution than creativity.

You can be sure that the offers that you make will be more important than the words that describe them.

What you will require from your agency, above all, is the ability to analyse information and draw correct inferences from it. Unless the people on your account have this ability, all the serious thinking will depend on you and your colleagues. In this case all you will need is a strong media department, a competent production department and an efficient account handler. You should expect to save money because of your limited use of the agency's resources. Many mature direct marketing accounts are run like this. The disadvantage is that there is no external pressure to innovate. Without it, you will need an extraordinary internal creative resource (in the broad sense) if the business is not to stagnate and, eventually, decline. You should think carefully about isolating yourself from a source of good ideas in order to save 5 or 6 per cent on your advertising. It is sometimes the right decision, but most often it is not. If your company is inexperienced in direct response, it is not even a serious option. You will need a marketing orientated direct marketing agency.

Listing your priorities

Taking stock of what you will need, you may attempt a list of priorities such as:

1. *Commitment.* The personal interest in your business of someone, probably an account director, who is obviously respected and influential in the agency.
2. *Compatibility.* An interest in concrete results rather more than abstract advertising values. Curiosity about your business and what makes it work.
3. *Teamwork.* A group of people who seem to enjoy working together, who have not built departmental barriers.
4. *Analytical strength.* An ability to handle results and other information, drawing fast, accurate conclusions from it.
5. *Media skills.* The ability to plan from back data and the enthusiasm to negotiate well.
6. *Vision.* An ability to be creative over the whole range of your activity—offers, media ideas, terms of business, new products and, of course, ads. More particularly, the ability to create from the basis of results evidence and observation of the market place.
7. *Range of skills.* Knowledge and experience of all the media you use. These may include direct mail.

8. *Production capability*. The ability to turn out work quickly and accurately at reasonable cost without sacrificing quality.
9. *Management*. The ability to run an agency tightly, with good employee relations, sound financial management, strong administration and real interest in clients' business.
10. *Adaptability*. A willingness to learn new tricks.

Assembling your priorities enables you to see the kind of agency you require. It may be that no one agency, willing to accept your account, will score strongly on all of these features. In this case, you may still prefer to use an agency that demonstrates commitment, compatibility, teamwork and analytical ability, even if it is weak in the media area. You will then need a good media independent.

This situation often occurs because on the whole, it is best not to be an agency's largest or smallest account, but to be closer in size to the largest than to the smallest. Being the largest account tends to provoke a touch of servility, which gets in the way of clear communications. The ideal is to be important, in a business sense, to the agency but not so important that the loss of your business would deliver a crippling blow to it.

If direct mail is an important ingredient in your marketing mix you are unlikely to find your ideal agency outside a list of direct marketing agencies. In this case, you will need to dismiss from your initial list those direct marketing agencies with insufficient media advertising experience. If your account is big enough, you may split the work between two or more agencies. However, you should be careful to ensure that the business is important to each and that there will be some synergy between your advertising and your direct marketing activity.

More often than not, effective direct response advertising is the work of direct marketing agencies. However, this is not always the case, and other factors may be important to you. If your business is based near Manchester, you may not want a London agency. It will be less expensive and will foster day-to-day communications if you select an agency near you. Most of the larger provincial agencies are relatively adaptable because they are less typecast than London agencies. Between them they generate quite a high proportion of the more effective direct response work. Your short-list may then include both general and direct marketing agencies.

Assuming your list of priorities is similar to the one above, you can find out how well an agency measures up by a combination of desk research, seeing agencies that are possibles, and talking to their clients. You may also wish to supplement your desk research by visiting the Advertising Agency Register, approaching the British Direct Marketing Association and talking to media owners. If you invite agencies to pitch, you are creating an entirely artificial situation in which their performance may have little bearing on the service they will subsequently deliver. I confess to ambivalent feelings on the matter. As an agency head, I loved competitive pitches. They created an opportunity to stimulate excitement, generate camaraderie and test our cunning and our intellectual ability in a kind of management game.

How pitches are won

Pitches are enormous fun when you win and they help bring staff closer together. They are, however, almost invariably all but decided on the basis of the relationship you have established with the client beforehand. The secrets of a high success ratio in pitches are:

1. To discover if the issue is already decided in someone else's favour and the pitches are cosmetic. This is often the case. In the circumstances you naturally withdraw.
2. To involve at least one key person in the client's organisation with your solution before the event and to do everything you can to establish the right personal chemistry.
3. To make an inventory of the skills you need at the outset, appoint the pitch team immediately and keep them on a strict timetable.
4. To ensure you are the last to pitch. The questions will tell you what others presented (more or less) and you can destroy their solutions in your answers.
5. To keep your team late the night before, not to finish off the work, but to rehearse until they are word perfect and to convince them you are going to win.
6. To recognise that the document comes last. It will never win the business and, only very rarely, lose it.
7. To discover who your potential enemy is on the client side, disarm him with flattery and make him agree with you on an undeniable matter of fact.

8. To recognise the person everyone else defers to and direct the main thrust of the presentation to him.
9. To finish the presentation on a big idea.
10. To follow it immediately by requesting the business.

From this description, you will see how artificial is the business of winning pitches. I have worked in an agency where we went through a streak of being unable to lose. I have worked in another where we could scarcely win. The difference was the confidence transmitted by the successful team. The presentations, in content, were often nowhere near as good. But they were presented with a style which only people who expect to win can muster. They had little or no bearing on how we would handle the business.

Agencies are sometimes chosen on little more than a whim. In one pitch, my agency was one of three that refused to enter. The client was left with two. One of these was the sole survivor of the four short-listed by the marketing department, being the only one willing to pitch. The other had been nominated by a group director. It was already decided that they would win. Unfortunately, he could not attend the presentation and another director took his place. The two agencies presented and each was congratulated by the substitute director and sent on their way. 'Who recommended the first agency?' asked the director. 'They were our recommendation in the marketing department,' said the marketing manager. 'And the second one? 'They were recommended by (director's name)? 'Really,' said the substitute director. 'What does he know about advertising? Let's appoint the first one.' There was not one word of discussion about either presentation.

This type of story has given pitches a bad name. They deserve it. Yet I have been the beneficiary of similarly casual appointments. One client told me he had decided on my agency because I looked less like an advertising man than anyone he had met. He reasoned I must be good to survive. Besides, he couldn't stand advertising people. Another client stopped me three-quarters of the way through a presentation. 'We've heard enough, haven't we?' he said to his two colleagues. They nodded. 'You've got the account,' he said. There was still one other agency to pitch. Worse, they were allowed to do so without any chance of getting the business.

The value of pitches

From the prospective client's point of view, pitches have three values:

1. They test how well an agency team works under pressure.
2. They test how efficiently an agency gathers supplementary information and give some indication of how the personal chemistry will work out.
3. They enable the buck to be passed to the boss, so that he makes or endorses the decision.

In my view, only the last of these three values is decisive. It is the real reason for most pitches. Some clients are alleged to use pitches cynically to gather ideas at little or no cost. If so, they will be disappointed. When my agency won, it was almost always offered the losers' pitch documents. They were valueless, being based on even greater ignorance of the client's business than we had demonstrated.

The artificiality of the whole procedure is further underlined by the trade press announcements of pitch victories. The client is, nine times out of ten, quoted as saying that the winning agency 'showed the best understanding of our business'. What this means is that a rapport was struck before the pitch and the agency was able to involve the client in its solution. It had fathomed out, through personal contact, how the client thought about the issues raised in the brief and delivered the solution the client wanted, with the addition of a smart creative twist.

It is, of course, perfectly possible to see if a rapport can be established without going through the exciting nonsense of a competitive pitch. It is also possible to find out how an agency performs under pressure and what its teamwork is like, simply by talking to its clients. However, this would remove a lot of the fun from the business.

Split-run testing

Direct marketing clients sometimes prefer to test prospective agencies by split-running their mailing packages against one another. This has the advantage of producing a decision based on results, so that the manager making the decision cannot be blamed for making the wrong one. It is a ludicrous way to select an agency since it measures nothing other than a creative team's ability to have a good first shot at a problem they have not met before. I say this in no spirit of embitteredness. My agency did extremely well out of such testing, our success ratio being even higher than it was from pitches. Furthermore, the client paid for the mailing package.

There are only two grounds on which such testing is justifiable:

1. The agency is being selected purely as a creative resource in the narrowest sense.
2. There is a second test after each agency has had time to assimilate the results of the first test and any research that has been done on the reactions of recipients.

Running a two-stage test measures the learning rate of an agency based on its ability to make inferences from known facts and research data. In one case, in which my agency was involved, there was very little difference on the first test but we were more than 100 per cent better second time around. The principle can be applied to direct response media advertising and especially to inserts.

However, it is critical to ensure that the test is properly controlled (e.g. the inserts are delivered interleaved on an A/B basis) and that it is of sufficient size to be reliable. It is an even poorer guide to effectiveness in media advertising because the agency has no control over size or insert format and none over media buying. It tests only what is usually the least important variable.

In my early experience of direct response advertising I worked on a mail order account that was divided between the agency I worked for and a competitive agency. During the second campaign, two of our ads were split-run against two of theirs. We won both tests. At the end of the campaign my new boss went to see the client, a man of military bearing, awe-inspiring presence and ferocious temper. It was the first time they had met. Not liking what he took to be my new chief's self-importance and pomposity, the client said we were fired. My new boss, somewhat shaken, requested an opportunity to present our case and raced back to London to start me working on it. The client listened politely when I presented the case, which included the split-run test results. When I had finished he told me what a good job he thought I had done and how much he had come to respect my intelligence. This was for the benefit of my boss who, he correctly deduced, was thinking of firing me for losing the business. The client concluded with the words, 'You sail away with all your flags flying. But sail away you must.' I have never been fired with such exquisite style before or since. At the time, I thought this was rather unfair. I soon discovered that the client, on the strength of their losing the split-run tests, had obtained a spectacular deal from the other agency to handle the entire account at a guaranteed production cost amounting to only 1.5 per cent of billing. He had taken two known pieces of information and acted on them in preference to being guided by split-run tests of, admittedly, somewhat dubious statistical significance. The known facts were that he could not get on with my new boss and that the other agency would rather run the account at a loss than lose it altogether. He had spent most of his life in mail order and his faith in isolated split-run test results reflected his experience. So much for split-runs as a method of deciding between agencies.

However you decide on the appointment of an agency, it is important to ensure that the expectations of each party to the relationship are realistic. The level of service, terms of business and remuneration of the agency are all matters which, in the UK, are often not discussed at all until after a competitive pitch. This has always struck me as extraordinarily unbusinesslike. It is as if it were somehow improper to talk about money.

Managing the relationship

If you have picked the right agency and each party's expectations of the relationship are realistic, you are all set for a mutually profitable relationship. However, business relationships require good management. Right up until the day you have to let them go, your aim should be to make certain you get the best the agency can deliver.

The one surefire way to do this is to ensure you are the agency's favourite client. This does not involve letting them take you to lunch or dinner or being undemanding and compliant. Far from it. Favourite clients are nearly always extremely demanding and keep stretching the agency staff to the limit of their abilities. They challenge a great deal of what the agency says, but also listen attentively to well-reasoned arguments. They are exacting, quality conscious, they demand efficiency and, above all, commitment. They have, in the agency's eyes, one saving grace. They recognise good work, even to the extent of singling out the individuals responsible for it and ensuring that they, and their boss, are aware of how much their efforts are appreciated. A letter of thanks costs a few pence and can be worth thousands of pounds in extra commitment and enthusiasm.

Some agencies like to talk of partnerships with clients, but it must be made clear who is the senior partner. The buck stops with the client and the client must remain in control. He can stimulate the junior partner to greater efforts through encouragement, even defer to the junior partner in areas of specialist expertise, but he must remain the boss.

My cleverest clients always sold themselves to the agency in the same way the agency sold itself to them. The object was to secure £1500 worth of service for every £1000 spent on it. The ploy always worked. The first step is to get the catalyst in the account group on the client's side and work outwards from there, getting to know more people in the agency as time goes on. Time spent with people who do the actual work on the business is usually better spent than time spent with the agency head. The agency head is probably in the relationship for the money. The staff are in it for the satisfaction and the kudos. It is cheaper to give them what they want than it is to give the boss what he wants. It is also far more beneficial.

Much of the success of the agency depends on the efficiency of media buyers and production staff. They seldom receive any appreciation from clients. Any opportunity to single them out and pat them on the back is well taken. You will probably be the only client who has bothered to do so in years. The adrenalin of shared success is a powerful stimulant. It is vitally important to people to believe their efforts are valuable. They are much happier working on a client's business that is going from strength to strength than one that is in the doldrums. But do they know you are successful? And do they know you think their efforts have helped?

If you have a good account handler that person will have done his or her best to communicate your success and your appreciation to other members of staff. But it is my experience that this should not be assumed. In any event, a phone call or letter from you carries far more weight.

When things start to go wrong it is usually through garbled communications. Most of the time you must rely on an account handler to pass on briefings accurately and to answer the questions that arise on the basis of some knowledge of your business. This is not always easy and, unless you have devoted a good deal of time and effort to educating this person, it is next to impossible.

Signs that communications are not right can be picked up quite quickly from contact reports. Have all decisions been recorded? Have views been stated accurately? And did you receive the contact report promptly? To circumvent problems of mis-communication the marketing staff of many clients write their own creative briefs. This is often for reasons of informing other concerned individuals in their own organisations. However, there is no reason why—time permitting—the account group should not write the brief and submit it for your approval. They will learn the business faster if they have to do this.

In a good agency, briefs are signed-off by a board director or account group director. Contact reports are read—at least on a sample basis—by the chief executive. The good chief executive queries items in contact reports to keep the staff thinking that he reads them all. In this way he controls their speed and accuracy as best he can in the time available.

Next to the account group the people you need to spend most time with are not the creative people but the media people, and anyone who is doing response analysis work. The creative people need to be seen every now and again. Enough to keep them informed and enthusiastic, but not so much that your agency is racking up cost charges for unproductive time. The media people have to form a trusting relationship with you in which they can make decisions on your behalf, following buying price criteria which you have agreed. Your relationship with the media people will be on a day-to-day basis and you will need to be able to short-circuit the account group.

It is always a good idea to keep one eye on the clock. One sign of weak account management is too many agency people at meetings. Another is too much time spent at lunch. Each person-hour could be costing £50–£100. An alcoholic lunch can render six people useless for an afternoon. In a few months, a director of the agency will be round with the begging bowl if over-populated meetings are allowed to drag on.

The social side

Relationships are cemented sometimes by social occasions and never more so than by the celebration of a mutual triumph. However, they do tend to be somewhat overdone with no perceptible benefit. When I ran an agency I had many clients that I never invited to lunch, dinner, or even breakfast. My parsimony in this respect was well known and jocular references to it among my clients were not uncommon. Yet, although I scarcely ever socialised with my clients, I formed genuine friendships with them through mutual trust and willingness for us each to help one another when help was needed. My lack of sociability was caused by my enthusiasm for work and my clients understood this. Those of my staff who spent most heavily on entertaining were those whose client relationships I had to watch most carefully. It takes more than convivial lunches to form a solid business relationship—especially when the cost of the lunch and the time spent drinking are both recharged to the client.

In remarking on my carefulness with the petty cash, one of my clients wisely remarked that he detested being taken to lunch by agencies. 'When I am the host,' he said, 'I am in control.'

It is a good idea to have regular meetings at your own offices and at the agency's office alternately. It is important for agency people's understanding and involvement with your business that they should come to see you. It is also important to meet more of the agency's staff than can practicably be ferried to your offices and be expected to sit through a long meeting, when only part of it concerns them. Meetings at the agency are a good way of seeing these people and keeping a finger on the pulse of the place.

If you set about managing the relationship in this way, you will generally get value for money. The problems of the inevitable comings and goings of agency staff will be alleviated to a large extent by the spread of your influence through the agency. The more people who are involved and who are committed to your success, the more quickly the relationship will come back on course after the loss of a key member of the team.

How to complain effectively

Selling the idea of working on your business does not entail putting up with anything less than superb service. You have a right to expect the best the agency is capable of and your demand for the best will give those concerned better job satisfaction. If you have occasion to complain you should do so promptly and clearly so that a festering sore does not develop. There is nothing an agency management hates more than a client who puts up with some poor aspect of service for months and then sacks the agency. Complaints are usually best made at director level. It is not always easy, but it is good relationship management to tell the person you are complaining about that you are going to do so and to explain why. However, nothing this person says in mitigation should deflect you from making the complaint.

You may find that you are not getting as much of someone's time as you were promised. Perhaps it is the person who most impressed you at the presentation, and as that person has also impressed other prospects since, his or her time may now be over-committed. In this case, the agency management is to blame. It is their problem and they must resolve it to your satisfaction.

Stamina

On the whole, most people in the agency will continue to become more effective or more efficient on your business for several years. If they do not do so, it is a sign that they are not enthused by it. This is either your fault or theirs. Most often it will be yours. It may not be your fault at a personal level. It may be that your company is excessively bureaucratic, slow moving, or committee-ridden. If this is the case, perhaps you should consider your own future. If the bureaucracy is getting to a bunch of part-timers, what is it doing to you? The people who will benefit least from a long spell on your business are the creative people. They do tend to get tired on an account, especially a large account, after a period of time. There is no rule as to how long this will be and much will depend on the success of their work and your appreciation of its value. The agency should begin to see the warning signs before you do. The account group can readily detect a lack of enthusiasm for new briefs and should report this, asking for a change. However, their request will not always be granted and you may have to raise it yourself.

I hope the foregoing comments, based on the experience of such relationships from an agency viewpoint, will make it clear to you that I do not believe that a client who is promiscuous in agency relationships gets good work. Such a client is unwilling to offer loyalty and so gets none in return. Every agency has some talented people in it and no agency is peopled solely by talented people. The trick is to make your account so popular it is seen as a privilege to work on it. That way you will always get good people. When there is an exception, it is best to complain quickly and have a change made. Only in the last resort should you change agencies because it will cause a damaging break in continuity and will waste a great deal of valuable management time.

Managing the money

There are a number of ways of remunerating an agency, both direct and indirect, through commissions. There are also a number of ways in which an agency spends a client's money. All expenditures need careful monitoring and there are certain things you need to know if you are to appoint an agency. It is a good idea to look at the last available report and accounts of any agency you are contemplating employing. For a start, you need to be sure it is in good financial shape. If it is on the borderline it will be delaying supplier payments and the cost of extended credit is likely to find its way onto your production charges. It will also be interested in extracting every penny it can from you. At the other extreme, it may be unduly profitable. In this case the profit will generally be obscured by large bonus payments and excessive remuneration of certain directors. A reasonable level of profit for a direct marketing agency will not be more than 20 per cent of its income in fees or commissions. Most general agencies operate at a somewhat lower level of profit. In some case direct marketing margins may be higher when, for example, a direct marketing agency group provides other services such as bureau, telemarking, or lettershop services. Nevertheless, you should not expect your agency to seek a margin better than 20 per cent on response advertising.

Agencies measure profitability of individual accounts by means of time-sheets. The majority of staff complete these and they are collected on a weekly basis. A minority of staff, mainly administration people, do not complete time-sheets. Their cost is apportioned across all clients in proportion to the income that each client provides, or in proportion to the time-sheet cost that each client generates.

Time-sheeting is notoriously inaccurate. Many members of staff do not fill in their time on a daily basis but rely on memory to complete their time-sheet at the end of the week. It is almost impossible to remember how the time was spent if they do this. Others are late with their time-sheets. Under-employed members of staff fill in the time they should have spent working and allocate it to some unfortunate client. On the other hand, clients get a free ride with busy people because they work more hours, sometimes many more hours, than a standard working week. This has the effect of making their chargeable hours cheaper.

It is always better to have good people on your account—not only are they more effective, they also cost less because they tend to be very fully employed. Most agencies cost time on time-sheets as a multiple of the individual employee's salary. This is the fairest and least inaccurate method. However, some have flat rates for particular categories of employees. The relevance of all this is that, however the agency is remunerated, it will gauge whether it is making a profit or loss on your business from the aggregate of time-sheet information. If it is making less than its required margin, you may expect to be asked to pay more at the next review. The theory is that inaccuracies balance out over a number of employees and over a prolonged period and, in any event, time-sheet costs are the best guide available to what handling the business is costing the agency.

There is no reason why an agency should not be open with their clients about time costs and most will willingly provide analyses on a monthly or quarterly basis on request. If this goes down to individual employee level, as it should, the client can readily see who is spending how much time on the business. Sometimes, mis-codings occur and a person's time is allocated to the wrong client. Usually, this will be picked up by the account director, but it is more likely to be picked up if the agency knows it has to send you time cost analyses.

Fee payments

It is, on the whole, better for both parties if the agency is remunerated on a fee basis rather than depending on the lottery of commissions, which bear little relationship to time spent. For the agency, it gives an assurance of profit, providing it has its forecasts right and keeps its house in order. For the client, it is easier to control fee payments than commission costs.

On the whole, I am not in favour of open-ended time cost agreements. They are justified when the workload is unpredictable but this is seldom the case. An agency should be capable of forecasting its required fee income for the period of a six- or 12-month agreement. In practice, many are not very good at this and the client can expect to hear from the agency if it has underestimated, but not if it has overestimated. This is another good reason for requesting time cost analyses. The possession of this information enables the client to come to a better informed conclusion on the case for increased fees. In some cases, economies can be suggested.

When adjustments are needed these should not be applied retrospectively except by prior agreement. Sometimes work is requested which is clearly additional to that outlined in the agreement. It would be unreasonable and short-sighted to expect the agency to rack up a loss on this.

Misunderstandings about money can be averted by use of

an agreement which sets out the agency's terms of business and appends a description of the work required against the fee. Setting and agreeing fees also requires a clear statement of what is, and what is not, covered. For example, will the agency mark up artwork or production costs, rebating media commission only? It is best to avoid complications like this by agreeing that everything will be charged on a strictly net basis, unless a good case can be made out for protecting the agency against unexpected shifts in expenditure. Even these are best covered by subsequent agreements to compensate the agency for losses incurred through unpredictable changes.

Volume discounts

Most agencies enter agreements with suppliers of finished artwork and other materials which award to them volume discounts. The argument is that volume discounts are not earned by individual clients but by the total business of the agency. In many cases, the cost of work is marked up in order for the volume discount to be applied. It is not a true discount. It is appropriate to ask an agency for details of any such agreements so that you are satisfied that they are genuine volume discounts. There is no absolute certainty that this will be the case, but it is certainly not the case if the agency has not guaranteed any level of expenditure to a supplier over a period.

You might feel more comfortable if no such agreements existed, or if the discounts were passed on to you. However, a fee adjustment would have to be applied because most agencies are very dependent on such agreements to deliver a reasonable margin of profit.

Finished art and production costs are a grey area and there is no perfect way of controlling them. It is important to query charges that seemd quite excessive or are over budget. However, querying every charge is a mistake. It increases the tedium of handling your business and leads to every charge being marked up to allow for the loss occasioned by awarding you a rebate, the loss of cash flow and the time spent on handling your queries. You will get better value if it is enjoyable to work on your business. Agency production charges are high, especially in London, because most work is done overnight at excessive labour cost. Out-of-town artwork make-up and filmsetting cost little more than half of London prices but it generally takes three days for what, in London, is turned round during the night. There is little difference in quality between out-of-town work and London work except where the pick of London studios and typographers are used. Some clients place much of their own production work to avoid these high costs. It is usually a mistake. Production costs may account for 10 per cent of a budget but the difference between good and bad may be much greater than this. It is generally better controlled by quality-conscious art directors in an agency unless production quality is relatively unimportant.

Agency charges are not, on the whole, unreasonable. When I ran an agency the time charges we received for professional work, such as legal advice, were generally at a much higher hourly rate than we would charge, even for the most senior people's times. It is important to control costs but also to recognise that your agency will be more productive if it is making a decent margin on your account.

The value of experience

However experienced an agency may be in response work, it must employ many young people who are not. They bring enthusiasm, energy and, one hopes, ideas to the business. They also think they know more than they do and sometimes make very expensive mistakes. As a clever client you will have got to know as many of the experienced people in the agency as possible, including the heads of the various service departments. Often, a proposal may be put to you that has not been checked for its feasibility with any of these people. It should not happen but it does happen. It is a good idea to ask if the technical implications have been checked thoroughly and to insist that they are. Quite often, account handlers try to re-invent the wheel, even though the person who invented a perfectly round wheel is sitting one floor up or down from them. This happens because they spend all their time working on the business of two or three clients and are largely unaware of what the agency has done for other clients. Service department heads are aware of the work of all clients in so far as it concerns their specialisation. They are very useful people to cultivate, but few clients take the trouble.

As an agency grows, some long-standing clients feel they no longer get the experienced attention they enjoyed when it was smaller. On the other hand, there is now a greater depth of experience overall in the agency and a greater breadth of specialised services. The best way to take advantage of what the agency now has, while continuing to receive a high degree of personal attention, is to stay in touch with the key specialists in the agency and not allow yourself to be confined to contact with the account group. Doing this, you will often find that the agency can provide useful information and services that no one in the account group had drawn to your attention.

Many clients, through their own success, find it necessary to delegate regular contact with the agency to subordinates. It is important to ensure that your subordinates learn how to get the best out of the agency, just as you did. It is also worthwhile to stay in occasional touch with people who are important to your business, not just with the agency's chief executive. Relationships often wither when the responsibility for maintaining them is delegated. Everyone loses when this occurs. Having to make a change of agency can easily wipe out six months, or even a year, of progress.

Keeping them on their toes

Agencies are extremely neurotic organisations. Experience has taught them that clients are often fickle, susceptible to approaches from competitors, and easily swayed by the prospect of pastures new. Many clients exploit this neurosis by flirting with competitive agencies, even awarding them one-off assignments. If this works, then there is something wrong with the relationship. If the relationship is solid there are much more productive ways of ensuring high-quality work and attention. Challenging people with problems and encouraging them when they get the answer right is much more productive.

Stimulating an agency to be proactive should be as easy as listening sympathetically to their ideas and finding something good about those you cannot pursue. If they keep meeting the 'not invented here' syndrome, the ideas will dry up. I once had a client who countered every proposal with one of two objections. The first was that it had never been tried before; the second was that it had. It did not leave me with a great deal of scope to help him improve his business.

If the ideas you did not request are not forthcoming you either have the wrong people on your account or you are doing something to discourage them. It is important to find out which cap fits and act accordingly. If the ideas gradually dry up over a period, in spite of the encouragement, it is clearly time to have a chat with the key person in the account group. He or she may have become overloaded or simply got tired of working on your account. It is then best to ask for this person's solution to the problem. Most people will give an honest answer and you can then commit them to their solution.

In performance terms, it is results that count. Direct response work carries its own disciplines and your obvious interest in the results and frequent comment on them will be stimulus enough to keep the agency on its toes. In my agency I wandered around much of the time asking people about the results of various tests and individual ads or mailings. I did so more out of interest than as any management principle. Occasionally the reaction to my question was, 'I'll have to look it up.' I never ceased to be amazed at what people could not remember. It is a sad fact that if the results do not appear to be important to you, they will soon cease to be important to anyone else.

The pay-off

Questions to ask of a prospective agency

Before getting too far down the track with an appointment it is necessary to give a prospective agency an outline of what you expect and to ask these questions, some of which I was never asked in 11 years of running an agency.

The business
- Can we have a copy of your last report and accounts?
- What margin do you expect to make on a typical client's business?
- Are you willing to work on a fee basis with all other charges strictly net?
- Do you have any volume discount agreements with suppliers or any other arrangements giving you a margin that is hidden within net charges? If so, would you be willing to pass copies of these agreements to us prior to your appointment?
- What are your terms of business?
- Can we have details of the number of employees in each department?
- Can we have a table showing growth rate over the last five years (or since formation, if less than five years ago)? To include income, profit and end-of-year payroll.
- Do you have any subsidiary or associate companies

which are preferred suppliers? If so, can we have details of any that are relevant to our business?
- What is the minimum acceptable income from a client?
- Do you have any interests or client relationships that may conflict with our business?

The philosophy and management style
- What is the agency's declared policy or philosophy? How is this communicated to employees?
- Does the agency have a business strategy? If so, what—in outline—is it? If not, what are the agency's medium- and long-term goals?
- Can we have a breakdown of clients by years/months with the agency?
- Can we have a similar breakdown for employees?
- Can we have a breakdown of clients by size?
- Can we have a list of those clients for which you are the sole or main agency?
- Do you object to our contacting any client for a view on the quality of work and standard of service they are receiving from you?
- Can we have a copy of the organisation chart?

Success on behalf of clients
- Can you give details of any clients who have (a) awarded you additional assignments since appointing you or (b) whose business with you has grown very significantly?
- How many of your clients have appointed you through the recommendation of another client (either as a direct or indirect result of recommendation) or because a client changed jobs?
- What achievements on behalf of clients are you most proud of?
- Can we see evidence of the media planning and buying skills in your credentials presentation?
- Can we see evidence of response analysis and forecasting experience in your credentials presentation?

Specific to relationship
- What do you chiefly look for in a client relationship?
- What features do you look for in a client company or its management style?
- How do you nominate people in the agency to work on an account? Who do you think might be appropriate to work on ours? Can we have details of their current

commitments and recent experience? Also of any service
department heads who would be involved?

- How do you like to manage an account of our size and
workload?
- What is your minimum period of contract on a fee
basis?
- What is the probable total or hourly average charge
likely to be?
- Do you believe, on the basis of the information you have
about us so far, that you could work productively with
us? If so, why do you think you would be our best choice?

These questions may come in stages. The financial questions
can be asked without giving the agency any details of your
account beyond an outline of the sort of work entailed and its
potential size. The answers to all of them should be sought
before either getting too involved with the people who might
work on your account or spending a lot of time in the agency.
Having seen a credentials presentation, spend time
wandering around and talking shop with the people; you will
then have a pretty good idea of what makes them tick and
how you would get on with them. If you want them to enter a
competitive pitch, that is up to you. It will probably waste
your time and their money to ask for any more than a basic
presentation of how they would tackle the assignment
without supporting creative work.

Depending on your needs, you will need to ensure that the
agency has the various skills and services you will require.
These may include an ability to handle personalised
mailings, brochure production, or, even, database
management if you believe in putting all the responsibility
under one roof.

Ten ways to get the most out of an agency relationship

1. *Involvement*

You will get the best if yours is the agency's favourite
account. It can be so easily, because few clients bother to
involve the agency in the business so that their people share
in the triumphs and the disasters, the problems and their
solutions. The people on your account will become committed
and more productive as time goes on. And, as time goes on,
you can involve more of the backroom people in the agency.
A simple congratulatory letter can be worth thousands of
pounds in extra effort.

2. *Fun*

Agency people work, for the most part, long hours under pressure. They put up with this because they have a low boredom threshold and would not swop their chaotic but incident-filled lives for a more peaceful, well-ordered existence. I have known several thousand agency people, only one of whom did not have a good sense of humour. He was in the business because his father founded the agency. He did not last. Any opportunity to share an internal joke or hilarious incident, any genuine opportunity for celebration, should be taken. It will bring extra commitment.

3. *Encouragement*

Agencies are neurotic and their staff are insecure. They respond far more positively to encouragement than threat. Castigation should be employed sparingly but forcefully. Above all, ideas must be encouraged and must receive a rapid response. Keep the ideas coming by praising the effort even when some of the ideas are impracticable. Always explain why when you cannot adopt an idea. They may be able to adapt it so that it works. If not, they will learn something.

4. *Honesty*

If you have to hide things about your business from your agency you have the wrong agency. Almost all security leaks come from a client's own staff except those that occur accidentally, for example, at printers. If you are not satisfied with something, have it out with the agency straight away. Do not invent false deadlines, then spend three weeks approving something you demanded in 48 hours.

5. *Demands*

Brief clearly with all the necessary supporting facts and then be demanding. Undemanding clients are not respected. Clients who throw down intellectual challenges offer enjoyment and job satisfaction. Clients who like finished jobs to look wonderful are seen as professional and foster pride in the agency's work. Give them just enough time to respond well to a brief.

6. *Dialogue*

There are a good many things you understand better than anyone in the agency. If they are relevant, take the trouble to explain them. There will also be things they may understand better than you do. Listen. It is not a sign of weakness to change your mind in response to a strong argument. Take every reasonable opportunity to widen dialogue. The more people who know one another in the two organisations, the stronger the commitment.

7. *Results*
You pay the agency for achievement, they charge for time. Never let them forget what you are paying them for. They will either be worth less or more than you are paying, scarcely ever the exact amount. They are usually worth more when they are improving your results or devising ways of developing the business. Ensure they understand how important results are to you.

8. *Administration*
Be known to demand value for money. Do not be a scrooge to the extent of sacrificing quality illogically, or souring the relationship by querying each invoice. Ask for time-sheet analyses to be sent to you regularly. Query items that puzzle you. Query inaccuracies or ambiguous points in contact reports. Ensure you have regular direct contact with the media people on your account and agree a system that will enable them to buy distress space at pre-agreed target buying prices, if necessary. Ensure there is a key number system and standby copy to cope with this.

9. *Personal*
Form a trusting relationship but do not allow this to spill over too much into your personal life or the lives of your staff. It is not necessary and you do not want to end up in someone's pocket.

10. *Firing*
If it is not going right, say so. Have the people on your account changed if necessary. If that does not work, fire the agency. Do not ask them to re-pitch. It is ridiculous to ask an agency that knows the business to pitch against agencies that don't. What are you going to learn about them you do not already know? And how can you compare their pitch performance fairly? Until you fire them, stay loyal. Do not award projects to other agencies unless absolutely necessary. If you do, explain why. Do not let your agency find out about it from another source.

12 A look into the future

The proposition

It has been fashionable among direct marketing people to assert that direct marketing expenditure will exceed general advertising expenditure by the year 2000. It will not. And for good reason. Such a proposition depends, in my view, on ignorance of how both advertising and direct marketing work. What I hope will happen is that the argument will go away as the roles of advertising and direct marketing merge into a continuous process of making known, creating desire and building loyalty so that it will be impossible to say where one process ends and the other begins. That is what I hope will happen, though I am by no means confident that it will.

In this chapter we shall see how it would not be economically viable to supplant the majority of advertising with direct marketing even if the advertising audience could endure a plethora of advertising containing calls to immediate action. Moreover, it is unlikely that public tolerance will reach such a level. Whenever advertising has been refined to a formula in which it has sacrificed charm in favour of ramming information down the public's throat, as it last did in the 1960s, the public has switched off. It is impossible to conceive of a situation in which the majority of advertising messages were followed by a telephone number and an instruction to enquire without also sacrificing much of the quality which makes a high volume of advertising tolerable. Such commands do not lend themselves to being voiced in a bedside manner. We do not wish to leap out of our armchairs in the middle of a commercial break to dial an 0800 number unless we have a very good reason for so doing. Neither do we wish our glossy magazines to be jammed full of coupons, credit card symbols and large telephone numbers. If our mail contains five catalogues, three charity appeals, four sweepstakes promotions and two magazine subscription offers for each personal letter, we shall dismiss these mailings as junk and stop bothering to open them.

As a result, such activity will cease to be as effective as it is today and so the volume of it will recede. Direct marketing is nothing if not measurable. All good marketing depends on an appreciation of human psychology. An elementary understanding of this is sufficient to realise that most people are, at least mildly, sceptical and that they also suffer from inertia. Or, rather, they enjoy inertia. It is simply not in human nature to respond instantly to advertising messages unless they are peculiarly apposite at a particular time. Such calls to action, then, will find their natural level, however well targeted direct marketing activity may become. This natural level is no doubt some long way in excess of the present level. How far in excess, no one can say. But it will certainly not reach the dizzy heights forecast by those who like to look at straight line growth charts and imagine they will continue that way indefinitely.

At the present time there is still chronic under-investment on maintaining customer loyalty as opposed to chasing new business.

The segmentation of many markets into more and more niches presents the consumer with alternatives that increase in number more rapidly than the disposable income to indulge such refined tastes. The effect is to reduce brand loyalty, and to shorten the average lifetime value of a customer.

This disturbing trend has begun to provoke a reaction from marketing people in the form of a belated recognition of the value of an established customer. Loyalty is valued most when disloyalty becomes a real threat. The British importers of Volvo cars are on record as saying that it costs five times as much to make a new customer conquest as it does to secure a repeat sale. Like many manufacturers and distributors, though by no means all, it is relatively simple for Volvo to establish the identities of their end users—and to stay in touch with them. Yet it is not difficult to think of many products where it may continue to make more sense to communicate with established customers in-pack or via the media than through the mail or by telephone.

There is also insufficient recognition of the wastage inherent in much advertising activity. As markets become splintered into more and more segments, we can expect to see more tightly targeted product launches. Some of these launches will be discreet, being confined to established customer bases. Many financial products, software products and ancillary products are more efficiently marketed to known users of a companion product than to the world at large. These weaknesses—under-investment in customer loyalty and inadequately targeted advertising—will be corrected over time and, as a result of this correction, we can expect direct marketing expenditure to grow. What direct marketing will not do is replace advertising except where advertising is being misused to do what direct marketing can do more effectively.

The need for advertising

In Chapter 2 we discussed the theory (or a theory) of how advertising works. We looked at the process of making known what is available for sale (the first purpose of advertising) and we examined the process of image matching, stating that consumer or business users of a product or company almost invariably 'image match' before they trouble to 'fact match'. This process of developing awareness and image matching occurs over time. Sometimes over a long period of time. It may start long before the consumer is in the target market. A 10-year-old child may aspire to own a personal computer. A school leaver might dream of the day when a gleaming red Ferrari stands outside the front door.

Advertising is one of a number of influences that help to create such aspirations. PR is another. Role models are yet another: an admired older person or colleague may sport a particular wristwatch which reflects a personality seen as worthy of emulation. Since such influences occur over time, repetition is beneficial, whether the time period is short or long.

Thus advertising investments have a cumulative effect. On the whole, though not invariably, heavily advertised products outsell less heavily advertised products. There is even a cut-off point below which it is not generally worth advertising at all. Unless a minimum impact and consistency is affordable it is better to save the money and buy distribution some other way.

In many product fields it is necessary to establish with multiple retail head offices that sufficient is being spent on advertising to build or maintain market share. A failure to do this will prevent listing or provoke de-listing of a product. We can readily see that weight and consistency of advertising carry a significant benefit. Further, that the effect of advertising is cumulative and its visibility, to stockists or distributors, may be a factor. While notions of the sheer volume of advertising required before its cumulative benefit starts to diminish have changed, there is little dispute that these cumulative benefits exist. In this context one advertising exposure has little or no effect, consistent advertising exposure has a major effect. In sharp contrast with this, there is generally no cumulative benefit from direct response advertising whether this is carried through media or the mail. The sole exception is broadcast media and, even in this case, the required impact level is extremely low. We are here discussing benefit solely in terms of response. The first ad in a series will almost always pull the highest response and response will continue to tail off over a series until a stable level is reached. If our first ad pulls 100 replies, the second may pull 95, the third 70 and the fourth only 65. This pattern will not always prevail but, much more frequently than not, the general shape of the downward curve will remain the same.

Responders are 'fact matchers' or immediate buyers. There are far fewer of them in the market at any one time than there are image matchers. Furthermore, they do not include all fact matchers or buyers. They include only those who are willing to seek information or make a purchase in a specialised way—by telephoning or writing to the advertiser. The reason diminishing returns set in immediately in a direct response schedule is that there is a limited supply of such people within any media audience.

The limitations of direct marketing

It is impossible for a direct marketed product to capture a very large share of market against conventionally distributed products. This is because it becomes progressively more expensive to build market share as the pool of potential responders gets smaller. The conventionally distributed product may have relatively high marketing costs in advertising, sales promotion and dealer margins, but these costs remain fairly stable. The direct marketed product has escalating marketing costs once it has reached an optimum market share. This share may be quite low. A real life case history will help to bring this point home. The identity of the product is disguised for reasons of confidentiality. The product is a financial service bought on an annually renewable basis. The advertiser acts as a broker for the product and relies on direct response advertising to secure enquiries which are then converted to sales by in-bound telemarketing.

The total market is 9 million users and this number is growing at a slow rate. For purposes of simplification we shall assume that the market is static. The marketing department had produced a forecast growth projection (Table 12.1) from a current user level of 1.300 million (a market share in unit terms of 14.4 per cent) to a level of 2 million (22.2 per cent share) in four years' time.

Table 12.1   Forecast growth (millions)

Users	Base year	Year 1	Year 2	Year 3	Year 4
Total users	1.300	1.475	1.650	1.825	2.000
Additional users required		0.175	0.175	0.175	0.175

On the face of it, this does not seem an exaggerated ambition. It represents an average annual growth rate of 10 per cent. But first, since the product is subject to annual renewal, there will be lapsed users. From research data it was possible to ascertain the loss rates of customers within a number of different categories. The most significant differences were between recently acquired customers and established customers. The more recently acquired customers were fairly disloyal but the position stabilised after three years. It follows that the more new customers are obtained the higher the average loss rate would be. Loading into a computer model, the effect of losses produced the picture shown in Table 12.2.

Table 12.2   Growth requirement (millions)

Users	Year 1	Year 2	Year 3	Year 4
Total users	1.475	1.650	1.825	2.000
Less Renewals	1.045	1.177	1.315	1.457
New users	0.430	0.473	0.510	0.543

Now it can be seen that an even growth rate of 175 000 extra users a year (Table 12.1) requires an escalating new user target, rising from 430 000 new users in Year 1 to 543 000 users in Year 4. With this revelation we may start to become a little concerned that we need to hook more fish from the pool as the stock becomes depleted. Unless we can recover some lapsed users we shall have had to find 1.956 million new users by the end of the fourth year. Put another way, we are virtually starting from scratch to reach our 2 million user target.

The next step was to assess the number of consumer contacts (responses) that would be needed to supply 1.956 million new users. To make the figures meaningful in terms of market penetration, we also had to look back to see how many contacts had already been made. At this stage an assumption had to be made on the basis of relatively scant back data.

While the conversion rate on enquiries was well known and recorded, the number of repeat enquiries was not known. We could not be sure how many enquirers had also enquired at some time in the past. An assumption had to be made and the assumption was that unconverted enquiries would, on average, enquire again once every four years.

Loading this assumption into the program it was then possible to display the total number of new contacts needed to meet the four-year target. The figures are shown in Table 12.3.

Table 12.3 Consumer contact requirement (millions)

Past contacts	Year 1	Year 2	Year 3	Year 4	Cumulative
3.263	0.921	1.014	1.092	1.163	7.453

From the knowledge you have gained, you will quickly appreciate that the shape of the curve produced by drawing a graph from these figures is an inversion of a direct response curve. It already looks as if the target may be impossible or, at least, impossibly expensive to achieve. However, this can best be demonstrated statistically. You will recall that the target market consists of 9 million individuals, of whom 3.263 million have already contacted us. This leaves 5.737 million who have yet to contact us. In the first year we need 0.921 million to contact us, or 16.1 per cent of the available market. By the fourth year, the available market has shrunk to 2.710 million. Of this 2.710 million we need 1.163 million to contact us; that is, 42.9 per cent of the available market. The magnitude of the task, then, is not represented by the difference between securing 0.921 million contacts in Year 1 and 1.163 million contacts in Year 4. It is more nearly represented by the difference between securing contacts from

16.1 per cent of an available market in Year 1 and 42.9 per cent of an available market in Year 4. Unless we know exactly who these people are (of which, more later) we shall need at least 2.66 times the weight of expenditure to achieve this result. This will increase our cost-per-enquiry by at least 111 per cent between Year 1 and Year 4 because we shall have gained only an extra 26 per cent of enquiries for an extra 166 per cent of expenditure. This simplified example understates the case against one dimension and overstates it against another. The case is understated because, in our simplification, we have assumed that the minority who have so far resisted contact with us are the same as the majority who have contacted us. This is clearly not so. They are more loyal to their current service provider and need more persuasion to respond to us.

However, the case is overstated in that the figure of 9 million people in the target market is not actually constant. About 4.5 per cent of people drop out of the market each year and are replaced by new entrants. As nearly as one can say, these two factors roughly balance out. We are thus left with a problem of a potential hike of 111 per cent in our selling costs. Few businesses have a sufficient margin to tolerate such an increase without running into a loss. Fewer still could do so without recognising that it would be more profitable to stick at about 1.5 million customers than to strive for the 2 million target. A target market share of 22.2 per cent is an impossibly ambitious aim for a product relying on direct marketing technique. There are two 'direct marketing' solutions and two 'classical marketing' solutions. The direct marketing solutions are:

1. Increase the retention rate of existing customers.
2. Build a market universe database, overlaying present and lapsed customers and all enquirers. Concentrate all promotional effort on lapsed customers, past enquirers and non-enquirers. Withdraw all media advertising.

The classical marketing solutions are:

1. Diversify distribution channels.
2. Segment the market by launching additional products designed to appeal to non-users of the core product.

All of these solutions look as if they have possibilities, yet none is a 100 per cent solution. Let us examine each one in turn.

The direct marketing solutions

1. *Increase retention*

This entails an examination of what is done now to retain customers. This examination will reveal opportunities to improve retention. To these opportunities can be attached forecast achievements. The cost-per-additionally-retained customer can now be compared with the cost-per-new customer. If the cost comparison is favourable we can put each forecast to live test.

Since the loyalty rate is already averaging 83 per cent a year and a 4.5 per cent loss is inevitable (they are represented by people dropping out of the market), our scope for improving retention is limited to the gap between 83 and 95.5 per cent. Clearly, we cannot afford to incentivise all customers to remain with us because we shall be spending money on the 83 per cent we would already retain to keep the 12.5 per cent we would otherwise lose. Furthermore, the incentive will be insufficient to keep all of the 12.5 per cent. They may have experienced poor service or they may have received a competitive offer that it would be unaffordable to match.

The robustness of our solution will depend on our skill at identifying potential losses and according them special treatment. What is certain is that we shall not be 100 per cent successful in targeting these people and we shall not be 100 per cent successful in retaining those we have actually targeted. Realistically, we might get halfway between our present retention rate and the maximum possible retention rate. This is a potentially good solution, but it is not a total solution.

2. *Build a market universe database*

This is often a realistic possibility in business-to-business marketing. It is seldom so in consumer markets. The solution works in developed markets where there is a constraint on growth that can be described in terms a computer can easily recognise.

Such a case is credit product marketing. It is possible, through the use of a credit scorecard, to eliminate all households or individuals that the credit provider does not wish to grant credit to. Thus the market is being delineated negatively. The market is described in terms of those we would like to do business with, not in terms of those who have any predisposition to do business with us. Such market definitions can be refined by examining the characteristics of responders and profitable customers which can be replicated for non-users on the electoral roll. From these data we can construct a response scorecard, a sales scorecard, or a profit scorecard so that we can select only high potential suspects for targeted marketing. What we must recognise, in so doing, is that we no longer have a market universe database. We have made assumptions about who will be most responsive on the basis of insufficient evidence and will have omitted some people who would have responded if we had targeted them.

The difficulty of applying such an approach to most markets is that few can be delineated so clearly. Most markets are delineated by a set of attitudes. It does not matter if we are theoretically insufficiently wealthy to own a Porsche. If we are set on having one, we may make all sorts of sacrifices in order to realise our ambition. Back to image matching. It is impossible to build a market universe database for such a product, for to do so would require responses to market research questions. Since we could not afford to interview every household, we would have to fall back on postal research. If we are lucky we may accumulate responses from 40 per cent of the target market after considerable time and cost. And we shall be left with the problem of keeping the information up-to-date. Even if we could build a market universe database we must still incur the cost of maintaining it and the cost of communicating with the people whose names are on it. This may be readily recoverable if we know *when* to communicate with them. Mailing is expensive and a mis-timed mailing to the right suspect will not produce the response we want.

Currently, marketing databases are being paraded as a panacea for all marketing problems. They are not. The Pareto Principle applies. It is sensible, in most circumstances, to build a database of the minority of people upon whom a majority of future profit will depend. It is not sensible, except in rare cases, to attempt to build a market universe database.

In the particular case we are considering it may be sensible to build a customer database which includes unconverted enquirers and lapsed users. These two groups are disproportionately likely to be responsive to future promotion. Doing so will probably prove a worthwhile investment but it will not solve the longer term market penetration problem by itself. What it will do is become a larger part of the solution as time goes on, providing we are able to market to these discreet groups profitably. It will also give us more precise information of what is happening on our marketplace.

The classical marketing solutions

Turning to the classical marketing solutions, these are to diversify distribution channels and to launch additional brands to segment the market.

1. *Diversify distribution*

There is a limit to the number of people who will opt for any particular channel of distribution, given a choice. Many people will always prefer to walk into a shop rather than pick up a telephone. They feel more at ease and reassured when they can see who they are talking to. Some people like to deal by correspondence, but they are a minority. Unless a wide range of ways to buy is available, it may become progressively more expensive to increase market penetration. This is because the size of the target market is artificially reduced to that part of the population that is prepared to deal in a particular way. Before we start to push up against the outer limits of what is achievable from one distributive channel, it is likely to be less expensive to open up an alternative distribution channel. For the cost of getting our last 1.163 million enquirers we could open up quite a few shops or shops within shops. Or we could do a deal with compatible chains of outlets—perhaps estate agents or travel agencies—and train their staff to sell our product. This will ensure that some business walks in off the street and increases the gearing on our advertising spend. Our advertising becomes across-the-line or double duty advertising. This is the way in which the mail order business began to change in the USA many years ago. The largest mail order company was Sears Roebuck. Today you can deal with Sears Roebuck in-store, by phone, or by mail. Since then, such diversification has also taken place in reverse, with big stores spawning catalogues. Diversifying channels of distribution offers the consumer freedom of choice and raises the threshold on our possible market penetration.

2. *Segment the market*

Quite early in the history of automotive mass production and marketing, General Motors overtook Ford as the world's largest car maker. The reason was branding. Market segmentation. General Motors recognised that it is easier to secure high market penetration with a number of brands than with one brand. This is not simply because several brands can create the opportunity to enrol more dealerships, although that is important in the automotive market. It is that the higher the market penetration, the more necessary it is to appeal to different kinds of people. The appeal of any one brand becomes less precisely targeted, the more its market share grows. Of course, what is called 'badge engineering' is not the total answer. If brands are recognisably different, with different price, value and quality attributes, the segmentation job will be more effective. There will always be some consumers who opt for the cheapest alternative, others for the alternative offering the best reassurance of quality, and so on. It is cheaper to offer each market segment what it wants than to try to get every market segment to want the same thing. Curiously enough, this fact has been clearly demonstrated in direct response advertising.

Diminishing returns from mail order catalogue advertising investment have been reduced by promoting additional brands. The segmentation of markets by one company has been extraordinarily successful in fast moving consumer goods and in some durables and service markets. Pedigree Petfoods has a market share of about two-thirds of the prepared petfoods market. GUS has about 40 per cent of the catalogue mail order market. Such achievements would be impossible without a portfolio of brands.

In the case we have chosen to examine it is clear that we can recycle unconverted enquirers faster if we trade under several identities. We can maximise our chances of conversion. Not only that, but we can be more precise in targeting product attributes to match the needs of alternative market segments.

I have used this example of a financial service because it illustrates a number of points. Firstly, a marketing problem is capable of more than one solution and that the answer is more likely to be found in a combination of solutions. Secondly, direct response activity is subject to diminishing returns and, for this reason alone, direct marketing is most unlikely to take over the world of marketing with the facility that its most blinkered protagonists project. Thirdly, it is generally an enormous waste of time and money to build market universe databases, although there will always be specific exceptions to that principle. This is the second compelling reason why direct marketing will not take over the world of marketing.

Why marketing needs all-rounders

This leaves one major point, the fourth point, which is the most important in its implications for the future. Problems are solved by people who have open minds. They are not solved by people who cannot see past their own preconceived and packaged solution. It is for this reason that I look with disfavour on the splintering of the marketing services industry into specialised cells exhibiting a deep knowledge of very little. There is no breadth of vision offered by such a configuration of services. There are increasing numbers of people who know a lot about a little, but diminishing numbers of people who know a little about a lot. It is inevitable that, as the extent of knowledge grows, there is more call for specialisation. Yet this brings with it the opportunity to chase down more and more blind alleys of ever-increasing length.

There are currently two solutions to this problem, neither of which is satisfactory. The first is within the marketing services sector. Many advertising agency groups, some PR company groups and some sales promotion agency groups, have accumulated networks of specialist subsidiaries. The theory is that, within the group, there will be a specialist capable of solving any marketing problem from corporate style to database management. Even if this were wholly true, it leaves the problem of who calls in the relevant specialist. Such groups are controlled by people who have limited knowledge of most of the marketing disciplines under their control. Furthermore, they are remote from the majority of their clients. Each subsidiary is run by someone who specialises in the service the subsidiary provides. More often than not, he or she has little knowledge of, or interest in, the disciplines of associated companies. Frequently, chief executives see themselves as being in competition with associates. This is scarcely surprising since they are running a separate profit centre and the Group Board will constantly be comparing their achievements with those of their fellows. The chief executives bring up their staff to think the same way.

At the present time, there is no concerted effort to give anyone the most rudimentary training in all the disciplines within such a group. Instead, the group is more likely to buy a management consultancy company staffed largely by people with no practical experience of what any of the associated companies do. The effect of specialisation is to put the onus on the client to select the skills that are necessary without the benefit of experienced external advice. In order to select the required skills it is essential to have a preconceived idea of where the answer to any marketing problem is most likely to lie. This brings us to the second solution to the difficulties posed by specialisation of marketing services.

This solution requires the marketing department to arrive at a correct allocation of resources between alternatives without independent advice. In this scenario, the ultimate decision maker, who is either the marketing director or managing director, is the fount of all wisdom and makes, or approves, the choices. The theory is that the marketing department contains people with sufficient knowledge of each of the marketing disciplines to provide management with the necessary advice to make good decisions. This theory is not replicated in practice. There are four reasons why. Firstly, it is not easy to give one's boss advice. Secondly, it is well nigh impossible for the most progressive marketing department to keep up with the latest developments in all the various specialisations. Thirdly, the marketing department spends the majority of its available time dealing with expediencies. Fourthly, decision making without external advice becomes introspective.

The whole point of external advisors is that they can draw parallels between markets and different companies in similar situations. They are often seeing a problem similar to one they have met before and carry with them a knowledge of attempted solutions that succeeded, or failed, and why. The whole point of agencies is that they adopt a different point of view, that of the consumer, when they are doing their job well. Yet agencies are necessarily left out of the consultative process when, through lack of breadth in their experience of the different marketing disciplines, they cease to be worth consulting. Worse, they are now often considered to be partial in their advice.

The effect has been to throw the marketing department back on its resources and to prevent agency groups from cross-referring business between associates. Not surprisingly, few clients use a portfolio of specialist marketing services drawn from any one group. Most prefer to choose their sales promotion, PR and direct marketing agencies without reference to their general advertising agency. This may sometimes work out well enough in practice but it leads to many missed opportunities, because it relies upon the client to recognise the need for new skills and services. For much of my life I have been a specialist in direct marketing. I know from experience that companies that had the role of direct marketing in their operations explained to them over ten years ago have now only just 'discovered' it. The average elapsed time between the introduction of a basic idea and its adoption is, at a guess, somewhere between five and ten years, and the adoption then depends on a change of senior management.

In their book, *Managing Knowhow*, Karl Erik Sveiby and Tom Lloyd distinguish between service companies and know-how companies. While all know-how companies are service companies, many service companies are far removed from being know-how companies. The features that distinguish the know-how company are:

- non-standardisation
- creativity
- high dependence on individuals
- complex problem-solving

It is doubtful whether many large agency groups, put together by mergers and acquisitions, have fully recognised what is special about their business and reacted to it with sufficient sensitivity. To do so would involve painful de-structuring and rebuilding in a different format. Any such drastic change inevitably places established client relationships at risk.

Enforcing a change

The account group system, in which a client's business is understood and handled by a relatively small number of people, even in a large agency, has stood the test of time. The present difficulty is that this group of people no longer possess the range of skills and experience required to help their client at a strategic level. The problem can only be solved by restructuring an agency group into a series of mini all-purpose 'agencies', depending only for the most refined and specialised skills upon service departments that meet the whole of the agency's needs within their specialisations.

The likelihood is that the problem will be avoided for as long as possible and that it will be forced upon agencies by their larger clients, who are more concerned with how well their marketing allowable is spent than with how it is divided between different interests. At present one can envisage considerable cultural difficulties involved in putting together teams of people drawn from different disciplines. The emphasis on quality control in general advertising agency work is much stronger than in sales promotion or direct marketing work. The emphasis on cost control in these more readily measurable activities is much stronger than it is in general advertising. However, these differences of attitude are not entirely logical and would gradually disappear within a cross-discipline trained team of people.

Similarly, it is not easy to establish a correct relationship between advertising, sales promotion and direct marketing in many marketing departments. It is much simpler to do this in a service organisation, such as a bank, than in a packaged goods manufacturing business. Banks, like FMCG companies, market branded services, but these brand identities are subservient to the corporate identity. This is reflected in the status and role of product managers within the marketing department. The bank is aware that its success will largely depend on uptrading established customers and that this will depend on cross-selling. Furthermore, its customer marketing database is derived from a central source—customers' accounts and supporting transactional data. Thus the direct marketing manager will occupy a key role and may be elevated in status above individual product managers.

Until relatively recently, below-the-line activity in FMCG companies was often decided at quite low management levels and there was little continuity of relationship with sales promotion agencies. Each promotion was often the subject of a competitive pitch. The objects of the below-the-line activity were:

(1) to secure increases in net effective distribution;
(2) to protect/increase linear footage;
(3) to secure sampling;
(4) to cause an immediate uplift in sales;
(5) more rarely, to induce repeat sales.

The activity was often seen as tactical rather than strategic and could safely be left to product managers working within agreed budgets. The name and address data produced by many promotions were dumped.

Since the cost of data collection and retrieval has declined sharply there has been a gradual realisation that sales promotion could play an expanded role. There is no distinction between sales promotion and direct marketing in this context. Below-the-line activity can now be used more effectively to induce loyalty but, of even greater importance, it can be used to cross-sell. This is affinity group marketing taken to its ultimate when the virtues of one brand are borrowed by another. This is easier to establish in a company organised on the Japanese model than one organised on the American model. In the Japanese model, corporate identity is king. In the American model, individual branding is king.

Looking at the effect of this within the marketing department, one can see a structure that supports brand identity. Product or brand managers are, in effect, set in competition with each other and have no interest in cross-selling. They each may 'own' their customer data. Such a structure is inimical to the successful introduction of programmes designed to build lifetime customer values. It is necessary to establish that customer data are owned by the company and that a senior executive must be their custodian.

Marketing is a continuous process and depends on the impression that is made on each person over his or her effective 'life' as a consumer. Departmental structures and excessive specialisation of services impede this process because they create sectional interests which prevent innovation. It is necessary to keep questioning why things are the way they are because what made logical sense at some time in the past probably no longer does so. Unless marketing people are educated to make dispassionate judgements about the utility of all the tools at their command, it is difficult to see how marketing will become more efficient. There are better grounds for optimism that client companies will recognise this more readily than agencies or other suppliers. Change to these organisations will have to be forced by their clients, although it may be encouraged by the spread of interactive media.

The effect of these changes will be to increase the volume of one-to-one communications and interactive advertising. However, this volume will not increase steadily and will not occupy the dominant share of marketing budgets. The maintenance of strong brand or corporate identities is a very important reassurance to consumers. It is therefore an essential part of the loyalty building process. It is equally important to consumers that their choice of a product is endorsed by their peers. It is impossible to create this impression without public media advertising or a strong PR programme.

Technology and isolation

A major influence between now and the end of the century will be the effect of technology and labour costs on the isolation of the consumer. It is now possible to open and maintain a bank account without ever entering a bank. More commonly, few customers will enter their bank branch on a regular basis. Since the branch is the prime vehicle for establishing human contact and cross-selling, this represents a major marketing problem. Increasingly, retailing is becoming dehumanised. With a sharply declining availability of school leavers the only logical reaction must be to reduce labour needs. Meanwhile the introduction of electronic fund transfer produces a wealth of transactional data about individual shoppers. Increasingly, it will be possible to refuel one's car without any human contact. The spread of in-home entertainment, especially of feature film videos, increases isolation further. The possibility of electronic home shopping is another isolating influence. The growth of one-person households is yet another. It is inconceivable that these influences will not create a need for more warmth and a greater desire for shared experiences.

What is more difficult to predict is precisely how marketers will step in to meet the need. There will certainly be an increase in one-to-one communication. However, it is likely that all interactive advertising will become more attractive—especially that which offers an obviously shared experience. The popularity of charity Telethons is an example of the power of a shared experience. The popularity of radio phone-ins is another, while broadcast media competitions attract prodigious numbers of entries. Even newspaper campaigns—for example, petitions to stop seal culls, or save the whale—have attracted up to half a million responses. In the USA, cable TV shopping has proved extremely successful using a home-spun but chatty presentation style. The reason for this success is because, increasingly, people feel isolated.

While these changes repesent a powerful argument for an increase in direct response activity, it would be a mistake to assume that the role of brand identity will be diminished. When there is less human contact and less advice is available, the reassurance offered by an established brand becomes more important.

What is certain is that less people will be paid to sell things in the future and that the role of advertising, especially of direct advertising, will be expanded to fill the gap. Products which offer added-value services will almost certainly achieve an increased share of the market.

There have always been, as long as anyone can remember, mail order businesses which have successfully projected a warm personality to their customers. JS & A, quoted earlier in this book, is one. On a larger scale, another American company, L. L. Bean, with rigorous attention to customer service, is another. I believe that such skills will become increasingly demanded and that consumers will be willing to pay a little more for good service from companies that project an image of caring for them as individuals. Before the large mail order companies became as automated as they are today, they provided a valuable social service.

Finlay MacDonald, recounting the days of his childhood on the Isle of Harris in the 1920s, in his memoirs *Crowdie and Cream*, referred to the extraordinary customer service given by Williams and Oxendale at that time. One order read: 'Dear Sir, Please send me COD a dress like the one you sent Mrs MacLean for her sister's wedding—only blue and one size larger.' The order was satisfactorily fulfilled. Finlay MacDonald quoted a typical ending to a customer's letter: 'Hoping you are keeping well. We are all fine here despite the cold weather.' In quoting this he said, 'Such informality did not betoken naïveté; it exemplifies the breakdown which can take place in the mores of business formality in the course of a long and honourable association.'

The challenge for marketing

The challenge for marketers will be to approach this standard of service when more people feel as isolated as the residents of the Isle of Harris did in the days of MacDonald's childhood. Of course, it will be impossible to provide the same degree of personal attention but it will be essential to avoid the obvious ignorance of a customer's needs that is apparent when the skill to exploit technology is less advanced than the technology itself. More than this it will be essential for companies to adopt a better service orientation.

It is reasonably predictable that companies that use direct marketing methodology to improve customer service will increase their market share and their profitability. It is equally predictable that most companies will not do this at least for a long time to come. Direct marketing targeting and interactive technique will become increasingly exploited but not as fast, or as well, as technology will permit.

Meanwhile, in the UK expenditure on direct response press advertising was roughly equal to that on direct mail in 1988. Each medium enjoyed a half share of about £1 billion revenue. The growth in direct mail volume through the 1980s was steady, not spectacular—increasing by 50 per cent in the five years between 1983 and 1987. With low inflation in direct mail costs, the direct mail share of the advertising market was exactly the same in 1987 as it had been in 1983—7.7 per cent. Over the same period, Nielsen Clearing House reported an increase in coupon distributions of 57 per cent. There is little evidence to support claims that have been made as to the growth of direct marketing activity. It is possible that improved targeting has resulted in reduced mailing volumes in many cases. Consumer direct response advertising in the UK in the first half of the eighties was heavily dependent for its growth on the financial sector. After the October 1987 crash, a reduction of 13.5 per cent in financial direct response advertising (1988 over 1987) showed growth to be 9 per cent. Direct marketing remains dependent for much of its volume on comparatively few industries and it cannot realistically anticipate the lion's share of the majority of marketing budgets. Yet there can be little doubt that the division of markets into narrower segments, the escalation of media costs, the spread of consumer credit, the buoyancy of the service sector, the increase in the cost of salespeople's time, and the reduction of data storage costs have created a set of circumstances in which—the odd hiccough apart—direct marketing's influence will become ever more widespread. It will not, however, take over the world of marketing with the facility that its most ardent protagonists would have us believe.

The pay-off

The notion that direct marketing will supplant advertising is based on a misunderstanding of the functions of each. It is further based on a misreading of what the pioneers of modern direct marketing, including such notables as Lester Wunderman and Stan Rapp, have said about its development. To some degree, it is based upon confusion about the definition of direct marketing. Direct marketing is a method of increasing the gearing on advertising, public relations and PR investment with the object of speeding, increasing and prolonging the return on these investments.

Except in a few areas it does not compete with advertising or even compete with salespeople's efforts. It supplants such activities only where they are being used ineffectively to perform tasks which direct marketing can perform at less expense or with greater effect.

This is often only at the margins.

Much direct marketing effort depends upon the goodwill generated by advertising and other means of establishing powerful brand or corporate imagery. This is because its object is to supply a direct linkage between a brand or company and willing customers. It is generally a part of the persuasion process, not the whole of it. In some cases, it is more efficient to carry loyalty building promotion on-pack or in-pack than via the mail. However, the vehicles used to carry direct marketing communications are of less significance than the philosophy that lies behind direct marketing's increasing influence.

As markets continue to splinter, as customer loyalty continues to decrease, as advertising costs increase and as database marketing skills increase, this philosophy becomes ever more attractive. In virtually all business-to-business markets and most consumer durables and service markets, it makes inescapable sense to identify and cosset customers and prospects. More often than not, rather than attempt to reach these people by direct mail, it will be more efficient to identify them through their response, not only to direct response media advertising, but often to advertising whose main function is not to produce direct response.

The fences that have been built around the different marketing disciplines will gradually be taken down so that the marketing allowable will be spent more accountably and more efficiently. This process seems simple and obvious enough but it will be slowed down by the structure of both marketing departments and marketing service groups, and by the lack of vision of those content to graze within their fenced-off paddocks. They will be superseded by a new generation of marketing and advertising people who will work across the mythical line that is drawn between advertising and other marketing expenditures. When Independent Television started in 1955, most large agencies sprouted TV, cinema and radio departments (in one or two cases they were separate companies) because the creative people employed in the agency did not understand the medium. Fortunately, a new generation of creative people, educated by television, succeeded them before the separation between TV and print media became final.

When direct marketing has ceased to be seen as new and threatening it will be absorbed and will find its natural level, just as every innovation has always been absorbed in the past.

13 Contacts and associations

Newspaper Publishers Association Ltd.

Address: 34 Southwark Bridge Road
            LONDON
            SE1 9EU
Telephone: (071) 928 6928

The NPA represents the national newspapers as opposed to magazines or regional newspapers. Advertising and its acceptance falls within the scope of the NPA's activities and, in conjunction with the Institute of Practitioners in Advertising and the Incorporated Society of British Advertisers, it has established the National Newspapers' Mail Order Protection Scheme (MOPS). See below.

Those magazines which are distributed free with national newspapers are represented by the NPA and mail order advertising within them is covered by MOPS.

Periodical Publishers Association

Address: Imperial House
            15–19 Kingsway
            LONDON
            WC2B 6UN
Telephone: (071) 379 6268

The PPA represents magazine publishers and, like the NPA, includes the acceptability of advertising within its terms of reference.

The National Newspapers' Mail Order Protection Scheme Ltd. (MOPS)

Address: 16 Tooks Court
            LONDON
            EC4A 1LB
Telephone: (071) 405 6806

MOPS was established in 1975 to formulate a code of practice and regulations to ensure that mail order advertisers soliciting money in advance of fulfilling customers' orders operated within well-defined and controlled guidelines.

The function of MOPS is to safeguard readers' money. It does this in two ways. Firstly, it requires would-be sell-off-the-page advertisers to apply for permission to advertise in national newspapers. This process involves the advertiser in giving information and undertakings, enabling MOPS to take an informed view on the security of readers' money.

Secondly, MOPS reimburses readers if the advertiser goes out of business without fulfilling the order, or fails to give a refund for returned goods.

The scheme is funded, at least in part, by fees payable by mail order advertisers and their agencies. Advertisers' fees are on a sliding scale, representing about 1 per cent of large expenditures, but a higher percentage of small expenditures. Agencies pay a modest flat fee. Calls on MOPS are further safeguarded by a readers' account system, in which readers' money is held by an independent stakeholder until the goods have been despatched. This system is employed when goods of a very high value are involved, or the advertiser is not highly capitalised. A bank guarantee is an alternative way of safeguarding MOPS in similar circumstances.

Many mail order ads do not fall within the scope of MOPS protection. They include classified ads, two-step ads, mail-in premium ads requiring proof of purchase of a retail distributed product, and service product ads such as club memberships or magazine subscriptions.

Associations

The Advertising Association

Address: Abford House
             15 Wilton Road
             LONDON
             SW1V 1NJ
Telephone: (071) 828 2771

How and when it started
The Advertising Association was founded in 1926. It was set up as the professional body to represent all those in the advertising business as it was at the time. The business of advertising was very much smaller, and mainly limited to

the published media, outdoor advertising and some direct mail.

Its role
With the massive growth in advertising the Association has expanded enormously and comprises a 'federation' of 29 trade associations and professional bodies. As such, its membership varies from advertisers, agencies and media and support services. The principal purpose of the Association is therefore those tasks which have a bearing on all of its membership, serving all interests equally.

Help to members
The Association lobbies legislative proposals at a national and international level. It campaigns for the freedom to advertise and to improve public attitudes to advertising.

It is concerned with the process of training and development within the advertising industry. The Advertising Association publishes advertising statistics for both the UK and Europe, and instigates research projects on advertising issues.

The Association also organises seminars and training courses for those involved in the advertising and media fields. Advertising Association members also benefit from the comprehensive library facilities in the Advertising Association Information Centre, which contains one of the most impressive collections of literature on advertising in Europe.

The British Direct Marketing Association
Address: Grosvenor Gardens House
                35 Grosvenor Gardens
                LONDON
                SW1W 0BS
Telephone: (071) 630 7322

How and when it started
The BDMA goes back in some form to the twenties, but in its present form it started in the late sixties.

Its role
Its role, as the major British association for the direct marketing industry, is to further the interests of both clients using direct marketing, and agencies servicing these companies.

Help to members
The BDMA gives its members direct marketing contacts, information and advice. All BDMA members must adhere to a code of practice although many of its stipulations are anyway contained in both current legislation and other codes.

Their code covers all aspects of direct marketing and by every available media. The BDMA represents direct marketing interests in the political forum, as well as to the press.

For company members who wish to use direct marketing, the BDMA give advice on how to start, suggest who might be best able to serve their needs, and give any other information available, free of charge. For agency members, the BDMA adds credibility and support.

The BDMA sends each member bi-monthly newsletters, monthly bulletins and regular mailings. Books and publications can be bought direct from the BDMA booklist at discounted prices. Direct marketing information and statistics are freely available to members by phone.

The BDMA Diploma in Direct Marketing is a recognised asset in the industry, which until recent years had little recognised training or educational courses.

The Advertising Standards Authority

Address: Brook House
                  2–16 Torrington Place
                  LONDON
                  WC1E 7HN
Telephone: (071) 580 5555

How and when it started
The ASA was formed in 1963, in order to set standards in advertising, in line with other trade associations for other forms of media.

Its role
Is to set standards for advertisements transmitted by all forms of media, except television and radio.

Help to members
It administers two self-regulatory codes of practice on behalf of its members – the British Code of Advertising Standards and the British Code for Sales Promotion.

It handles formal complaints raised by members of the public about an advertisement or a promotion by one of its members, and monitors such advertisements and promotions.

14 Legislation and standards

Lists

Legislation

The Data Protection Act 1984 is the main law to affect the list industry. This act has a widespread impact for the majority of businesses, since it was passed to regulate computer activities. The rapid advance and intricate development of computer storage systems during the late seventies and eighties, led to similar advances in information processing. The British Data Protection Act was instigated as a result of the need for British to fall in line with the Council of Europe Convention on Data Protection.

Originally there were fears that the principles laid down by the European Convention would be so strictly adhered to, that it might have forced list brokers out of business altogether, since the use of data, obtained for one purpose would not have been permitted to be used for any other.

When the Data Protection Act was passed in 1984, many people in the list industry were able to breathe a sigh of relief, for the final Act was not as restrictive as the White Paper had been when it was issued in 1982. But this could still be an issue.

Three definitions from the Act affecting the direct mail industry

'Data subject': 'an individual who is the subject of personal data', i.e., the customer on a list whose personal details can consist of a name and address together with other details such as recency of purchase, income and family data.

'Date user': 'a person who holds data'. Those who store and control the content of data intended for processing. In direct mail terms this could include the list owner, the list broker and the list manager.

'Computer bureau': 'a person carries on a computer bureau if he provides other persons with services in respect of data'. The definition continues to explain that this could be either as an agent, or by allowing others the use of equipment for processing data. For example, list brokers, computer bureaux and printers, and mailing houses.

The Data Protection Act 1984 requirements

1. All those holding computerised information which specifically refers to named individuals must apply to register with the Data Protection Registrar, who oversees the imposition of the Act, more details of which are given below. Those who register become bound to operate within the terms of registration.
2. For those data users and computer bureaux involved in the list industry, this means a licence for all data activities has to be obtained for each individual company (rather than every list having to be registered separately, as was first imagined).
3. The Data Protection Act only requires registration from those companies processing personal data held on computer. Information held on a manual or card system does not require registration.
4. Harm caused through the disclosure or destruction of data, by these processing data, to the data subject, was made an offence under the Act. The courts were given the power to enforce the correction of harmful or faulty information, with the payment of compensation to the data user where applicable.
5. Data subjects are able to view any information held about themselves by a specific data user or computer bureau, on payment of an administrative charge. Under the Act this information is required to be given.

How to register

Data users must apply to the Data Protection Registrar at the following address:

Office of the Data Protection Registrar,
Springfield House,
Water Lane,
Wilmslow,
Cheshire
SK9 5AX

When registering the following information must be given:

1. Details of the personal data being held.
2. The purpose for which the data user intends use.
3. The sources of the data.
4. Those to whom the data will be disclosed.

5. The countries outside the UK to which the data may be transferred.

An entry free is charged for registration, which is renewable. Refusal of registration can be made where:

1. Insufficient information in the particulars are given.
2. The applicant is considered likely to contravene the principle of the Act.
3. Insufficient information leads to the possibility that an application could contravene the Act.

Four areas of difficulty

1. It may be, in certain circumstances, worthwhile for the data users to register each list on which a name reoccurs so that an enquirer is forced to pay several fees, rather than just a single one.
2. The source of a data subject's name must also be disclosed to the data subject at their request. However, if the source of a name is an individual, not a company, the user can refuse to reveal it.
3. Data users should ensure that a print-out of information is a complete file. It is customary for print-outs of portions of the file to be taken.
4. Data users must establish that enquirers are genuinely who they claim to be. This is especially difficult for those who only deal with customers through the post. Thus, for instance, it would be prudent that copies of information should therefore only be sent to known addresses, unless a genuine change of address can be established.

Offences under the Data Protection Act 1984

The data user can fall foul of the law, committing a criminal offence, when he knowingly does one of the following:

1. 'holds such data of any description other than that which he has registered.
2. holds or uses any such data for other than a registered purpose.
3. obtains such data, or information to be contained in them, from any source which he has not described in his entry in the register.
4. discloses such data to any person not described in his entry.
5. directly or indirectly transfers such data to any place outside the UK which is not named in his entry.'

(quoted from *Direct Response Magazine*)

Further reading

The eight data protection principles together with other practical guidelines, are contained in eight, allegedly clear and readable booklets written by the Data Protection Registrar. These can be obtained from the address given above and are available free of charge.

The Lindop Report (HMSO, Cmnd 7341) written in 1978, details background to the Data Protection Act. Apart from Chapter 17, 'Direct Marketing' (page 139), other relevant sections include Chapter 28 'Data Handling Bureaux' (page 252), Chapters 18 and 19 on the regulation of the Act (page 149ff) and Chapter 2 on 'Privacy and Data Protection' (page 9).

The Data Protection Act is explained in detail in Sizer and Newman's book entitled the *Data Protection Act: A practical guide* (Gower, ISBN 0-566-02445-4).

Self-regulation

The industry has itself reacted to the Data Protection Act, by bringing about a code of practice in the form of the Mailing Preference Service. In the words of the Data Protection Registrar:

> The Service offers a facility for individuals to suppress the receipt of unwanted mail which I feel accords well with the requirement of fair processing of personal data contained in the First Data Protection Principle.

The Mailing Preference Service has three fundamental principles:

1. To delete names of those who do not wish to be on non-customer mailing lists, so that they no longer receive unwanted mail. MPS exclusion can be carried out on both non-customer mailing lists and, by direct removal requests, from both in-house and outside lists.
2. To add names of those who wish to be included on our lists, so that they receive more mail.
3. All members of the scheme are encouraged to recommend others in the industry to comply with the scheme.

This benefits the direct mail industry by:

1. Helping to improve the image of direct mail. Those aware of the scheme are impressed by the concern of the industry to adapt to people's needs.
2. Reducing wasted mail, by avoiding the cost of sending

mailing packages to those who do not wish to receive them and who are therefore less likely to respond.

3. Attracting new names who enjoy receiving direct mail, and as such are more likely to respond.

How the scheme operates

Members of the public contact the service direct to be included in the scheme. Those companies who subscribe to the service are sent updated copies of the file (either held on computer tape or printed onto a hard copy as required), on a quarterly basis. Names remain on the file for three years. Change of addresses are the responsibility of the members of the public, as explained to them on entry to the scheme.

Registration

Everyone involved in direct marketing is encouraged to join the service. Membership is renewable annually, the fee is based on the scale of operations, calculated by the quantity of items mailed in a year. A separate fixed fee is set for those members who derive no direct benefits from the scheme (e.g. list owners, and computer bureaux, etc.).

An application form to register with the Mailing Preference Service, together with further details are obtainable from:

The Mailing Preference Service
1 New Burlington Street
LONDON
W1X 1FD
Telephone: (071) 437 070

Creative

Legislation

The copyright laws

Current law regulating copyright mainly dates back to the Copyright Act 1956. The reason for this legislation is to protect those who engage in creative activity, whose value is derived from the ideas, skill and labour to produce a unique object. The nature of work which can be viewed as creative, varies widely. It could be a drawing, a record, a video or musical cassette, a computer program, or an architectural plan. All of which may or may not have been published. Copyright laws affect those creating direct mail packages in two ways:

1. Advertisements can contravene copyright if material is included which is the copyright of another party. This can be:

   (i) Testimonials
   (ii) Photographs or other illustrative material
   (iii) Written material

2. Advertisements themselves have a copyright in their own right as company literature.

Who owns copyright?   The author of the work is the first owner of a copyright. The author is not necessarily an individual, in the case of company literature the author is deemed to be the company, rather than the employee who undertook the work.

How long does it last?   Copyright generally lasts for the lifetime of, and for 50 years from the death of, the author. In the event that the work is published after the death of the author, copyright lasts for 50 years from the date when the work is published. The exception to this is those industrial designs which are considered appealing to the eye, for which copyright currently lasts for 15 years only. Future legislation is likely to bring these into line with the other works.

How does one obtain copyright?   Copyright arises automatically. There is no need to register a copyright. The idea or principle behind a creative work cannot constitute a copyright. It is the work itself which is protected. A mark on the product is not necessary for copyright to be enforced. However, such a mark does act as a warning to those who might be in danger of infringing copyright.

How does one prevent an infringement on another person's copyright?   Those who wish to use a piece of work which might infringe copyright, must obtain the permission of the author (be it an individual, or a company). The process of finding the author may not be straightforward, but is essential to avoid infringement.

The degree of infringement   Infringement can be either to a primary or secondary degree. Primary infringement is where an author's work is reproduced exactly, or in a recognisable form without prior permission being obtained. However, if it can be proved that the second piece of work was arrived at independently, this does not constitute infringement.
   Secondary infringement occurs when selling or importing

copies of the infringing product is carried out (something that mail order traders may be in danger of doing). People are only liable if this infringement is committed knowingly.

In cases when the act of copyright infringement is of urgent concern, a court may issue an order to restrain the infringer, or to seize the goods which are causing this infringement.

FURTHER READING
An excellent booklet which explains copyright is available free of charge from Pinset & Co. at the following address:

Pinset & Co.
Post & Mail House
26 Colmore Circus
Birmingham
B4 6BH
Telephone: (021) 200 1050

OTHER USEFUL PUBLICATIONS
Copyright, W. A. Copinger and E. P. Skone James, Sweet & Maxwell.
The Visual Artists' Copyright Handbook, Henry Lydiate Publications.
Layman's Guide to the Copyright, Designs and Patents Bill, Department of Trade and Industry, October 1987.
Government introduces Bill to reform Copyright, Designs and Patents Law, Press Notice, Department of Trade and Industry, 30 October 1987.

Libel
Libel and slander both amount to defamation of someone's good reputation, to which everyone is naturally entitled. Libel occurs when someone publishes something which damages a third party's reputation. In direct mail, libel can occur when either a picture, photograph, name or words used in a mailing is, albeit unknown to the publisher, libellous.
  For libel to be upheld:

1. The statement complained of must be brought by the person to whom it refers.
2. The statement must be false, though this can be by implication.
3. The statement must be published so that a third person can read it and can interpret the statement as defamatory.

The degree of defamation need not be large, but it does have to cause ridicule, lower the reputation and image of the person or cause hatred to them. There are cases where libel is caused unwittingly. However, this is still an offence in law, and a person's innocence will only have an effect as to the degree of punishment for the offence.

In advertising libel can occur if someone's photograph is used in a way that defames him. For example is the picture is touched up to cause the individual ridicule or harm. Similarly, copy which mentions a named individual can be deemed libellous, if defamatory.

The Financial Services Act 1986

For those who have to create a mailing to do with a financial service, the Financial Services Act 1986 will obviously carry the most dramatic impact. Financial companies will be aware of various specialist aspects of legislation which affect their business. For further information, a good source is *Marketing Insurance: A Practical Guide*, N. Dyer and R. Anderson, pages 380–405. Also of interest is *Financial Services Direct Marketing*, by Tony Martin, part of this series (to be published in Spring 1991).

The ramifications of the Financial Services Act 1986 for advertisers using direct mail   The Financial Services Act 1986 covers 'dealing in, arranging deals in, managing or advising on those things which are classified in the Act as investments'.

For those 'carrying out investment businesses' in Great Britain, namely the client company, there are two points of interest:

1. The activity of advising on investments. In cases where a joint affinity or cooperative mailing includes literature for a financial service, whilst the financial company is likely to be aware of the ramifications of the Act, the company sharing the mailing may also have to be authorised under the FSA, if their literature can be seen as endorsing that of the financial company.
2. The activity of arranging deals which require special explanation. In cases where an outside company database is used to select likely prospects for the investment business, this collaboration might be seen as 'arranging deals'.

The ramifications of the Financial Services Act 1986 for direct marketing agencies   Direct marketing agencies are affected by the clause which states that 'a person who issues, or causes to be issued, an investment advertisement' must be authorised under the Act. An agency has a responsibility to ensure that a mailing package has been approved by the client, and also that the person who has given this approval is authorised under the Act. This second point requires an agency to consult a register of authorised businesses from the board.

If a knowingly false or dishonest statement is included in a mailing, in order to induce people to buy or sell their investments, a criminal offence has been committed which could result in a two-year sentence.

The Act also prohibits artificial closing dates for investments or for the terms for which they are available to be given.

The Medicine Act 1968

This Act, which made new provisions for medicinal products and their associated uses, also made provisions for advertising that would have an impact on the design and content of direct mail packages.

Under the Act
1. Any person with commercial interests in the sale of medicines, or related products, who issues a false or misleading advertisement relating to medicinal products is guilty of an offence.
2. Any person who holds a licence authorising him or her as being able to recommend such a product, and who falsely recommends such a product due to commercial self-interest, is also guilty of an offence.

   Defence of the above two charges is given to those who acted unknowingly.
3. Advertisements and direct mail packages can be prohibited or regulated by appropriate government ministers. This ensures that sufficient information is supplied about the medicinal product, that this information is not misleading, and that the safety of such products is preserved.
4. The Act also stipulates that a 'data sheet' (a standard sheet providing a breakdown of the contents of the medical products as for prescription) must be supplied along with any direct mail advertisement sent directly to a practitioner in the medical field. The exception to this is when such a sheet has been sent to the same practitioner within 15 months prior to the advertisement being sent.

   There must be a consistency between the particulars

contained with the advertisement and data sheet. The licensing authority holds the power to require to see copies of advertisements, together with their relevant data sheets.

Competitions

A competition or other form of prize-winning event offered as an incentive in a mailing must comply with the two pieces of legislation which follow:

The Gaming Act 1968

Section 42 of this Act prohibits advertisements (or mailings) which inform, or invite queries from the public about premises where gaming is currently taking place, or which will take place in future.

Likewise, those advertisements which invite the public to subscribe money to be used for the purpose of gaming, either in this country or abroad, are prohibited.

The Lotteries and Amusements Act 1976

This prevents the sale of lottery tickets through the post. The Act also stipulates that it is unlawful to conduct prize competitions, unless some exercise of skill is required of the recipients. Amusements with prizes must be devoted to purposes other than private gain.

Standards

The British Code of Advertising Standards

Background

In 1961 the first British Code of Advertising was drawn up by the Advertising Association in order to bring printed advertising into line with television advertising, which had recently drawn up its own code.

Today's code remains much the same as the very first BCAP code. It is administered by the CAP Committee under the general umbrella of the Advertising Standards Association. The responsibility for upholding the code lies with the advertiser.

What the code covers

The code voluntarily regulates advertising of all types except those transmitted by radio and television. The IBA has its own code for broadcast advertising. Thus, not only direct response advertisers, but also other advertisers adhere to these guidelines.

What are the aims of the code?

It is in the interests of all those who advertise to uphold standards of belief and trust, for otherwise advertising will not be deemed credible by the very same public it is designed to convince. If an advertisement is offensive, then the image of the advertising industry itself is in effect tarnished. The code seeks to ensure that the content of each advertisement meets standards, rather than judging each advertisement for its artistic appeal, or success according to any other criteria.

What happens when the code is contravened?

An advertiser comes under scrutiny as a result of either a formal complaint made by a member of the public, or as a result of the monitoring process which is carried out on a continual basis by the Advertising Standards Authority.

Contraventions of the code result in a formal request made to the advertiser to alter his practices immediately. In certain cases, compensation must be paid to affected parties.

What does the code lay down?

The code requires that an advertisement:

1. adheres to British law
2. is decent
3. is honest
4. is truthful

The fourth of these points is discussed in some depth. Truthfulness is crucial to political advertisements, advertisements where prices are quoted, whose which use the word 'free', testimonials used within advertisements and for guarantees.

The code also states that an advertisement must be recognisable as such. An advertiser must be sure that the product or service is available as it was advertised.

Advertisements must be responsible to both the consumer and to society in general. For example, violence should not be encouraged, special rules must be adhered to in the cases of health-related products, cosmetics, cigarette and alcohol advertisements, and other sensitive areas.

The Acts which affect advertisers include the following:

1. Consumer Safety Act 1978 (adherence to given standards must be kept).
2. Hallmarking Act 1973 (the quantity of metal used in a product must be stated by the advertiser). Goods must conform to their description/or to sample supplied. Size/weight must be clearly stated within an advertisement. Goods sent on approval, if returned by the consumer, must have postage paid by the latter.
3. Post Office Act 1953 (Section II) not all goods are suitable for offer by mail order e.g. unsafe items. The address of an advertiser must be clearly stated in the body of the advertisement.
4. Mail Order Transactions (Information) Order Act 1976.
5. The European Communities Act 1972.

The code contains a special section for mail order and direct response advertising. Mailing and packaging must be carefully considered as to their design (children have access to packages delivered at home). In cases where cash with order is chosen as the method of payment, mail order advertisers are obliged to return all advanced payments where the unwanted goods are returned by the consumer within seven days of fulfilment.

Repayment must also be met by the advertiser in cases where a consumer wishes to be reimbursed due to a delay in fulfilment, or when a product does not match its description in the advertisement.

All orders must be fulfilled within 28 days of the order being placed. Exceptions to this must clearly state the terms of despatch.

A refund should be offered to a consumer as soon as an advertiser is aware that fulfilment will be delayed.

Financial services and products, advertisements offering either employment or business opportunities, limited editions, and advertisements concerning children are all other areas for special consideration, and detailed in the code itself.

Further information
The Code of Advertising Practice Committee
Brook House
2–16 Torrington Place
LONDON
WC1E 7HN

The British Code of Sales Promotion Practice

The first edition of the current code was published in 1980. The code is based on the principles of the International Code of Sales Promotion Practice.

What happens when the code is contravened?

This code is administered by the Advertising Association. The monitoring of promotions and dealing with public complaints similarly result in the termination of malpractice, and compensation being met where necessary.

What are the aims of the code?

The code protects the consumer from malpractice of those marketing techniques which give, usually on a limited basis, offers and incentives including premiums, vouchers, coupons, samples, and all types of prize promotions, etc.

The fundamental principles are similar to the Code of Advertising Practice. All promotions should be legal, decent, honest and truthful. A consumer must be able to understand the terms of the promotion fully and easily. No disappointment should be caused by it. The guidelines of the code stipulate that:

1. The consumer's right to privacy be protected, e.g.:

    (i) precision must be ensured in the compilation of the list
    (ii) written permission must be sought from competition winners, before they can be used as a part of any company publicity.

2. Those under 16 be protected in particular, since this age-group are more susceptible and easily taken advantage of.
3. All consumers be protected from safety risks.
4. Promotions should not mislead consumers by their presentation, or publicity, e.g. the terms under which the promotion operates must be both clear and complete.
5. Promotional products must meet satisfactory standards of durability, and should not cause offence to their recipients.
6. Over-exaggerated claims about the produce, e.g. its quality, must not be made.
7. Claims of 'savings' made by the consumer must comply with the following Acts:

    The Price Marking (Bargain Offers) Order 1979
    Trade Descriptions Act 1968, section II.

8. The availability of a promotional product must be given, where limited. Where a delay occurs, consumers must be informed immediately.
9. Faulty or damaged goods must either be replaced, or a refund made.
10. It is only acceptable to call an offer 'free' when there is no cost to the consumer, other than possibly postal or incidental expense incurred in claiming the free offer. Such charges cannot be raised deliberately to recoup the cost of the free offer.
11. Entry and judging conditions should be clearly stated, prizewinners must be notified individually, and a complete list of prizewinners must later be made available for anyone wanting to see this information. A closing date should be clearly stated in the rules of entry, and prizewinners, unless otherwise stated, must receive their prize within six weeks of the closing date. All promotions with prizes should conform with:

   (i) The Lotteries and Amusement Act 1976
   (ii) The Prevention of Corruption Acts 1889–1916
   (iii) The Income and Corporation Taxes Act 1970

12. Sales promotions should allow for a free decision to be made, and should not be unfair to competitors. Business incentives should not come between the employee and his duty to his employer.

Further information

A copy of this code is available from the CAP Committee at the address given on page 348. As well as giving further detail, the code also lists government legislation which should be adhered to in the context of promotions.

Mail order legislation

Throughout the sixties and seventies, a series of Acts were passed to protect consumers. Many of these Acts have a direct effect on the type of mail order transaction that can be offered. Most of these particular laws are based on the fact that the consumer needs certain information to assist him or her in the decision whether or not to purchase goods.

When the consumer buys at a retail outlet, legislation requires that such goods be marked with, or be accompanied by, such relevant information. In the case of buying direct, however, the advertisement or direct mailing acts as a substitute point of sale.

The measures that protect the mail order buyer are numerous. Just to indicate their extent, the following section sets out the major Acts, their dates, together with associated implications for the mailer.

The Trading Stamps Act 1964

Under this Act, promoters of trading stamp schemes were restricted to companies or industrial and provident societies. Other groups or individuals were prohibited from promoting such schemes.

Thus a mail order company could still promote a scheme under this Act, so long as the following clauses of the Act were also adhered to:

(i) The company is registered.
(ii) A statement of its value in relation to current currency must be clearly indicated on a stamp.
(iii) The holder of trading stamps of a value of under 50p has the right to demand to exchange the stamps with the promoter for their aggregate cash value.
(iv) There is an implied warranty on the part of the promoter of such a scheme, that goods can be given in exchange for the stamps, and that their quality will be assured, etc.
(v) Catalogues and stamp books must include the name and address of the promoter.
(vi) Advertisements, by any media, which refer to the valued of trading stamps are prohibited.

The Trade Descriptions Act 1968

Under the Acts those who

(i) give a false trade description to goods, or
(ii) supply or offer to supply any goods to which a false trade description is applied will be guilty of an offence.

A trade description can be any indication made about a 'good' or part of a 'good'. This can include quantity, size or other measurement, method of manufacture or production, composition, strength, performance, results of tests or approvals, place or date of manufacture, and any other relevant history. A false trade description is one that is misleading.

A trade description can be applied to goods directly, e.g. by their markings, or indirectly (e.g. an oral statement which clearly refers to such goods).

Under section 5, an advertisement which includes a false trade description constitutes an offence under the Act, whether or not the goods to which it relates have yet been manufactured.

Under section 8 of the Act, where necessary or helpful to consumers, instructions or trade descriptions are to be attached to goods. Section 9 extends this to advertisements. The Board of Trade is given the right to make an order to require this type of information to be given.

False or misleading indications as to the price of goods is also an offence under this Act. Prices cannot be more than indicated, similarly prices cannot be lowered unless they have been offered at a higher price for at least 28 days.

A recommended price is strictly the price suggested by the manufacturer.

Other offences include false representations about:

  (i) Royal approval or award, etc.

 (ii) the supply of goods or services

(iii) services offered, i.e. giving false or misleading statements about these.

The import of goods with either infringing trademarks or false indication of origin, is prohibited under the Act. The Act is enforced by local Weights and Measures Authorities reporting to the Board of Trade. The local authority inspector has the right to seize goods and make test purchases in order to oversee the Act.

Unsolicited Goods and Services Act 1971

This Act stipulates that the recipient of unsolicited goods (where the recipient has no prior anticipation of such goods), has the right to do as he wishes with them, on the following conditions:

  (i) that the recipient notifies the sender of their arrival within six months of their receipt

 (ii) that the sender does not use his right to collect the goods within the 30 days after he receives the sender's notification.

The sender of unsolicited goods commits an offence when he demands or threatens the recipient for payment for the goods.

Unsolicited books, or other publications which describe illustrated human sexual techniques, were also made an offence under this Act.

Trade Descriptions Act 1972

This Act requires imported goods to be marked with, or accompanied by an indication of origin. An offence is committed if a person or company supplies or offers goods without such information.

The 1972 Act was followed by further Trade Descriptions Orders in 1981 (see page 356).

Textile Products (Indication of Fibre Content) 1973

Article 4 of these regulations requires full details of the fibre content of goods in the case of a textile advertisement to be given.

Consumer Credit Act 1974

This Act aimed to 'establish for the protection of consumers a new system, ... of licensing and other control of traders concerned with the provision of credit, or the supply of goods on hire or hire-purchase, and their transactions ...'

The Act requires a consumer credit business or consumer hire business to obtain a licence from the Director General of Fair Trading (newly appointed under this Act). Such a licence is mainly given on an individual, rather than a group basis.

A licence will not be granted to anyone who has committed unfair practices, e.g. fraud, sexual or racial discrimination, and the terms of a licence can be changed or a licence be removed altogether if an offence against the Act is committed.

An offence is committed when credit practices are carried out either without a licence at all, or under another name, or alternatively when the Director General is not informed of changes in the particulars of such a business.

Section 43 stipulates that any advertisements which indicate that the advertisers are willing to provide credit or hire-purchase agreements, must be regulated as to their form and content.

Specific information must be included, while other information is excluded and the advertisement must be balanced so as not to mislead the reader.

Under this Act an advertiser commits an offence if he is only prepared to enter a credit agreement, rather than being prepared to accept cash for the sale of the goods or services.

The deliberate conveyance of false or misleading information in an advertisement is an offence against this Act, both by the advertiser and the publisher of the advertisement.

Section 50 makes it an offence to send a minor any literature inviting the minor to borrow money, obtain goods on credit or hire, obtain services on credit, or even apply for information on borrowing money or obtaining credit, or hiring goods. A credit or hire-purchase agreement must conform to the form and content set out by the Secretary of State so that the hirer is aware of the rights and duties imposed by the agreement, the amount and rate of credit charged, and the protection available under this Act.

An agreement must be signed by both the hirer/debtor and owner/creditor. The owner/creditor is also obliged to supply a copy of the agreement, give notice of the cancellation of any rights, give information to the creditor about the return of goods or credit terms which come into force in the event of the death of the debtor or hirer.

The local Weights and Measures Authority enforces this Act.

The Mail Order Transactions (Information) Order 1976

This Order protects only consumers, not those who purchase in their business capacity. It stipulates that any advertisement or direct mail solicitation, inviting payment to be made with order, must give the advertiser's true name (either surname, or corporate name), or registered business name, and the address where the business is managed.

The Consumer's Transactions (Restrictions on Statements) Order 1976

This Order ensures advertisements state that a consumer's statutory rights are not affected where other terms and conditions are either made to or for the consumer. Where a wholesaler or manufacturer expects to sell goods direct, they too are included under the above terms of the Order.

The Unfair Contract Terms Act 1977

This Act stipulates that certain terms and conditions are prohibited from being included in a contract.

Article 5 covers the sale and supply of goods. No manufacturer or distributor is permitted to write into a contract that they are not responsible for those goods that prove defective while in consumer use, as a result of their own negligence.

Any written assurance or promise that defects will be made good either by repair or replacement, constitutes a binding guarantee.

Any liability under the 1893 Sale of Goods Act or the 1973 Hire-purchase Act cannot be avoided by any contract term.

The Consumer Safety Act 1978

This Act requires that goods be safe, and that appropriate information be provided, and inappropriate information excluded in respect of goods. These regulations cover:

(i)   The composition, contents, design, construction and finishing of goods
(ii) The approved standards of goods and the manner in which information is given
(iii) The tests which form these standards
(iv) The instructions of warning that goods do not meet the required standards. The supply and sale of dangerous goods or components. This Act is enforced by the Weights and Measures Authority.

The Price Marking (Bargain Offers) Order 1979

This Order regulates the practice of promoting products or services at a lower price than their market value. A price can only be expressed as 'lower' when it correlates with either a past price, or an intended future charge. Alternatively, if the terms of sale have changed, the quality of the goods has altered, or when goods are offered in different combinations.

The Trade Descriptions (Sealskin Goods) (Information) Order 1980

This Order requires sealskin goods to be clearly marked as such and the country given in which they were killed.

Trade Descriptions (Origin Marking Order) 1981

The Order prohibits the supply, of offering to supply, new goods (specifically clothing and textiles, domestic and electrical applicances, footwear and cutlery) without a mark or other indication of origin. Where such goods are sold by mail, under this Order the indication of origin must be given on the advertisement, unless the advertisement states that goods are returnable if the customer is not satisfied, and such goods are marked with, or accompanied by their country of origin.

Trade Description (Country of Origin) (Cutlery) Order 1981

This Order clarifies that the country of origin which should be indicated for cutlery is where the initial manufacture took place, rather than where any subsequent silver-plating or other ancillary process occurred.

Fulfilment

As well as ensuring mail order transactions provided sufficient information, safety and conditions of hire-purchase and other credit arrangments, consumer legislation also makes provision for the fulfilment and supply of the goods and services.

Sale of Goods Act 1979

This Act brought in measures on the contract of the sale of goods—both actual sales and agreements to future sales.
Under this Act a sales contract becomes:

(i) Void when unbeknown to a seller his goods have perished in transit
(ii) Under warranty when a seller has not fulfilled a condition in a sales contract.

All charges must be disclosed to the buyer before the contract is made.
Goods must correspond to their description, and samples must correspond with the goods they represent.
There is an implied condition that goods will be of a merchantable quality, except when defects have been pointed out to a buyer, prior to their purchase.

Unless otherwise agreed, the goods remain the seller's risk until the property is transferred to the buyer, but once this has occurred, the buyer has responsibility for the property, whether delivery has been made or not.

Delivery for goods, unless otherwise agreed, must be concurrent with the payment for them.

If a seller sends goods to a buyer, this fulfilment must occur within a reasonable time-limit. Unless otherwise agreed, the seller pays for delivery. In the event of the wrong quantity or goods of the wrong description being delivered, the buyer holds the right of refusal, but if he accepts the goods, he must pay for them at the agreed rate.

A buyer also holds the right of refusal on goods sent in instalments, when this method of fulfilment has not been agreed by him. Any instalment that is not delivered or not paid for can constitute a breach of contract.

When a seller sends goods to a buyer in a distant place, the buyer bears the risk of damage in transit. The buyer is only deemed to have purchased goods after he or she has had a reasonable opportunity of examination, and he or she informs the seller otherwise.

Unless otherwise agreed, the buyer is not required to return goods he or she is dissatisfied with, but must notify the seller if refusing to accept them for any deterioration of the goods between their delivery date and their return, the seller is liable.

When a buyer does not pay, the seller has a right either to seize the goods or to stop their transit, and action can be taken. A buyer can take action against the seller for non-delivery and breach of warranty.

The Supply of Goods and Services Act 1982

This Act brings the hire of goods and all methods of payment for services into line with the Sale of Goods Act 1979.

In the case of the supply of a service, there is an implied degree of care and skill contained, and an implied time for the service to be carried out.

Index